Interpreting NAFTA

The Science and Art of Political Analysis

Frederick W. Mayer

COLUMBIA UNIVERSITY PRESS   NEW YORK

Columbia University Press

Publishers Since 1893

New York   Chichester, West Sussex

Copyright © 1998 Columbia University Press

All rights reserved

Library of Congress Cataloging-in-Publishing Data

Mayer, Frederick.

   Interpreting NAFTA : the science and art of political analysis /
Frederick W. Mayer.

     p.   cm.

   Includes bibliographical references and index.

   ISBN 0-231-10980-6 (alk. paper). — ISBN 0-231-10981-4 (pbk. :
alk. paper)

    1. Canada. Treaties, etc. 1992 Oct. 7.   2. Free trade—North
America.   3. North America—Commercial treaties.   4. United States—
Commercial policy.   5. United States—Politics and government—20th
century.   I. Title.

HF1746.M39 1998

382'.917—dc21   98-3019

To Mary Kay

Contents

Section III: The Politics of Ratification

Preface

In August 1992, I took leave of my position at Duke University to spend what I expected to be a year in Washington, D.C. I had won an International Affairs Fellowship from the Council on Foreign Relations, a program designed to take young scholars away from academia and expose them to the world of actual foreign policy making. Because my academic interests were in international negotiations, specifically the relationship between domestic politics and international processes, my hope was to find a perch close to the action for the biggest international negotiation going: the negotiation among the United States, Mexico, and Canada to reach a North American Free Trade Agreement, more commonly known as NAFTA.

The natural place to be was at the Office of the United States Trade Representative (USTR), the lead agency for international trade negotiations, where a number of previous Council fellows had worked. But by the summer of 1992, when I had to decide where to locate, the NAFTA negotiations appeared to be nearing the end, which meant that the next hot arena would likely be the Congress. I had not really considered working on the Hill, but I learned that Senator Bill Bradley was looking for a fellow to handle foreign policy matters and that he intended to be involved with NAFTA when it came to Capitol Hill. My colleagues warned me that being a fellow in a Senate office might not involve much actual contact with the senator and that there was no guarantee that Bradley, only the fourth ranking Democrat on the Senate Finance Committee, would actually be a pivotal player, but the prospect of working for Bill Bradley was alluring.

As a young man, I had played basketball—on a club team at Harvard and then for one year in a semi-pro league in England—hardly the level of Bradley's brilliant Princeton and NBA careers, but enough to feel some kinship. I had read John McPhee's homage to Bradley at Princeton, *A Sense of Where You Are*, and Bradley's autobiography of life in the NBA, *Life on the Run*. Later, I had admired Bradley's career in the Senate and, like many Americans, saw him as one of the most attractive political figures of our time. At Duke, I often assigned my politics classes the book *Showdown at Gucci Gulch*, an account of the 1986 tax reform effort in which Bradley plays a starring role. Bradley was a personal hero, and when I was offered the position, I could not turn it down.

Seeing one's hero up close is risky. Certainly few of the political heroes of my youth have held up well to close scrutiny. But my time with Bradley did nothing to diminish my admiration for him. He is demanding and some-times intimidating, but he is also extraordinarily disciplined, principled, and intelligent. He is what he seems to be: a political figure less interested in the pursuit of power than in the uses of power for public good. The decision to work for Bradley did not cost me a hero, and, as it happened, I could not have chosen a better spot to observe the politics of NAFTA.

I came to Washington favoring NAFTA. I thought then and now that it was good policy, that it would produce economic benefits for the United States and few of the costs alleged by its critics, that on balance it would do more good than harm to the environment, and that it was important for U.S.–Mexican relations. Bradley was even more deeply committed. He had been interested in Mexico since his involvement with the Mexican debt crisis of the early 1980s. As was his style, he had systematically taught himself about Mexico: reading Mexican history, making annual trips to talk with a wide circle of Mexicans, and keeping abreast of the current political and economic scene in Mexico. He saw in NAFTA not just a sensible trade agreement but a historic opportunity, a unique chance to redefine U.S.–Mexican relations. He was determined not to let the opportunity pass.

From the moment I arrived that August, Bradley was deeply engaged with NAFTA. When candidate Clinton appeared to be wavering, Bradley talked at length with him, arguing that NAFTA was both good policy and good politics. When the process of negotiating side negotiations created a political vacuum of support in 1993, he thought of ways to lay the groundwork for the eventual campaign for NAFTA. When the side negotiations foundered, he intervened to help find common ground, eventually personally brokering some of the final deals. When Finance Committee Chairman Moynihan decided to oppose NAFTA, creating a leadership vacuum in the Senate, Bradley stepped forward as the de facto leader, forming a bipartisan group to make the case for NAFTA to his colleagues. And when at the end it became apparent that the vote in the House of Representatives was the key obstacle, Bradley did what he had done during the tax reform effort seven years earlier: he walked over to the House side of the Capitol to personally persuade undecided representatives.

Bradley's engagement thrust me into the middle of a political maelstrom. I quickly discovered that I was not only going to get to observe the politics of NAFTA, I was going to be a participant in them. In my first weeks, a memo I wrote on why Clinton should support NAFTA was faxed to Little Rock. As the side negotiations proceeded, I talked constantly with officials at the office of the United States Trade Representative; staffers on the Hill; environment, labor, and business lobbyists: and Mexican and Canadian off-icals, trying to assess where the pitfalls were and to suggest when and how Senator Bradley might need to intervene. With Amy Dunathan of Senator Chafee's office, I organized the ad hoc whip effort in the Senate, tracking the projected vote count, assembling profiles of undecided members, dis-tributing information and arguments to other Senate offices, and coordinat-ing with the White House and business community efforts. And I monitored the public politics of NAFTA, keeping on top of the press coverage and public opinion polls, assessing the nature of the larger political problem facing NAFTA as the congressional vote neared, and discussing with Senator Bradley and other NAFTA advocates strategies for solving it. By the end of my fellowship in August 1993, I was too deeply involved to leave and decided to continue through the fall, commuting weekly from Durham.

All this was heady stuff for an academic normally safely distant from events. To be in the East Room of the White House with Bill Clinton, Gerald Ford, Jimmy Carter, and George Bush for the "kickoff" of the fall campaign for NAFTA was exhilarating. (I was standing in the back, squeezed against the wall.) To have the Senate vote count on my computer, to be receiving more phone calls than I could possibly return, to be in the middle of the biggest game in town were all very exciting. When NAFTA passed, I felt the kind of thrill I once got from winning a championship basketball game. I suspect Bradley felt much the same.

This book clearly grows out of my personal engagement with NAFTA, but I have tried not to write merely a personal account. My goal has been to write NAFTA's story, not mine. When I returned to Duke, I decided that I wanted to put my experience in a larger context, to understand as best I could the political process in which I had been a minor player. To that end, I assembled thousands of newspaper articles, hearing transcripts, press releases, reports, advertisements, and other documents about NAFTA, and interviewed nearly two hundred participants on both sides of the issue. Out of this I gained an even greater appreciation for the extraordinary complexity and richness of the politics of NAFTA, and I learned much that would have been helpful to me at the time. I also developed great respect for professional historians, who must take the innumerable fragments of history and try to make of them a story that is at once compelling and fair. I have tried to do this in telling the NAFTA story.

This book also reflects my personal experience in a second way, the experience of trying to live in two worlds—the academic and the political— and a desire to reconcile them. This is not an easy thing to do. At about the time I began work in Bill Bradley's office, I published an article in *International Organization*, a respected academic journal, that used highly abstract game theoretic techniques to make an argument about the relationship between domestic politics and international negotiations. Being understandably proud of the article, I gave a copy to one of my colleagues in the office. I never made that mistake again. The article, with its elegant and abstract economic illustrations, was paraded about to hoots of laughter, and became the source of good-natured joking for the rest of my time in Washington.

When I returned to academia and began thinking about writing a book, I found myself asking what of the academic literatures I knew might actually be useful to practitioners. What of my training had been useful to me? As I reflected on the reaction to my article, I came to the conclusion that my Hill colleagues were at least partly wrong. The kind of abstract spatial modeling that I had learned in graduate school from my mentor Howard Raiffa had, in fact, been quite useful to me as a political strategist. I found that thinking in this way often helped me to identify what was important, formulate useful questions, and think strategically. And although the language was foreign to practitioners, in truth the concepts were not too far from the intuitive understandings of experienced negotiators and lobbyists. But this kind of thinking was far from sufficient.

First, to understand what was going on and to operate in the political arena, I needed to know a lot about the institutional context in which I was working. I had to learn how Congress works, how its committees are structured and operate, what the "fast track" process really did, what informal rules governed interactions between senators, who talked to whom, and much more. I had to learn how the executive branch is organized to negotiate trade agreements and to deal with Congress, which agencies handled what, how they operated, and who really knew what was going on. And I had to learn about the political institutions and habits of Washington, who the lobbyists were and where they were coming from, which groups could cause trouble or give help, how information gets around, and much more. I left Washington with a renewed appreciation for the importance of political institutions.

Second, to make sense of what I was observing as the politics of NAFTA heated up, I had to recognize that this was not just about interests. Rational choice theories of politics are predicated on the assumption that individuals are motivated by interests. But how could I understand the extraordinary level of opposition to NAFTA—my meetings with angry union leaders, the burning of Bill Bradley in effigy by a chapter of United We Stand America, the shrill warnings that NAFTA would destroy the environment—in these terms? How could a trade agreement that would likely have only modest effects on the United States induce such vehement opposition? As I listened to the opposition, I came to see that it was not so much what NAFTA was that mattered, but what it symbolized. I found that thinking in terms of framing, narrative construction, and other sociological concepts not only helped explain what I observed, but suggested strategies for addressing the problem. I left Washington with a new appreciation for the importance of symbolic politics.

These reflections about what a political strategist needs to diagnose political problems and to prescribe political strategies are reflected in the analytic framework developed in this book. The framework draws on several literatures in political science, economics, and sociology. There is indeed quite a bit of academic literature of value for the practitioner. But the value comes from judicious application of multiple lenses, not from the pursuit of single theories about the way politics works.

I have received help from many quarters in writing this book. The Council on Foreign Relations provided me with an invaluable fellowship without which this would not have been possible. Mike Aho, then director of economic studies at the Council, and a former Bradley aide, involved me in a NAFTA study group supported by the Ford Foundation, which has generously supported the subsequent research for this book.

I am grateful to the many people with whom I worked in Washington, from whom I learned an enormous amount, and who consistently demonstrated generosity, patience, good humor, and professionalism. Among these were Bradley legislative directors Ken Apfel and later Trudy Vincent; Bradley aides Mike Dahl, Mark Schmitt, and John Depres; former aide Gina Depres; my interns, Greg Pogarsky and later Heather Miller; the staff of the Senate Finance Committee, particularly majority counsel Marsha Miller and her assistants Eric Biele and Debbie Lamb, and minority counsel Brad Figel; Senate staffers Amy Dunathan, Seth Brewster, Kevin Dempsey, and Bill Reinsche; and my counterpart in the House, Matsui aide Diane Sullivan; the tremendously professional and dedicated staff at the USTR, including Chip Roh, Bryan Samuel, Ira Shapiro, and Nancy Leamond; Bob Kyle at the National Security Council; and many individuals in the advocacy community with whom I interacted, including business strategists Sandy Masur, Ken Cole, and Gail Harrison, and environmental strategists Doug Siglin and Ken Berlin.

I am enormously grateful to the many people I interviewed, who without exception gave generously of their time and spoke with candor. Unless otherwise noted, all quotes in the book come from these interviews. I am particularly indebted to Chip Roh, whose careful reading of the manuscript saved me from innumerable errors. I am also grateful to my colleagues at Duke, my department chairs Bruce Kuniholm and Phil Cook for their consistent encouragement, and especially to Jay Hamilton, Jim Miller, and Rob Sprinkle for their most helpful comments on early drafts. I am indebted to Mac Destler, George Downs, Peter Katzenstein, John Odell, and Carol Wise for their supportive comments and gentle criticisms. I thank also my terrific students at Duke, who heard much more than they wanted about the politics of NAFTA, two of whom—Jenny Schulstad and Michael Campbell—served as research assistants.

Finally, and most important, I am deeply grateful to my wife Mary Kay Delaney, and our three boys, Paul, Michael, and David, who together endured a move to Washington and back and many late nights thereafter with great good cheer. Mary Kay did much more than endure, however. Our conversations about her own work in the anthropology of education contributed enormously to my thinking about the usefulness of constructivist approaches to political analysis and to the nature of theory for practice.

Durham, North Carolina
December 3, 1997

1 Introduction

In June 1990, Carlos Salinas de Gortari, president of Mexico, and George Bush, president of the United States, announced their intention to negotiate a free trade agreement between their countries. The general public paid little attention. Trade negotiations are generally not the stuff of headline news. Nevertheless, the event was a historic turning point, a break from the animosity and indifference that had always characterized U.S.–Mexican relations, and the beginning of an extraordinary three-year saga that would alter the political landscape of North America: the creation of a North American Free Trade Agreement (NAFTA).

This book is, first, a history of the saga, beginning with the decision to negotiate, continuing through two years of international negotiations, and culminating in the tumultuous battle in the United States to approve the agreement. It draws extensively on interviews, primary documents, press accounts, and the author's own experience as an aide to U.S. Senator Bill Bradley during the last 15 months of the NAFTA effort, in which capacity the author was responsible for managing the ad hoc whip effort to win Senate approval.

Second, this book is a political analysis of those events, an application of relevant theories of international relations, comparative politics, legislatures, organizations, interest groups, and public opinion. The analysis aims to answer three basic questions: Why did the nations of North America decide to negotiate? Why did the agreements take the form that they did? And, why was ratification so fiercely contested in the United States?

Finally, the book is an argument about the nature of theory for practical political analysis, where the goal is not to demonstrate the validity of general theories about politics but to explain *an* event and potentially to inform action *in* the event. It develops a broad theoretical framework that crosses between international relations and domestic politics and among rational choice, institutionalist, and symbolic constructivist approaches to analysis. It argues that to interpret NAFTA one needs to see it as simultaneously international and domestic, and at once about the politics of interests, institutions, and ideas.

A Brief History and Some Puzzles

In February 1990, Mexican officials asked the United States to consider negotiating a bilateral free trade agreement. In the United States, the Bush administration quickly agreed. Canadian Prime Minister Brian Mulroney's government at first decided not to join the talks, but after a summer's reflection, it changed its mind. By the end of 1990, all three governments had committed to negotiate a NAFTA. There are puzzles here.

Mexican politicians had long carefully distanced themselves from the United States. Suggestions throughout the 1980s that Mexico enter into a free trade agreement with the United States had been firmly rejected. The conventional wisdom was that no Mexican president would risk public censure from too public an embrace of the "colossus to the North," yet little more than a year after taking office, Salinas was staking his presidency on just such an initiative.

For its part, the United States had just completed a free trade agreement with Canada, its largest trading partner. Most observers thought that it would be some time before the United States would be ready to add another member to the club. The thought that a free trade area including Mexico might be a high priority of the U.S. government, after decades of a foreign policy that ranged between belligerency and neglect, was hard to hold, yet the Bush administration eagerly embraced the idea.

Canada had gone through a grueling national fight during the 1987 national elections over the recently negotiated Canada–U.S. Free Trade Agreement (CUFTA). When the Canadian economy went into recession shortly after the election, the public blamed the CUFTA. The last thing that Prime Minister Mulroney wanted to do in 1990 was reopen the issue by embarking on another free trade negotiation. Yet by August 1990, the Canadian government had reversed its position and asked that it be allowed to join the talks. Given all this, why did Mexico, the United States, and Canada decide to negotiate?

With Salinas, Bush, and Mulroney in agreement, the NAFTA negotiation was born—almost. In Canada and Mexico, the head of state can commit his country to negotiate, but in the United States, the rules of the U.S. trade policy–making game in effect required the president first to obtain permission to negotiate from Congress. In the spring of 1991, President Bush asked for extension of authority to negotiate. Historically such requests had not been controversial, and most observers did not anticipate a problem this time. They were wrong. The fight in Congress became the hottest issue of the spring, with an unusual coalition of unions, environmental organizations, and other citizens' groups pitted against the business lobby and the administration in a battle that gave the first clear indication that NAFTA was not going to be trade politics as usual.

The president won the skirmish in May, but not before agreeing to address some of the environmental and labor concerns that the opponents had raised. The promise put new issues on the trade negotiating agenda, issues that would expand in importance as the NAFTA process proceeded. Why did the president feel compelled to link these new issues—environment and labor—to the trade agenda?

The NAFTA negotiations formally began in June 1991. The three governments had hopes that they would conclude quickly, perhaps by the end of the calendar year. After all, the basic form of the agreement had already been established in the CUFTA, and all three countries agreed on the final outcome of the negotiations: free trade. But these hopes soon proved unrealistic. The talks made little progress in 1991 and dragged on through the summer of 1992. Not until August, with the U.S. presidential election looming, did the negotiators finally reach an agreement—and then only after two weeks of intense final talks in Washington's Watergate hotel.

The final deal was a sweeping trilateral agreement to eliminate, over time, most barriers to trade and investment in North America and to strengthen intellectual property rights. The negotiators accomplished much of what they had set out to do. Yet questions remain about the particular form of the agreement. Why were some sectors of the economy excluded from the agreement altogether, and others given lengthy grace periods before the free trade agreement took full effect? What accounts for the elaborate rules of origin that determined what goods would count as "North American"? How was it that Mexico was able to reduce protection in such politically powerful sectors as finance, telecommunications, and agriculture?

The negotiations concluded in the middle of the U.S. presidential election campaign and immediately became an election issue. Independent candidate Ross Perot began warning that NAFTA would create a "sucking sound" of U.S. jobs going to Mexico. President Bush, of course, was squarely for the agreement. The question was, where would Bill Clinton position himself on the issue? Clinton delayed a decision as long as possible, sought advice from all quarters, and then took a middle ground. He would support NAFTA but would insist that the labor and environment issues be addressed with supplemental agreements before he would submit the package to Congress for a vote. That a trade agreement became a central issue in a U.S. presidential campaign was surprising. Candidate Clinton's particular position seemed a curious formulation.

Whatever his motivations, Clinton's campaign stance established the agenda in 1993 for the new administration. Before the president would send a bill to Congress for ratification, the United States would seek to negotiate these supplemental agreements. Mexico and Canada reluctantly agreed and hoped that the talks could be concluded swiftly. But the talks dragged on, through the spring and summer, until they finally closed in the early morning of Friday, August 13. By then, Canada was in the midst of its national election; Mexico was beginning the party battle to decide the successor to Salinas; and the window was rapidly closing for Congress to consider the agreement before it went into effect January 1, 1994. As with the commercial negotiations themselves, there are questions about both process and substance: Why did agreement take so long, and why did it take this form?

In August, when the supplemental agreements were reached, President Clinton could finally come to Congress with an implementing bill. But by then public opposition had swollen so much that it appeared impossible for the president to secure the votes needed to pass the agreement in Congress. An extraordinarily broad and motivated alliance of labor unions, environmental groups, citizen and human rights groups, along with Ross Perot, Jesse Jackson, and Pat Buchanan, appeared to be too popular, vocal, and powerful for supporters of NAFTA to overcome. Public opinion polls and focus groups were not encouraging to NAFTA's supporters. At town meetings around the country, members of Congress back home for the August recess got an earful from irate constituents. NAFTA had become a major national issue, vying with health care reform for top billing. In the House of Representatives, where NAFTA's prospects looked dimmest, Majority Leader Richard Gephardt announced his opposition and Democratic Whip David Bonior claimed that he had the votes to kill the agreement.

Herein lies perhaps the biggest puzzle of all. The vast majority of the credible economic analyses showed net gains for all three countries, with very little dislocation for workers in the United States or Canada. This conclusion should not be surprising, since most of the changes required by NAFTA were in Mexico, where numerous sectors enjoyed trade protection, rather than in the considerably more open United States or Canada. For only a few sectors of the economy—generally low wage, currently protected sectors such as apparel and glass—could one confidently project losses for U.S. industries or workers. Even those studies that disagreed about the direction of the economic effects of NAFTA agreed on one point: Those effects would be small. How, then, could a matter with relatively small and probably positive effects on the U.S. economy (or for that matter on the environment, immigration, workers rights, or any of the other issues raised in the context of NAFTA) have become such an enormous political issue? What accounts for the alliance between such normally bitter rivals as Ralph Nader, Ross Perot, and Pat Buchanan? What accounts for the vituperative rhetoric that characterized the opposition: "sucking sound," "environmental disaster," and "economic Munich"?

By September 1993, NAFTA was in political trouble. Speaker of the House Tom Foley and the White House agreed that the House of Representatives, where the agreement was in the greatest trouble, would vote on November 17. Faced with the strong possibility of defeat, NAFTA's advocates mounted a furious counterattack. On September 14, former Presidents George Bush, Jimmy Carter, and Gerald Ford joined President Clinton in the East Room of the White House to kick off the campaign for NAFTA. What followed was an all-out campaign on many fronts. The president, his cabinet, and an army of other administration officials; the former presidents and a host of other prominent Americans; CEOs and lesser officials of American business; and important elements of the environmental and Hispanic American community joined in lobbying Congress. In the media, NAFTA supporters filled the newspaper op ed pages with testimonials; cabinet officers, members of Congress, and even the president appeared on television talk shows; the business lobby commissioned and ran election-style television commercials; and, most remarkably, Vice President Al Gore engaged Ross

Perot in a debate on a popular cable television talk show, CNN's "Larry King Live." A less visible business-funded effort modeled after the grassroots organizing tactics of the opposition began to generate phone calls and letters from constituents in key Congressional districts. As the date neared, and NAFTA still lacked votes, the administration scrambled together a package that would win more support: A new development bank to clean up the environment along the U.S.–Mexican border won a couple votes; adjustments in the terms of the sugar, citrus, and vegetable agreements won some more. On November 17, NAFTA passed in the House by a margin of 234 to 200. Three days later it easily passed in the Senate, 61 to 38. But why did victory require such an enormous effort? What understandings of the political problem informed the strategies for and against NAFTA? And what strategies made the difference?

The Nature of Political Analysis

This book has two goals. The first is to answer the questions raised by the history: to interpret NAFTA. The second is to argue for and to develop a general analytic framework for political analysis. The two goals are mutually reinforcing.

To some extent the questions raised by the overview history will be answered by the fuller account provided in subsequent chapters. But narrative, no matter how complete, cannot be completely self-explanatory. We need theory to guide our inquiry. Empirical questions cannot profitably be addressed, indeed cannot even be asked, without some structuring assumptions that direct our attention to what is important, connect causes and effects, and enable us to discern patterns in the otherwise inchoate mass of data. Understanding political processes requires both a rich knowledge of the history and an analytic framework to interpret it.

The impulse of most contemporary political science is to demonstrate the truth or falsity of general propositions—the more general the better. The preferred form of empirical research, therefore, is to articulate a highly parsimonious theory and to test it as rigorously as possible, preferably using econometric techniques.

This book, however, is concerned with political analysis: the science and art of analyzing particular political circumstances. Political analysis does not seek to demonstrate general truths about the nature of politics. It seeks to explicate particular political contexts and processes in such a way that not only explains after the event but also might be useful to actors in the event. The ultimate purpose of political analysis is to inform strategy.

The analytic framework used in this book has two dimensions. One dimension is the *level* of the analysis, or more particularly of the core units or actors in the international system. Can international relations be understood as a purely international process in which the core actors are nations and/ or international institutions or must one attend to domestic processes within nations at either a group or an individual level? The second dimension is the *mode* of politics. Can political processes, at whatever level of analysis, be understood best as rational choices, institutional processes, or responses to symbolic constructions? The different levels and modes are not mutually exclusive possibilities; indeed they are both logically complementary and practically synergistic. Taken together, they constitute an integrated framework for political analysis.

The framework is considerably more complex than is the norm in political science. This complexity reflects the task facing political analysis. First, because political analysis is concerned with the particular event, it must necessarily be much more attentive to context. The issue for political analysis is not which strategy on average is most likely to work (although that information is useful), it is what strategy is most likely to work in a particular context.

Second, because political analysis is intended to be used, it must be sufficiently rich to include those dimensions of strategy available to the actor; it must have "policy handles." If one is negotiating an international agreement (or analyzing the negotiation after the fact), one needs a framework in which the choices of negotiators matter. If one is trying to build a winning coalition in Congress (or to analyze after the fact how one was built), one needs a theory that predicts swing votes and identifies ways to bring pressure on those legislators. To be useful, analysis needs to do more than predict general trends, it needs to identify specific points of leverage.

Third, because the impulse of political analysis is not to prove or disprove highly general theory, it does not need to engage in battles over what theoretical approach is generally correct. The issue is not whether the rational choice, institutional process, or symbolic constructivist approach is correct (and which are, therefore, incorrect), or whether domestic politics does or does not matter, but rather which lenses are most useful for interpreting a particular phenomenon. Of course, it is not enough to say that events are complicated and that there are many potentially valid ways of interpreting them. The question is which approach to take when. This can be partially predicted on the basis of observable characteristics. Some processes are more amenable to rational choice models than others. Some processes are more amenable to international level theory than others. But to an equally large extent, the political analyst must be something of a scientific naturalist, equipped with a variety of analytic tools and alert to what is happening. It may not be possible to predict when symbolic politics will play a significant role, for example, or what form those politics will take, but an analyst aware of the potential for such processes and of the forms they may take can recognize and analyze them when they happen.

Organization of the Book

The book is organized in three sections, reflecting three stages of the history of NAFTA. The first section concerns the decision to negotiate, the second the negotiation of the commercial treaty and the supplemental agreements, and the third the politics of ratification in the United States. Individual chapters consist of two parts: a historical narrative followed by an analytic commentary on that history. The narratives are intended to provide as full an account of events as space allows. The commentaries are intended to make an argument about what techniques should be applied to particular questions and particular stages of the history and to demonstrate how such application illuminates the history. The analytic framework and the basic argument are developed in chapter 2.

Deciding to Negotiate

Chapter 3 chronicles the decision by Salinas, Bush, and Mulroney to negotiate NAFTA, addressing the question of why each country chose to act as it did. The analytic commentary at the end of the chapter explores the uses and limits of international relations theory to understand their decisions. The chapter considers, in turn, three systemic theories of international relations — realism, institutionalism, and constructivism — theories respectively based on interests, institutions, and ideas. The chapter argues that each illuminates some aspect of the decision, but that systemic theory is ultimately insufficient. To understand the motivation and timing of the decision, one must attend to domestic politics.

Chapter 4 focuses on the skirmish in the United States to obtain fast-track negotiating authority to proceed. The history underscores the necessity of considering the effects of domestic policy-making processes on international relations. Although President Bush announced his intention to negotiate in 1990, the United States did not actually choose to enter into negotiations until Congress acted in 1991. The chapter argues that the timing is inexplicable without an understanding of domestic institutions. The rules governing the granting of fast track negotiation authority, and the implications of that authority, together created an opportunity and a motive for political opposition. The ensuing fight nearly derailed the negotiations, delayed their beginning, and altered their character. Thus the first section of the book concludes that the decision to negotiate NAFTA must be understood as both a domestic and an international phenomenon, a decision made by three national systems interacting in a larger international system.

International Negotiation

Chapter 5 describes the negotiation of the commercial agreement and argues that to make sense of the process and outcome of international negotiation requires close attention to the configurations of interests and institutions in the domestic arenas of all three countries. The analytic commentary at the end of the chapter uses simple spatial models to demonstrate the value of a two-level games framework, in which the bargaining space available to international negotiators is constrained by domestic factional interests. The analysis suggests that the central negotiating challenge was to coordinate domestic and international bargaining in such a way as to make possible international agreement.

Chapter 6 describes the negotiation of the supplemental agreements on labor and environment. This chapter argues that to explain the outcome requires attention not only to the interaction of domestic interest groups but also to the dynamics within interest groups. It extends the two-level bargaining model to a multilevel model that includes intra-organizational bargaining among individual-level actors. The chapter also points to the necessity of considering the larger context in which these negotiations took place, in particular the looming shadow of the ratification fight in the United States.

The chapter, however, concludes that a purely interest-based model is ultimately insufficient to explain the motivation of individuals in these groups and the nature of the gathering storm over ratification, and suggests the necessity for considering the role of symbolic politics.

The Politics of Ratification

Chapter 7 describes the politics of advocacy in the United States, with particular attention to the motivation and tactics of NAFTA's opponents. The chapter argues that the disagreement between the magnitude and pattern of U.S. domestic opposition and the economic and other interests at stake challenges rational choice theories of political behavior. To make sense of the character of domestic opposition to NAFTA requires interpretation through a symbolic constructivist lens. Many opponents (and many supporters) based their position not on what NAFTA logically would do to their interests but on what NAFTA symbolized to them. The chapter does not argue that this was "irrational," however. First, given their values and understandings of NAFTA's meaning, individuals adopted reasonable stances. Second, given the costs associated with acquiring and processing information about NAFTA, and the likely low payoff from such an investment, individuals quite rationally chose to rely on relatively simple symbols and stories to form their judgments. Third, supplying such symbolism was quite rational for policy entrepreneurs who had interests in NAFTA or in using NAFTA to further other interests. Taken together, supply and demand create a market for meaning. But rational choice cannot explain the form of the exchange—which symbols were demanded and which were supplied.

Chapter 8 describes the campaign to pass NAFTA in Congress and the eventual success of the campaign. The analysis considers the problem of political diagnosis faced by NAFTA's advocates in the fall of 1993. The problem was partly institutional. The rules of fast track, the organization of Congress, and bureaucratic inertia in the administration all presented significant obstacles to assembling an implementing bill and bringing it to a vote. The problem was partly about interests. The configuration of interests mobilized against NAFTA and the ability of those groups to affect the votes of members of Congress threatened NAFTA's prospects if it came to a vote. And the problem was partly about the social construction of NAFTA. NAFTA's symbolic meaning to the general public, to members of interest groups, and even to members of Congress created political pressures and perceptions of those pressures that threatened to overwhelm NAFTA.

To pass NAFTA, all three problems needed to be solved. The chapter argues that strategists in the Clinton administration, Congress, and the business community pulled together a coherent and effective strategy that involved management of institutions, bargaining with interests to build a supporting coalition, and symbolic communication to reconstruct the meaning of NAFTA for the interested public, key opinion leaders, and members of Congress.

The concluding chapter pulls together the analytic and historical threads of the book. It argues that a practical theory of politics must cross boundaries. Political processes may involve the competition of interests, the operation of institutions, and the creation of symbolic constructs. Such processes may operate among nations at the international level, among groups in domestic political arenas, and among individuals situated at various locations in the political landscape. Theories that deal with only one cell of the matrix, while useful, are necessarily incomplete. Attempts to drive out competitors are misguided. The goal should not be parsimony for parsimony's sake. The question is not which one theory is correct, but which approach (or approaches) is most appropriate for the problem at hand. The compleat political analyst needs a full toolbox and the ability to judge which tool the task requires.

2   A Framework for Political Analysis

Facts do not speak for themselves; they must be interpreted. If we are to move beyond a recounting of the events of NAFTA to an interpretation of them, we need theory. And if the nature of the understanding we seek is of a form that not only provides a satisfactory explanation after the fact but also might have provided useful guidance to actors in these events, we need a theoretical apparatus of some complexity.

The previous chapter discussed briefly the nature of theory for practical political analysis and argued that its form will necessarily be more complex and less universal than is the norm for contemporary political science. This chapter develops a framework for political analysis of international relations that will be applied and further developed in subsequent chapters. The framework has two dimensions. The first is the *level of analysis*, the assumptions made about the degree of aggregation or disaggregation most useful for analyzing international relations. Although, in principle, there are numerous possible levels, the framework consolidates them into three: international, domestic, and individual. The second dimension of the framework is the *mode of analysis*, the assumptions made about the nature of political behavior and of the ways in which these combined behaviors result in outcomes. The framework categorizes these modes as rational choice, institutional process, and symbolic construction, roughly the politics of interests, institutions, and ideas (figure 2.1).

Together, these dimensions define a matrix of possible theoretical approaches into which the prominent theories of international relations can be placed. The matrix is not intended to represent alternative and necessarily competing approaches, however. On the contrary, it is intended to suggest the possibility of a coherent and integrated approach. There are no necessary contradictions among rational choice, institutional process, and constructivist approaches or among theories that focus on the international, domestic, or individual level. Indeed, these approaches are naturally complementary, notwithstanding the sometimes fierce intellectual warfare waged among different schools of thought.

The question is not which approach is *right* but rather which ones are most useful for modeling the phenomena we seek to explain. The politics of NAFTA operated on many levels and in many modes. NAFTA was about the behavior of nations, of domestic pressure groups and political institutions, and of individuals within domestic groups and institutions. These behaviors were at times choices made rationally; at times executions of previously established rules, routines, and habits; at times responses to symbolic constructions.

But one cannot consider everything at once. The purpose of analysis is to focus on what is important, not to capture every complexity. The issue is which approach gives the greatest analytic leverage for the question at hand. This book argues that the choice of level and mode of analysis depends on the context and the question being asked. Under some conditions, treating nations as unitary, rational actors is an extraordinarily useful fiction. Under

Mode of Politics

Level of Analysis	Rational Choice	Institutional Process	Symbolic Response
International	Realism	Regime Theory	Epistemic Communities
Domestic (Group)	Political Economy	Organizational behavior	Cultural anthropology
Individual	Public Choice and Institutional Economics	Cognitive Psychology	Constructivism, Symbolic Interactionism

FIGURE 2.1 Dimensions of a framework for political analysis, with a partial mapping of relevant theoretical approaches.

others, however, such an approach may obscure critical features of the system and lead analysis astray. These conditions can be partially specified beforehand. But part of the art of political analysis is to be quick on one's feet, to recognize the nature of political processes even when they could not have been accurately predicted. In this regard, the political analyst is something of a scientific naturalist, for whom science is a tool for sharpening observation, not a substitute for it.

Before proceeding, it is worth reiterating what the book is *not* arguing. It is not arguing for the *general* truth or falsity of any one theory or theoretical approach. It is interested in the extent to which a particular theoretical lens, applied to a particular question at a particular moment in time, allows the analyst to explain observations, predict events, or perhaps most importantly, prescribe a strategy for actors in the event. Whence comes the unusual structure of the book, with historical narratives first and analysis second. The point is to explicate history, not to use history to justify theory.

Dimensions of the Analytic Framework

Theories of politics may be based on different levels of analysis and on different assumptions about the nature of political processes. This section sketches out a framework with three levels of analysis—international, domestic, and individual—and three modes of political logic—rational choice, institutional process, and symbolic construction. Together these categories define a matrix of possible theoretical approaches, as illustrated in figure 2.1.

The Level of Analysis

On what level should analysis focus? In one sense, the answer is a given for the study of *inter*-national relations: The forum is the international arena in which nations are the core actors. Yet the nation is not necessarily the appropriate aggregation on which to focus analysis. The behavior of nations in the international arena may be best explained as the outcome of domestic political processes among groups or institutions within nations, or by the behaviors of specific individuals within those groups or institutions.

Many levels of analysis are possible. This chapter adopts the common three-level taxonomy proposed by Kenneth Waltz: international, domestic, and individual.[1] It begins with international-level or systemic approaches, because they are the most parsimonious and because systemic theories dominate the field of international relations. It then turns to domestic-level analysis, in which the core actors are subnational institutions and groups acting and interacting in domestic political arenas. Finally, it considers individual-level analysis, in which the core actors are individuals acting and interacting within domestic groups and institutions.

International Level Analysis

One possibility for theory is to focus exclusively on the political processes in the international arena. Such an approach presumes that intranational politics can be safely ignored in explaining national behavior. The dominant theories of international relations all make this assumption, although they differ with respect to their characterization of the nature of the international system: rational choice in the case of realism and neorealism,[2] institutional process in the case of neoliberal institutionalism or regime theory,[3] or symbolic response in the case of constructivist theories of international relations.[4]

There are obvious reasons for basing international relations theory on the nation. One is that nations must be at least the nominal actors in the system if the object of study is *inter*-national relations, as noted above. A second is the inherent parsimony of the approach. By dispensing with domestic politics, the analyst has many fewer variables to consider.

NAFTA, viewed through this lens, was a purely international phenomenon, the outcome of national behaviors in the international arena.

Domestic Level Analysis

A second possibility for a theory of international relations is to treat the behavior of nations as the consequence of domestic politics: the behaviors of domestic interest groups, domestic political institutions, or subnational communities of shared belief. Nations are the nominal actors in the international system, but national behavior is determined by the action and interaction of bureaucracies and legislatures, political parties, business and union lobbies, and other advocacy groups.

NAFTA, viewed through this lens, was about the interaction of three domestic political systems—about the way in which the actions and interactions of domestic interest groups, political institutions, and subnational communities determined the international process.

There is obviously an extremely rich array of possibilities here, in part because of the proliferation of actors, in part because of the complex possibilities for interactions among them, and in part because once one admits the possibility of disaggregating the nation, it is hard to know where to stop. Should the analyst treat a coalition such as the AFL-CIO (American Federation of Labor and Congress of Industrial Organizations) as the unit of analysis or consider it to be comprised of its member unions? Is the appropriate unit of analysis class groupings, industrial sectors, or firms?[5] Adding to the analytic complexity is the phenomenon of such transnational actors as multinational enterprises (MNEs) and other international groups and institutions operating in domestic political arenas.

Not surprisingly, given the proliferation of possible variables, the field of international relations has tended to avoid entanglement with the complexity of domestic politics and has left these matters to comparative politics and political economy. One exception to this, on which this book will later draw, is two-level games theory, an approach to modeling the interaction between domestic and international levels.[6]

Individual Actors

Finally, the behavior of nations in international affairs can be treated as the consequence of the actions and interactions of individuals. These individuals may be located at the pinnacle of national institutions, heads of state, for example; within domestic groups, members of Congress or union members, for example; or in the general public. In this conception of international relations, national behavior may reflect either the particular choices of powerful individuals or the collective consequences of numerous individual choices. In either case, however, understanding how nations behave in international affairs requires attention to individual interests, habits of thought, or worldviews.

Obviously, we are a long way from a general theory of international relations once we entertain the possibility that understanding international affairs requires understanding particular individuals. For that reason, most theories of international relations have steered far clear of such entanglements. One exception to this is the small but important literature on elite decision making for foreign policy making.[7] The literature on intraorganizational politics, within interest groups or within Congress for example, has generally not focused on matters of foreign policy and has been largely ignored by the field of international relations.

NAFTA, viewed through this lens, was about the behaviors of particular individuals at different locations in the political process, including heads of state Salinas, Bush, and Mulroney; leaders and followers within groups in all three countries, for example Ross Perot and members of his organization United We Stand America; or individuals in the general public.

Modes of Politics

Theories of politics also differ in the assumptions they make about the fundamental nature of political behavior and political processes. These core assumptions determine what attributes of circumstance the political analyst must consider to explain and predict international outcomes. Although there are many variants of theory, they can be classified into three broad paradigms: rational choice, institutional process, and symbolic response.

The distinctions among these approaches to international relations correspond to the major cleavages not only within political science, but more broadly in the social sciences. The relationship among these approaches is generally thought to be a contest, an orientation that has led to considerable tension among advocates of each school. This need not be so, as this chapter will argue below. But first, it is useful to consider the ways in which these approaches do differ and how their application to NAFTA would lead to different interpretations.

Rational Choice

One approach to the analysis of politics, and thus a basis for theories of international relations, is to assume that the behavior of actors in the system (at whatever level of analysis one adopts) is determined by rational choice. This means actors have stable preferences or interests, consider the alternative choices available to them, predict the consequences of their choices, evaluate likely outcomes in terms of their interests, and choose the strategy with the highest expected value. Strong rational choice theories assume complete information and perfect ability to process it. Weaker theoretical forms relax these assumptions and allow for incomplete information and less than complete ability to process it, particularly in mapping from alternatives to outcomes, but all assume behavior is essentially interest-maximizing.

Rational choice approaches are also divided on the degree to which preferences themselves are "rational." One stance is that preferences be *substantively* rational, i.e., that actors always seek to maximize the same set of core interests—power or wealth, for instance. Other approaches allow for the possibility that interests may change or be selectively triggered by different circumstances. All rational choice approaches, however, assume some degree of *procedural* rationality, i.e., that actors are strategically rational in pursuit of their interests, whatever the origin of those interests.[9]

Rational choice approaches seek to predict how individual choices will aggregate into collective action. Rarely are outcomes dictated by any one actor. Rather, they are the consequence of choices jointly made by two or more players in a game. The essence of politics, therefore, is strategic interaction among competing or complementary interests. The dominant metaphor is that of a game or a negotiation.

Rational choice methods, adopted from economics and game theory, have had tremendous success in establishing themselves as the dominant mode in contemporary political science.[8] The methodology has great virtues of clarity and parsimony. From relatively simple assumptions, one can make clear predictions. The essence of many apparently complex phenomena can be profitably viewed as relatively simple games. The approach has been applied to the behavior of individuals in groups and organizations, to contests among interest groups, to bureaucratic behavior, to legislatures, and, of course, to international affairs.

Rational choice approaches to international relations could locate rationality at any of the levels identified above: nations, domestic groups, or individuals. The dominant rational choice approach in international relations—realism—takes the nation as the core actor. Contemporary structural realism assumes that nations are both substantively and procedurally rational.[10] There have been relatively fewer attempts to connect rational choice processes involving lower-level actors to international relations, with the exception of the two-level games approach noted above.

NAFTA, interpreted solely through a rational choice lens, could be viewed as a game among three nations, each seeking to maximize its national interests; the interaction of three domestic games among groups within Canada, Mexico, and the United States; or a game among key individuals situated at particular locations in the political process. Rational choice models, we will see in later chapters, need not be confined to one level of analysis. NAFTA can also be profitably viewed as a two-level game in which domestic groups bargain at one level to determine national strategies at the next or as an extraordinarily complex multilevel process in which individuals, located in interest groups, business organizations, governmental agencies, or in the general public, interact to determine the stances of groups in intergroup bargains (or of legislators in Congressional bargaining) that in turn determine national stance in the international bargain.

Institutional Process

A second approach to the study of politics generally, and thus a basis for understanding international relations, is to assume that the behavior of actors is determined by preexisting institutions. In this concept of politics, rules, norms, routines, and other institutions limit options for action and at least partially predetermine their selection, thus channeling behavior along established paths. Political behavior is less a choice than an execution of programs. Political outcomes are determined by these predictable processes (and the sometimes quite unpredictable interaction among them). The central metaphor for political behavior is that of a machine, or to put it in more contemporary language, a computer program.[11]

There are strong and weak institutional theories. The strongest forms hold that behaviors are solely determined by institutions and that the nominal actors are largely irrelevant to outcome.[12] Weaker forms hold that institutions restrict choice but do not determine it, that actors are boundedly rational.[13] Institutional approaches also differ on the question of the genesis of institutions. The stronger forms tend be silent on the question, taking institutions as given. Weaker institutional approaches may treat institutions as artifacts of earlier rational choice games, although they insist that the institutions are "sticky"—i.e., once created they persist even though they would not be the outcome of a current rational process—and therefore have some independent effect at any given moment.

As with rational choice approaches, institutional process approaches can be applied at any level of aggregation. International regime theory, the main thrust of which is weak institutional theory, maintains that international institutions restrict national behaviors in international affairs, serving in particular to facilitate cooperation when it might not otherwise occur.[14] Comparative politics has focused much attention on the relationship between domestic institutions and national behavior, although relatively less on the *interactions* among national systems.[15] And at the level of the individual, scholars have investigated the ways in which elite decision makers display bounded rationality with international consequences.[16]

An institutional process interpretation of NAFTA would emphasize the way in which preexisting structures determined the outcome. It might treat the choice to negotiate NAFTA as a manifestation of the international trade regime, or the predictable selection of three domestic trade policy-making systems, or the reflexive behavior of habitual free-traders. To the extent that it considered domestic opposition at all, it might treat unions, for example, as boundedly rational institutions responding in now-routine fashion to trade liberalization.

Symbolic Response

A third approach to the study of politics, and thus a potential basis for theories of international relations, assumes that political behavior is a matter of neither rational choice nor institution process, but is rather a response to the way in which political circumstances are symbolically constructed. In this conception of politics, symbols and symbol systems—including language, ideas, and narratives—affect not only what actors believe about the world, and thus how they predict the consequences of action, but also how they value the actions available to them. The essence of politics, therefore, is a contest among competing constructions.

This approach to politics draws on a rich intellectual tradition largely outside of political science. The approach derives from the early work of sociologist George Herbert Mead and his successors in the Chicago school of sociology; from cultural anthropology, particularly the work of symbolic interactionists such as Clifford Geertz; from social psychologists such as Jerome Bruner; as well as from literary criticism and cultural studies.[17]

Although symbols operate on individuals, symbol systems are socially constructed by communities of shared identity and therefore may operate at several levels of aggregation. Until quite recently, however, there has been relatively little attention given to constructivist or interpretivist approaches in political science.[18] There is now a renewed interest in the role of ideas in politics, more specifically in international politics. At the international level, neoliberal ideology is given credit for creating and maintaining a world economic order.[19] Less grandly, ideas are said to be useful for facilitating international cooperation,[20] and transnational communities of shared belief are said to be helpful in facilitating cooperation on particular international issues.[21] There is also much interest in the role of symbol systems at the national and subnational level, sparked in large measure by recent dramatic expressions of nationalism and ethnic politics.

The politics of NAFTA, viewed through a symbolic lens, might be seen as a contest of ideas at several levels. The decision to negotiate and the form of the commercial agreement could be seen as the triumph of the dominant neoliberal worldview over a discredited economic nationalism. The fierce domestic politics of NAFTA in the United States could be seen as the manifestation of competing symbolic interpretations. Opposition to NAFTA, in particular, might be viewed as a response to what NAFTA had come to symbolize to unions, environmental groups, and economic populists.

An Integrated Framework

The dimensions of level and mode together define a matrix of nine cells, as illustrated in figure 2.1. Most approaches in political science (and in other areas of the social sciences) can be located in one or another of these cells, as illustrated. There is a tendency to view the approaches as competitors and to see the task of scholars as one of determining which approach is right. This is unfortunate. For the political analyst, far more can be gained by treating the approaches as complementary and by considering the possibility of integrated, multilevel, multimode analysis. Each approach, as suggested by the applications briefly described at the end of each preceding section, yields some insight, although none alone is sufficient. The sections that follow argue that, far from being inconsistent, the approaches are logically complementary and that thinking across levels and modes provides useful analytic synergies.

Logical Complementarity of Modes and Levels

There is no inherent contradiction among rational choice, institutional process, and symbolic response. If institutions and symbol systems did not exist, it would be rational to create them.

There are many reasons why it is rational to establish institutions that substitute for reason and to maintain them even when they are no longer optimal (assuming they ever were). For example, the first time one drives home from work, one might choose the route that minimizes travel time. Thereafter, however, letting habit take over is more efficient. Establishing and maintaining institutions as facilitators of collective action is also reasonable.[22] In a world of no transaction costs, perfect information, and no problems of enforcement, institutions would be unnecessary. But in the presence of any of these barriers to efficient negotiation, institutions can reduce transactions costs, improve information, and reduce fears of defection.[23] Given that there are costs of creating an institution, the logic of sunk costs may make it efficient to maintain institutions even when they are less than optimal.

Reliance on symbolic shorthand is also often rational. As Downs has argued, to the extent that actors engage in political behavior in circumstances in which their individual actions have little or no chance of changing the policy outcomes—voting, for instance—it is irrational for them to bear the costs of acquiring and processing information needed to inform rational behavior.[24] In these circumstances it is more efficient to rely on symbolic communication for cues about action. Moreover, it is also possible that what is being consumed is the symbolism itself. As will be argued further in chapter 7, the logic of "rational ignorance" creates a market for symbols, a market for meaning.

There is also no logical inconsistency in thinking of theories at different levels of aggregation, provided that we do not insist on substantive rationality at every level. If, for example, we assume that domestic interest groups are rational actors whose strategic interactions produce national behaviors in international affairs, one cannot also assume that the nation is substantively rational. Such an assumption implies that strategic interaction necessarily leads to socially optimal outcomes, an assertion both empirically and theoretically flawed. The nature of institutions and of symbol systems, however, is that they allow for aggregation. The institutions of the nation-state, for example, allow for bargaining among subnational interests to determine the "national interest" to be pursued by procedurally rational nations in the international arena.

Most theories of politics operate within one mode and at one level of aggregation. There is good reason for this, not least because a single approach is more parsimonious. But what is gained in clarity may come at the expense of accuracy. Combining levels and/or modes of analysis in one model can provide greater insight into political phenomena and, most importantly, can be more useful for informing strategy in a particular circumstance. The issue for the political analyst is to balance the two.

There is no inherent reason why analysis need be confined to one level or one mode. In some circumstances, a model that crosses borders may more than make up for its complexity with its superior fit with the observed data. This discussion has already touched upon the potential virtues of a multilevel or nested bargaining model, in which, for example, nations maximize "interests" determined by the outcome of contests among subnational entities, each of which is maximizing its own interests. We could also consider the interaction between two types of political behaviors at the same level of aggregation, for example between a commercial interest maximizing its economic interests and a citizens' pressure group responding to a symbolic construction. Finally, we may also want to consider processes in terms of one mode of analysis at one level of aggregation and another mode at another level. For instance, nations may behave quite rationally given their "interests" as determined by a domestic politics of symbols.[25]

The Science and Art of Application

So far, this chapter has argued that the politics of NAFTA operated at different levels and in different modes and that there are many potentially useful analytic approaches for analyzing them. But, the reader may protest, one cannot analyze everything in every way. How can one apply such a complex framework? To be useful, a model cannot consider every complexity. Rather, it must abstract sufficiently from the detail to direct attention to what matters. Similarly, one cannot analyze every event through every possible theoretical lens.

Parsimony is a virtue. Yet excessive parsimony may substitute clarity for accuracy. The issue is what can be safely suppressed without doing too much violence to the problem at hand. In deciding what approach to take, the analyst should not abandon the pursuit of parsimony, but this cannot be the only consideration. Some analytic approaches are better for some contexts and some questions than others. Under some circumstances, the complex intrigues of domestic politics may matter little to international outcomes. In others, the costs of such simplifying assumptions may be too high. Under some circumstances, actors may be safely treated as rational interest maximizers. In others, however, such an assumption will lead analysis astray. Determining the appropriate approach is the essence of analytic judgment.

There is a science and an art to this judgment. To some extent, the likely form of politics, and therefore the appropriate approach to take in analyzing it, can be predicted beforehand. On the question of the mode of analysis, first, the greater the potential impact of some event on interests, the more likely actors are to behave in rational self-interested ways. In the NAFTA, the specific terms of the commercial agreement had considerable implications for particular firms. We should expect a domestic politics of interests during the negotiation of that agreement. Conversely, the less is at stake, the more likely habits or symbols will matter more. Second, the more extensive the preexisting institutional arrangements, the more important institutions are likely to be. In the NAFTA, the basic constitutional and legal provisions governing trade decision making in the United States, specifically the fast track process, were long established and elaborate. We should expect this domestic institution to matter most at the stages of authorizing negotiation and ratifying agreement (and to matter less during the negotiation itself, a much more ad hoc institutional arrangement).

The appropriate level of analysis can also be partially predicted. First, to the extent that interests converge at one level—for example, the domestic level—and diverge at the next higher level—here, the international level— the higher level process will be more important than the lower level process. (Of course, collective action failures are possible even with converging interests.) As will be argued in chapter 3, for this reason realism might be more appropriate for international security than for international trade, and in the case of NAFTA, an exclusive focus on the international level is likely to be of limited usefulness. Second, the greater the strength of institutions at a given level of aggregation, the less significant political processes below that level are likely to be. In the case of NAFTA, for example, strong national constitutional structures gave the heads of state considerable latitude in initiating negotiations; consequently, ignoring domestic politics at that stage of the process was more likely to be appropriate. (Chapter 3 will argue, however, that even here, domestic politics matters.) Conversely, only weak national institutions governed the negotiations themselves, so that domestic political processes were more likely to matter.

Although the relative importance of interests and institutions, and the level at which they matter most, may be reasonably predictable, it is somewhat more difficult to know beforehand when an issue will have symbolic resonance. In the case of NAFTA, although one might have anticipated the potential for significant symbolic politics in the United States at the ratification stage (and before), anticipating the extent and the character of that opposition would have been very difficult. This is where the art of political analysis comes into play: As mentioned before, the analyst must be something of political naturalist, equipped with a set of analytic categories that allow for keen observation. One might not have been able to know beforehand that NAFTA would evoke a symbolic reaction, but when it did one could have recognized this reaction for what it was.

Interpreting NAFTA

As described in chapter 1, the rest of this book is divided into coverage of three broad historical stages: the decision to negotiate, the international negotiations, and the US ratification process. At the end of each chapter, an analytic commentary interprets the historical narrative. In each case, the choice of analytic approach reflects a judgment about what is most useful for understanding the history.

Deciding to Negotiate

The decision to negotiate a NAFTA involved two steps: first a decision by the three heads of state to initiate the process, and second, in the United States only, a legally mandated legislative process to authorize the negotiation.

One would expect that the decision to initiate negotiations, of all the stages of the process, would be most amenable to an international level analysis, particularly a rational-choice, realist, approach. Viewed through this lens, the three nations "decided" to negotiate the NAFTA because it was in their interest to do so. At first glance, this interpretation is consistent with the record. But further reflection shows that two important puzzles are not solved by this interpretation: If NAFTA made sense in 1990, why didn't it make sense earlier, and why do nations need to negotiate to persuade each other to do what they should want to do anyway? These puzzles can be partly addressed by institutional and symbolic theories at the international level, but the analytic commentary of chapter 3 will argue that they can best be addressed by considering domestic political processes.

The second step of deciding to negotiate involved the debate in the US Congress in spring 1991 over whether or not to authorize President Bush to proceed. The fast track fight affected both the timing and the agenda of the subsequent negotiations. The key questions here are why there was a fight and why it turned out as it did. The analytic commentary of chapter 4 will argue that answering these questions requires attending to both interests and institutions in the US political arena, as well as to the relationship between them. Powerful domestic groups had competing interests in the fast track process because that institution had profound implications for the ultimate outcome of the whole NAFTA process. The rules governing fast track extension (another institution) created both the opportunity and the context for the contest of those competing interests.

International Negotiations

The NAFTA was negotiated in two installments: first the commercial negotiations from June 1991 to August 1992, and then the supplemental negotiations from February to August 1993. Both negotiations raise questions about process and outcome. Although it is possible to talk about them as purely international processes, we must ultimately consider the roles of subnational aggregates, particularly of domestic interest groups, to make sense of either.

In all three countries, powerful domestic interests had stakes in the outcome of the commercial negotiations. The extent of their power to influence those talks depended in part on national institutional arrangements, but given the inherently ad hoc nature of negotiation itself, institutions played a relatively smaller role at this stage. The analytic commentary of chapter 5, therefore, focuses on the relationship between domestic interest politics and the international negotiation. It develops simple two-level bargaining models to interpret the observed processes and outcomes.

The supplemental negotiations on environment and labor shared many features with the commercial negotiation: Both were negotiations among nations in which domestic interest groups played important roles. They can, therefore, also be interpreted as a two-level game. However, the commercial and the supplemental negotiations differed in important ways. First, unlike

the concentrated economic interests that dominated the commercial negotiations, large-membership organizations played a pivotal role in the side
negotiations. The behavior these pressure groups cannot be explained without consideration of a yet deeper level of bargaining—the individual level
between group leaders and group members. Second, the supplemental negotiations were conducted under much closer public scrutiny and in greater
proximity to the upcoming legislative battle in the US Congress. The ability
of particular groups to influence the bargain cannot be explained fully without reference to this broader political environment in which the negotiation
took place. For both of these reasons, therefore, the analytic commentary of
chapter 6 argues for considering the deeply nested and contextually embedded nature of negotiation processes.

Ratification

The third stage of the NAFTA story involves the politics of ratification in
the United States. The problem here is to explain both the character of the
political battle that developed in 1993 and the eventual outcome. As with
the authorization process in 1991, basic constitutional differences among
the three countries partially explain why only the United States had a significant ratification fight. In Mexico, because of the extraordinary strength
of the ruling party, and in Canada, by virtue of its parliamentary system,
opponents had little opportunity to prevent ratification. In the United States,
however, a different institutional arrangement created just such an opportunity.

A purely institutional perspective, however, cannot explain the level of
political engagement in the United States, particularly the extraordinary
level of grassroots opposition. To that issue the book turns in chapter 7. The
strength and the pattern of opposition presents a puzzle. On the one hand,
the likely effects of NAFTA in the United States, whether on the economy,
the environment, labor standards, or any of the other dimensions of concern
raised in the course of the NAFTA debate, were likely to be exceedingly
small. For example, on the politically sensitive question of NAFTA's likely
effect on the numbers of jobs in the United States, the vast majority of studies
predicted modest net gains, and every sensible economic analysis predicted
tiny effects, one way or the other.

Yet if the "real" impacts of NAFTA were likely to be small, the political reaction to it was anything but. How can we account for the vociferous opposition by unions, grassroots environmental groups, citizens' lobbies, Ross Perot's United We Stand America, and Pat Buchanan? Chapter 7 argues that these political dynamics can only be understood as a response to NAFTA as symbol. It argues that opposition leaders, through the stories they told about NAFTA, constructed a kind of narrative politics in which opposition to NAFTA became less a matter of calculated self-interest than an affirmation of identity. It takes as text the rhetoric of opposition and analyzes the way in which the meaning of NAFTA was constructed.

Finally, the book turns to the vote in the US Congress, the last stage of ratification, and to the nature of the political strategies employed on both sides of the battle. The analytic commentary to chapter 8 argues that to make sense of those strategies now, and more importantly to inform successful strategy in the moment, required thinking across levels and modes of politics. In the end NAFTA was won in part by manipulation of institutional rules, in part by deals to satisfy domestic interests (including some deals that had to be negotiated internationally), but in large measure by a countervailing symbolic campaign of support for NAFTA. Part of the political problem faced by advocates at the time could have been predicted. Commercial interests facing loss of tariff protection were sure to mobilize. However, much of the opposition was hard to predict. To be sure, there were warning signs for the attentive, particularly in 1991. But the crucial matter then was whether the analyst had the right tools in hand to interpret what was happening when it did.

Taken together, the analytic commentaries that follow each historical chapter develop more fully the framework for analysis sketched in this chapter. They constitute an argument about how the political analyst should employ the tools of political science, adapting them as needed, to interpret political phenomena such as NAFTA.

Section I

Deciding to Negotiate

3 Why a North American Free Trade Agreement?

In 1990, Mexico, the United States, and Canada decided to negotiate a North American Free Trade Agreement. A year earlier, even the most enthusiastic advocates of such negotiations thought they were a decade away. Mexico, almost everyone agreed, was not yet ready for such a bold move. The United States was preoccupied with efforts to complete the huge multilateral Uruguay Round of the General Agreement on Tariffs and Trade (GATT) negotiations. Canada was still digesting a free trade agreement with the United States completed two years earlier, an agreement so politically unpopular that the idea of entering into new free trade negotiations was practically unthinkable.

Yet in early February 1990, a year and a half after he took office, Mexican President Carlos Salinas de Gortari decided to ask the United States to negotiate a free trade agreement with Mexico. Within a month, United States President George Bush had agreed to pursue the possibility. In June, Bush and Salinas publicly announced plans to investigate the possibility of negotiating a bilateral agreement.

Canadian Prime Minister Brian Mulroney initially chose to keep Canada on the sidelines. Over the summer, however, Canada decided that it would like a seat at the negotiating table. At the end of August, just as the Bush administration was planning to ask Congress for authority to negotiate with Mexico, Canada asked to join the talks. Mexico and the United States hesitated, fearing that the Canadians would merely complicate negotiations, and not until January did the three countries finally agree to make the talks trilateral and to negotiate a North American free trade area.

Why did Mexico turn north, seeking formal links to a neighbor it had so long kept at a distance? Why did the United States agree to negotiate a free trade agreement with a country it had so long ignored? And why did Canada first decide to stay out and then change its mind?

Mexico Looks North

To appreciate the boldness of the Mexican decision, we need to place it in the context of the troubled history of relations with the United States. Heroic opposition to American aggression is a central theme of Mexican history. At the foot of Chapultapec Castle in the heart of Mexico City is the monument to the "Child Heroes," Mexican cadets who in 1847 jumped to their deaths rather than surrender to the approaching American troops of General Winfield Scott. Since the United States took a third of Mexico by force in the Mexican-American war, Mexicans have had many good reasons to regret their proximity to the United States. Every Mexican knows the aphorism: "Poor Mexico. So far from God, so close to the United States." Fear of U.S. intervention has continued to be a central theme of modern Mexican politics. As the Mexican writer Jorge Castenada has noted, "In nearly all domestic conflicts in modern Mexico, the winning side—since the Revolution, the government side—has raised the specter of national disintegration due to foreign intervention."[1]

A history of distrust created a habit of distance from the United States. Throughout the Cold War, Mexico was a consistent critic of U.S. policy in Vietnam, in Cuba, and in Nicaragua. In economic matters, Mexico had pursued an independent path as well, tightly restricting foreign investment and limiting foreign trade. In keeping with the spirit of the Mexican revolution of 1910, Mexico organized its agricultural sector in a system of farm communes known as *ejidos*, maintained a state-owned oil monopoly created when it nationalized foreign-owned oil companies in 1938, and maintained high levels of state ownership and control elsewhere in the economy. The move toward a free trade agreement with the United States represented a sharp break with this past.

The Mexican Debt Crisis

During the administrations of Luis Echeverría (1970–1976) and José López Portillo (1976–1982) Mexico pursued an "import substitution" approach to economic development.[2] The idea, popular at the time throughout the developing world, was to nurture domestic manufacturing through subsidies and protection, on the theory that economies with larger manufacturing sectors grow more rapidly. In addition, in part as a legacy of the revolutionary tradition in Mexico, the Mexican government greatly expanded its role in the Mexican economy through state ownership and extensive regulation.

Mexican trade protection in this period involved both high tariff and nontariff barriers. The maximum tariff was 100 percent, with an average tariff rate near 20 percent. More formidable, however, were license requirements for imports. In 1960, 38 percent of imports were subject to import permits. By 1982, every import into Mexico required a permit, applications for which could be denied if domestic substitutes were available or for whatever reasons Mexican officials did not deem the import acceptable.[3] Moreover, Mexico declined to join the GATT, the basic international agreement adhered to by most of the world's trading community.

State ownership of "strategic industries" increased dramatically during the 1970s. From 1970 to 1982, the number of *parastatals* (state-owned enterprises) increased from 391 to 1155, and their share of the national gross domestic product (GDP) rose to 18 percent.[4] Petroles Mexicanos (Pemex), the state-owned oil company, continued to enjoy its monopoly status in that most important industry. Extensive government regulation governed the remaining private sector.

For most of the 1970s the strategy appeared to be highly successful. The Mexican economy grew at an average of over 7 percent for the decade, led by strong industrial expansion.[5] When large oil deposits were discovered in the mid 1970s, there appeared to be no reason why the boom wouldn't last indefinitely. But the oil discovery masked deep structural problems that would make expansion unsustainable and create economic disaster in 1982.

High oil prices created a glut of dollars on the world market in the mid 1970s. Banks found themselves with cash and looked for people to lend it to. Mexico was only too happy to borrow, using the funds to prop up its increasingly uncompetitive state enterprises and to fund a huge fiscal deficit. Expansionary monetary policy and an artificially high peso also helped sustain the binge. By 1982, Mexico's total external debt was $92 billion.[6]

Then the wheels came off. A world-wide recession made it harder for Mexico to sell goods abroad to obtain the foreign currency it needed to repay its debts. Tight monetary policy in the United States and elsewhere in the developed world raised real interest rates and made it more difficult to pay old debts with new loans. Furthermore, the peso devalued relative to the dollar, making it more expensive to pay back the largely dollar-denominated debt. By the summer of 1982, commercial banks had stopped lending to Mexico. In August, Mexico effectively declared bankruptcy, becoming the first developing country to suspend payments on international debts.

In the throes of this economic crisis, President López Portillo responded with the populist gesture of blaming the financial community and nationalized the banks as one of his last acts in office. The powerful Mexican financial community, long an ally of the ruling Partido Revolucionario Institucional (PRI) party, was outraged.[7] The move was popular with the public but soon proved economically disastrous. Capital fled Mexico, unemployment soared, and real wages plummeted.

The de la Madrid Administration

Since the Mexican Revolution, the PRI had ruled Mexico without serious challenge. As Mexico's constitution allowed the president only a single six-year term, the question of succession hinged on the selection of the next PRI candidate by his predecessor. López Portillo's hand-picked successor was his planning minister, Miguel de la Madrid, who inherited the mess when he took office at the end of 1982.

Despite his ties to López Portillo, de la Madrid presented a sharp contrast to his populist predecessor. With a graduate degree in public administration from Harvard, de la Madrid was more of a technocrat who believed in market economics and free trade. With the strong encouragement of the international finance community, de la Madrid first moved to stabilize the domestic economy. In his inaugural address in December, the new president condemned the "economic populism" of his predecessor and announced a program of economic austerity. He raised taxes, cut the budget, lifted price controls on most items, and negotiated the terms of Mexico's debt with its creditors and the International Monetary Fund. The policies sparked sharp criticism from the Mexican left. The Socialist Workers Party, for example, said that "severe austerity, hunger, unemployment and misery, along with repression of the masses and cuts in democratic and labor liberties will be certain under the government of Miguel de la Madrid."[8]

De la Madrid, a cautious politician by nature, was careful not to move too quickly. He moved most cautiously on the trade front, but in 1985 he began to reverse Mexico's protectionist policies. In July, de la Madrid cut the percentage of imports requiring import licenses to 65 percent, down from 100 percent at the beginning of his term. Then, at the end of the year, he took the dramatic step of applying to join the GATT. Mexico had come close to applying before, in 1979, but populist opposition by a coalition of intellectuals, small business owners, and labor union leaders had persuaded López Portillo to back away. This time, de la Madrid carefully cultivated support in the private sector first, orchestrated a Mexican Senate panel recommendation in favor of joining GATT, and then appeared to respond to the Senate demands. There was no backlash.[9] Over the next year, Mexico negotiated the terms of accession to GATT, agreeing to cut its maximum tariff to 50 percent and to work to lower it further.

In 1987, de la Madrid faced another economic crisis. The stock market crashed; the peso fell precipitously; and inflation spiked up again. De la Madrid's response, unlike that of his predecessor, was to accelerate economic reform. At the end of 1987, de la Madrid issued decrees that lowered Mexico's maximum tariff to 20 percent (which lowered the weighted average tariff to 11 percent) and eliminated import license requirements for all but a quarter of imports.[10] The decrees had been carefully worked out with key factions of the business community—including especially Augustín Legoretta, former president of the National Bank of Mexico and president of the Coordinating Council of Entrepreneurs (CCE), and Vincente Bortoni, president of the National Confederation of Industrial Chambers (CONCAMIN), a coalition dominated by large manufacturing interests—and with the largest labor unions as part of an overall pact to restrain prices and wages.[11]

As the Mexican economy began to open in the 1980s, international trade became more important to Mexico. Mexican exports nearly doubled in real terms from 1980 to 1989, going from $15.2 billion in 1980 to $29.6 billion in 1989 (in constant 1987 dollars). As a percentage of GDP, exports rose from 12 percent, where they had been for decades, to 20 percent. In the same period imports soared from $19.3 billion to $31.1 billion, although they dipped precipitously during the economic crises of the mid 1980s.[12] All of this meant that by the end of the decade, much more of the Mexican economy was tied to international commerce than at the beginning.

Most of these ties were to the United States. Two-way trade between Mexico and the United States soared from $18.4 billion in 1979 to $51.5 billion in 1989 (measured in current dollars). For Mexico, this represented more than two-thirds of both imports and exports. Mexico became the United States' third-largest trading partner after Canada and Japan. Foreign direct investment in Mexico, which had fallen to less than $1 billion a year in 1982 and 1983, rose to an average of $3 billion a year in the last three years of the decade. The accumulated value of that investment rose fourfold during the decade to $26.6 billion, two-thirds of which was from the United States.[13] The growth in trade and investment represented a kind of "silent integration," which in both countries created interests that had a stake in freer trade.

Some portion of the overall increase in commerce came from rapid growth in the *maquiladora* program, which allowed foreign businesses to locate in areas of northern Mexico near the U.S. border, import components duty-free from outside, assemble them, and export the finished product without duties. The program began in 1965 as part of Mexico's strategy to improve the economy of its border region and support the United States' efforts to reduce incentives for illegal immigration. During the 1960s and 1970s, the program grew very slowly. In 1980, 620 plants employed 119,546 workers, mostly women, and mostly in textiles and light manufacturing. But in the 1980s, the program took off, driven in part by a fall in the value of the peso. By August 1989, 1699 plants employed 443,682 workers and the numbers were growing rapidly. The biggest growth came in electronics and transport equipment, which by the end of the decade accounted for 38 percent and 20 percent of the total, respectively.[14] Unlike the early sweatshops, many of the new plants were efficient modern facilities with high levels of productivity.

Despite the growing importance of the United States in the Mexican economy, de la Madrid was cautious about establishing formal economic ties with the United States. Mexican politicians have always been leery of appearing to be too close to the United States, and differences over policy in Central America kept relations cool between the governments for most of the decade. But quietly, the United States and Mexico were laying the groundwork for more extensive trade and investment cooperation. In 1985, they signed an agreement governing subsidies and countervailing duties. In November 1987, the two countries agreed to a "Framework of Principles and Procedures," in which they agreed to consult with each other whenever disputes arose. The understanding was a breakthrough of sorts. Sectoral accords on steel, alcoholic beverages, and textiles followed. But the agreement was very modest compared with the free trade agreement the United States was then negotiating with Canada.

Mexico sat on the sidelines while Canada and the United States negotiated a free trade agreement in 1986 and 1987. A similar agreement with the

United States seemed only a remote possibility, although the idea received support in some quarters. In his announcement of candidacy for president in 1979, Ronald Reagan had proposed a "North American Accord" among Mexico, Canada, and the United States. "The key to our future security may lie in both Mexico and Canada becoming much stronger countries than they are today," he said. At the time, the idea was received very coolly in Mexico, although López Portillo was pleased by the respect Reagan showed for Mexico when Reagan visited to push the idea. Others in the United States continued to promote the concept periodically. The economist Sidney Weintraub, a noted expert on Mexico, published *Free Trade Between Mexico and the United States?* in 1984, calling for just that.[15] But de la Madrid had no intention of moving faster than the political climate would allow. During his administration "there was no idea of a free trade agreement," he later asserted.[16]

Salinas Takes Over

Senator Bill Bradley (Democrat, N.J.) had been taking an interest in Mexico since his chairmanship of the Debt Subcommittee of the Senate Finance Committee thrust him into a prominent role in the effort to restructure the Mexican debt. He started making annual private trips to Mexico in 1985 to learn more about the country and to get to know its leaders. Bradley became the foremost advocate in the U.S. Senate for forgiving some of the debt if Mexico pursued economic reform. "Clearly they needed an open trading system and the Mexican economy needed to be modernized," he recalled. Bradley became an advocate of a free trade agreement between Mexico and the United States, not only for its economic merits, but also as a way to begin to bridge the "cultural divide" between the two countries.

In 1987, on one of his visits to Mexico, Bradley met with de la Madrid's young planning minister, Carlos Salinas de Gortari. Bradley found Salinas very impressive. Salinas, a Ph.D. political economist from Harvard, was the "most economically oriented" of the Mexican cabinet officers, "a very precise thinker," recalled Bradley. The two men shared similar views about Mexican economic reform. But when Bradley urged Salinas to consider a free trade agreement with the United States, "Salinas said 'No, no.' I don't think he thought Mexico was ready for it," recalled Bradley.

Shortly afterward, de la Madrid tapped Salinas to be the PRI candidate and his presumed successor. For the first time, however, a PRI candidate faced a significant electoral challenge, this time from Cuahtémoc Cárdenas, the son of a former president and the leader of a liberal coalition promising political reform. Salinas won a narrow victory in an election marred by allegations of vote fraud and a widespread belief that Cárdenas had actually won a plurality of the vote. From this shaky beginning, Salinas quickly proved to be an effective politician in office, launching an aggressive anti-corruption campaign and a highly publicized rural development program known as "Solidarity."[17]

Salinas brought into office cabinet ministers much like himself, most importantly Jaime Serra Puche as Minister of Commerce and Trade and Pedro Aspe as Finance Minister. Both Serra and Aspe were Ph.D. economists, trained in the United States. Like Salinas, they believed in market economics and in free trade and understood the importance of international financial markets in determining the flow of capital around the world. In their view, to grow economically, Mexico needed to attract foreign capital. And the way to make Mexico attractive to foreign capital was to complete the transformation of the Mexican economy.

Where de la Madrid had been cautious, Salinas was bold. In the first year he announced further unilateral tariff reductions, the elimination of most remaining import licensing requirements, and privatization of the vast majority of Mexico's state-owned enterprises, most importantly the banks that had been nationalized by López Portillo. Salinas also moved to secure closer economic relations with the United States. In this, he was helped by the election of George Bush in 1988. As a Texan, Bush was familiar with Mexico. Before he took office, he invited Salinas to his home in Houston. The two men quickly developed a personal friendship. Bush directed Treasury Secretary Nick Brady to work with Pedro Aspe on a debt relief package that would finally put the debt problem to rest. The Brady plan, as it became known, committed the United States to a position in favor of significant debt relief.

The two countries also began a more intensive dialogue on trade matters. In October 1989, the United States and Mexico reached an "Understanding Regarding Trade and Investment Facilitation Talks," which went somewhat beyond the framework agreement of two year earlier. The convention affirmed their intention to enter a series of proactive negotiations, not just consultations as needed when problems arose, to deal with such cross-sectional issues as intellectual property, services, and investment, although little real progress was made.

In December, while in the United States to sign the accord, President Salinas met with leaders of the U.S. business community. He found great enthusiasm for further trade and investment liberalization. At his urging, Jim Robinson, Chief Executive Officer (CEO) of American Express, and Colby Chandler, CEO of Eastman Kodak, both of whose companies had experience operating in Mexico, formed a task force of the Business Round-table, an elite business organization composed of the CEOs of the largest U.S. corporations, to consider ways to strengthen U.S.–Mexican trade relations and to make recommendations to both governments.

Still, the vision on both sides of the border was of incremental progress. The thinking in both capitals was that such a dramatic move as a free trade agreement was many years off. In Mexico City, the idea just seemed too politically risky, particularly given that it had originally come from the highly unpopular Ronald Reagan. "Every time the idea came up, we kept on leaving it behind us," recalled Jaime Serra. "Our analysis was clouded by the political and ideological background of the proposal."

In Washington, free trade negotiations with Mexico seemed premature to most pundits. Better to let the fallout from the Canada agreement settle and to finish the multilateral Uruguay Round of the GATT before starting something new. The American academic Sidney Weintraub, a leading proponent of free trade with Mexico, voiced the prevailing view: "In the next 10 years we may see a free-trade agreement with Mexico, but it won't come before then. We'll see a series of agreements on textile quotas, steel, intellectual property and so on. We'll see a series of negotiations that will conclude in a free-trade agreement."[18] Mike Aho, director of international economic studies at the Council on Foreign Relations, and former aide to Senator Bill Bradley, stated that "I don't see any comprehensive agreement between Mexico and the United States before the next century."[19] Aho, however, hedged his bets. A free trade agreement might come earlier, he predicted, if the Uruguay Round stalled.

The Decision in Davos

At the beginning of February every year, heads of state, finance ministers, politicians, and corporate leaders gather in Davos, Switzerland, for a week of informal discussions at the World Economic Forum. In 1990, Carlos Salinas was to address the opening session. For Salinas, the trip to Europe was a great opportunity to promote what his administration was doing in Mexico and to interest international investors. He had just finished another renegotiation of the Mexican debt, an agreement that would be announced in Davos, but Salinas knew that for his reform program to work he needed an infusion of foreign capital. "We were still facing some confidence problems," recalled Jaime Serra, who accompanied Salinas to Davos. Here was a chance to sell the Europeans on what Salinas was doing in Mexico.

But what Salinas discovered in Davos was that Europe was more interested in looking inward than outward at Mexico. The deadline of 1992 for completing negotiations for a European Union loomed. And the talk in Davos was about the fall of the Berlin Wall and the stunning changes in Eastern Europe. Salinas urged the Europeans not to lose sight of the rest of the world. "May these splendid signs of change not cloud Europe's global vision, nor turn its attention away from our continent—particularly Mexico—and from other regions of the world," he implored the gathering in his keynote address. But Salinas quickly concluded that the Europeans were doing exactly what he urged them not to do. "We realized that the world was moving very quickly," recalled Jaime Serra. Mexico would need to do something dramatic if it wanted attention.

Salinas and his cabinet officers talked late into the night, for the first time discussing seriously the option of a comprehensive free trade agreement with the United States. From an economic point of view, a comprehensive agreement made a great deal of sense. First, it was consistent with the whole economic reform program under way. "We wanted our economy to be competitive," said Serra. Opening markets piecemeal would create distortions. "You can't open up in cookies if you don't have competitive wheat," he explained. To be competitive, Mexican industry needed competitive inputs, including better services and cheaper capital. Second, by combining negotiations, Mexico would be in a better position to obtain concessions in areas in which it had comparative advantages, for example in agriculture. If issues were handled separately, the U.S. would only negotiate seriously in sectors such as financial services in which it wanted something. Third, and most significant in the context of their experience in Davos, a free trade agreement with the United States would be the kind of bold move that would attract attention in the international financial markets and bolster confidence in the direction that Mexico was heading. Still, the politics made Salinas and his advisors nervous. The meeting broke up without a decision.

Late that night, Carlos Salinas decided: Mexico should seek a free trade agreement with the United States. Jaime Serra met with United States Trade Representative (USTR) Carla Hills the next day. At their meeting, Serra suggested to Hills that their deputies handle the minor issue about which they were meeting. Serra told Hills his government would like a free trade agreement with the United States. Hills told Serra she would have to consult with her president.

The United States Responds

The Mexican proposal came as a surprise to United States Trade Representative Carla Hills and her staff. Their initial reaction was not enthusiastic. For the USTR, the top priority was finishing the multilateral Uruguay Round of the GATT, which was taking much longer than initially expected. The thinking was that there were not enough resources to negotiate both the Round and a bilateral agreement with Mexico. Jules Katz, the deputy USTR and chief negotiator for the GATT negotiations, recalled his reaction:

> I had some concerns. First, 1990 was the year we were going to finish the Uruguay round, and free trade negotiations with Mexico might be distracting. Second, I had concerns about how far the Mexicans would go. They had always insisted on special and differential treatment. Third, there might be undesirable diversionary effects on the Caribbean and Central America.

In Mexico, Salinas and Serra worried that things would move slowly if they relied only on Hills and the USTR, so they decided to open some other channels of communication. Serra and Jose "Pepe" Cordoba, Salinas's Chief of Staff, flew to Washington to meet with Secretary of State James Baker, Secretary of Commerce Robert Mosbacher, and Secretary of the Treasury Nicholas Brady, as well as USTR Hills.

Mosbacher, like Bush a Texan, supported the idea. Indeed, he had been pushing it himself for some time. This was important, since it meant that the usually protectionist Commerce Department would not stand in the way. Brady was less receptive at first. He told Serra that he would prefer to separate negotiations on financial services from other issues. I'm not trading banks for avocados, he told Serra. Serra responded that if avocados weren't on the table, he wasn't trading banks. Serra persuaded him that the talks needed to be comprehensive.

The Mexican delegation knew that the key was Baker, clearly the most influential cabinet officer in the Bush administration. Without Baker's support, Mexico would not pursue the agreement. In Baker, however, Serra and Cordoba found a strong ally. Baker, another Texan, viewed stronger ties with Mexico as a cornerstone of the U.S. foreign policy. In his confirmation hearings before the Senate Foreign Relations Committee in 1989, Baker had told the committee: "It is time that we regarded Mexico with the respect and the seriousness it warrants. Whatever the past, we must all be aware that America's relationship with Mexico means a very great deal. I happen to believe, Mr. Chairman, that it is as important as our relationship with any other country in the world."

Baker responded to the Mexican initiative with enthusiasm. As Robert Zoellick, then counselor to the Secretary and Baker's closest aide for international economic issues, recalls, he "saw the free trade agreement with Mexico as part of an overall strategy of building our continental base." Baker advised President Bush to accept the Mexican proposal.

On a Sunday evening in late February, Carlos Salinas called George Bush. Would the United States be willing to enter into free trade negotiations with Mexico? he asked. The answer was "yes." Bush would direct his administration to work on the details. The two leaders agreed to quietly build support during the spring and to use the occasion of Salinas's visit to Washington in June to announce the agreement.

At the USTR, Carla Hills asked her staff for an assessment of the policy and political implications of a free trade agreement. They concluded that an agreement was both more technically and more politically feasible than many at the USTR had originally thought. Chip Roh, Assistant USTR for North America, led the effort. He recalls that "[t]he analysis made the USTR more optimistic. Traditional [trade] malcontents such as steel, etc. wouldn't be opposed. There was a lot of interest in the investment community. Mexico was reforming and its economy was getting better. In short, it seemed doable."

Administration officials began conferring with key political players around Washington. The support of House Ways and Means Committee Chairman Dan Rostenkowski and Senate Finance Committee Chairman Lloyd Bentsen were essential. Any agreement would eventually have to pass through their committees. As Jules Katz recalls, "Bentsen and Rosty were not overwhelmingly supportive. They were concerned that we were loading one more thing onto the political process. But they didn't put up a red light."

In March, a delegation of prominent American CEOs led by Kodak's Chandler and American Express's Robinson traveled to Mexico to consult with Mexican officials and business leaders. The group had come together in the fall, at the suggestion of Carlos Salinas, who thought they could be helpful in furthering the bilateral trade relationship. Their purpose now was to encourage Mexico to move more quickly to reduce trade barriers. As they made the rounds, they discovered that Serra was now thinking more boldly than they were and was now talking about comprehensive free trade negotiations. Robinson and Chandler agreed to help organize U.S. business support for the idea by the time of the announcement in June.

In late March, Canadian Prime Minister Brian Mulroney arrived in Mexico for a state visit. The agenda included signing a Memorandum of Understanding committing Canada and Mexico to continuing discussions on trade matters, but little else. In Mexico, Mulroney heard that the Mexicans were pursuing a much more extensive bilateral agreement with the United States, along the lines of the Canada–U.S. Free Trade Agreement (CUFTA). His reaction was to wish the Mexicans well, but he made it clear that Canada had no interest in taking part in the talks. As Jaime Serra recalls, Mulroney told the Mexicans they didn't want to change their agreement, that politically it would be very expensive.

Announcing the Decision

Mexico and the United States had hoped to build support for free trade negotiations before going public with the plans. This was particularly important for the Mexicans, who feared a nationalist backlash against closer ties with the United States. The politics "had to be handled carefully" recalled a senior Mexican official. "In Mexico, the easiest thing to do is to organize 100,000 people in a demonstration and put them in front of the U.S. embassy. . . . The hardest thing to do is to persuade them to do a free trade agreement with the United States."

A leaked story in the Wall Street Journal on March 26 scuttled the careful orchestration. The story revealed that there had been secret talks between high level officials of the United States and Mexico and that the two countries had agreed to pursue a free trade agreement. The Mexican embassy issued an ambiguous statement: "It cannot be confirmed that a free trade agreement will be realized between the two countries." President Salinas was silent. "We are trying to cool things off so that it cannot be exploited by the ultranationalists," an unidentified senior Mexican official told a Canadian reporter.[20] During a State Department press conference in Washington, Secretary Baker acknowledged that there had been talks with the Mexicans but was at pains to assert that they were "very preliminary," implying that nothing had been settled yet.

An unrelated incident in April complicated the domestic political problem in Mexico. Bounty hunters paid by the United States Drug Enforcement Administration (DEA) abducted a Mexican doctor, Dr. Humberto Alvarez Machain, and transported him across the border to El Paso, Texas, where he was arrested for complicity in the 1985 torture and murder of Enrique Camerena, a DEA agent. The United States had previously requested that Alvarez be extradited to the United States, but Mexico, which had a tradition of refusing extradition, had not turned him over. At first, the United States denied any involvement in Alvarez's abduction. But on April 27, *The Washington Post* reported that the abduction had been planned by the agent responsible for the Camerena case. Few stories could have touched a rawer nerve. Mexico was in an uproar over this breach of national sovereignty. The Mexican press gave the case extensive coverage. The Mexican Congress called for a formal investigation. A furious President Salinas threatened to throw all DEA agents out of Mexico and to suspend joint antidrug efforts. Vice President Quayle was dispatched to Mexico to apologize to Salinas. In a private meeting, Salinas tore into the vice president. This was a violation of Mexican law, an assault on Mexican sovereignty, a return to the wild west. At a press conference Quayle later acknowledged (with considerable understatement) that President Salinas had "expressed to me his strong displeasure with the Dr. Alvarez incident."[21]

Despite the incident, Salinas pressed ahead with plans for a free trade agreement. As he had done when orchestrating Mexico's accession to GATT as planning minister under de la Madrid, he convened a Senate "consultation forum" and charged it with making recommendations to him about options for Mexican trade policy. In its report to Salinas delivered on May 21, 1990, the group recommended "the negotiation of a free trade agreement" with the United States but stated that "this agreement . . . would preserve the country's political and economic sovereignty and leave Mexico free to establish its trade policy with the rest of the world." The next day, Salinas told the senators that he intended to follow their recommendations. He would discuss a free trade agreement with President Bush when he visited Washington in June, but he sought to demonstrate the limits to what he was proposing. Mexico will seek "free trade with the United States . . . but not a common market like the example of today's Europe," he said.[22]

In the United States, consultations with the private sector and with Congress had identified some opposition but also strong support. The labor unions were clearly unhappy, but union opposition to free trade with Canada had been easily overcome. Producers in agricultural sectors likely to face stiffer competition from Mexico expressed alarm, as did a smattering of smaller, mostly labor-intensive industries. But this opposition was more than offset by the very strong support coming from such major business associations as the Chamber of Commerce, the Business Roundtable, and the National Association of Manufacturers. There were a few warning signs. When Jaime Serra traveled to Chicago to meet Rostenkowski in his home district, Rostenkowski told him he was supportive but warned that this was not going to be easy. Still, the Bush administration did not anticipate any major problems.

On Sunday, June 10, Presidents Salinas and Bush met at the White House, the fourth meeting of their presidencies. "The two presidents . . . are convinced that free trade between Mexico and the United States can be a powerful engine for economic development, creating new jobs and opening new markets," they said in a joint statement. The next day, the Business Roundtable endorsed the plan and issued a report from its task force calling for a comprehensive trade and investment pact. President Salinas met with the CEOs of the Roundtable, thanking them for their support. He emphasized the competitive advantages of a free trade agreement. "Europe of 1992 will be the largest market in the world if we don't get an agreement," he said.[23] Appearing on "NBC News" later that day, Salinas responded to a question about the potential for job loss in the United States. "Where do you want Mexicans working, in Mexico or the United States?" he asked. "Because, if we cannot export more, then Mexicans will seek employment opportunities in the United States. We want to export goods, not people."[24]

Although the June announcement in the United States was carefully orchestrated to get maximum positive coverage, some reactions were negative. Union response was particularly sharp. Speaking for the AFL-CIO (American Federation of Labor and Congress of Industrial Organizations) at a hearing in the House of Representatives, Mark Anderson, director of the union's trade task force, said that the union viewed the prospect of a free trade agreement between Mexico and the United States with "considerable alarm." Anderson asserted that a free trade agreement would encourage greater capital outflows from the United States, lead to an increase in Mexican imports, and further harm the U.S. industrial base. "A free trade agreement with Mexico, a country where wages and social protections are almost nonexistent when compared with our own, simply invites disaster for U.S. workers," Anderson asserted. Moreover, the vast differences in regulatory structures and social protections "cannot help but create serious difficulties for U.S. production."[25]

For its own membership, the AFL-CIO sounded the alarm in the *AFL-CIO News*. The weekly newspaper linked the proposed free trade agreement to the existing *maquiladora* program, about which it had been running articles for some time. A free trade agreement with Mexico would be more of the same. "More American jobs would be jeopardized—on top of the tens of thousands that have already been lost to so-called maquiladoras—without any substantial benefit to the poverty-wage workers of Mexico," the newsletter said.[26]

In Congress, Democratic members with ties to organized labor voiced reservations about moving ahead too quickly with the Mexico negotiations. House Majority Leader Richard Gephardt (Democrat, Mo.) urged the USTR not to rush into an agreement before looking more closely at the effects of the *maquiladora* program. Representative Don Pease (Democrat, Ohio) warned: "Before we try to enter into an agreement, let us try to figure out what the likely impact would be. There are bound to be some winners and losers."[27] At a House Ways and Means Committee hearing on June 14, Charles Rangel (Democrat, N.Y.) urged that Mexico improve its drug enforcement before the United States negotiated free trade. "The [cocaine] epidemic is a threat to our national security," Rangel said.[28] But for now, the voices of concern were largely ignored by the Bush administration.

The Mexicans wanted to move quickly. They "had a great concern about timing," recalled Jules Katz. "They wanted it complete before the end of Bush's first term and before Mexico entered into their election cycle. They definitely didn't want it to carry over to 1993." They also felt that the longer the talks took, the more risks they ran in the financial markets. Mexican strategists were always cognizant of investor confidence. "My time constraint," recalled Jaime Serra, "was mostly driven by market expectations." Serra and Hills, and their deputies Herminio Blanco and Jules Katz, had laid out a timetable at an all-day meeting in Los Angeles in late July. "We thought we could do this reasonably fast," recalled Katz. "I said, let's work back from the future. Let's set a date of the end of 1991, which gives us 1992 for the legislative process. We knew we had to get fast track authority. But we thought we could begin the prenegotiation process [in which] we could present ideas and concepts. Then the negotiations could go smoothly."

In August, President Salinas formally requested a free trade agreement with the United States. In September, President Bush notified Congress of his intention to enter into negotiations with Mexico. Under the terms of U.S. trade law, the Congressional notification began an important clock. Unless either the Senate Finance Committee or the House Ways and Means

Committee voted to block the talks within 60 legislative days (days that Congress is in session), the president would be automatically authorized to negotiate with Mexico under fast track rules.[29] The 60–legislative day period was expected to expire sometime early in the spring. With little significant opposition in either committee, there appeared to be no obstacle to proceeding.

In November, President Bush traveled to Mexico for his sixth meeting with President Salinas. A crowd of 75,000 Mexicans gave Bush a hero's welcome. "This relationship is of vital importance to my country," he told the crowd. "We will never neglect it. We are neighbors and we are friends."[30] The day before, Bush had lunch with Salinas at Agualeguas, the ancestral home of Salinas, near the Texas border. Bush talked about the luncheon in his speech.

> It was in Agualeguas that I saw many similarities of our backgrounds. Both of us are the sons of senators. Both of us were raised to believe in public service and both of us know that what is true for two people is true for two nations. Friendship makes us stronger. I know that my country is also stronger because of Mexico's contribution to our cultural heritage—a rich bequest: architecture, language, and culture. And in a more personal way is the heritage bestowed on the Bush family. Our son Jeb has lived in your country, his wife Colomba was born in your country. . . and their union has given Barbara and me three beloved grandchildren. So when I speak of Americans and Mexicans I can only say *somos una familia,* we are one family.[31]

There was, however, one item of business aside from good will. The two governments issued a joint communiqué announcing that they were now "contemplating the way in which Canada might consider joining such negotiations." The Canadians had changed their minds; they wanted to be at the table after all.

The Canadian Dilemma

In March, when they had first learned that the United States and Mexico intended to negotiate free trade, Canadian Prime Minister Mulroney and Trade Minister John Crosbie had stated that Canada would not take part.

John Weekes, who eventually would be Canada's chief NAFTA negotiator, recalls the first Canadian response. "Our initial reaction was, 'Oh my God, why would we want to do that?' " The U.S.–Canada free trade negotiation had been a huge issue in Canada in 1988, perhaps the dominant issue of that year's election campaign. The Canadian public had been equally divided on the merits of the agreement at that time, but when the Canadian economy went into recession shortly thereafter, most Canadians seemed to attribute the accompanying high unemployment to the free trade agreement with the United States. In a poll taken for *Maclean's* magazine in May 1990, when asked whether the free trade agreement had "hurt, made no difference or helped jobs and economic conditions in Canada," only 7 percent thought it had helped and 57 percent thought it had hurt.[32] Given the state of public opinion, there was little political appetite for entering into negotiations that might provide an opportunity for Canadians to vent their displeasure.

Canadian trade officials, however, found the idea of being left out of the talks equally troubling. If Canada did not join, the United States would be the center of a hub-and-spoke arrangement, which would make locating a business in Canada relatively less attractive than locating it in the United States. Moreover, sitting on the sidelines, Canada would forfeit any leadership role it might hope to play in future trade negotiations. Within the Canadian government, Trade Minister John Crosbie, Finance Minister Michael Wilson, and Canadian Ambassador to the United States Derek Burney argued that there was both an economic and strategic logic for having a seat at the table.

Moreover, the politics did not appear unfavorable. The conservative government had a comfortable majority in Parliament; the business community supported joining the talks; and the Canadian public did not seem nearly as alarmed at the prospect of an agreement with Mexico as the Mulroney government had originally anticipated. The *Maclean's* poll that found virtual unanimous condemnation of the free trade agreement with the United States found the Canadian public evenly divided on the merits of joining a NAFTA. Indeed, Canadians were less negative than Americans.

The issue was taken up by Mulroney's cabinet during the summer, and the Canadians decided to ask to join. Prime Minister Mulroney was a guest at President Bush's home in Kennebunkport over the Labor Day weekend. Mulroney told Bush that Canada would like to be included. On September 24, Trade Minister Crosbie informed the House of Commons of the change of view: "The government has decided that Canada should involve itself."[33]

The announcement drew predictable criticism from opposition parties, Canadian labor unions, the coalition of environmental activists who had opposed CUFTA, and Canadian nationalist groups such as the Council of Canadians. Maude Barlow, president of the Council, called for a rollback of CUFTA instead. "We want our country back. As long as the free-trade agreement is in effect, no future [Canadian] government will be able to determine the fate of this country."[34] But the opposition in Canada did not have the same sting that it had before.

At first neither Mexico nor the United States was particularly enthusiastic about having the Canadians join the party, particularly if they were only there for defensive reasons. When Canadian Ambassador to Mexico David Winfield first broached the subject with Jaime Serra in the summer, Serra asked Winfield why Canada had changed its mind. Winfield told him that Canada really wanted to take part, but that Canada did not want to renegotiate the CUFTA. The Mexicans worried that the Canadians weren't serious and that their presence would create problems. This perspective was shared by Bob Zoellick at the State Department in Washington. "I was quite tough on this," recalled Zoellick. "I didn't want the Canadians to [mess] it up." Senate Finance Chairman Lloyd Bentsen also expressed strong reservations in a letter to Carla Hills in September. On a trip to Mexico City later in the fall, Bentsen explained his opposition to reporters, "If my wife and I want to settle something we don't want any third parties involved."[35]

At the USTR, however, Jules Katz advocated including Canada. As Katz recalled, "the State Department wanted to say 'no' to the Canadians. . . . The veterans of dealing with the Canadians thought they were only going to cause trouble. My view was: How can you say 'no'? There wasn't any reason for them to cause trouble since what we were trying to do was basically the CUFTA with improvements and extensions." Moreover, if the long-range goal was to have a hemispheric arrangement, negotiating a series of bilateral agreements didn't make sense. Katz persuaded Carla Hills that the Canadians should be included.

The issue raged on through the fall, with Canadian trade officials lobbying the Mexicans and the U.S. State Department, assuring them that Canada was serious and would not create problems. Eventually the trade ministers—John Crosbie, Jaime Serra, and Carla Hills—met in New York to discuss how to include Canada. Out of the meeting came a "nonpaper," an informal document that asserted that if any party became obstructionist, the other two parties could continue alone. Not until early in 1991 was it agreed that Canada would be part of the talks. The three countries of North America would seek to negotiate a North American Free Trade Agreement, thereafter almost always referred to simply as NAFTA.

By the time it was finally decided to include Canada, however, any hope of getting a quick start on the talks was dashed and Jules Katz's optimistic timetable of July was moot. Iraq had invaded Kuwait, and the United States was increasingly preoccupied with the buildup of its forces in the Persian Gulf. At the USTR all attention was on the desperate and ultimately futile effort to finish the GATT talks in Brussels. The Canadian request to be included and the agonizing over whether to let them in "threw a monkey wrench in the process," recalled Chip Roh. NAFTA would now have to wait until 1991.

Interpreting the Decision to Negotiate: The Uses and Limits of International Relations Theory

This chapter began with three questions. Why did Mexico, with its history of closed trade policy and cool relations with the United States, seek a free trade agreement with a neighbor it had so long kept at a distance? Why did the United States decide to embrace the overture from the southern neighbor it had so long ignored? Why did Canada, mired in recession and still recoiling from the political aftermath of the CUFTA, first decide to stay out and then change its mind?

With what analytic lens should we examine these questions? A logical place to begin is with international-level theories of international relations. The decision to negotiate NAFTA was a decision to cooperate in an important realm of international affairs, just the kind of matter international-level theories are designed to address. The issue is how well these theories explain the decision and whether one can safely ignore domestic processes at this stage of the NAFTA story.

Each of the international-level theories presented in this chapter provides useful insights. However, international-level theory is ultimately insufficient to explain the decision to negotiate NAFTA and could not have predicted it. To explain why and when Mexico, the United States, and Canada agreed to negotiate NAFTA requires looking beneath the international level to domestic processes.

International-Level Theories of International Relations

International-level, or "systemic," theories of international relations share the presumption that nations are the core actors in an international system, the attributes of which determine national behavior in international affairs. These theories differ, however, in the assumptions they make about the nature of state action, about the character of the international system, and therefore, about the nature of international politics. They differ most starkly on the question of whether national behavior is driven by interests, by institutions, or by ideas.

International Interests: Neorealism

The dominant theory in contemporary international relations is neorealism, or structural realism, an international-level, rational choice theory in the realist tradition that goes back to Thucydides.[36] Neorealism is most closely associated with the work of Kenneth Waltz. Although this theory is largely consistent with the older realist tradition exemplified in this century by the work of Hans Morgenthau, it is more purely systemic in that it obviates any need to consider national characteristics. At its core, neorealism has three tenets. First, states have clear interests, primarily in security. Second, they are rational actors; they have well-ordered preferences, predict accurately the consequences of their actions, and choose the course of action that maximizes their interests. Third, the international system is fundamentally anarchic, so that international outcomes are determined solely by the balance of power and the strategic interplay among states.

As has been noted elsewhere, neorealism is to international relations what neoclassical microeconomic theory, and particularly the theory of oligopoly, is to commercial relations.[37] There is only the most sketchy of theories of the state, as there is of the firm in microeconomic theory. State preferences are given, stable, and essentially symmetric. Furthermore, because the international system is anarchic, i.e., it lacks an overarching coercive power, the system is more a market than a hierarchy. However, because the number of powerful actors is relatively small, large states are not "price takers" but rather interact strategically to maximize their interests.

The Decision to Negotiate: A Neorealist Interpretation   To apply structural realist theory to an international economic issue necessarily requires some modification.[38] Realism and structural realism were developed primarily to deal with issues of war and peace, not economic cooperation. Its emphasis, therefore, on security as the primary value being maximized needs to be expanded to include a somewhat broader concept of national interest, one that includes economic power and wealth. In addition, structural realism's focus on the balance of power is problematic when dealing with international economic issues. Other characteristics of the international system that might matter for economic policy are market power and comparative economic advantage.

A modified structural realist interpretation of the history would argue that Mexico's decision to seek a free trade agreement with the United States was a strategic move in an international game. Lower trade barriers between the United States and Mexico would provide gains from trade, make Mexico more competitive in a world of emerging regional blocs, and most importantly, help Mexico attract much-needed foreign capital. With the fall of the Berlin wall, Europe was preoccupied with the east and Mexico was compelled to look north. The United States decided to negotiate with Mexico because it would benefit from increased trade with Mexico, because a more prosperous Mexico would make the United States more secure, and because a regional agreement would help the United States compete more effectively with Europe and Japan in the long run. Canada decided to join the talks primarily because it recognized that it was better off joining Mexico and the United States at the table than watching them negotiate a bilateral agreement without it.

The extraordinary parsimony of neorealist theory is apparent in this application. Only a tiny portion of the story told in this chapter really matters. Personal revelations at international gatherings, infighting in the United States between the USTR and the State Department, political scars in Canada from past fights over free trade with the United States—none of this detail is relevant. All that matters is the international circumstance in which these three countries found themselves at the moment of decision.

Obviously this is thin description, but parsimony is a virtue, not a vice, if theory can direct our attention to what really matters and successfully predict outcomes on the basis of observable conditions. So the real question is how well the theory actually explains the decision to negotiate. As a first cut it does quite well. Deciding to negotiate is certainly not inconsistent with the tenets of realism. The descriptions of national interests are not inconsistent with how decision makers in all three countries understood the choice. But closer inspection reveals puzzles of some consequence.

Unresolved Puzzles   One set of puzzles relates to the timing of the decision. If a free trade agreement with the United States was in Mexico's interest in 1990, why wasn't it in Mexico's interest before? If anything, Mexico's need for international capital and its marginal gains from more liberal trade would have been greater if it had sought a free trade agreement with the United States in the previous decade. Why did López Portillo respond to the economic crisis in 1982 by raising protection and nationalizing banks? Why didn't de la Madrid initiate free trade negotiations during his term, perhaps in 1985 when the debt crisis was most acute? And what are we to make of de la Madrid's assertion that he would not have entered talks in 1990 because it was politically too risky? A theory that looks only to international circumstance has difficulty explaining this record.

Second, consider the relationship between the fall of the Berlin Wall and the subsequent opening of Eastern Europe, and the decision to negotiate NAFTA. This was clearly of great importance in Salinas's thinking, but it makes little sense from a realist perspective. The opening of Eastern Europe should have had little real effect on Mexico. Aside from West German investment in East Germany, the amount of investment actually going into Eastern Europe was trivial. The Mexicans might have believed that there would be investment diversion, but that type of explanation is not available in a realist model.

Third, consider the timing of the Canadian decision. Why did Canada decide in March to stay out of the talks and in August ask to be included? Nothing of significance changed in the international system between March and August. One could argue that these fine matters of timing are largely noise, irrelevant to eventual outcomes, but the Canadian question delayed the opening of the talks, a delay that had significant consequences, as we will see in the next chapter. Of course, part of the delay had to do with the hesitancy of the United States and Mexico to agree to include Canada, a delay equally difficult to explain given that both countries had an interest in moving quickly.

Deeper puzzles surround the form of cooperation. First is the question of why countries need free trade agreements. Neorealism is compelled to argue that international agreements do not matter. If the international system is inevitably anarchic, why should Mexico, Canada, and the United States seek an agreement to govern their future trade relations? Whatever they agreed upon would be worth no more than the paper on which it was written. If that is the case, why bother going to the trouble of negotiating?

Second, neorealism cannot adequately explain why *negotiating* is necessary at all. Consider the underlying economics of what was being proposed. From a neoclassical trade economics perspective, opening markets is in a country's national interest *regardless of whether other countries do it or not*. There are circumstances where this proposition does not hold, but they did not apply here.[39] This is not an international "prisoners' dilemma" game, in which nations face a choice between cooperating and defecting and in which the dominant strategy is defection. Here, the dominant strategy for each party is to cooperate by opening its markets. Why, then, did Mexico, Canada, and the United States need a negotiation to compel themselves to do what they "should" have done on their own anyway? Or, to turn the question on its side, why did these countries have "irrational" protection in the first place?

International Institutions: Regime Theory

Perhaps the most prominent international-level challenger to neorealism is regime theory, a theory that international institutions matter—that internationally held rules, norms, and organizations affect the choices nations make. The community of scholars advocating a role for international regimes, or institutions, is far from monolithic. Two issues in particular divide it. The first is how significant a role regimes play: whether the international landscape is essentially anarchic and only occasionally punctuated by relatively weak regimes or whether the landscape is in fact quite structured by international institutions. The second is an ontological debate between those who see institutions as creations of rational-actor states and those who see international regimes as generative of states and their interests.

Mainstream regime theory comes down on the side of a modest role for institutions and for ontological primacy of the state.[40] Like structural realism, it is ultimately a rational-actor, state-centric theory. Regimes arise through the interaction of rational-actor states in an anarchic system. Regime theory parts company from structural realism, however, in that it allows states to rationally choose in one moment and to be boundedly rational in another. The metaphor of a repeated prisoners' dilemma game in which players develop norms for cooperation, particularly as popularized in Axelrod's *The Evolution of Cooperation*, is central to this orientation.[41] Although mainstream regime theory concedes an ontologically primary role to self-interested actors, it allows state behavior to be channeled and moderated by international institutions and therefore directs some portion of our attention to the character of those regimes.

The primary role of international institutions is to facilitate mutually advantageous cooperation in circumstances where it might not otherwise occur. Regimes can do this by reducing uncertainty associated with cooperative moves; by raising confidence that others will not exploit cooperation; by lowering transaction costs, often by providing a focal point for coordinating cooperation; or by altering payoff structures, as when the International Monetary Fund (IMF) gives loans on the condition of more open (cooperative) trade policies. Regimes arise when there are international public goods, when there are barriers to cooperation in procuring those goods, and when the density of transactions makes it more efficient to incur the costs of creating an institution rather than to deal with problems on an ad hoc basis.[42]

As noted above, mainstream regime theorists join with structural realists in asserting the ontological primacy of self-interested states. Nevertheless, this theory differs in an important regard from structural realism: At the moment of decision, regimes are an independent force and must be treated as (partially) exogenous variables. Regimes created at one moment tend to be "sticky," to change more slowly than the conditions that led states to create them. Because of the lag, at any one moment of decision, international rules, norms, principles, and processes may not be what states would create at that moment, but given sunk costs and continuing benefits, states maintain the regime.

International Regimes and the Decision to Negotiate   Given the apparent weakness of the international regime between Mexico and the United States, the key initiators of NAFTA, it might appear that international institutions could have had little to do with the decision to negotiate NAFTA. But regime theory can help to explain some of the anomalies not explained well by structural realism.

First, regime theory provides a way of thinking about what Mexico, Canada, and the United States were doing when they decided to negotiate a free trade agreement: They were agreeing to create a new regime. If the negotiation succeeded, new rules would govern commerce among the three nations, rules that would constrain their subsequent actions. The importance these countries attached to the decision to negotiate (and the subsequent effort that would go into actually negotiating) suggests that they certainly believed that regimes matter.

Second, regime theory provides a way of interpreting the timing of Mexico's decision. During the 1980s, international regimes facilitated Mexico's evolution toward embracing a free trade agreement. Mexico's debt crisis provided an opportunity for the international financial regime, particularly the IMF and its conditionality rules, to push Mexico in the direction of greater economic openness. Greater openness led to increased international trade and investment, particularly involving the United States, which deepened the economic relationship between Mexico and the United States, making for a more dense issue area and a need for stronger institutions. A series of small steps—accession to the GATT in 1985, a "framework agreement" with the United States in 1987, an "understanding regarding future negotiations" in 1989—opened information channels, created confidence, and lowered the transaction costs of subsequent negotiation. Each step ratcheted Mexico forward to a position in which the creation of a free trade agreement with the United States was both more feasible and more desirable for Mexico.

Third, regime theory helps explain the particular form that cooperation took. To the question, why a free trade agreement? there is an answer: because that was the choice available under the existing international regime. The possibility of a free trade agreement, the general form of which was defined by the rules of GATT and the specific form by the precedent of the CUFTA, served as a focal point for cooperation. The choice before the three countries, therefore, was not an infinitely variable one. It was, rather, a choice between a free trade agreement or the status quo. Here is a clear example of institutions functioning as "switchmen" in Max Weber's terms.[43]

Regime theory suggests that more of the historical narrative is relevant to the questions in which we are interested. It relates the debt crisis, the growing volume of international commerce in North America, and the existing pattern of international agreements to the decision to negotiate NAFTA. As a supplement to structural realism, regime theory solves some of the puzzles left by that theory, perhaps most importantly, why nations would be interested in an international agreement. It does not, however, solve all the puzzles.

Remaining Puzzles   Two sets of puzzles remain, the first about the decision to cooperate, the other about why that decision took so long. First, although the modest growth of arrangements between the United States and Mexico during the 1980s may have made a free trade agreement both somewhat more possible and more desirable, they hardly compelled the next, much larger, step in 1990. Like structural realism, regime theory cannot explain the apparent relationship between the fall of the Berlin Wall and the decision to negotiate NAFTA or the difference made when a much bolder Carlos Salinas replaced the more cautious Miguel de la Madrid.

Second, although regime theory provides a way of thinking about why a free trade agreement would be desirable, it cannot satisfactorily address why there was a problem cooperating in the first instance and why it was so difficult to overcome without protracted negotiations. Mainstream regime theory is designed to explain how nations solve prisoners' dilemma–like problems. But the *inter*-national trade problem is not a prisoners' dilemma game. Regime theory shares with structural realism an inability to solve the puzzle of why countries would need to negotiate to do what they rationally should do unilaterally.

International Symbolic Politics

A third international-level approach to international relations adopts the position that internationally held symbol systems—ideas, ideologies, worldviews, and the like—affect the behavior of nations, independent of interests or institutions. After a long period of neglect, symbolic, constructivist, and ideational approaches to international relations have recently received more attention from scholars, in part because of the inadequacy of rational choice theories in explaining the extent and, more importantly, the form of international cooperation. Symbolic theories span a spectrum from weak to strong, anchored on one end by modest extensions of rational choice theory and on the other by constructivist approaches derived from sociology and cultural anthropology. Along this spectrum lie four roles for international symbolic constructs.

In the most limited conception of the role of symbols, international symbol systems derive from and ultimately serve national interests. The perspective is essentially economic: Ideas are solutions to collective action failures. As with international institutions in regime theory, symbolic constructs here help reduce uncertainty, lower transaction costs, and provide focal points for coordination.[44] Note that this is quite a benign role for symbolic constructs. They are essentially a public good, created and maintained either by a hegemon, a nation sufficiently large to have a private interest in the public good, or by a collective of nations who manage to negotiate the establishment of the public good.

A second role for symbolic systems is to establish beliefs about cause and effect. Predicting the consequences of policy is often extraordinarily difficult, making it virtually impossible to map precisely from option to outcome. Actors must contend with deterministic complexity, environmental uncertainty, and strategic indeterminacy. Symbolic constructs, more specifically shared causal beliefs, connect choice and consequence. Take, for example, the competing ideologies of liberal trade and mercantilism. Both involve, among other things, mechanisms for connecting policy choices to predicted outcomes. Although each has a complex undergirding of economic reasoning, for the political actors who rely on them, they are largely symbolic constructs. As several scholars have argued, the international convergence of belief around the consequences of adopting liberal trade policies may help account for the level of international economic cooperation among those nations sharing the economic orthodoxy in the second half of the twentieth century.[45]

A third role for symbolic constructs is to frame issues so as to make some dimensions of consequence more salient than others.[46] International issues may invoke competing national objectives, for example human rights and physical security, making evaluation difficult. The United States, when confronted with the recent conflict in Bosnia, had interests in both human rights and security. To the extent that the conflict was framed by stories of "ethic cleansing" and metaphors of the Holocaust, the human rights dimension was most salient and the U.S. "interest" became one of preventing genocide. To the extent, however, that the conflict was seen as an intractable civil war and the metaphor of Vietnam was invoked, the security dimension was most salient and the U.S. "interest" became one of avoiding a costly and ineffective entanglement. Different framings, structured by available symbol systems, can trigger different interests.

A fourth and strongest role for symbolic constructs is to determine national interests themselves. The "epistemic community" literature takes the stance that conceptions of national interest can derive from the internationally held symbolic constructs of these communities of shared belief and value.[47] An international environmental community of shared belief, Haas argues, can lead to the greening of national conceptions of self interest. In a sense, symbolic constructs become not merely facilitators within an international system but creators of it.[48] Symbolic systems, of course, may serve more than one of these functions. Ideologies—Marxism, for example—can be at once definers of categories for thinking about possible actions, sets of beliefs about the way the world works, framers of issues, and value systems. Similarly, collectively held historic metaphors (such as Chamberlain's attempted appeasement of Hitler at Munich) also involve, although less expansively, categorization of potential action (appeasement or not), beliefs about the relationship between choice and outcome (appeasement emboldens aggressors), framings of the dimensions of consequence (loss of security), and normative implications (heroic nations fight to stop aggression).

International Symbolic Politics and the Decision to Negotiate International symbolic theories can help explain aspects of the decision to negotiate NAFTA not well handled by realist or institutionalist approaches. In particular, this perspective allows for an understanding of the specific timing of decision and its relationship to dramatic world events.

Viewed through this lens, Mexico's decision to seek a free trade agreement represents the triumph of an international liberal trade ideology over the ideology of import substitution that had dominated thinking in Mexico and other developing countries. It was no accident that the decision to enter NAFTA came in Davos at a gathering of the world's economic elite, almost all of whom shared the same worldview, or that the deciders for Mexico were products of training in liberal trade economics at leading U.S. universities.

The new Mexican elite, welcomed at Davos, became members of an international epistemic community whose liberal trade ideology provided a focal point for cooperation, defined causal beliefs about choice and consequence (free trade leads to economic growth), framed the issue so that some interests were more salient than others (economic efficiency), and established value preferences (free trade is good, protectionism is bad).

Thinking in terms of the power of international symbolism also helps explain why the fall of the Berlin Wall could have served as a catalyst for NAFTA. The event symbolized for the international elites gathered in Davos not only the end of the Cold War, but also the increasing importance of economics in world affairs and the trend toward a new competitive regionalism in the "new world order." These ideas were all in circulation before the fall of the Wall, of course. Gorbachev's USSR looked far less menacing that its predecessors; economic issues recently had been taking a front seat more often; and with European economic integration and the CUFTA, regional economic arrangements were proliferating. When the premier symbol of the Cold War and the old world order—the Berlin Wall—"fell," all of this became clear to the Davos contingent.

A symbolic lens can also provide a different perspective on the question of why Mexico would seek a free trade agreement. For Mexico, deciding to seek a NAFTA was a symbolic action intended to dramatize a new Mexico to itself and to an international audience. It was part affirmation of a new sense of identity and in part a pragmatic way of signaling a distracted international financial community.

Limitations of International-Level Theory

Taken together, the three strands of international-level theory can explain much about the decision to enter into the NAFTA negotiations. But purely international theories, alone or collectively, are ultimately inadequate to explain fully the decision to negotiate NAFTA. Most notably, none adequately addresses the core puzzle first identified in the discussion of structural realism: Why do nations need to negotiate agreements to do what is (or is perceived to be) in their national interests? The reason is simple: Systemic theories mis-specify the nature of the problem. The problem in international trade is not fundamentally *international*. It is, rather, a problem of *domestic* politics. Nations negotiate international free trade agreements to solve a domestic problem.

International systemic theories have been largely used to consider security rather than trade issues. For issues of security, the variance of interests within nations is relatively low: All share an interest in security. With low internal variance (and assuming strong national political institutions) domestic politics can be more safely ignored and nations presumed to be unitary, if not always completely rational, actors. National interests, however, are usually at least partially in conflict with each other. For this reason the international security can generally be characterized as a multiparty prisoners' dilemma game. This specification of the problem dominates contemporary international relations theory.

In international trade relations, however, changes in trade policy inevitably make winners and losers of domestic interests. When the interests of domestic factions differ strongly, the fiction of a unitary national actor becomes harder to maintain, not just descriptively, but also predictively (whose view of the national interest will prevail for purposes of acting internationally?) and normatively (what is the national interest when there are winners and losers and limited opportunities for internal side payments?). Furthermore, in contrast to security, national economic interests vary little. As noted earlier, the international trade game is not a prisoners' dilemma in any significant way.

So what *was* the game in the case of NAFTA? Why didn't Mexico, the United States, and Canada simply do what was in each of their individual interests? Indeed, why hadn't they done it long ago? What accounts for the pattern of protection that raised the cost of capital, energy, services, and industrial inputs in Mexico; sugar and tomatoes in the United States; and milk in Canada? (These examples will be discussed at length in chapter 5.) These questions cannot be answered by looking only at the international level. They require consideration of politics at a lower level of aggregation.

Domestic and Individual-Level Theory and the Decision to Negotiate

Subsequent chapters will develop an extensive framework for thinking about domestic-level and individual-level politics of international relations. This chapter, however, considers briefly the nature of such theories and applies them in a more ad hoc fashion to the puzzles raised earlier about the decision to negotiate NAFTA.

Domestic-Level Theory

Domestic-level theories based on interests, institutions, and symbols all provide some insight into to the decision to negotiate NAFTA. A focus on domestic interests, in particular, suggests answers to the core puzzles of why nations protect and why they might need a free trade agreement to end protection, and it provides additional insight into the timing of Mexico's decision to pursue such an agreement.

Protectionist policies primarily arise from and are maintained by the interplay of domestic interests. The classic formulation of this phenomenon comes from the work of E. E. Schattschneider, whose core observation was that concentrated producer interests in protection tend to outweigh the more diffuse general consumer interest in free trade.[49] In current political science language, concentrated interests face less of a collective action problem than do diffuse interests in mobilizing to influence policy. International free trade agreements, therefore, serve as vehicles for solving this domestic political problem by bundling together many issues at once and by bringing international pressure to bear on domestic politics. (Chapters 4 and 5 will further develop this thinking.)

Mexico pursued NAFTA in part to help overcome domestic political obstacles to economic reform, including a more open trade policy. The Salinas government, carrying on from its predecessor, was intent on completing Mexico's abandonment of state interventionist and import substitution policies in favor of free market and free trade policies. Some of this it was doing unilaterally, but NAFTA enabled Mexican officials to link numerous reforms together, thus partially overcoming the political logic of protection. (The way in which linking issues can overcome obstacles to free trade is explored further in chapter 5.)

Equally important, a free trade agreement helps to lock in free trade, thus preventing domestic interests from unraveling reforms at a later point in time. This was of critical importance for attracting international capital. NAFTA could make Mexico more attractive to foreign investors not simply by dramatizing Mexico's economic reforms, as suggested above, but perhaps more importantly by ensuring that domestic political forces could not (so easily) reverse them. U.S. policy makers saw NAFTA in much the same light, as a way both to accelerate and to secure more liberal economic policies in Mexico.

For the most part, domestic symbolism worked against a free trade agreement in all three countries. This lens, therefore, does little to explain why they decided to negotiate NAFTA, but it can help explain why they had not done so earlier. In Mexico, embracing the United States ran counter to Mexican political culture. Mexican presidents had always been wary of appearing to be too close to the Americans. In Canada, too, symbolically getting too close to the United States threatened Canadian identity, but Canada had overcome this obstacle when it negotiated the CUFTA. In early 1990, however, the more proximate symbolic problem was CUFTA itself, which had become a symbol of economic failure, and the fear that negotiating NAFTA would stir up a hornets' nest. The U.S. domestic symbolic politics of NAFTA was not particularly salient in 1990 but would become much more so as time went on, and as chapter 7 will show, would become the central dynamic by the end of the process.

The configuration of domestic political institutions also played a role in the decision to negotiate NAFTA, albeit a somewhat more subtle one. The Mexican Constitution, coupled with the near monopoly on power enjoyed by the PRI, gave the Mexican president great power to make a bold decision, even when it might be opposed by strong domestic interests and ran against Mexican political culture. The Canadian parliamentary system and the fact that the Conservative Party was in power gave the Canadian Prime Minister the capacity to take actions that might also engender considerable domestic opposition. Both of these institutional arrangements stand in contrast to those in the United States, where, as the next chapter will demonstrate, a pledge by a U.S. president to negotiate did not actually mean the United States had decided to negotiate.

Individual-Level Theory

Individual-level analysis attends to the interests, habits, and constructed understandings of particular individuals, who may either be elite decision makers or members of domestic groups or the general public. Because the decision to negotiate NAFTA was largely made by elites, however, it is most appropriate to concentrate on them here. Viewed through an individual-level lens, the decision to negotiate NAFTA becomes a story about Carlos Salinas, George Bush, and Brian Mulroney.

A considerable but often neglected literature on foreign policy decision making by elites considers the way in which leaders think, learn, and decide.[50] One strand of the literature emphasizes individual strategic calculations, demonstrating, for example, how interests in personal power compel leaders to take certain actions. Another strand focuses on the way in which personal histories and experiences establish habits of thought and action, illustrating, for instance, how early traumas or triumphs affect subsequent perception and behavior. Still another strand addresses the ways in which individuals construct understandings of the world and locate themselves in it, considering the stories leaders tell about world events and the actions they take. The possibility that leaders apprehend the world symbolically provides a mechanism through which social constructions may influence individual action. Political biographers, of course, apply all of these lenses to their subjects, although not always systematically.

It is well beyond the scope of this book to attempt a biography of the key figures who decided to embark on NAFTA. Nonetheless, certain obvious characteristics of Carlos Salinas, in particular, are worth noting. First, Salinas received a Ph.D. in political economy from Harvard, an experience that not only affected his thinking about economic policy but also likely made him more comfortable with the United States than most of his predecessors (although Miguel de la Madrid had also a degree from Harvard, a master's in Public Administration). Second, Salinas clearly viewed himself as a reformer, who hoped that his place in Mexican history might be that of the president who brought Mexico into the modern era and into full membership in the international community. Third, by temperament, Salinas was a bold politician, notwithstanding his initial reputation as a technocrat. It is hard to imagine Salinas's cautious predecessor, Miguel de la Madrid, initiating NAFTA, as de la Madrid himself admitted.

George Bush's personal makeup was perhaps less crucial to the U.S. decision to negotiate NAFTA; other recent presidents might well have made the same choice (and all of the living presidents would later support NAFTA). But Bush was a free trader, he saw foreign policy generally and NAFTA in particular as an important part of the story that would be told about his presidency, and perhaps of greatest significance, he was comfortable with Mexico. Like many Texans, Bush had none of the reflexive aversion that characterizes some American attitudes about Mexico.

It is harder to say what role Mulroney's personal makeup played in Canada's decision to join the talks. Other individuals in his position might have also felt compelled to do the same. Yet Mulroney too was ideologically comfortable with free trade, and it is worth recalling that it was Mulroney who surprised most political observers in 1984 when he decided to push for a free trade agreement between Canada and the United States, without which there would have been no NAFTA.

Considering these personalities, NAFTA appears to be something of a historical accident, the product of a particular moment in which the three leaders of North America were of like mind and impulse. It is hard to imagine Bill Clinton, Ernesto Zedillo, and Jean Chrétien initiating NAFTA, although to be fair, all would later operate in very different political environments, different in no small measure because of the intervening politics of NAFTA.

Conclusions

The preceding analysis has demonstrated how different analytic lenses provide different interpretations of the decision to negotiate. International-level, or systemic, theory provides insights into national motives for seeking free trade agreements but does not adequately solve certain puzzles, most notably why nations protect some products and why they need to negotiate to eliminate protection. Domestic-level theory provides a way of explaining these puzzles by identifying the international trade problem as the consequence of domestic interests. Nations protect not because it is in their interest to protect but because in domestic politics concentrated interests have the power to obtain and defend protection. International free trade negotiations are a vehicle for overcoming this tendency, but the ability of nations to pursue negotiations depends on the strength of interests opposed to free trade, the arrangement of national political institutions, and the nature of symbolic constructs that may make foreign cooperation politically risky. In the end, however, neither international nor domestic factors may fully determine national choice in a particular instance. For that, it may also be necessary to consider the understandings and motives of particular individuals placed in key positions in the national decision making process.

The Mexican decision to seek a free trade agreement with NAFTA was a strategic gambit, taken largely by Carlos Salinas, on both the domestic and international levels. On the domestic level the strategy was to use international negotiation to overcome domestic political opposition to economic reform, a way of accelerating Mexican market opening and of locking it in. Implicit in Salinas's decision was a judgment that the domestic political constraints that may have inhibited his predecessors were not insurmountable. On the international level, the strategy was intended both as a signal to the international investment community and as a means to obtain trade concessions not otherwise obtainable from the United States. The U.S. decision to take Salinas's offer, a decision made by George Bush and his inner circle of advisors, was at once a foreign policy gambit to help Salinas with his domestic problem, a strategy to maintain momentum toward freer international trade, and a domestic political calculation that interests in Mexican market opening would outweigh interests in maintaining what remained of U.S. protection. Prime Minister Mulroney's decision, first to stay out, then to ask in, reflected in the first instance a calculation about the domestic political costs of engaging in free trade, costs essentially resulting from symbolic association with the unpopular CUFTA, and in the second instance a judgment that those political costs had been overestimated and that the Canadian national interest was better served by being at the table with the United States and Mexico.

Why did Mexico, Canada, and the United States decide to negotiate NAFTA? Because of the confluence of many factors, international and domestic, and because national leaders in all three countries seized the strategic opening before them.

4 Domestic Politics Matters: The Fast Track Fight

For Mexico and Canada, once Salinas and Mulroney committed to NAFTA, the decision was made. For the United States, the situation was different. Under the U.S. Constitution, Congress, not the president, regulates foreign trade. To negotiate a NAFTA, Bush would first need to obtain "fast track" negotiating authority from Congress.

Fast track is the standard process by which Congress delegates authority to the president to negotiate on its behalf and commits itself to both to limited debate (hence "fast track") and to an up-down vote, without amendment, on the agreement reached by the president. The process had been invented in 1974 for the Tokyo Round of the General Agreement on Tariffs and Trade (GATT). Since then, Congress had granted the president fast track authority for free trade negotiations with Israel and Canada, as well as for the ongoing Uruguay Round of GATT. Historically, Congress had granted this authority with relatively little fight. The process of obtaining negotiating authority had never been the focus of protracted political maneuvering. Indeed, outside the small circle of trade insiders, no one even knew what "fast track" was. Certainly few envisioned this previously obscure process would become a defining issue for the negotiations to follow.

The 1988 Trade Act had authorized the fast track for three years, with a provision that gave the president two more years if he requested it, subject to a veto by a majority of either house of Congress. Bush needed to ask for the extension by the beginning of March 1991. By then, a remarkably diverse collection of interest groups had mobilized to oppose fast track or to insist that conditions be attached to its approval. Predictably, some opposition came from industries that stood to lose in free competition with lower-cost Mexican producers (glass and brooms, for example) and from organized labor, which (rightly or wrongly) felt threatened by the prospect of competition from cheaper Mexican labor. But these predictable interests were joined by a host of organizations concerned about the environment, food safety, family farmers, human rights, worker rights, and other issues—all newcomers to the politics of trade.

Together, the opposition nearly scuttled NAFTA before it began as nervous members of Congress balked at the prospects of facing down angry constituents. In February 1991, fast track looked dead. Only a major effort by the Bush administration succeeded in reversing the tide, and in May, Congress voted to grant the president two years of negotiating authority; the president had won. But the critics had not entirely lost. Their efforts linked new issues to the trade agenda and forced Bush to agree to address the labor and environment issues they had raised. In so doing, they changed the course of the international negotiation and transformed the domestic politics of NAFTA.

This chapter details the fast track fight of 1991, seeking to answer three questions: Why did fast track, a previously obscure procedural matter, become such a heated issue? How were advocates for environment and labor able to force linkage of their concerns to the negotiating agenda? Why, in the end, did the president obtain the authority he sought?

Getting Started

At the end of 1990, the Bush administration established an interagency group to coordinate its fast track efforts. The group was chaired by Josh Bolton, general counsel at the Office of the United States Trade Representative (USTR), who had been pushed by Bob Zoellick for the role. Ideally the process would have been run out of the White House, but as Zoellick recalled, "Josh knew substance, knew the Hill, knew the agencies."

The task facing the administration was created and structured by U.S. trade law: The president needed fast track negotiating authority from Congress before he could begin the NAFTA negotiations. From a presidential perspective, the fast track provided great advantages. Most notably it ensured that once the president negotiated an agreement and proposed legislation to implement it, Congress would be forced to vote on the implementing bill without amendment and within no more than ninety legislative days. Unfortunately for the administration, the fast track process expired June 1, 1991. By the end of 1990, all could see that the NAFTA negotiations would not be completed before the expiration date. But fortunately for the administration, when Congress last renewed fast track in 1988 (primarily for the Uruguay Round of the GATT), it provided for the possibility of a two-year extension. To get it, the president needed to make a formal request on or before March 1, 1991. The extension was automatic unless either the House or the Senate voted to deny it within ninety days.

In the fall of 1990, however, there was little reason for the administration to be concerned about a vote in May. Despite rumblings from labor, there was not much to suggest that the opposition would include more than the usual suspects. Chip Roh, the Assistant USTR for North American Affairs, later recalled the mood: "In November and December we were making early rounds on the Hill, talking with Ways and Means and Finance Committee staffers and other key committees. There was not much interest. Everyone said, 'That's next year's issue.' There was nothing to indicate significant problems."

The Opposition

On January 15 a coalition of labor, environment, farm, consumer, religious, and human rights groups held an all-day forum on the Hill to bring attention to their concerns about fast track and NAFTA. Its organizers had not expected to garner much attention. But the Washington trade community packed the room, and C-SPAN was there. The event started a buzz around Washington: Something was going on here.

The traditional view of the trade policy-making problem is that concentrated protectionist interests tend to outweigh the more diffuse consumer interest in free trade.[1] In the case of NAFTA, however, free trade threatened few economic sectors. Farmers of certain agricultural products, most notably citrus fruit, sugar cane and sugar beets, and warm weather vegetables such as tomatoes, and manufacturers in currently protected labor-intensive sectors such as apparel, brooms, and glass were rightly concerned about increased competition. Compared to the collection of industries who stood to gain from free trade, however—banks and other financial institutions, the big three automakers, corporate agriculture, virtually the whole of American big business—these potential losers did not look like much of a political threat. Where necessary, too, the blow could be softened with promises to negotiate longer transition periods or other measures to deal with special circumstances.[2] The significant opposition, therefore, came not from the traditional source—protectionist producers—but rather from a new coalition of labor unions, environmentalists, and grassroots groups.

Labor Opposition

Labor unions did not just oppose fast track in the spring of 1991, they excoriated it. The response was partly visceral on the part of the rank and file and partly strategic on the part of the union leadership. Workers' reactions to the prospect of free trade with Mexico were conditioned by their negative experience with U.S.–Mexico trade to date and their general suspicion of the Bush administration. Savvy union leaders recognized the significance of the procedural vote for their ability to influence the terms of the eventual agreement and were determined to make a stand against the extension of fast track.

In 1965, Mexico and the United States established a program intended to help develop the border economies of both countries. The maquiladora program allowed U.S. businesses to locate assembly operations in free trade zones along the U.S. border in northern Mexico and to import components from the U.S. duty free, assemble them in Mexico, and reexport them to the United States without tariff. American businesses began moving operations from the Rust Belt to northern Mexico to take advantage of cheaper labor.

The program began slowly, but when the peso was devalued after 1982, the number of firms grew rapidly. By 1989, around 1500 maquiladora plants in Mexico employed nearly 400,000 workers.[3] Workers in Mexico earned a fraction of what their U.S. counterparts earned, perhaps one eighth, perhaps less.[4] The stated purpose of the program was to encourage economic development on both sides of the border and to reduce immigration pressures. For the unions, however, the real purpose was clear: to allow U.S. manufacturers to substitute cheap Mexican labor for expensive U.S. workers.

In the mid 1980s, the AFL-CIO (American Federation of Labor and

Congress of Industrial Organizations) began an information campaign about the maquiladoras. Union workers in the 1980s were suffering from layoffs and corporate downsizing. Here was a perfect example of what was really happening. Big multinational corporations were moving jobs to places where workers came cheaper. A November 1986 *AFL-CIO News* article entitled "Runaways to Mexico Spread Economic Woe," was typical:

> For American business, it's a bonanza. The Mexican government pro-
> vides soldiers and police to stifle union organizing. On-the-job safety
> regulations are virtually nonexistent or rarely enforced. . . . But the
> deal has been costly for an American workforce already battered by
> the influx of foreign-made goods. In the past decade alone, by the
> most conservative estimate, the jobs of 90,000 American workers have
> gone south of the border.[5]

The stories about companies going to Mexico, or using the possibility of a move to force union concessions in negotiations, gave workers a way of focusing their anger about what was happening to them. According to Mark Anderson, research director for the AFL-CIO, workers "connected the layoffs and downsizing in the United States to transfers in production to Mexico in the mid 80s. It was a very visible thing to members. It wasn't theoretical. They *knew* about Mexico."

What made matters worse in union eyes was that the Reagan Commerce Department was actively promoting business relocation. In 1986, union protests spurred Congress to cut off funds to the offending program. A private consulting firm took up the slack with the Reagan administration's blessing. In December that year, a group of union activists led by William Bywater, president of the International Electrical Workers union, marched to the Commerce Department demanding to see Secretary Malcolm Baldrige. On the steps, an angry Bywater told reporters what he would say to Baldrige when he saw him: "I'll tell him to keep his nose out of Mexico and pay attention to the United States."[6] Baldrige was not available.

By the annual AFL-CIO convention in Bal Harbour, Florida, in February 1988, the maquiladoras warranted an official policy statement from the executive council.

> The Maquiladora Twin-Plant Program has resulted in the loss of tens
> of thousands of U.S. jobs, economic depression along the border and

other areas of the United States, and sweatshop conditions in Northern Mexico for hundreds of thousands of young workers—a workforce cynically selected as most susceptible to intimidation and least likely to organize and militantly defend its rights.[7]

The statement marked a subtle shift of emphasis. The early focus of the education efforts was on the cost to American jobs. Gradually, however, the spotlight was turning to the plight of the Mexican workers and to the environmental degradation that surrounded them. The unions focused especially on toxic dumping. The AFL-CIO produced a film about toxic dumping at a Steepen Chemical plant in Mexico and worked with ABC's "20/20" and NBC's "Dateline" on features about toxic hazards. At the annual Bal Harbour meeting in February 1989, the AFL-CIO Executive Council released a report entitled "The Maquiladoras: The Hidden Cost of Production South of the Border." The report documented toxic poisoning, inadequate waste water facilities, denial of health and safety protection, pollution of drinking water supplies, and endangerment of the ecosystem.[8] In 1989, too, the union was a founding member of the Coalition for Justice in the Maquiladoras, along with a number of grassroots environmental and citizen groups, including the Texas Center for Policy in Austin; the Border Ecology Project in Nagos, Arizona; and the Quaker American Friends Service Committee. A central focus of the Coalition's efforts was investigating and publicizing workplace and environmental conditions in the maquiladoras.

The new focus on the environment was strategic. Mark Anderson later described the reasons for the shift: "Environment became a means of drawing attention to poor company practices in the border. . . . Nobody cared about a worker losing his job in Illinois. They were much more sensitive to toxic dumping in Mexico."

It was against this backdrop of awareness of the maquiladoras, of stories about runaway plants, exploited workers, and toxic dumps, that union workers heard President Bush announce his intention to negotiate free trade with Mexico. "All of that activity made this issue different from other issues," recalls Mark Anderson. "We already had two or three years of education about maquiladoras with our members. When NAFTA surfaced our first reaction was, 'Bush wants to make it worse.. . . This was piling on.'"

In the fall of 1990, unions faced a strategic decision: Would they simply oppose fast track authority for NAFTA or would they hold out the possibility of support (or of more tempered opposition) in exchange for some concessions. Union leaders recognized that simply blocking agreement was not enough. "The irony was that we needed to do things with the Mexicans to deal with the problems on the border," recalled the AFL-CIO's Anderson. "If we simply defeat[ed] NAFTA, we [wouldn't] make things better. The status quo was no good." There is some evidence that top union leadership considered making a deal for better worker adjustment assistance. In August 1990, Jules Katz, the Deputy USTR who would be the chief negotiator for NAFTA, called Tom Donahue, Secretary-Treasurer of the AFL-CIO, to tell him that President Bush had decided to go ahead with the negotiations. Donahue warned that the unions would fight. As Katz recalls, "I said, 'I hope we can work together.' Donahue said there is a price attached: adjustment assistance. I said, 'I'm with you on that. I'll fight for it in the administration.' "

It is unlikely, however, that there was ever a serious possibility of such a deal. The more prevalent union view on adjustment assistance, recalled Mark Anderson, was "adjustment to what? Adjustment is an attractive theoretical concept, but if the economy is not producing stuff to increase general employment, it loses its allure." Donahue and Katz had no further conversations about such a quid pro quo.

The problem for union leadership was that union rank and file was so spontaneously and unambiguously negative that it precluded any possibility of bargaining with the administration. Union leaders are elected officials; they were in no position to make a deal. Steve Beckman, chief strategist for the United Auto Workers (UAW) on NAFTA, recalls:

> From the beginning of the fast track debate, this was a visceral issue with members. NAFTA was very much a gut issue. Members understood that it was a direct threat to their jobs. If we had wanted to make a deal we couldn't have.

The union leadership also recognized clearly that fast track limited their ability to affect the terms of the agreement. They had learned from experience with the Canada–U.S. Free Trade Agreement (CUFTA) that once the administration had fast track, it would be able to negotiate what it wanted and force the Congress to take it or leave it. They needed to kill fast track, whether they wanted to push for a better agreement or whether they wanted to block any agreement. By the end of 1990 union lobbyists were on the Hill urging fast track's defeat.

The Environmental Awakening

Although the environmental problems of Mexico were of great concern to many environmentalists, the Washington environmental community was slow to link its interest in these problems to the upcoming trade negotiation. Unlike labor unions, environmental organizations in the United States had no history of involvement with trade negotiations. They had largely ignored the CUFTA. They had no staffers who dealt with trade and environment issues. It is all the more remarkable that from this beginning environmental organizations would succeed in making their issues concerns in the fast track debate and would become important players in the process.

The roots of this success were with a small group organized in the spring of 1989 by Stewart Hudson, a young staffer at the National Wildlife Federation (NWF). Hudson put together an "Ad Hoc Group on Trade and Environmentally Sustainable Development" to talk about the idea that trade, and trade agreements, might be bad for the environment. Of immediate concern was the ongoing Uruguay Round of the GATT. Participants in Hudson's group were worried that international trade agreements were becoming ways of attacking domestic environmental laws, which could be struck down as trade restrictive by unaccountable trade tribunals.

After the Bush-Salinas announcement in June 1990, the group saw a great opportunity. Mexico provided a way to make the connection between trade and environment clear. The maquiladora program, which some depicted as a trial run for a free trade agreement, had resulted in numerous easily documented environmental problems. The population explosion around factories in the program had overwhelmed the local environmental infrastructure, leading to obviously unsanitary living conditions. As these environmentalists saw it, the environmental horrors of the maquiladora demonstrated how free trade without accompanying environmental provisions was harmful to the environment.

Second, the environmentalists argued, companies fleeing environmental regulation in the United States for the "pollution haven" of Mexico illustrated the necessity of making comparable enforcement a part of any free trade agreement. The environmentalists pointed to the case of furniture makers in Los Angeles who had moved to Tijuana to avoid installing ventilation hoods in their factories and to statements by Mexican recruiters of American businesses who made low regulatory compliance costs part of their pitch to attract new investment.

And, third, they believed, Mexico provided a clear example of how trade law might undermine environmental law: the case of tuna and dolphins. The U.S. Marine Mammal Protection Act requires that tuna be caught in ways that do not harm dolphins. In June 1990, a small environmental group filed suit to block imports of Mexican tuna on the grounds that Mexican fishers did not protect dolphins as required by the U.S. Marine Mammal Protection Act. The environmentalists won and imports of Mexican tuna were banned. In October, the Mexican government decided to challenge the ruling on grounds that it was an illegitimate restraint of trade prohibited by GATT, and alarm bells went off throughout the environmental community. If this act could be challenged in this way, environmentalists feared, so too could other environmental, health, and safety standards.

In November, Hudson circulated a draft document laying out the National Wildlife Federation's concerns. The paper made the rounds of environmental organizations in Washington and found its way to several interested Congressional offices. Still, the rest of the environmental community did not rush to get involved. As Hudson recalled, "I couldn't get the mainstream environment groups interested."

Building a Coalition

One of the key early members of the ad hoc group was long-time labor rights activist Pharis Harvey, head of a small outfit called the International Labor Rights Education and Research Fund (ILRERF). Harvey had been involved for years in the effort to get "human rights and labor rights factored into trade." The effort had been frustrating. Although the 1988 trade act had made the opening of a discussion between labor and trade a negotiating objective, Harvey felt that no one in the Bush administration had taken it seriously: "They just went through the motions with a wink and a smirk. It was clear that this wouldn't go anywhere unless we had broader international cooperation." When NAFTA came along, Harvey saw an "opportunity to build a regional discussion of the issue and the potential of getting more serious consideration. [NAFTA] was an opportunity to get it into the public debate."

As the issue of fast track extension approached, Harvey focused on the process itself. The issue was "largely about participation and process," he recalled. "Most of us viewed fast track as a truncation of the democratic process. [It was] a way in which the administration kept debate closed." Moreover, he didn't buy the argument that fast track was necessary to NAFTA. "I understand it with GATT when you have 140 countries, but I thought it was overreaching in a bilateral agreement," he said, forgetting Canada for the moment.

The strategic problem was how to engage the public in the dialogue he desired. Harvey contacted his old friends in Canada who had been active in fighting the CUFTA. They brought a delegation to Washington to talk about how you went about building a broad citizen's coalition. As Harvey recalls, they had two pieces of advice: "First, you need to develop a strong international effort. They felt they had failed because they had no effective counterpart in the U.S. Second, don't just say no. Integration is going to take place with or without you. If you simply oppose you will be dismissed."

In mid-November 1990, Harvey, Stewart Hudson, and Cam Duncan of Greenpeace decided to hold a one-day forum January 15, 1991, on Capitol Hill to attempt to draw attention to their concerns. Their idea was to have panels on labor, environment, and agriculture issues, with representatives from Canada, Mexico, and the United States on each to demonstrate the international nature of their concerns. Members of Congress, their staffers, and the press would be invited. On November 20, the idea was discussed at a larger meeting of the growing coalition of potential opponents who had met to discuss how best to press for inclusion of various social concerns in the free trade negotiation. The group now included, in addition to the NWF and Harvey's ILRERF, representatives of the AFL-CIO, the UAW, Greenpeace, the Natural Resources Defense Council (NRDC), the Family Farm Coalition, and the Community Nutrition Institute, among others.

On the basis of past experience, neither Harvey nor Hudson expected much of a crowd for their January 15 forum. Harvey's wife prepared coffee for a hundred people. When they walked in that morning, however, more than 400 people packed the room beyond capacity. It seemed that the whole Washington trade community had turned out. In addition to a huge turnout of Capitol Hill staffers and representatives of various nongovernmental organizations, "every trade lawyer in town was there," recalls Harvey. Hudson described it later as just "dumb luck, the synergy of labor, environment, and other issues coming together." But he also pointed to a particular Washington phenomenon.

> You have to understand that there is an industry in town representing business clients. As I looked around the room, I realized that the [Washington trade lawyers] of the world are our allies. They want it to become an issue! What happens is a buzz. You could just see the memos going out to corporate clients. "There is a big force out there opposing fast track. If you retain us . . ."

Initially there was almost no media coverage, but C-SPAN had been there and the network would eventually broadcast the forum three times. And word began to get out. The Bureau of National Affairs *International Trade Daily* reported the event January 20th. Washington insiders now knew about it. The forum hadn't represented a real coalition, just provided evidence of how widespread the opposition was. But on February 12, Harvey and Hudson and other participants from the January forum held a press conference at the Methodist Building on Capitol Hill to announce the creation of a coalition of sixty-two environmental, labor, religious, consumer, and community groups intent on opposing fast track authority unless the administration agreed to address the host of social concerns they represented. The coalition took the name Mobilization on Development, Trade, Labor, and the Environment, or MODTLE. (They would later be dubbed a "motley crew" by editorial writers.) Now there was a real coalition that might cause fast track some problems.

We've Got a Problem Here: Rethinking Strategy in the Administration

As the political landscape changed, the administration fast track team was faced with the challenge of reassessing the situation and of devising a new strategy to cope with it.

In January 1991, Nick Calio, Deputy Assistant to the President for Congressional Relations, joined the team. Calio was worried. Because Calio was responsible for the House of Representatives, he knew there was trouble brewing. He was particularly concerned about what position Congressman

Richard Gephardt (Democrat, Mo.) would take. As the majority leader and as a long-time player in trade matters, Gephardt could be very influential with House Democrats. If he opposed fast track, it might not win. Moreover, Gephardt was increasingly critical of fast track.

"The agreement was in trouble in January," Calio recalled. "I knew it was a big problem." Calio shared his assessment with the Bolton group. Bolton agreed that they had a problem. "I was not exactly the bearer of bad news," Calio recalled. "They knew there were problems. But they were not attuned to what it would take to win."

In February 1991, as members of Congress began to focus their attention on fast track, critics drowned out supporters. At hearings in both houses, witnesses representing an extraordinary spectrum of American political institutions gave members as earful as they spoke of their concerns about NAFTA's potential impacts on the environment, labor rights, workplace safety, human rights, drugs, and immigration — in addition to more traditional concerns about economic impacts. At the Ways and Means Committee hearing February 21, the AFL-CIO's Tom Donahue issued a thundering condemnation of fast track for NAFTA:

> This is an unusual occasion. It is not every day that a sovereign nation seeks to negotiate an agreement that is certain to destroy the jobs of tens of thousands of its citizens. . . . We believe that the substance of the administration proposal is harmful and ill-conceived, and we believe that American workers will pay for it with their jobs. . . . We are alarmed by the effort to limit discussion and debate, the effort to circumscribe the role of Congress in what will be a wholesale restructuring of the economy of North America.[9]

At the same hearing, David Ortman of Friends of the Earth (testifying on behalf of Friends as well as the National Wildlife Federation and the Texas Center for Policy Studies) said that these environmental groups were not prepared to support fast track unless environmental concerns were addressed as part of the negotiation. Pharis Harvey said "an agreement that deals only with narrowly defined trade and investment rules may have serious adverse effects on the environment, on labor standards, on human rights, on agricultural interests and consumers, both in the United States and Mexico."

Other members of the opposition coalition also testified. Linda Golodner, of the National Consumers League and the Child Labor Coalition urged that Congress be "given the opportunity to ensure that child labor issues, as well as human rights, environmental, agricultural, and labor concerns are an integral part of any negotiated trade agreement." Joseph Kinney of the National Safe Workplace Institute said, "it would be a real travesty to put pressure on a regulatory climate that we produced by having unfettered, unthoughtful, in effect homicidal trade relations with Mexico."[10]

House Democrats were coming under increasing pressure to oppose fast track. In their view, they didn't owe the Republican president George Bush anything and they were hearing bad things from the people who normally supported them: labor, environment, citizen's groups, and the like. For members not versed in the details of trade policy, the composition of the opposition gave them pause, at the very least. The Democratic National Committee, responding to union pressure, went on record in opposition to fast track. Members were beginning to stake out positions that the administration might not be able to meet. Meanwhile, Majority Leader Gephardt was sounding more like someone poised to oppose fast track. In a speech to the UAW February 6, he said "I believe every member of Congress should be against the negotiation of . . . a treaty with Mexico that doesn't stand up for the rights of American workers."[11]

Dan Rostenkowski (Democrat, Ill.), Chairman of the Ways and Means Committee, and his Finance Committee counterpart, Lloyd Bentsen (Democrat, Tex.), both supporters of NAFTA and defenders of the fast track process, had been around long enough to know that this was not business as usual. NAFTA appeared to be touching a nerve that was generating opposition from a host of new players in trade politics, many of them traditional Democratic constituencies. Union opposition was bad enough, but when joined with environmentalists and others, the resulting coalition made Democrats very nervous. Both chairmen set up ad hoc whip groups to poll the membership and see what the vote looked like. The preliminary counts were encouraging in the Senate, but the situation in the House was precarious.

Josh Bolton, Nick Calio, and others in the administration had been making the rounds on the Hill and coming to the same conclusion. As they assessed it, their strategic problem had two aspects. First, they needed to find a way to buy time. The opposition had the momentum and control of the debate. Members were beginning to lock themselves in. "In February and March, our main objective was to get members to keep their powder dry," recalls Calio. Then, second, they had to gain control of the debate and find a way to give members some political "cover," particularly on the environmental issues. They believed they could win without labor's support and they could win without environmental support, but the combination of labor and environment was formidable. "We could see that environment was a problem if labor was a problem," Calio recalled. There was, of course, no prospect of winning labor support. The administration concluded that they had to find a way to neutralize the environmental issue.

The new strategic importance of environmental issues gave one group in the administration an important opening. Back in August, Dan Esty, a young assistant to Environmental Protection Administration (EPA) Administrator Bill Reilly, had noted the rising attention to trade and environmental issues. The EPA had never been part of the discussion on trade matters. Here was an opportunity. Esty wrote a memo to his boss. Esty recalled, "I told him, 'Environment is going to be a big issue with NAFTA. That creates an opportunity for us. Let's make it a top focus.' " Reilly agreed, and gave Esty a green light. Unlike most staffers at the EPA, Esty was no stranger to trade issues. Before coming to the EPA he had been a trade lawyer at Arnold and Porter, a top Washington law firm. He knew Josh Bolton and others at the USTR. Esty suggested that Reilly approach Carla Hills about setting up an EPA-USTR trade and environment working group. Reilly took the idea to Hills, and she agreed that it would be wise to get out in front on the issue. A small working group started meeting late in the fall.

Now with fast track in some trouble, the administration needed to reach out to elements of the environmental community. Esty and Reilly knew where to turn. Reilly had been president of the World Wildlife Fund before coming to the EPA, and he knew the leadership of the environmental organizations. He had been talking especially to his friend Jay Hair, president of the National Wildlife Federation. He had reason to believe that the NWF and other "moderate" environmental groups might come around to support fast track. Those groups saw NAFTA in much the same terms that the EPA did, as an opportunity. On February 19, Esty set up a meeting for the staff at the USTR and representatives of six environmental organizations, including the NWF.

The USTR's Chip Roh later described the meeting as "culture shock." This was new terrain for both sides. The trade officials knew next to nothing about international environmental issues. The environmentalists knew less about the arcane world of trade negotiations. Nevertheless, the meeting began a dialogue that would continue throughout the rest of the NAFTA process.

The Bolton group had one more problem: convincing the Bush administration to do what needed to be done. The administration's initial response
to the environmental charges had been simply to refute them. "Our first
reaction was to say: 'They shouldn't be opposed to this,' " recalled Chip
Roh. In January, Carla Hills had been clear that labor and environmental
concerns should not be considered as part of the free trade negotiation. Hills
had now come around to the view that the administration would need to do
more, indicating in her testimony before the Ways and Means Committee
on February 20 that the administration was willing to consider bilateral social
issues "relating to the environment, drug enforcement, standards in the
workplace, and emigration," and that it was currently studying how to deal
with these issues, "whether that be in the trade agreement or in a separate
document."[12]

During the last weeks of February, the administration team talked fre-
quently with staffers at Ways and Means and Finance about their respective
problems. On March 1, Carla Hills met with Dan Rostenkowski and Lloyd
Bentsen to discuss the situation and how to deal with it. Rostenkowski and
Bentsen told Hills bluntly that they wouldn't have the votes to pass fast track
unless the administration gave them some help in countering labor and
environmental objections. Hills understood the situation and expressed willingness to work with the chairmen on this, but she intimated that she was
having some difficulty convincing others in the administration to be flexible,
most notably Bush's chief of Staff, John Sununu. They agreed that it might
be helpful if Bentsen and Rostenkowski went on record with their concerns.
Over the next few days, staffs worked to iron out the details. Rostenkowski
and Bentsen would write to the president, urging him to consider certain of
the problems raised by the opponents of fast track and requesting a report
on how the administration intended to respond to them. Drafts of the letter
went back and forth. It was cleared with key Republicans on the trade
committees.

On March 7, Chairmen Rostenkowski and Bentsen delivered an open
letter to the president. The letter stated sympathy for the "legitimate concerns" raised by members of Congress, including "the disparity between the
two countries in the adequacy and enforcement of environmental standards,
health and safety standards and worker rights." These issues, it said, should
be addressed "either within the agreement itself or through some appropriate
alternative context, within the same time frame as the trade negotiations."
The chairmen requested that the president provide an action plan to

Congress by May 1. "Such an action plan is essential to the Congress as we deliberate on your fast-track request."[13]

The letter was a stroke of political genius. First, it solved Carla Hill's internal problem. "We needed a vehicle so that we could move forward to start to allay fears of potentially anti-fast track vote," recalled Calio. A request from the chairmen of the two most important committees in Congress could not be denied. Without Bentsen and Rostenkowski, fast track was dead.

Second, the letter bought time. While the administration considered how to respond to the Bentsen-Rostenkowski request, they could ask members of Congress not to take a position. "The March 7 letter let us say: 'Wait, we're working on it. Give us a chance,'" recalled Calio. And it made it more difficult for outside groups to attack NAFTA. Although there was never any possibility that the labor unions would support fast track, the administration was talking to them about the action plan. Calio recalled, "It was worth the effort of talking with [labor]. While they were talking, they couldn't blast it."

Third, the Rostenkowski-Bentsen letter regained control of the issue by framing it in terms that the administration could meet (and the Mexicans accept). The letter carefully mentioned only environment, health and safety standards, and worker rights (it had nothing on wage disparities, for example) and did not insist that these matters be addressed in the NAFTA negotiations themselves. A senior official in the Mexican embassy later said, "It was a very skillful letter. It established a framework that allowed you to control the debate."

Finally, the gambit undercut Gephardt. Now whatever he decided to do would be defined in relation to the Bentsen-Rostenkowski letter and to the administration's response. As a senior Republican Hill staffer recalled, "We were supportive of the letter because we thought it would put the issue to bed. . . . We were trying to nip [the environment and labor opposition] in the bud. The administration and the Republicans and Bentsen and Rosty all were trying to undercut Gephardt."

On March 12, Carla Hills was back before the Ways and Means Committee. She thanked Chairman Rostenkowski for his letter and promised that the administration would meet the request. "I agree with your characterization of these issues as legitimate ones that deserve to be addressed in a meaningful way," she said.[14] So it was agreed that there would be an "action plan."

Devising an Action Plan

It was one thing for the administration to promise to address environmental and labor concerns, quite another to decide how to do it. "When we agreed to the Action Plan it was a 'place holder.' " recalls Calio. The administration had until May 1 to decide what should be in the place. For the next month and a half, its contents would be negotiated within the administration, with members of Congress, and with key interest groups.

The heart of the administration's strategy was to use the Action Plan to split the environmental community. "We had a very clear strategy to neutralize the [environmental] issue," recalled the EPA's Esty. "Our problem was to smoke out the real environmentalism from labor protectionism in the guise of environmentalism." It was not that the environmentalists directly controlled many votes on the Hill, in the same way that the labor unions did. But they had very high standing with the public and a proven ability to generate favorable press coverage. Members of Congress did not want to be antienvironment. If the fast track vote became defined as a litmus test on the environment, it would be very difficult for members to vote for it. And some members who wanted to help the unions but avoid being labeled protectionist might find it tempting to use the environment as an excuse to vote no. To prevent that, some environmental groups had to be persuaded to give their blessing, not just sit on the sidelines.

Fortunately for the administration, the environmental community was far from monolithic. As the EPA's Esty recalled:

> The environmental community breaks down on several fracture lines. Some groups are national in focus. They perceive that they have the ability to shape environmental policy. Other groups are more grassroots. They distrust national processes. The second fault line is between those in the environmental community who think that economic growth can be good for the environment and those who subscribe to the limits-to-growth model in which economic growth translates into pollution.

Esty identified a set of environmental groups that might work with the administration, all large national organizations. On March 9, President Bush summoned the leaders of the National Wildlife Federation, the National Audubon Society, the Natural Resources Defense Council (NRDC), the Environmental Defense Fund (EDF), and the Nature Conservancy to the White House. The hope was that some might endorse fast track—indeed Chief of Staff Sununu's insistence on this matter led NWF's Jay Hair to turn down the invitation. None of the groups were prepared to go that far yet, but the Audubon Society and the NRDC did put out statements implying that they might support fast track if their concerns were addressed.

The White House call also had another effect. To this point, most of the mainstream environmental groups other than the National Wildlife Federation had not really been active on fast track. But, said the NWF's Hudson, "the Bush meeting brought other groups into the picture. When the president of the United States calls you to a meeting, it is a wakeup call. A lot of groups got involved then."

Over the next six weeks, the NWF's Stewart Hudson, Justin Ward from the NRDC, and others worked with the USTR and the EPA to fashion a deal. The environmentalists laid out several conditions for their support. First, the trade agreement would need to include provisions that protected the sanctity of U.S. environmental laws. Second, there needed to be some mechanism to ensure that Mexico enforced its environmental laws. Third, the administration needed to commit to a plan to clean up the environmental mess on the border. Fourth, environmentalists needed a seat at the table for the negotiations and all future trade talks. The administration was willing to talk about all of these issues. Indeed, the interests of these groups were not far from the interests of the EPA.

As the administration wooed the moderates, the environmental coalition began to fragment. A free trade agreement, particularly one negotiated by the Bush administration, could only make environmental matters worse in the eyes of the more radical environmental groups Greenpeace and Friends of the Earth as well as the Ralph Nader organization Public Citizen, now increasingly active in the coalition. These groups were deeply suspicions of the administration and the business community pushing for free trade. The whole agenda was defined by the very people they had been fighting for years. To them, free trade was just a backdoor way to deregulate. Leadership of the environmental opposition shifted from the NWF's Hudson to Public Citizen's Lori Wallach. As Hudson recalls, Wallach told them: "You people don't know how to run a campaign." She did. She began working more closely with Mark Anderson of the AFL-CIO, Steve Beckman of the UAW, an outfit called the Fair Trade Campaign, and others out to kill fast track. As the rift in the environmental community deepened, the administration grew increasingly confident that it could break the coalition.

Winning Gephardt's support was proving to be a more difficult proposition, however. Gephardt advocated a much broader agenda for the negotiations. The traditional approach to trade, in his view, was far too narrow and outdated. What was needed was a new approach to trade policy. On March 27, Gephardt sent his own letter to President Bush.

I am prepared to lend my full support to a North American Free Trade Zone if the agreement fights for American jobs and exports, preserves the world's environment, and defends the rights of Mexican workers. . . . I request that you not limit the talks to what used to be traditionally known as "trade issues"—tariffs, trade-related investment restrictions, dispute resolution and the like—but rather that we address North American Free Trade systematically. . . . To do so will require discussing issues like transition measures, wage disparity, environmental protection and worker rights.[15]

Gephardt called for an "escape clause" to deal with unanticipated surges in Mexican imports, "a very strict rule of origin," and measures to ease the transition, deal with wage disparity, the environment, worker rights, and human rights abuses in Mexico. He joined Bentsen and Rostenkowski in calling for a response on these matters by May 1.

Gephardt's letter was taken very seriously in the administration. As Majority Leader and someone to whom many members looked for guidance on trade issues, Gephardt's views could not be taken lightly. Nevertheless, there was disagreement on how far to go toward meeting his broader demands. The Action Plan would address the environmental issues, but these were not really Gephardt's central concerns. The administration was not going to propose a European Community–style social charter or address wage disparities. It might be willing to provide funds for "worker adjustment" programs that would support workers who lost their jobs as a consequence of free trade. The administration was divided on this issue, however. Chief of Staff Sununu argued against doing anything. As Nick Calio recalls, the view was "On policy grounds, why pour money into a program that doesn't work? Also, why should we do this for people who aren't going to support NAFTA anyway?" The political strategists disagreed. "[We] recognized that there were going to be dislocations," recalled Calio. "And we had to do something to get Gephardt and hold other Democrats. My assessment at the time was that we had to have it [worker adjustment assistance]."

Nonetheless, the initial drafts of the Action Plan did not include labor adjustment provisions. When drafts of the plan were shared with the Hill in late April, however, Bentsen and Rostenkowski made it clear that they wanted worker adjustment. Both liked labor adjustment programs, particularly those controlled by their committees. Moreover, they were convinced that it was a political necessity. They conveyed their strong displeasure to the administration. In a one-on-one meeting with the president on April 23, Gephardt made clear he would need an adjustment provision too. Just before the May 1 deadline, the administration decided to include worker adjustment. The package was complete. Now the problem was to sell it.

Organizing a Campaign for Fast Track

While the administration worked behind the scenes to negotiate a deal on the Action Plan that would win over some environmentalists and satisfy the Democratic leadership, it also worked with its allies on the Hill, in the business community, and with the Mexicans to put together a campaign for fast track. The campaign had two fronts, a direct lobbying effort and a public relations effort.

Nick Calio coordinated the administration's legislative lobbying effort at the White House. He set up a master whip list, rating each member of Congress on the standard 1–5 scale (where 1 = support, 2 = leaning yes, 3 = undecided, 4 = leaning no, 5 = opposed).[16] Every administration contact with members was logged. The consultations were producing information on raw political votes, as well as member concerns. This intelligence allowed for targeted lobbying. If a member had a concern about the environment, for example, Bill Reilly would call. The political intelligence fed back to the policy debate about the Action Plan as well. "All of the information was funneling into our meetings and being assimilated as we moved toward a final policy decision," recalled Calio.

The administration began working closely with the pro–fast track whip operations in the on the Hill. Rostenkowski set up an ad hoc whip operation in the House. The stalwarts of the ad hoc bipartisan whip group were Bob Matsui (Democrat, Calif.), Bill Richardson (Democrat, N.M.), David Dreier

(Republican, Calif.), and Jim Kolbe (Republican, Ariz.). Later, Bob Torri-celli (Democrat, N.J.) joined the whip group. Torricelli's addition was con-sidered a coup, because of his close ties to unions and to Dick Gephardt. Chairman Rostenkowski kept a close eye on the situation. Because he was worried about the pressure the unions were putting on younger members, he brought some of them into the whip operation, most notably Tim Penny (Democrat, Minn.) and Mike Kopetski (Democrat, Oreg.). In the Senate, Bentsen's group included Democrats Max Baucus, Bill Bradley, Alan Cran-ston, Dennis Deconcini, and Phil Graham and Republicans John Chafee, Jack Danforth, Bob Dole, Richard Lugar, and Bob Packwood, together more than half the Finance Committee. The Senate group was much more closely held, with Bob Kyle, chief trade counsel for the Senate Finance Committee, and Brad Figel, his Republican counterpart, the only staffers allowed in the meetings. The Hill whip groups shared information and intelligence with the administration.

The magnitude of the opposition to fast track had surprised the business community, which as a consequence got off to a slow start on its lobbying efforts. Early in the spring, many in the administration were grousing that the private sector wasn't doing its share. In April, however, the business community's effort began to gather steam. At the Business Roundtable, Jim Robinson, the American Express CEO who had been instrumental in efforts to promote the concept of a free trade agreement, prodded his fellow CEOs to begin working on the issue. At a meeting in April, Robinson put on a combat helmet from Desert Storm to make his point. "I want 2000 sorties a day," he told them. Each CEO was given three members to see personally. Staffers followed up to make sure the assignments were kept. Robinson threw himself into the effort. Before the battle was over, Robinson would see or talk by phone with almost 200 members personally.

The Business Roundtable sponsored the creation of a new National For-eign Trade Council, an ad hoc group of 500 companies and trade associa-tions, and coordinated its efforts with the MTN Coalition, a group of com-panies largely concerned with GATT; with other business organizations such as the Chamber of Commerce; and with individual companies such as Gen-eral Electric, whose chief lobbyist, Bob Barrie, was perhaps the most active Washington representative. The lobbying effort concentrated on direct con-tact with members, but also produced a considerable volume of letters from business leaders, stacks of favorable editorials, and endorsements from an impressive list of opinion leaders. The intent was to leave no doubt that the business community was solidly behind fast track.

The Mexican government mounted its own lobbying effort. Because the Mexicans were new to the Washington game, they hired political expertise. "We don't know the ways of Washington well, so we get people who do," explained Herman von Bertrab, who headed Mexico's new NAFTA office in Washington. Among those retained by the Mexican government were the prominent Republican lobbyist Charls Walker and the prominent Democratic lobbyist Joe O'Neill (formerly of Lloyd Bentsen's staff). It was awkward for the Mexicans to lobby directly, but these well-connected lobbyists provided good access for them.

Off the Hill, the pro-NAFTA effort sought to counter the widespread negative images of Mexico and NAFTA through a public relations campaign involving editorials, radio ads, speeches, and other events designed to generate positive media coverage. The problem was that NAFTA's opponents had succeeded in connecting trade with Mexico with images of shuttered factories in the United States and environmental degradation in Mexico. News articles making the connection even appeared in papers whose editorial stance favored NAFTA. For instance, the solidly pro-NAFTA *Wall Street Journal* ran a story in September 1989 in which it reported that the maquiladora program was "helping turn much of the border region into a sinkhole of abysmal living conditions and environmental degradation."[17] In 1991, the opponents took their opposition to the editorial pages, emphasizing lost jobs, environmental degradation, and the antidemocratic nature of the fast track process. AFL-CIO president Lane Kirkland, for example, writing in the *Wall Street Journal* on April 18, once again connected NAFTA to the maquiladoras, and that program to the legacy of job loss in the United States:

> During the past decade, hundreds of U.S. companies, lured by Mexico's "comparative advantages" of rock-bottom wages and lack of effective government regulations and enforcement, have shut down factories in the States and relocated them to the *maquiladora* areas. While hundreds of thousands of American workers were losing their jobs to this dislocation, more than a half-million Mexicans working in *maquiladora* plants were joining the ranks of the most crudely exploited humans on the planet.

The result has been social and environmental conditions along the Mexican side of the border that rival any of the well-publicized disasters of the worst Stalinist regimes.[18]

To counter this, pro-NAFTA editorials emphasized job creation and international competitiveness and sought to portray the opponents as reactionary. A *Wall Street Journal* editorial, for instance, castigated liberals for turning their backs on Latin America:

Thirty years ago American liberals rallied around John F. Kennedy's Alliance for Progress in Latin America. Today many of those same liberals are uniting to defeat a U.S.–Mexico free-trade agreement because it might produce too much progress. The transformation of American "progressives" into a force for reaction is an astonishing event.[19]

The vast majority of editorial pages around the country endorsed fast track and offered similar assessments.

Mexico, too, got into the public relations battle. At the behest of its strategists at the public relations firm Bursen-Marsteller, President Salinas toured the United States and Canada early in April, making speeches and proselytizing about NAFTA. Salinas was accompanied by a retinue of cabinet officers and top Mexican businessmen wherever he went. In Austin, the last stop on the tour, Salinas became the first Mexican president to ever address the Texas State Legislature.

Rolling Out the Action Plan

The heart of the administration's strategy for passing NAFTA was the rollout of the Action Plan, a response to the letters from Rostenkowski, Bentsen, and Gephardt. Nick Calio coordinated an elaborate effort to maximize the political gain from the announcement. Because Majority Leader Gephardt was out of town until April 30, the administration chose May 1 as the big day. The week before, key members of Congress and favorable interest group leaders were briefed on the plan's contents.

The day of the announcement, a letter was hand delivered to Rostenkowski, Bentsen, and Gephardt early in the morning. The letter promised an administration "action plan" on labor and environmental issues. The president was "committed to working with the Congress to ensure that there is adequate adjustment assistance and effective retraining for dislocated workers," and promised to "develop and implement an expanded program of environmental cooperation in parallel with the free trade talks" and "expand U.S.–Mexico labor cooperation."[20] The president promised to appoint environmentalists to the trade advisory committees and committed himself to formulating a plan to clean up the border.

Bentsen and Rostenkowski immediately applauded the president for his responsiveness. The National Council of La Raza, perhaps the leading Hispanic group, endorsed NAFTA, a coup for the administration. But NAFTA's toughest critics were not won over. The MODTLE coalition held a press conference at the National Press Club to denounce the "inaction plan." Pharis Harvey, president of the International Labor Rights Education and Research Fund, blasted the plan as unresponsive to the numerous concerns about NAFTA that had been raised, including

> environmental destruction, suppression of labor rights and standards, growing wage disparities, increased immigration, dangers of pesticide use, human rights abuses, and the need for adjustment assistance for affected workers in industries. . . . The Administration's so-called "Action Plan" has concentrated on only two of these issues—labor and environmental standards—and on these issues their response is not an action plan, but an inaction plan. On the other issues there is a deafening silence. If this is any indication of how the administration plans to satisfy Congress and the general public, there is strong reason to deny them *carte blanche* authority to negotiate an unchangeable agreement.[21]

Although by now it was apparent that there were strains in the environmental coalition, the mainstream groups that the administration had been assiduously courting did not immediately endorse the plan. This caused some frustration in the administration. On May 8, the president met with a small group of environmental leaders including John Adams, executive director of the NRDC; Kathryn Fuller, president of the World Wildlife Fund; and Frederic Krupp, executive director of the Environmental Defense Fund. The president assured them of his commitment to addressing the environmental issues. Among other things, the president promised to appoint five environmentalists to the advisory committees. The group seemed impressed. Kathryn Fuller told a reporter afterwards:

> It is certainly fair to say that all the participants from the environmental community see the president's environmental initiatives in the trade negotiations very positively. For the first time, environmental issues are being intertwined throughout the negotiations and discussions on an international trade agreement.[22]

News of the meeting prompted consumer advocate Ralph Nader to fire off a letter accusing the environmentalists of having sold out.

On May 10, Jay Hair, president of the National Wildlife Federation, announced his organization's support of fast track in an editorial in the *New York Times*. The rift in the environment community was now out in the open. The editorial angered leaders of environmental groups who continued to oppose the treaty, such as the Sierra Club and Greenpeace. They recognized that the NWF endorsement effectively neutralized environment as an issue in the Congress. "At the very least," said a spokesperson for Friends of the Earth later, "we expected the big environmental groups to stay on the fence. Hair's endorsement was strong enough to hurt our position."[23]

Momentum was now clearly with the administration. But Dick Gephardt had not yet announced a position. His opposition could still make matters difficult; his support would all but assure victory. On May 2, Bush canceled a planned campaign trip to Missouri to avoid appearing with Gephardt's Republican challenger. The administration had been dealing with Gephardt for months, and there was some frustration. As Nick Calio recalled later, "An enormous amount of work went into getting Gephardt. We knew we would have to work hard at it. But we didn't know we were going to have to work that hard."

Finally on May 9, Gephardt announced his decision. He would support fast track, he said, but he intended to hold the administration to its commitments on labor and environment.

> I am not willing to write a blank check to this or any other administration on a trade negotiation. We're saying as clearly as I know how to say it to our government and the Mexican government that if this treaty is insufficient, if it does not adequately address the concerns that

have been over and over again offered by many of us, we retain the right and will amend this treaty and implementing legislation.[24]

Privately, the labor unions were furious with Gephardt.

The path to victory for fast track extension now seemed secure. Although there remained strong opposition to NAFTA in the Congress, members who were inclined to support free trade agreements now had some political cover on both the environmental and labor issues. A few key voices in the business community who had initially voiced reservations about the agreement were now satisfied. The textile industry was promised a restrictive rule of origin to discriminate against non–North American fabric. The pharmaceutical industry was assured that Mexico would pass a strong intellectual property law before the NAFTA talks even got underway. But there would be one more shoal to navigate, one that only a very few insiders even knew existed.

Playing with Rules

By the rules adopted in the 1988 Trade Act, the president would get a two-year extension of fast track authority unless either the Senate or the House voted to deny it to him. The rules made fast track difficult to stop, since failure to act gave the president what he wanted. Moreover, the extension would apply to both NAFTA and the unfinished Uruguay Round of the GATT. That put a lot of pressure on members who, given a chance, might have liked to oppose NAFTA but were hesitant to pull the plug on the unfinished multilateral Round. As the vote approached in the House, opponents now tried a last gambit. They proposed to give members just that chance.

In the House, the Rules Committee has enormous discretion concerning the terms on which a bill will be considered when it reaches the floor. Normally, this power is used to determine the length of debate, the types of amendments that may be offered, and the like. Sander Levin (Democrat, Mich.), a critic of NAFTA and of the fast track process, now proposed that the Rules Committee use its authority to separate the votes on NAFTA and GATT. The fast track is a rule of Congress, self-imposed, and therefore, something that the Rules committee could change, he argued. For a moment, it appeared that Levin might have the votes in Rules to carry the day. The pro-NAFTA forces counterattacked. The Speaker of the House, Tom

Foley, made it clear to Joe Moakley (Democrat, Mass.), Chairman of the Rules Committee, that he thought this was a bad idea. Moakley made it clear to the members of the committee that they were not to vote this way. The idea died, and with it the last real chance to defeat fast track.

On May 23, the House voted 231 to 192 against a resolution by Byron Dorgan (Democrat, N.D.) to disallow the president his extension. The next day the Senate followed suit, voting 59 to 36 against Fritz Hollings's (Democrat, S.C.) resolution. President Bush had fast track negotiating authority for two years. Nearly a year after the president had announced that the United States would negotiate a NAFTA, the United States could at last enter negotiations.

Interpreting the Domestic Politics of Decision:
The Role of Institutions and Interests

This chapter began with three questions: Why did an obscure procedural rule of the Congress become the focus of such intense political pressure? How were advocates of labor and environment able to force those issues onto the agenda and extract concessions from the Bush administration? And why did Congress approve the fast track extension Bush requested?

To answer these questions (indeed, even to ask them) we need a theory of international relations in which domestic politics matters. Unless the fast track fight was irrelevant, just so much fury signifying nothing, international-level theory will not do. But, as will be even clearer in subsequent chapters, the domestic political process through which the United States decided to negotiate did matter, both because fast track authority could have been denied and because the process of obtaining it altered the trajectory of subsequent events.

To interpret the history of the fast track extension requires consideration of both interests and institutions at the domestic level. This was a strategic game among competing domestic interest groups, which therefore can be profitably viewed through a rational choice lens. But domestic institutions also mattered: The game was played according to rules established at an earlier time; at stake were rules to apply at a later time. To explain what happened after the fact (and even more to have predicted what would happen or to have informed strategy in the event) requires an understanding of the complex intertwining of interests and institutions.

To understand what was at stake in the fast track fight, one first needs to understand why the fast track process matters. As seen through a rational choice lens, the fast track rule is an ingenious partial solution to the problem of international trade politics as traditionally understood, which is, in essence, a collective action problem among domestic interests. Fast track authority was necessary (and nearly sufficient) for determining whether or not there would be a NAFTA. Domestic pressure groups recognized the significance of fast track and mobilized in pursuit of their interests.

Thus the politics of fast track can be interpreted as a rational choice process among NAFTA supporters and opponents as well as a critical set of opportunists, most notably several environmental groups, who saw a chance to advance interests on side issues not directly at stake. This configuration of interests and interplay of strategies eventually necessitated a strategic response in the form of a promise by the Bush administration to address environmental (and to a lesser extent labor) issues now associated with NAFTA.

The fast track extension game cannot be understood simply in terms of rational choice, however. To understand the fight over the rule in 1991 and its outcome requires that we understand the institutional context in which the fight took place. In particular, we must see the peculiar rules operating in 1991 that initially created an opening for NAFTA's opponents and in the end worked to their disadvantage. These rules had been established in 1988 on the basis of a contest of interests, but interests operating with imperfect foresight (NAFTA had not even been proposed) and within an institutional context created at yet an earlier time. Institutions cannot be reduced to rational choice processes.

The Rules Matter: Effects of the Fast Track Process

As first formulated by E.E. Schattschneider, and as explicated by the mainstream literature on trade policy making ever since, the core problem in international trade is overcoming the tendency of concentrated interests in protection to overwhelm the more general interest in free trade. If policy is made piecemeal, establishing the level of protection one sector at a time, for example, gains to protection will be concentrated for firms in that sector, while the losses will be diffused among unorganized consumers. Given the much greater problem of collective action for the many small losers, the concentrated protectionist interests will be much more successful in bringing political pressure to bear on trade policy makers. Attempts to negotiate away these barriers one by one encounter the same problem: Concentrated protectionist interests are more politically powerful than diffuse free trade interests and thus are often able to prevent international agreement. Comprehensive trade negotiations, those that deal with many sectors simultaneously, help balance the contest of interests by adding together the many small benefits from each sectoral liberalization. But if Congress can subsequently revisit the terms of an agreement one sector at a time, the comprehensive agreement will unravel as concentrated interests block pieces of the agreement one by one.

The fast track process largely solves this problem. Under fast track, the president is required to obtain negotiating authority from Congress before entering negotiations, or more specifically from the two committees with jurisdiction over trade, and to consult regularly with those committees and with Congressional leaders during the course of negotiation. The Congress, in return, agrees to a ratification process (called implementation, because trade agreements are not treaties) that differs from the normal legislative process in three critical ways. First, the implementing bill is written by the president, not by Congressional committees (although they are consulted). Second, the bill may not be amended; Congress can either accept or reject it. Third, the bill must be considered within 90 legislative days after it is introduced (hence "fast track"), unlike normal legislation, which can be bottled up in committee, never put on the calendar for floor action, or in the Senate, filibustered by determined opponents.[25]

These features have complex effects. One obvious and initially surprising effect is to shift power from Congress to the president. Under normal legislative process, Congress writes legislation and then forces the president to accept or reject it. Under fast track, the president negotiates an agreement, submits it (or more specifically an implementing bill) to Congress, and compels Congress to accept or reject that. Hence the president can identify the set of possible agreements that would be acceptable to a bare majority of Congress and then commit to the one he or she most prefers, a clear advantage to the president.

If this were the only effect of fast track, it would be astonishing that Congress had adopted it. Normally, Congress is intensely jealous of its institutional prerogatives, but fast track helps solve an intra-Congressional bargaining problem. For most members of Congress, a comprehensive free trade agreement may be preferable to no agreement. But every member would prefer an agreement that reflected that member's parochial interests. For example, a member representing a rural district would prefer an agreement that exempted agriculture, and a member representing a textile-making district would prefer an agreement that exempted textiles. If trade-implementing legislation were handled under the normal legislative process, which provides an opportunity to bargain over the form of the bill before it is introduced or to amend it afterward, each member will be tempted to try to modify the terms of the agreement. "Logrolling" among members of Congress, in which each member buys support for his or her particular modification by agreeing to support changes proposed by other members, may then unravel the comprehensive free trade package. The fast track, however, by ceding to the president the writing of the legislation and by prohibiting amendments, eliminates the possibility of logrolling and forces members to consider the benefits and costs of the whole bundle of issues at once. The problem as formulated here is a classic collective action problem, essentially a multiparty prisoner's dilemma, to which the fast track rule is an institutional solution.

A second benefit to Congress has to do with the effect of the fast track process on the game between members of Congress and outside pressure groups. Fast track ties the hands of members (or, rather, allows the president to tie them) by preventing them from amending the agreement in ways that favor concentrated outside interests. By eliminating flexibility, the rule empowers members in dealing with those interests.[26] With fast track, the member can credibly claim to be unable to respond to special-interest demands. In this way, the fast track reduces the larger collective action problem among interests in the society.

Fast track limits the power of special interests in yet another way. By establishing a self-enforcing calendar for action, the rule ensures that an antagonistic chair cannot block a vote and, in the Senate, that the implementing bill cannot be filibustered. A member who happens to represent a district where losers are concentrated cannot, therefore, block implementation.

Taken together, the benefits of fast track to Congress outweigh its costs and go a long way toward overcoming the trade policy making problem as it has traditionally been defined. Most important for the NAFTA story, fast track makes it possible for the United States to negotiate and implement international trade agreements.

Fast track, however, does not serve every interest. First, some protected commercial interests will fare better in a world with less international cooperation and more trade barriers. Second, to the extent that fast track not only limits the power of narrow commercial interests but also reduces the effectiveness of broader interests—labor unions or environmental groups, for instance—those interests may also fare better without fast track. Third, domestic interests not aligned with the president may not be well-served by the concentration of power that fast track puts in his or her hands.

Interests and Institutional Choice

In the spring of 1991, interest groups understood quite well what effect fast track would have on the probability of a free trade agreement and anticipated reasonably well what form that agreement would take. Their actions reflected these understandings. To the question of why fast track became such an issue, we have an answer: because interest groups correctly anticipated the likely outcome of the extension of the fast track rule. The fight over the institution of fast track, therefore, can be profitably viewed as a rational choice process among competing domestic interests.

Consider three sets of interest groups. The first were supporters, including especially business groups, who expected to benefit from any NAFTA that President Bush would negotiate. They understood that fast track made NAFTA possible, and they fought hard for it (although they were somewhat surprised at how hard they had to fight).

The second set were opponents, interest groups who expected to lose from any NAFTA that Bush might negotiate. Unions, some grassroots environmental organizations, and highly protected sectors of the economy all preferred no agreement. They understood that a denial of fast track might be their best opportunity to prevent the agreement and fought hard to defeat extension of the rule.

A third set of groups were in a more interesting strategic position. Regardless of whether fast track passed or not, their interests would not be affected strongly. However, they could gain a lot if they could alter the form of the NAFTA that Bush was likely to negotiate. This set included, most notably, the mainstream environmental organizations interested in focusing attention on border environmental issues and establishing a precedent for considering the environmental effects of trade agreements. For them, the battle over fast track renewal represented an opportunity. By forming a tactical alliance with NAFTA's opponents, these opportunists could gain leverage to advance issues of concern to them.[27]

These groups clearly anticipated the effects of the fast track process, but such understanding is not inevitable (although that is often the assumption by rational choice theorists). In this case, the experience of the interested parties with the CUFTA may have been relevant. Fast track authorization of CUFTA had met no significant opposition. When Congress considered the completed agreement in the spring of 1988, however, unions and other opponents discovered that their ability to prevent agreement or to affect its terms had been severely limited by the fast track process. The lesson learned, they were ready this time. Unions and other opponents recognized that the fast track fight was their last best chance to prevent agreement. Business recognized that without fast track, agreement was unlikely. And groups seeking to link their concerns to the negotiating agenda recognized that the fast track fight represented their best opportunity to compel such linkage.

Side Payments and the Logic of Linkage

The creation of the "Action Plan" to deal with environmental (and to a lesser extent labor) issues can be understood as the outcome of a strategic game between a key set of "mainstream" environmental groups, their allies on Capitol Hill, and the Bush administration. In this instance, a particular constellation of interests and configuration of rules made possible a commitment strategy by these environmentalists, which forced new issues to be linked to NAFTA and required a side payment in the form of the Action Plan.

The balance of forces that arose for and against fast track gave the mainstream environmental organizations something of a swing vote. They recognized that if they joined in the fast track debate they could determine its outcome. If some of them endorsed fast track, it would pass; if they opposed it, it would not. That they were in this position depended on the fact that the Democrats controlled both houses of Congress and that Democrats were vulnerable to the strong opposition of labor and grassroots organizations. With a Republican majority or weaker opponents, the support of the mainstream groups would not have been necessary.

Unlike unions and the grassroots opponents, the mainstream groups did not view NAFTA as a significant threat to their concerns. They did, however, see NAFTA as an opportunity to advance their interests. They had long wanted more attention paid to the environmental problems on the Mexican border and to the environmental consequences of trade. Without NAFTA, they had not been getting anywhere on these issues. As opposition to NAFTA grew, they recognized that a credible threat to oppose fast track might compel the administration to address these interests. They formed a tactical alliance with the grassroots environmental opponents and stated their price.

The Bush administration, faced with a credible commitment by the entire environmental community to oppose agreement, reinforced by the public commitments of the chairmen of the two trade committees, began quiet negotiations with the mainstream environmental groups to explore what it would take to obtain their consent. At this point, the side issues had become linked to fast track extension. The Bush administration would only agree to so much on these issues, of course, in part because of ideological opposition but also largely because the business groups supporting fast track extension worried about the precedent of linking environmental issues to trade agreements.

In the end, the Bush administration made a modest side payment to the environmental groups in exchange for an announcement of support for fast track extension. The payment—a promise to address the border issues, to discuss greater cooperation with Mexico on environmental issues, and to put a handful of environmentalists on the trade advisory committees—was of a form that did not significantly diminish the expected value of free trade for business supporters. The support of key environmental groups split the environmental community, neutralized the environment issue for members of Congress, and gave most members enough political cover to support extension. Figure 4.1 provides a more formal graphical analysis of this game. As

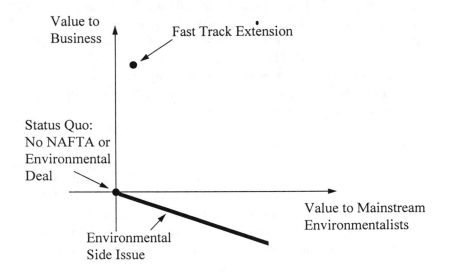

FIGURE 4.1   The Action Plan.

(A) The values of fast track extension (the expected value of NAFTA) and the range of possible resolutions of the environmental issues as yet unlinked to fast track. The value of fast track compared with the status quo is very positive for business but only very slightly improved for the mainstream groups. The environmental side issue is largely distributive: What gives value to environment takes value from business. Acceptable resolutions lie above and to the right of the two axes, drawn so they intersect the alternative of no agreement. Negotiated separately, the parties "should" agree on fast track but will not agree on any resolution of the side issues.

illustrated, the essential features of the politics of fast track extension can be modeled as a bargain between two players whose support was necessary for fast track's success—business and mainstream environment. The figure shows how a commitment strategy by the environmentalists compelled issue linkage and a side payment in the form of the Action Plan.

It is useful to recognize that the side payment was largely in the currency of an institutional change. The administration did not immediately put resources into the border region or agree to particular forms of cooperation with Mexico on environmental matters (or provide new funding for labor adjustment programs); it promised to put these issues on the negotiating agenda. All parties expected this commitment to be fulfilled, although they may have had different notions of its ultimate implications. This observation is a reminder that the form of a negotiation—who plays, on what issues, by what basic rules—is itself negotiated. These parameters reflect interests and power and may be altered if interests are sufficiently powerful and strategically skillful.

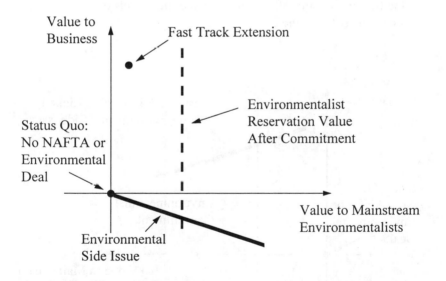

(B) The effect of the environmental groups' commitment strategy. With commitment, the environmental reservation value (minimum acceptable value) shifts to the right (dashed line). Now only points above the horizontal axis and to the right of the new environmental reservation value line are acceptable. No agreement is possible.

To the questions of why there was a fight, why a side payment was needed, and why Congress approved the fast track extension, we now have one set of answers: because of the particular constellation of interests and the strategies they pursued. This interpretation, focused exclusively on domestic-level rational choice politics, is not the only reason for fast track's success, however. Victory also depended on the particular institutional circumstances in which the game was played.

Institutions and the Context of Choice

The fast track fight of 1991 demonstrates that the choice of institutions is often a reflection of interest politics. But this does not eliminate an independent role for institutions. First, an obvious point, if the choice of rule made at one period were not binding (or at least constraining) at a later period, then there would be no reason to fight about rules. Interests could simply renegotiate the rules at a later time. Second, the choice of rules in one period must be made according to rules established at an earlier period. If the two periods are sufficiently separated, the effects of these rules may not be anticipated by the choosers.

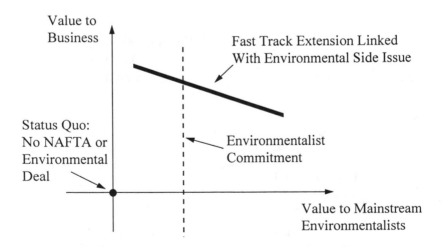

(C) The effect of linking fast track extension and the environmental side issue. Added together, the two issues create a zone of possible agreement to the right of the environmentalist commitment.

The history of fast track illustrates this last point nicely. The congressional game in 1991 was played according to rules laid down in 1988. In the 1988 Omnibus Trade and Competitiveness Act, Congress granted the president three years of fast track negotiating authority, primarily to finish the Uruguay Round of the GATT, with a provision that allowed for an extension of two more years if the president asked for it and neither house of Congress voted to oppose it. These were the rules by which the game in 1991 was played, and they mattered.

Had fast track authority simply been extended for five years in 1988, Bush would not have needed an extension in 1991. He would only have needed to announce his intention to negotiate under existing authority, in which case only a negative vote in either of the two trade committees—House Ways and Means and Senate Finance—where support for free trade was greatest, could have denied him fast track authority. The issue would probably not have been in much doubt; indeed, there would probably have been nothing

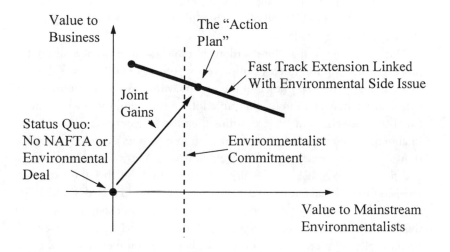

(D) The location of the Action Plan along the range of possible resolutions of the environmental issues. The Bush administration chose a point just sufficient to obtain the environmental groups' support. (Two years later, the Clinton administration would choose a point farther to the right on the line of possible resolutions.) This side payment transferred value from the business community to the environmentalists so as to create a possibility for agreement where none existed before, thus creating joint gains.

like the contest that arose over the issue of extension. There would have been much less mobilization of opposition, less of an opportunity to link environmental and labor issues, and no need for an Action Plan.

On the other hand, had fast track had been authorized in 1988 for three years without the extension provision, Bush would have needed new authorizing legislation in 1991 to negotiate with Mexico. Under these circumstances, the president would almost certainly not have obtained negotiating authority for NAFTA. (The enormous difficulty the Clinton administration had in obtaining fast track negotiating authority after it expired in 1994 reinforces this point.) As an ordinary trade bill, this legislation would have been open to amendment and subject to obstruction. Moreover, it would have been possible to authorize of fast track for completing the Uruguay Round of GATT without authorizing it for NAFTA, thus eliminating this important linkage.

As it happened, the rule established in 1988 made the extension process in 1991 itself something of a fast track process, an up-down vote on a previously established bundle in which not only NAFTA but also GATT was at stake. Opponents could not filibuster, could not amend, and could not split NAFTA from GATT, all of which made passing fast track much easier for NAFTA's proponents.

One could argue that the decision in 1988 was itself a rational choice process, reflecting the interests of players who bargained to create the legislation. The particular choice of three years with a two-year extension was a deal struck between those who wanted three years and those who wanted five. But the decision in 1988 regarding the rules for extension was not made in anticipation of NAFTA. Few if any then in Congress expected the extension to be used for a free trade negotiation with Mexico. Had the unions and the other NAFTA opponents understood in 1988 that the extension provision would make it more difficult for them to stop a NAFTA in 1991, they would have fought it more fiercely then. Yet the extension provision was scarcely even noticed. Foresight is not inevitable. Myopia is also logical, because of low interest in future events, because complexity makes it too difficult (or too costly) to assess the impact of rules on future events, or simply because the future is unpredictable.

The further back in time we go, the more difficult it is to imagine that choices made about institutions reflect foresight of their ultimate consequences and the less useful it is to consider the establishment of rules as the first stage in the same game.[28] The 1988 process was itself structured by institutions decided upon still earlier, most notably in 1974 when the fast track process was invented for the Tokyo Round of the GATT negotiations. At each point in time, a bargaining process operating in an institutional context created, among other things, a new institutional structure in which the next bargaining process took place.

Indeed, the whole possibility of a debate about authorization in the United States reflects Constitutional provisions that give Congress primacy in trade matters and create a need for authorization in the first place. Consider, in contrast, the Canadian process. Canadians were as divided about the prospects of a free trade agreement with Mexico as Americans were. Yet the nature of the Canadian political system provided no opportunity for opponents in Canada to prevent their Prime Minister from entering negotiations, and therefore, no opportunity to compel him to make the kinds of promises that George Bush had to make. These basic differences in political systems reflected choices made generations before and were not renegotiable. The designers of these two political systems certainly did not have NAFTA in mind, although their designs affected it.

Does one need to go back to the Constitutional Convention to explain NAFTA? Probably not, although if we were interested in the implications of constitutional choice, we might well find this interesting. For our purposes, and certainly for the purposes of participants in NAFTA, the genesis of rules established earlier is mostly irrelevant except to the extent such understandings provide a basis for assessing the stability of those rules. The analyst must bound the problem, which means that at some point, some institutions need to be taken as given. The task, then, is to understand the implications of those institutions for the game at hand.

A Note on Individual-Level Analysis

The preceding analysis has largely eschewed attention to particular individuals. But several players located in key spots in the policy making process adopted strategies that mattered to the outcome. It was not inevitable that someone in the environmental community recognize the opportunity, nor that the chairmen of the House Ways and Means and Senate Finance Committees demand action on the environmental and labor issues, nor that key figures in the Bush administration see the necessity of making a concession. Other individuals in these positions might well have behaved differently. Nevertheless, what mattered most was their understanding of the landscape of interests and institutions in which they operated.

Conclusions

The history of the fast track fight in the United States in the spring of 1991 clearly demonstrates a role for domestic process in international affairs. George Bush may have announced his intent in 1990 that the United States enter negotiations, but the United States did not decide to do so until Congress approved fast track negotiating authority in 1991. The political battle is a reminder that nations do not decide things as individuals do. A national decision requires a domestic political decision process.

To interpret the fast track fight, the political analyst needs to consider both domestic interests and domestic institutions. A rational choice lens can explicate the behavior of players and the outcomes of the battle, but it cannot, alone, completely explain the event. Institutions at a given time are partly exogenous and, therefore, play an independent role. To the question of why there was a fight in 1991, part of the answer is because the rules of the game allowed for it. To the question of why new issues were added to the agenda, part of the answer is that the particular rule governing extension of fast track created an opening for pressure groups to compel their addition. To the question of why, in the end, the Bush administration won, part of the answer is that the rules governing the vote in May favored extension.

Together, a consideration of institutions and interests in the domestic arena explains much of what happened in the spring of 1991. One limitation, however, should be noted. Our discussion so far has taken interests to be as revealed and has not inquired into the formation of those interests. If instead of procedural rationality, however, we are concerned with the substantive rationality of positions taken, that is, the extent to which the stance regarding NAFTA coincides with underlying interests, some puzzles appear. In particular, how was it that so many individuals, each with relatively little at stake in the negotiation and relatively little ability to influence its outcome, were able to organize such intense and determined opposition? We will return to this question in Chapter 7.

Section II

International Negotiation

5 Two-Level Bargaining: The NAFTA Negotiation

NAFTA had survived its first political challenge in the U.S. domestic arena; now the international negotiations could begin. The charge was ambitious: eliminate barriers to trade for all goods and services; eliminate barriers to investment and provide greater security for investors; and establish new rules for government procurement, intellectual property, and dispute settlement.

It would not be easy to reach these goals. No trade agreement so sweeping had ever been negotiated among countries at such different levels of economic development. Moreover, the negotiations would engage three different political systems, three different societies, and indeed, three different cultures. The process of establishing negotiating positions, of compromising from them, and ultimately of finding acceptable agreements would reflect not just the complexity of the issues on the international bargaining table, but also the necessity of simultaneously conducting internal negotiations in the domestic arenas of all three countries. In each country, negotiators had to consult with interagency committees, legislators, and a host of advisory committees from the private sector. The internal process was particularly intense in the United States, where the negotiations would be conducted in an atmosphere of much greater public scrutiny than any previous trade negotiation. Although the temperature would drop a bit from the heat of the fast track fight, reminders of the passions it stirred would follow the negotiations and serve as a forewarning that when the negotiators completed their job, the agreement would still have to go before Congress for its approval.

President Salinas, President Bush, and Prime Minister Mulroney urged their negotiators to move quickly in the hope that the negotiations would conclude by the end of 1991 or early 1992 at the latest, before the U.S. presidential campaign heated up. But this timetable would be completely unattainable. Before any real negotiating could take place, first the three countries had to agree on what issues to talk about and to decide on what positions to take. This process of defining the negotiation took the rest of 1991. Not until early 1992 were issues and positions sufficiently clarified that the negotiators could begin to negotiate the differences. Hopes remained high that the talks could be completed that spring, but the talks dragged on through the summer. Not until August 12, 1992, less than three months before the U.S. presidential election, did the negotiators finally reach agreement. By then it was too late for the U.S. Congress to consider the agreement in 1992. That would have to wait until after the election, when a new Congress and possibly a new president would decide what to do with it.

From the perspective of the national negotiators, NAFTA was a great success. The agreement did much of what the negotiators set out to accomplish and more than they expected. Its several thousand pages committed all three countries to eliminate, over time, most barriers to trade in goods and services; to open investment in most sectors of the economy, and to adhere to new rules for intellectual property, government procurement, and dispute settlement. Mexico, in particular, had agreed to a level of change that few would have predicted before the talks began.

Still, for all the movement toward some free trade ideal, perhaps equally interesting about the NAFTA are the deviations from it. If the agreement had been simply to free all trade and investment immediately, the text could have been a fraction of its actual length. What required the thousands of pages, and the bulk of the negotiating, were such matters as how slowly each country would move toward free trade for each product, how far and how fast each country would move to free investment, what "rules of origin" would determine how much of a product had to be made in North America to qualify for free trade, how conflicts between environmental and trade objectives would be handled, and what procedures would be used to settle disputes. The agreement is also interesting for what it did not include. A few politically privileged industries in all three countries were largely exempted: for example, Mexican oil, Canadian cultural industries, and U.S. shipping.

Only narrow classes of professionals and business persons were free to work across national borders. Few of the issues raised by U.S. environmental, labor, and other activist groups in the fast track debate showed up in the text. For all of these reasons, it is not just the *fact* of agreement but also the *form* of agreement that is of interest.

Why this NAFTA? Why its long phaseouts of protection for some products and immediate eliminations for others, its exemptions, its rules of origin, and its language balancing trade against environmental objectives? Why did the talks take so much longer than the politicians intended and conclude at almost precisely the moment they sought to avoid, in the heat of a U.S. presidential election?

Creating a Negotiation

Before parties to a negotiation can engage in the kind of give and take, offer and counteroffer that we think of as the stuff of negotiations, they must first decide what to negotiate. At the same time, as negotiators together define the issues, they each separately determine their objectives and their strategy. In simple bargains, such as buying a used car, the process of creating the negotiation can be as straightforward as making an offer. In the case of complex bargains like NAFTA, however, negotiations crystallize over time out of intricate interactions.

On June 12, 1992, the three trade ministers—Carla Hills for the United States, Jaime Serra Puche for Mexico, and Michael Wilson for Canada—met in Toronto to launch the negotiations. Each minister arrived with broad objectives, a general strategy, and an opening position.

For Carla Hills, the goal was to reach as broad an agreement as possible. The strategy was to use the existing Canada–U.S. Free Trade Agreement (CUFTA) as a starting point, and, if possible, to broaden it slightly to include agriculture. To her counterparts, Hills made it clear that the United States would insist on full market opening in goods, services, and investment. She intimated, however, that balanced against these liberalizing objectives, the United States would need a slow dismantling of trade protection for a few sensitive industries. Of course, she noted, U.S. immigration policy would not be on the table.

For Jaime Serra, the objective, too, was a broad agreement. As a Ph.D.

in economics, he privately believed that market opening was good for Mexico and that it made little sense to open piecemeal. "You can't open cookies if you don't have competitive wheat," he explained later. But he was cognizant that Mexican political realities limited how far and how fast he could move. Moreover, strategy dictated that he not appear too eager to open in those areas of greatest interest to the United States and Canada if he wanted to maintain leverage in the negotiation. To his counterparts in Toronto, Serra endorsed the idea of a broad agreement but hedged on whether it would be possible to open Mexican financial services. Of course, he said, Mexican oil was off limits. A prohibition against foreign involvement in the energy sector was written into the Mexican Constitution, and the subject was much too politically charged to be included in a negotiation.

For Michael Wilson, the overriding goal was to avoid reopening its existing agreement with the United States, particularly the dispute-resolution mechanisms and the politically important exemptions for Canadian cultural industries and agriculture that had been so hard to win. Canada would seek some improvements, particularly on the confusing rules of origin that had recently been the subject of a significant dispute with the United States but would insist that CUFTA be the core of NAFTA. Wilson reassured his negotiating partners that Canada intended to play a constructive role in the talks and that it welcomed the opportunity to gain open access to the Mexican market.

The three trade ministers established some ground rules for the negotiations. The most important was that there would be no backsliding from the CUFTA in any area of the agreement. NAFTA was to represent a step forward on all fronts. The ministers also agreed on how to organize the negotiations. A negotiation this complex has to be broken into parts so that teams of negotiators can work on the details. The standard procedure in trade negotiations is to establish working groups for each major issue. The ministers agreed to create 19 working groups; among the more significant were financial services, agriculture, market access, automobiles, intellectual property, services, and investment. These groups would report to chief negotiators for each country—Jules Katz for the United States, Herminio Blanco for Mexico, and John Weekes for Canada, who in turn would report to the trade ministers.

The organization of the negotiations closely resembled the earlier structure of the CUFTA negotiations. Chip Roh, Assistant U.S. Trade Representative (USTR) for North American Affairs and Katz's deputy, wrote a memo laying out a proposed list of working groups, taking the groups straight from the CUFTA. "It was hugely important that we had done the CUFTA," Roh later recalled. "We had a negotiating text. We knew how to organize it."

The trade ministers also discussed timing. Jaime Serra was eager to move quickly. His biggest concern was that the financial markets might lose confidence in the Mexican economy if the talks dragged on too long. "I didn't want this thing to hang on the tree forever," he recalled. "If it does, it goes rotten." On the other hand, he could not appear too eager if he wanted to retain bargaining leverage. He urged his counterparts to get it done fast. Carla Hills was in less of a hurry. The United States was hoping to wrap up the General Agreement on Tariffs and Trade (GATT) negotiations first. Still, she had an incentive to conclude the negotiations early enough that Congress could vote on an agreement before the 1992 elections, preferably well before them. Michael Wilson had less reason to hurry but did not want to appear obstructionist. The ministers agreed, therefore, on a breakneck schedule aimed at completing talks in 1991. They announced no deadline, however. In private and in public, the common line would be: "timing is dictated by substance."

The negotiating groups began work the week of June 17, 1991, and the chief negotiators met July 9 and again on August 6. Every week, the trade ministers talked in a lengthy conference call. On August 18, the ministers met for a second time face to face in Seattle. The chief negotiators met again on October 9, and the trade ministers met for a third time October 15 in Zacatecas, Mexico. Between international meetings, negotiators would consult with their private advisory groups and, especially in the United States, with interested legislators. For the negotiators the pace was absolutely frantic, so filled with meeting and briefing that there was no real time to negotiate. They felt torn by the contradictory admonitions from higher up to move fast, but don't compromise. By October it was apparent there would be no agreement in 1991.

Domestic Consultation

Left to themselves, the professional trade negotiators might well have reached agreement quickly. All sides, after all, agreed on the basic goal of free trade. But the negotiators were not negotiating for themselves, they were rather representing governments and, to a great extent, private interests in their societies. No international negotiation, no matter how secret, takes place in a political vacuum. Before they could negotiate internationally, therefore, negotiators had to consult domestically.

As in any trade negotiation, a domestic consensus about how to proceed formed on few issues. In the United States, for example, sugar producers wanted to maintain protection; sugar consumers wanted to reduce it. In Mexico, banks wanted to keep out U.S. and Canadian competitors, while capital-starved Mexican industry wanted more open banking competition to lower interest rates. In Canada, North American automakers wanted relatively high rules of origin to limit foreign competition (although General Motors [GM], Ford, and Chrysler did not agree on how high, as we shall see in later discussion); Japanese and European "transplants" wanted lower rules of origin. The negotiating teams of all three countries had to tread carefully to navigate through these domestic landscapes of competing interests.

All three countries used formal consultative processes to facilitate communication between negotiators and the private sector. In the United States, an Advisory Committee on Trade Policy and Negotiations (ACTPN), established by the Trade Act of 1974, coordinated more than 30 advisory committees on such broad topics as investment, intellectual property, agriculture, and labor as well as more narrowly focused topics such as chemicals, paper products, textiles, and dairy and livestock products. These groups met regularly with U.S. negotiators responsible for their areas. ACTPN members, appointed by the government, were almost all business representatives, although there were two labor union representatives and, as one of the Bush concessions to obtain fast track, an environmental representative. In 1991, the cochairs of the ACTPN were Jim Robinson of American Express and Kay Whitmore of Kodak, who were also cochairs of the Business Roundtable's trade task force. This consultative process was considerably more closed than the open politics of the fast track extension. Trade negotiations are conducted in secret, so only those with security clearances know the details of what transpires in the talks. Advisory committee members not only had privileged access, they could not transmit what they knew to others outside the process or to the media. Interest groups left outside were not happy.

Like the United States, Canada had an existing consultative structure, although as a parliamentary system in which the ruling party could be certain of legislative approval of whatever it negotiated, consultation was a less crucial function in Canada than in the United States. In the Canadian structure, created in 1986 for the Canada–U.S. negotiations, an International Trade Advisory Committee (ITAC) coordinated the efforts of 15 Sectoral Advisory Groups on International Trade (SAGITs), each with a more narrow purview. Canadian negotiators would meet regularly with these groups throughout the negotiation.[1] As in the United States, these advisors were appointed by the government and sworn to secrecy.

Mexico did not begin the NAFTA with a similar consultative structure in place. At the urging of Jaime Serra, the business community set out to create one. Rather than a government appointed committee, however, the Mexicans created a self-appointed private sector committee, Coordinadora de Organismos Empresariales de Comercio Exterior (COECE), which, as its name implies, coordinated communication between existing interest groups and the Mexican negotiators. Juan Gallardo, the head of a large soft-drink bottling company, became president of COECE. Although technically independent, the ties between COECE and Mexico's negotiators were probably closer than those between the private sector and national negotiators in the United States. Indeed, Gallardo and his group's members would travel with the negotiators to international sessions. "We'd meet with the USTR, and when we got back to our offices the business people were there. They were everywhere we went. We use to call them '*el cuarto de al lado*,' the room next door," recalled a senior Mexican trade official. Because labor support was more important politically to the Partido Revolucionario Institucional (PRI; the ruling party) in Mexico than to the Republicans in the United States or the Conservatives in Canada, Mexican negotiators consulted more closely with labor than did their counterparts.

In addition to the private sector consultative mechanisms, all three countries had more informal processes to link negotiators with the wider political environment. In the United States, the fast track process required consultation only with the House Ways and Means Committee and the Senate Finance Committee. But because they knew that in the end Congress as a whole would decide whether to accept the negotiated agreement, Carla Hills, Jules Katz, Chip Roh, and others at the USTR made themselves available to all members of Congress, by Jules Katz's count holding more than 400 meetings with members.

This effort did not satisfy everyone. Because many Hill staffers did not have the requisite security clearance, they could not attend closed briefings or read confidential negotiating documents for their members. Moreover, interest groups not represented on the trade advisory committees could not be briefed on the ongoing negotiations. The purpose of secrecy was to ensure that negotiations be conducted over the negotiating table and not in public. To those excluded, however, secrecy looked like a way to limit their influence, particularly since commercial interests had access they lacked. In response, the USTR held a series of public meetings throughout the fall, at which representatives of virtually the entire spectrum of interests could express their views, but this process was merely second best in the eyes of many NAFTA critics. Indeed, some groups protested that they were excluded from these meetings as well.

The Canadian negotiators had less need to consult so closely with their legislature, in that the Conservative majority in Parliament would almost certainly approve whatever the Conservative government negotiated. Nevertheless, how NAFTA was viewed by the wider population was a concern because the government knew that at some point in 1993 it would be forced to call a national election. Canada's negotiators consulted regularly with labor and environmental groups to try to defuse their concerns.

In Mexico, too, the issue was not so much whether NAFTA would pass the legislature—the PRI had an overwhelming majority in the Mexican Senate—but how NAFTA would be seen in the larger political environment. "There was a concern about a nationalist backlash," recalled an official in the Mexican Embassy. "This was always on our minds. That we would be charged with giving up the country. That's why we had to do it with support of the business community. . . . It was essential to build political support to defuse fears that we were giving up too much."

Defining the Issues

Through the summer and fall of 1991, through iterations of domestic consultation and international discussion, the issues came into focus and the range of possibilities began to narrow sufficiently for the negotiators to establish negotiating positions. The process had taken longer than the trade ministers had initially envisioned, and from the outside it looked as if little had been accomplished, but by mid-fall, the negotiators could at least agree on what they were negotiating in the major areas: market access, energy, autos, agriculture, services and investment, and financial services.

Market Access   In some ways the heart of the negotiations was the traditional territory of negotiating away tariff and nontariff barriers to the free movement of North American goods. At the very start, the parties agreed to two essential points that greatly simplified their task. First, there would be no exception from eventual elimination of quotas and tariffs. Second, tariff negotiations would start from "applied" (actual) rather than "bound" (maximum allowable) rates, which meant that the negotiations would proceed from much lower rates. That issue settled, the negotiators faced essentially two categories of problems: How fast should the tariffs come down? and What counted as a "North American" good?

The market access working group handled these questions for all but a few larger (and more problematic) sectors, such as autos, textiles, and agriculture, that had their own negotiating groups. Very early in the negotiations the parties agreed to put goods into four categories (A, B, C, and C+) depending on their "sensitivity" to increased imports, reflecting both how great an impact liberalization would have and how politically powerful its producers were. The more sensitive the good, the longer was the transition. For A goods, tariffs would be eliminated immediately; for B goods, in five years; for C goods, 10 years; and for C+ goods, the most import sensitive group, 15 years. It was the United States that insisted on the C+ category. This embarrassed Jules Katz, the veteran U.S. trade negotiator. "It was as if we were the developing country," he said later.

In September 1991, the parties exchanged initial positions, identifying the products they wanted to put in each category. Mexico, because it had higher tariffs across the board, had the longest list of sensitive industries, but all three countries listed numerous goods for which they requested lengthy phaseouts. The U.S. list included footwear and garments, glassware, brooms, and several other currently protected labor-intensive products.

With the lists on the table, the essence of the negotiating task was clear: trade "concessions" to shorten the transitions.

Energy   For many in the United States, one of the initial appeals of NAFTA was the prospect of better access to Mexican oil. Partly this was a matter of business opportunity for American oil companies and their suppliers, but also a more secure supply of Mexican oil might mean less reliance on insecure Middle Eastern supplies. Both dimensions weighed on the influential Texans with an interest in the talks: President Bush, Secretary of State James Baker, Secretary of Commerce Robert Mosbacher, and Finance Committee Chairman Lloyd Bentsen.

For the Mexicans, however, oil was a highly sensitive issue, a matter of national sovereignty. Mexico had nationalized its oil industry in 1938, after U.S. and British oil companies refused to abide by a Mexican Supreme Court decision in a labor dispute. An amendment to the Mexican Constitution prohibited foreign ownership of Mexican oil. So popular was this move against the foreign companies, one reporter wrote, that

> to raise money to indemnify the international oil companies, the government collected coins from school children and jewelry from matrons in an outpouring of national pride. People tell their grandchildren stories of lining up in front of the Palace of Fine Arts to drop their centavos into the collection box for the oil nationalization. And for schoolchildren whose grandparents forget, textbooks provide illustrated accounts.[2]

In addition to the historic sensitivity of the issue, there was also a contemporary powerful interest in maintaining the status quo. The nationalization had created Petroles Mexicanos (Pemex), an enormous state enterprise employing hundreds of thousands of Mexican workers.

On the other hand, Pemex was extraordinarily inefficient, in need of foreign capital. Although the Mexican Constitution prohibited foreign ownership of Mexican reserves and foreign exploration, drilling, and refining of "basic petrochemicals," it did leave open the possibility of foreign involvement in some service contracts and "secondary petrochemicals," i.e., products created from oil. The question was where to draw the line between basic and secondary petrochemicals.

From an economic efficiency standpoint, the more of the sector that was open, the better it would be. For these reasons, the Mexican government had already redefined some operations as secondary. Jaime Serra had to tread carefully, however, if he wanted to further loosen restrictions on these activities as part of the NAFTA negotiations. In July, when reports surfaced in the U.S. trade press that negotiators were discussing energy, an irritated Jaime Serra called Jules Katz at home and said "We are not discussing energy!" At the August meeting in Seattle, the Mexicans publicly announced "Five Noes:" no reduction of control over ownership, exploration or development of petroleum, including basic petrochemicals; no loss of control over storage and distribution; no foreign ownership of gas stations; no guarantees of supply to foreign countries; and no equity contracts for exploration.

The tough stand by the Mexicans may have reflected advice they were getting from the Canadians about how to deal with the Americans. "The Canadians may have told the Mexicans they had better figure out where the lines are at the beginning of the negotiation, because the U.S. is going to beat you and beat you again," recalled Chip Roh. "You need to know where your sacred territory is at the beginning." Roh also thought that the Mexican stand on oil was in part a strategy for making the issue a lightening rod for any popular dissatisfaction with the negotiations. "This was an incredibly clever ploy by Salinas and Serra," he said. "They let energy be the lightening rod for opposition. . . . And, in a sense, we played our part. We would say truly that they are being tough on oil." Mexican strategists later confirmed their strategic use of the oil issue. "For the critics of NAFTA, oil was a signal of whether Mexico was going to give in or not," said one Mexican official later. "This was the issue the public cared most about."

U.S. negotiators recognized the difficulty of the Mexican position. "My own political calculation was that we would come up short on energy and be disappointed, but that was OK as long as there weren't too many areas like it," said Chip Roh. Fortunately, after a period of initial optimism, the oil industry accepted the limits of what was possible and backed off on their pressure. "They never choked us," recalled Roh. "Some of the independent oil companies were unhappy, but the big oil companies had a correct conception that the Mexicans were not going to budge." Still, the U.S. negotiators continued to push for openings in petrochemicals and energy service contracts and for assurances that Mexico would continue to supply oil to the United States in the event of shortfalls.

Automotive Products   The stakes were high for the working group on automotive products. Trade in automobiles and autoparts constituted by far the largest volume of goods traded among the countries of North America: 14 percent of U.S. exports to Mexico, 30 percent of Mexican exports to the United States, and 6 percent of U.S.–Canadian trade.[3] The United States and Canada had traded autos and autoparts virtually freely since 1965, and both countries imposed relatively low tariffs on imports from third countries. Mexico, on the other hand, was almost completely closed to the import of automobiles. Mexican auto policies, first put in place in the early 1960s as part of the general import substitution strategy and most recently modified by the Auto Decree of 1989, were designed to force automakers to locate production in Mexico if they wished to sell there, and they worked. Of the nearly 500,000 cars sold in Mexico in 1992, just over 5000 were imported. Most of the trade between the United States and Mexico, therefore, involved the export of parts from the United States to assembly operations in Mexico, from which finished vehicles would be shipped back to the United States. The first question for the negotiators to settle was how far and how fast the Mexicans would dismantle their highly protectionist policies.

This matter proved difficult to resolve. The Mexican negotiators recognized that much of their auto industry would fare badly in open competition with the Americans and sought to stretch out the transition to free trade as long as possible. U.S. and Canadian negotiators pushed for faster opening but in the end accepted the longest possible phaseout. Their willingness to compromise reflected their close consultations with the "Big Three" automakers—General Motors, Ford, and Chrysler—and with major autoparts manufacturers whose production processes were adapted to the status quo and who, while eager to obtain better access to the Mexican market, worried that eliminating the restrictions quickly might make it too easy for European and Japanese competitors.

The other difficult issue concerned the auto rule of origin. Any regional free trade agreement discriminates against goods produced outside of the region in favor of those produced within it. This requires a rule that determines what is a regional good and what isn't. For a complex manufactured product such as a car, which can be assembled in one place from parts made anywhere in the world, this may not be a simple determination.

Establishing national positions on the rule of origin was complicated by differences of interest in the private sector. The U.S. automakers wanted the rule to preclude the possibility that Mexico would be used as an "export platform" for their international rivals, but not one that prevented them from using imported components. All three made careful calculations about the effects of various rules on their competitive position. GM, primarily because of a joint venture with Izuzu in Canada, needed to keep the percentage low enough for those cars to qualify for North American treatment and therefore pushed for 60 percent. Ford and Chrysler preferred a rule requiring 70 percent North American content. Parts makers in all three countries pushed for the highest possible content requirements.

U.S. negotiators consulted closely with the Big Three and the autoparts makers. "We needed a deal that was good for U.S. manufacturers and autoparts makers," recalled Chip Roh. "We needed their support." U.S. negotiators also talked with the United Auto Workers (UAW) union, which was demanding a rule of 80 percent, but the union position carried little weight given the UAW's almost certain opposition to the ultimate agreement. There was little discussion with Japanese or European subsidiaries in the United States. Because of the internal disagreement, U.S. negotiators did not establish a specific negotiating position on the rule of origin in 1991, merely arguing that it would need to be higher than the 50 percent rule used in the CUFTA.

The Canadians also were prepared to go higher than 50 percent, but intimated that they wanted a lower percentage than the United States. Like their U.S. counterparts, the Canadians consulted closely with their private sector. They faced many of the same pressures. The Big Three were also the biggest manufacturers in Canada. Canadian autoparts makers wanted high percentage content rules. Canadian negotiators, however, did not need to be quite as responsive to these pressures, and unlike the United States, Canada had a countervailing interest in a less restrictive rule. Japanese and European transplants had established assembly operations in Canada to build cars for both the Canadian and the U.S. market. If the rule of origin went much higher than 50 percent, they might not be able to continue to sell duty-free into the United States, thus negating the economic rationale for locating in Canada.[4] Canadian negotiators worried about this possibility and consulted closely with the transplants.

Mexico, too, had conflicting internal interests. Mexican autoparts suppliers wanted rules as high as possible. The Big Three also had operations in Mexico as did American parts suppliers, all of whom to varying degrees pushed for high rules of origin. But Mexico, like Canada, had European and Japanese transplant operations and hoped to attract more, which created incentives for relatively lower rules.

With all three countries hesitant to commit to firm negotiating positions, the auto working group made little progress on the rule of origin in 1991.

Agriculture   Historically, no sector has proven more resistant to trade liberalization than agriculture. Around the globe, governments protect and subsidize agricultural production, a reflection of a privileged political position that makes negotiating away these trade barriers extremely difficult. The situation was no different in North America. Canada, Mexico, and the United States all protected certain agricultural products; all three subsidized domestic production. Eliminating these policies had proven too difficult for the United States and Canada in the CUFTA. Now the question was whether the three countries could manage their domestic politics well enough to do more in the NAFTA.

For Canada, the answer was "no." The major problem was Canada's supply management programs for dairy and poultry farming, which were simply too entrenched to negotiate away. "We had absolutely no flexibility on that at all," recalled chief negotiator John Weekes. Moreover, Canada preferred that any concessions on agriculture be made in the context of the multilateral GATT talks, determining that it was better to be seen responding to pressures from Geneva than those from Washington. After months of discussion, the United States and Mexico finally agreed not to push Canada further and instead focused on negotiating a bilateral agreement, which was hard enough.

Truly free trade in agriculture between the United States and Mexico would alter the pattern of production in North America. The United States enjoyed a comparative advantage in grains, Mexico in such warm weather crops as fruits, vegetables, and possibly, sugar cane. Yet Mexico protected its grain producers, the United States its fruit, vegetable, and sugar producers. In principle, both countries would be better off if they utilized their comparative advantages, but in the fall of 1991, it looked doubtful that the negotiators could do very much to change the status quo.

For Mexico, the stakes were extremely high. Mexican agriculture was highly protected and subsidized, as well as highly inefficient. Fully 30 percent of the Mexican population was engaged in agricultural production, a percentage not seen in the United States since the nineteenth century. Most of the effort went to produce corn on collective farms called *ejidos*, which had been created by the land reforms that followed the Mexican Revolution. *Ejido* farmers worked small plots of land using primitive technology. Only an extensive system of price supports coupled with quotas on inputs allowed them to survive. Subjecting them to competition from the American corn-belt would be a dramatic step.

Few observers predicted this would happen. Yet, in the eyes of President Salinas and his advisors, the cost of inefficiency was too great a burden for Mexico. They envisioned sweeping reform, including assigning individual property rights to farmers, which would allow land consolidation into larger, more efficient farms, and moving from a scheme of distorting price supports to direct support for farmers. For the Mexican economic strategists, NAFTA fit nicely with this long-term strategy to transform Mexican agriculture. "If we don't take advantage of this opportunity now, we'll never do it," thought Jaime Serra. Serra was also prepared to negotiate a gradual phaseout of protection for corn, provided that in exchange the United States opened its markets for products that Mexico could produce more efficiently. But he was determined to extract a high price for any concessions he made on corn.

For the United States, the possibility of 90 million Mexican consumers for its more efficient corn producers was a great attraction. U.S. negotiators pushed for elimination of Mexican protection as quickly as possible. At the same time, however, they were under great political pressure not to trade away protection for the warm weather products Mexico hoped to export, among them citrus fruits, tomatoes, and sugar. The USTR heard an earful from threatened southern agricultural interests. The powerful Florida Agriculture Commissioner, Bob Crawford, told the USTR in August that unless protection was maintained, "Florida growers would be faced with an insurmountable economic threat, . . . a threat that we believe will put many Florida growers out of business."[5] In response, U.S. negotiators sought long transition periods and provisions that would allow temporary reimposition of tariffs in the event of import surges that threatened American producers.

The politics of sugar were particularly intense. In a free market, Mexican sugar growers would be very competitive with American producers. Yet, because U.S. sugar producers enjoyed an extraordinary package of strict import quotas and price supports, very little Mexican sugar was imported into the United States. Economists love to hate the U.S. sugar program, which keeps the U.S. price of sugar well above free market levels, by some accounts costing the American economy more than $2 billion a year.[6] Privately, U.S. negotiators felt much the same way, but they knew that with economic stakes this high, the same powerful sugar lobby that put the program in place would be watching them closely.

Financial Services   Because of high stakes and political sensitivity, financial services—banking, insurance, credit, and securities—were handled separately from other services. Regulations in all three countries made it difficult for foreign firms to provide these services, but by far the biggest gap between the status quo and a free market was in Mexico, where the government tightly restricted market access. No foreign banks or insurance companies could provide services in Mexico, and foreign holdings in Mexican banks were limited to 30 percent and in Mexican insurance companies to 49 percent. The central issue was how far Mexico would be willing to open its markets.

Mexico's stance in these negotiations reflected a battle between its financial service providers, whose interest was in maintaining protection, and other industrial concerns, whose interest was in opening up competition. For Jaime Serra, maintaining protection for Mexican banks while opening up in other areas was the equivalent of an *autogoal* in soccer (literally "own goal," as when a defender accidentally scores for the other team); it was self-destructive. Mexican financial services, particularly its banks, were highly inefficient, making the cost of capital in Mexico much higher than it otherwise would be. Serra recalled thinking, "If I tell a desk producer, 'You are going to be open to American competition in five years,' he'll say, 'They are going to kill me. They have better interest rates, better services, better wood.' That guy is right." In Serra's view, opening, while painful for Mexican financial institutions, was necessary for the rest of the Mexican economy.

But the Mexican financial service community was well connected to political power and obviously had a stake in maintaining its protected status. Moreover, opening was complicated by the fact that Mexico was in the midst of privatizing its banks, nationalized in 1982 by López Portillo as one of his last acts in office. Finance Minister Pedro Aspe, who was handling the bank sales, knew that if Mexico subjected its inefficient banks to American competition, the banks' values would drop precipitously. Powerful people were paying a lot for the banks, so Aspe and the banks resisted market opening.

Behind the scenes, both cases were presented to Salinas. The more protectionist view won the first round, and Mexico's negotiators went to the negotiating table with instructions to concede only a tiny fraction of market share. Their opening position envisioned a very gradual opening with a cap on aggregate foreign participation in the Mexican banking market at 5 percent.[7]

For the United States, opening Mexican financial markets was a high priority. Financial services companies played a central role in the business effort to support NAFTA, which made them influential in the business community. "In terms of resources of time and money we put more into it than any other sector," recalled an official of the Business Roundtable. "We viewed this as a test case of what could happen in the negotiation." For U.S. business, the Mexican position was completely unacceptable. The confrontation between the strong U.S. domestic interests pushing for market opening and the strong Mexican domestic interests in maintaining protection would make for a very difficult negotiation.

Other Services and Investment   Although formally handled by two separate working groups as the result of a ministerial decision early in the negotiations, at the staff level services and investment were effectively combined. The two issues tend to go hand-in-hand because the most common barriers to service provision are prohibitions against foreign ownership. Mexico's transportation, telecommunications, construction, and most other service industries were almost completely closed. Because American and Canadian services were generally more efficient than their Mexican counterparts, the Mexican market represented a tremendous business opportunity to these concerns. They pressed their negotiators to push Mexico to open up. The issue was how far Mexico would be willing to go.

As with financial services, the Mexican position in these talks was complicated by internal divisions. On the one hand, Mexican service providers were fearful of competition and pushed hard to maintain protection for as long as they could. The Mexican negotiators had to be sensitive to their concerns. On the other hand, the negotiators recognized that inefficient services in critical infrastructure sectors such as transportation and telecommunications constituted a drag on the rest of the Mexican economy. Business consumers of those services had an interest in greater access to cheaper, more reliable U.S. and Canadian providers. Mexico, therefore, tended to be more receptive than might have been expected to the aggressive U.S. and Canadian demands.

Early in the talks, the U.S. side insisted upon an important principle for the conduct of these negotiations. Rather than negotiating each liberalization from the status quo (as was being attempted in the Uruguay Round of the GATT), the negotiators would negotiate exceptions from openness. The approach adopted in NAFTA effectively reversed the burden of proof and gave considerable impetus toward market opening. The United States could consistently argue from principles of free trade and force the Mexicans to justify deviations from it. The Mexican negotiators, however, may not have found this situation undesirable. Outside pressure from the United States helped them in their internal negotiations with service providers and allowed them to push through reforms that they otherwise would have had difficulty obtaining.

Of course, each side did insist on some exemptions. All three exempted basic telecommunications. The United States insisted on excluding its politically powerful shipping industry, as it had always done in trade negotiations. Mexico insisted on excluding its railroads, which had been nationalized during the Mexican Revolution. Canada insisted on retaining exemptions it had obtained for its cultural industries in the CUFTA.

The Outside Political Environment

Through the summer and fall of 1991, the inside processes of international meetings at the levels of ministers, chief negotiators, and working groups, and of domestic consultations with advisory committees in all three countries, gradually gave form to the negotiation. Beyond this relatively closed circle, however, larger political forces were also at work.

In the United States, particularly, outside voices continued to criticize what was happening in the negotiations. The coalition of labor, environmental, and other citizen groups that had opposed fast track began shadowing the negotiators wherever they went. When the trade ministers met in Seattle in late August, the national Mobilization on Development, Trade, Labor, and the Environment (MODTLE) held a press conference nearby to protest its exclusion from the talks and to draw attention to its concerns. MODTLE rented a huge weather balloon, attached an anti-NAFTA sign to it, and floated it up to the forty-fourth floor where the negotiators could see it. (They later claimed not to have noticed.) At the Zacatecas meeting in October, NAFTA's critics held a three-day, trinational "parallel" forum on labor, environmental, and human rights issues. The press, shut out of the negotiations themselves, found that the opposition was the only story in town. As MODTLE organizer Pharis Harvey recalled, "the press was hungry. We got press coverage we couldn't get in between."

Because of the extraordinary level of interest in NAFTA, in August and September the USTR held public hearings to allow more general public input into the negotiating process. In San Diego, Houston, Atlanta, Washington, and Cleveland, the administration heard from witnesses representing business, labor, environment, and citizens' groups. Many of the witnesses—citrus growers, sugar beet growers, liquor distillers, shoemakers, a garment maker, a glass manufacturer (Anchor Hocking)—argued that the special circumstances of their industry required special treatment, often exemption, from free trade with Mexico. Other witnesses, however—the retailers' trade association, a Mexico-based autoparts maker, another glass manufacturer (Corning)—testified in favor of free trade. Union leaders warned that NAFTA could cause job losses and allow continued unfair trade practices in Mexico.[8] Other witnesses addressed environmental, health and safety concerns; child labor laws in Mexico; and the broad agenda of issues that had been raised in the fast track debate.

Most of the rising public interest in NAFTA was just background noise for the negotiators, but environmental opposition was not something they could safely ignore. The environmental community, including those groups that had endorsed fast track, was becoming increasingly unhappy with the direction the negotiations seemed to be taking and with the lack of progress on the parallel track promised by the Action Plan.

On August 1, 1991, the administration released a draft Integrated Border Environmental Plan, something that it had promised in May. The plan was panned throughout the environmental community. The plan, said Justin Ward of the National Resources Defense Council (NRDC) at the time, "is a big disappointment all around."[9] On the same day, Friends of the Earth, the Sierra Club, and Public Citizen filed suit against the USTR, alleging that NAFTA and the Uruguay Round of the GATT were major actions that required environmental impact assessments under the National Environmental Policy Act (NEPA). Public Citizen president Joan Claybrook said an assessment was necessary because "the United States negotiators are so closely intertwined with the needs and wishes of big business."[10]

Shortly afterward came the biggest bombshell: A GATT panel ruled that using the U.S. Marine Mammal Protection Act to prohibit imports of Mexican tuna was a violation of GATT obligations. The environmental community was outraged. "This case is the smoking gun," said Public Citizen's Lori Wallach. "We have seen GATT actually declaring that a U.S. environmental law must go."[11] Environment's allies on the Hill echoed the sentiment. Representative Barbara Boxer (Democrat, Calif.) and sixty-two other members of the House "strongly protested" the ruling.[12] Henry Waxman (Democrat, Calif.), chair of the House Environment Committee intoned, "This is a worst-case scenario come true—repeal of a vital environmental law because of conflict with a trade agreement."[13] Garry Studds (Democrat, Mass.), chair of the House Merchant Marine and Fisheries Committee, said, "the implications of the decision for a wide array of U.S. laws and programs are truly frightening."[14]

The connection to NAFTA was easily made. For environmentalists, here was as clear a case as one could want of the danger that free trade would undermine environmental laws, a case involving the very country the United States was negotiating with. Said Representative Boxer, "Mexico's challenge of U.S. environmental law that protects dolphins doesn't speak well for its claim to be a full partner in the protection of the environment under the U.S.–Mexico trade agreement."[15] The Mexican government scrambled to repair the political damage. President Salinas announced that Mexico would ignore the GATT ruling and that a new Mexican law would prevent killing of dolphins. Most environmentalists were not impressed, however. "We see these steps as cosmetic, a face-saving measure," a spokesperson for the Earth Island Institute's Save the Dolphins Project said.[16] For the rest of the NAFTA campaign, the image of a dolphin would appear on anti-NAFTA environmental literature.

Displeasure on the Hill with the course of the NAFTA negotiation was not confined to environmental issues. In June 1991, Marcy Kaptur (Democrat, Ill.) had founded a "Fair Trade Caucus" to serve as a "watchdog" group and to work with the Fair Trade Watch activists off the Hill. The Fair Trade Caucus regularly distributed information and analyses critical of NAFTA to other members of Congress. Just before the Zacatecas meetings in October, Majority Leader Richard Gephardt and four other Democratic Representatives active on trade issues—Sander Levin, Don Pease, Jim Moody, and Ron Wyden—sent a lengthy letter to Carla Hills warning the negotiators to pay close attention to their concerns and to keep to the commitments made in May. "We will hold the president to the commitments he has given to

Congress and the American people—both substantively and in spirit," the letter said. "If he keeps his commitments, Congress will do so as well."[17]

On the labor front, Senators William Roth (Republican, Del.) and Daniel Patrick Moynihan (Democrat, N.Y.), both members of the Senate Finance Committee, introduced a bill to ensure that current Trade Adjustment Assistance programs would cover workers adversely affected by any free trade agreement with Mexico. Moynihan took the opportunity to warn that his support for a worker adjustment bill to accompany NAFTA in no way indicated that he would eventually support the agreement. "I continue to have the strongest reservations about the free trade agreement with Mexico—the first free trade agreement we are being asked to consider with a country that isn't free," he said. "But, if such an agreement is negotiated and is passed by Congress, it ought only happen if the administration shows a new approach to the elemental issue of worker adjustment. Our bill will begin the debate on how this will be achieved."[18]

Year's End: Taking Stock

When the negotiations began in June, optimists hoped to reach agreement before the end of the year so that the U.S. Congress could vote on it early in 1992, before the presidential campaign heated up. The process had moved slowly, however. As Jules Katz recalled, "I wanted to write a text early and then negotiate from the text, but that didn't work out. The sheer mechanics of it were too complex. It took time to get people geared up." The first few months of more general discussions were necessary to exchange information, to feel each other out, and to begin to understand what might be possible in the negotiations.

Before the Zacatecas meeting in October, chief Mexican negotiator Herminio Blanco gave his assessment of the state of progress in the talks. "I would say we have finished the first stage, a very important stage of the negotiations, that is the interchange of information. We are entering the stage in which we must find among the three countries the formulas that will accommodate the interests of each."[19] In Zacatecas, the three parties agreed that it was time to put negotiating positions on paper. "You can spend years negotiating concepts, as we did in the Uruguay Round," said Jules Katz later. "Only once drafting starts do you really get down to negotiation." In all three countries teams of drafters set to work trying to craft language that reflected national bargaining positions.

The U.S. side moved slowly, however, in part because of a crisis in the GATT negotiations. Just when they were needed to draft NAFTA text, Jules Katz and others of the very small staff at the USTR were drawn away to Brussels. But the United States was slow for other reasons as well. "Carla had a concern that we proceed with 'deliberate speed' so as not to appear to be pushing this too fast," said Jules Katz.

The slow pace made the Mexicans extremely anxious about NAFTA's prospects in the United States. Negotiations were now threatening to carry on well into 1992. On the Hill, Democrats were warning that the agreement couldn't pass Congress if it came there during the election campaign. The press speculated that Bush would have to wait until after the election, particularly after Democrat Harris Wofford won an upset victory, partly on the strength of his opposition to NAFTA, in a special Senate election in Pennsylvania.

Behind the scenes, NAFTA's advocates worked together to accelerate the talks. As Bob Zoellick recalled, "You have to be careful, you can't substitute your judgment for theirs. But I worked with [Secretary of State James] Baker to try to move the process more quickly." Zoellick and Baker urged President Bush to invite Salinas to Camp David. A Salinas visit would create an opportunity to push the U.S. negotiators to move more quickly. "George Bush was dead fast committed," recalled Nick Calio. "He believed it was good policy and good politics. Anytime there was any discussion about holding back he just blew it away." The Mexicans liked the idea, too. "We thought that if Bush says, 'OK guys get going,' then Carla would take NAFTA more seriously and put more resources into the negotiation," recalled Jaime Serra. The U.S. negotiators meanwhile thought that the Mexicans were stretched too thin and were underestimating the difficulty of the remaining task. Just before the Camp David meeting, the negotiators finally exchanged draft proposed texts.

At their meeting at Camp David in mid December, the two presidents agreed to move as quickly as possible. The question, however, was how fast was possible. From the standpoint of the negotiators in the trenches, top officials did not have a clear understanding of how far apart the negotiating parties really were. In preparation for the Camp David meetings, National Security Council officials asked "What are the three or four key issues?"

There were hundreds, recalled a senior trade official. "We thought, OK, they don't see it. Let's do a composite text [a document that would combine the three negotiators' negotiating positions into one draft text]."

In early January 1992, negotiating group leaders and their lawyers put together the first composite text. Wherever there were disagreements, the text showed the three countries' respective positions in brackets. There were "thousands of brackets," recalled Chip Roh. In some chapters, there was so little agreement that virtually the whole text was bracketed. Some of the most contentious areas (agriculture, textiles, energy, automobiles, and dispute settlement) were left out entirely. Still, the text served two purposes: It demonstrated conclusively that agreement was not imminent and it clarified the task remaining.

Negotiating

With a single negotiating text in hand, the task of reducing the number of brackets began in earnest in February 1992. Early that month, the chief negotiators met twice, on February 4 in Ottawa and on February 9–10 in Chantilly, Va., to assess where things stood and to plan for an upcoming plenary session in Dallas. Carla Hills flew to Mexico to confer with Jaime Serra. Out of those meetings came a better understanding of what needed to happen.

In Dallas, February 17–20, all the working groups and the chief negotiators assembled in one place for the first time for a "jamboree" negotiating session. Together the three delegations numbered 400. The negotiators set up shop on the partitioned floor of a huge open design center. Jules Katz recalls the week as "very productive." "It was a process of beginning to hone issues, of finding out where the stumbling blocks were," Katz said. For the first time, countries began to move off their opening positions on a range of issues. One clear breakthrough came in agriculture. For the first time, the Mexicans agreed in principle to convert their corn quotas to tariffs and to discuss phasing them out.

Plenty of obstacles still remained. The essential problem was that in issue after issue, because Mexico was the most closed and highly regulated economy of the three, the Mexicans had to make the lion's share of the concessions. This reality had been acknowledged at the level of the chief negotiators and above, but the acknowledgment did not always translate into flexibility on the part of the Mexican negotiators. A senior U.S. trade official complained that the understanding between Bush and Salinas about a broad pact "somehow . . . hasn't gotten across to the individual Mexican negotiators."[20]

After Dallas, the negotiators met more regularly. Katz recalls a "jagged curve of progress. A good meeting followed a bad meeting." Still, over the next two months enough progress was made that "by April we could see the deal," recalled Chip Roh. Mexico had moved a long way on investment and services, and the negotiators were confident of an agreement. On financial services, Mexico had not come quite so far, but the U.S. team thought they might have reached the limit of what was possible. The negotiators were quite pleased with how much they had been able to accomplish in agriculture. Finally, Mexico was prepared to phase out its restrictions on auto imports.

There were more than a few loose ends, of course. Energy talks remained unfinished, but in the minds of the negotiators that was just a question of acknowledging tough political realities. The auto rule of origin remained up in the air. The Canadians were unhappy about certain features of the dispute settlement procedures and about the continuing challenges to their exemptions for cultural industries. Still, the basic form of the agreement looked clear to the negotiators. "But we couldn't close it," recalled Roh. "We were a month away for months." And while the deal remained undone, parts of it started to unravel.

First, a tidal wave of U.S. environmental opposition rose up and threatened to swamp the whole process unless changes were made. Then the financial community decided that it did not like the trajectory of the talks and threatened to withhold its support if Mexico did not make further concessions.

Domestic Pressures on the International Negotiation: Greening the Text

During the winter the environmental community had become increasingly unhappy. The tuna-dolphin case had sparked a firestorm. The draft border plan and draft environmental review had been widely panned. Now, in late February, the USTR released its final Environmental Review and the

Environmental Protection Agency (EPA) produced its final Integrated Environmental Border Plan. Environmental critics could see no improvements from the fall drafts. The plan committed the United States to spend only $379 million on border cleanup; Mexico promised $460 million. These commitments fell far short of the billions of dollars environmentalists believed were needed.

The NRDC's Justin Ward was not impressed. "They've produced a plan to plan," he said, and complained that the blueprint was "just a small laundry list of public works projects" long overdue.[21] Mary Ellen Kelly, an activist in the Border environmental coalition, said that the plan was a "risky strategy" for the Bush administration. "They are gambling that they can turn the environmental issues into a high-profile side show and that nobody's really going to look at the content of this plan and whether the money's really there. I just think the Congress is smarter than that on this one."[22]

Then, in March, the Washington journal *Inside US Trade* published a leaked copy of the NAFTA negotiating text from the Dallas meetings. Public Citizen's Lori Wallach recalled that "the NAFTA text showed up like a little lost baby on the doorsteps of citizen activists of all three countries, with little tags that said 'liberate me.' "[23] For the first time, the environmental community that had been outside of the negotiations could see what was going on inside. They did not like what they saw. The Sierra Club's John Audley stated the view of many in the community. "It's pure and simple, the document does not pay any attention to anything but expanding trade. . . . The best you get is meaningless language or no mention of the environment. Yet when you get to the sections about environment and health, such as food standards, you get language to protect economic activity from environmental standards."[24]

The key issue had to do with balancing trade and environmental objectives. Regulatory standards—for example, a limit on pesticide residues on food—can have trade consequences—for instance, if imports exceed residue standards. The Mexicans were concerned that the United States used regulatory standards for protectionist reasons and wanted language in NAFTA that would require they be the "least trade restrictive" available, the principle that was operating in the GATT. The U.S. negotiators tended to the see the issue in much the same light and worried less about undermining environmental standards than about erecting barriers to free trade. Their perspective was shared by the U.S. business community, with whom they were in close consultation. The convergence of these interests resulted in language in the draft agreement stating that "sanitary and phytosanitary measures shall not be applied in a manner which would constitute a disguised restriction on international trade."[25]

The leaked text became a lightening rod. Environmentalists reunited across the spectrum to demand changes in the text. In May, an environmental coalition including not only the Sierra Club and Friends of the Earth—NAFTA opponents—but also the Natural Resources Defense Council and the National Audubon Society—fast track supporters—presented the USTR with a list of demands. The groups urged that NAFTA require that environmental standards be maintained or raised, that there be greater public participation in the administrative process, that there be a commission to monitor the environmental impacts of trade and to ensure compliance with environmental regulations, and that there be greater funding to protect the environment, paid for by industry.

The environmental groups enlisted the support of Max Baucus, chair of the International Trade Subcommittee of the Senate Finance Committee. To reporters he complained that when he pressed Carla Hills on environmental concerns and worker displacement "I get glazed eyes and a blank look. . . . I just don't get the sense that they are addressing the major concerns that a lot of us have."[26] In letters to Carla Hills and EPA Administrator William Reilly on June 3, he pressed the environmental groups' agenda and made clear his determination that they be addressed. In the House, Bill Richardson (Democrat, N.Mex.), one of the leaders of the effort to pass fast track, warned that the agreement would "go down the tubes" unless Congressional environmental concerns were met:

> What will decide the fate of the free trade agreement in the Congress of the United States will not be the commercial trade side, will not be intellectual property rights, or banking or many of the other bilateral issues that have been negotiated extensively over the past two or three years. What will decide the passage of the free trade agreement in the Congress probably next year will be the issue of the environment.[27]

The messages from the Hill got the administration's attention. Negotiators received a charge to "green the text."

Over the next two months, U.S. negotiators would insist on reopening portions of the text to address some of the environmentalists' concerns. The Canadians, who had originally pushed for "greener" language, were not unhappy with the American change of heart, but the Mexicans were not pleased. Only when persuaded that some concessions were politically necessary did they agree to reopen discussions.

In the end, the negotiators modified NAFTA's language to shift the burden of proof from demonstrating that a regulation was least trade restrictive to demonstrating that there was some legitimate environmental reason for the standard. The final text would read, "Each party may . . . adopt, maintain or apply any sanitary or phytosanitary measure necessary for the protection of human, animal or plant life or health in its territory, including a measure more stringent than an international standard, guideline or recommendation."[28] The negotiators also added language in the investment chapter stating that no country may lower its environmental, health, and safety standards to attract investment. But they stopped short of providing any mechanisms to enforce the provision.

International Pressure on Domestic Interests: Opening Mexican Financial Services

From the outset, the financial services negotiations had been among the most difficult. The United States and Canada had been pushing Mexico hard to open its markets, but domestic interests in Mexico had succeeded in severely constraining the flexibility of Mexico's negotiators. Mexico's initial offer of a long transition to a 5 percent permanent ceiling on total foreign investment in financial services met with sharp public criticism in January 1992 when United States and Canadian business communities learned of it. Privately, these well-connected interests pressed for much greater opening of Mexican financial services.

At the Dallas meeting in February, Mexico made a significant concession, offering to accelerate market opening and to raise the ultimate foreign investment ceiling to 12 percent. The Mexican financial services community fiercely resisted any more concessions. With many investors having paid high prices for banks on the promise of continued protection, and with a number of banks still for sale, the Mexican financial services community and the government had a joint interest in holding the line on further opening. U.S.

and Canadian negotiators, while still hoping for more, recognized the difficulties faced by their Mexican counterparts. The new Mexican proposal became the basis for negotiation, and through the spring, the financial services negotiation gradually moved toward an accommodation, one that would only very partially open the Mexican market.

In early May, representatives of the U.S. and Canadian financial services communities were briefed on the process of the negotiations. They were furious. In the words on one U.S. business advisor close to the negotiations, "market access was bad; national treatment was bad; there were too many reservations." In his view, the U.S. negotiators had not been driving a hard enough bargain. He suspected that they had gotten caught up in the push to finish the negotiations before the Democratic National Convention and were therefore too eager to make a deal. This proposition was strongly disputed by negotiators at the USTR, who viewed the problem more as a consequence of the Treasury Department's insistence on conducting the financial services talks separately, which meant they had little leverage in the negotiation because they had nothing to give the Mexicans in exchange for financial market opening.

The USTR and the Treasury Department got hit with a lobbying barrage. Top priority was eliminating the permanent ceilings on investment. The U.S. Coalition of Service Industries, a group dominated by financial service interests, publicly described these ceilings as "totally unacceptable." Privately, Carla Hills and Treasury Secretary Nick Brady agreed to meet with a group of CEOs from the nation's biggest financial organizations. The business delegation issued a clear ultimatum: They would not bankroll the pro-NAFTA lobby unless the agreement was improved for them. "There was a lot of gnashing of teeth," recalled one participant. But Hills and Brady agreed to go back to the Mexicans for more.

Now the Mexican negotiators who had resisted further opening were faced with a credible threat from key players in the United States, in particular from the financial firms the Mexicans had counted on as allies in the push for NAFTA. The U.S. finance community communicated its position to the Mexicans directly, so there would be no misunderstanding. "The Mexicans knew that this was going to be a fight," recalled an advisor to the business community, "and they couldn't win if the five largest banks in the country were against it." The question for them was how far they needed to bend. Mexico's Finance Minister, Pedro Aspe, talked with top American officials. The Treasury negotiators were making many new demands, he complained. "Aspe said, 'You tell me what is important,'" recalled Bob Zoellick. Zoellick conveyed his sense that the U.S. financial services community was dead set against the ceilings.

In mid May, Mexico abandoned its demand for permanent ceilings, asking instead for a lengthy transition and for safeguards to prevent rapid increases in foreign holdings. This proposal became the basis for the ultimate agreement. U.S. and Canadian firms objected to the length of the transition, insurance firms being the most adamant about the matter. Eventually, the U.S. and Canadian firms accepted the safeguard proposal in exchange for more rapid opening in insurance and securities. In the end, we got "a pretty good agreement," conceded a senior advisor to the business community, but it had not been easy. "Financial services was the hardest for the Mexicans. It required the biggest club to get it," said an official at the Business Roundtable.

Negotiating in Two Directions: Tradeoffs in Agriculture

In the agricultural negotiations, the obvious tradeoff was Mexico opening its grain markets and the United States opening its warm fruit and vegetable markets. Although this made sense in terms of economic efficiency, both countries had significant domestic obstacles to making this exchange. For all of 1991, the talks remained largely stalled. The big breakthrough had come in Dallas in February, when Mexico surprised many observers by agreeing to discuss converting its corn quotas to tariffs and then gradually eliminating them. In exchange, the United States agreed to discuss opening its market for fruits and vegetables.

U.S. negotiators understood that there would be winners and losers, although they believed that the exchange was good for the United States. In the words of a United States Department of Agriculture (USDA) official involved in the talks, the U.S. negotiators expected "a differing impact across the country, certainly in the southern-tier states, those that border Mexico, particularly, and Florida, which competes directly."[29] The idea of trading off their interests did not sit well with fruit, vegetable, and sugar growers. They rallied to pressure for additional "safeguards."

The sugar issue was particularly contentious. The Mexican negotiators had initially asked for an enormous increase in the United States's quota for Mexican sugar, from 7200 tons a year to 1.5 million tons a year. They felt that they were making major changes in their agricultural system and the United States should too. Some in the Bush administration were sympathetic to the Mexican position, but U.S. sugar interests mobilized to fight it. Luther Markwart, executive vice president of the American Sugar Beet Growers Association called the Mexican request "outrageous, unconscionable, and greedy." The request "doesn't even justify the dignity of a response by our negotiators," he huffed.[30] The sugar lobby worked the corridors of the Capitol, and the administration heard an earful from the Hill.

The USTR and the Agriculture Department argued, however, that Mexico was not now a net exporter of sugar, and that it was highly unlikely to pose a threat to U.S. producers in the immediate future. Sugar growers saw other threats, however. If Mexico began using corn sweeteners in place of sugar—as a way of dealing with its surplus corn growing capacity or because it was importing cheap U.S. corn sweeteners—Mexico might become a sugar exporter in short order. Alternatively, Mexico might import sugar from other countries such as Cuba and export its own product.

In the end, the negotiators struck a complicated compromise deal, one that kept the Mexican sugar quota at the low level of 25,000 metric tons for six years but partly opened the door thereafter. If Mexico were a *net* exporter of sugar in the first six years, the quota would go to 150,000 tons thereafter. The *net* exporter provision was intended to take care of the possibility of Cuban transshipment or displacement, since imports from Cuba would count against Mexico in calculating its trade position in sugar. But there was no provision in the agreement to preclude the possibility of substituting corn syrup for sugar. Later, some in the United States would claim this was an oversight. Jaime Serra disputes this contention. "Of course we thought about fructose," he said. As a senior advisor to the Mexican government put it, "Each side was using the other for doing what it should be doing anyway. It was *not* a mistake that corn sweeteners were not included." U.S. sugar producers were furious.

For growers of warm weather fruits and vegetables, Mexico posed a direct threat. Florida and California agricultural interests pressed their case hard, in public forums, in private meetings, and especially though their representatives in Congress. The Florida Agriculture Commissioner called for exempting winter produce from NAFTA altogether. "Mexican growers enjoy economic advantages: free or subsidized land, child labor, no minimum wage laws, no worker compensation and occupational safety laws, no stringent environmental and food safety controls," he charged. "Mexico can compete on an uneven field with unfair leverage to win."[31] In the end, these products were not altogether exempted, but the political pressure forced the U.S. negotiators to insist on the longest 15-year phaseouts for protection on citrus fruits, tomatoes, onions, eggplants, chili peppers, squash, watermelons, and other products and on protection from import surges during the transition period. Like the sugar provisions, these phaseouts did not satisfy the special interests.

Endgame

President Bush had hoped that the NAFTA negotiations would be completed before the Democratic National Convention in mid July, but there were too many issues remaining in autos, agriculture, environment, energy, financial services, and elsewhere. The pressure was now on to finish by the time of the Republican National Convention in mid August. Carla Hills was on the schedule to deliver a keynote address; she would need an agreement in hand.

Inside the Bush campaign, NAFTA was seen as a good issue for the president. If made him look presidential and it put Clinton on the defensive. Bob Zoellick, now in the inner circle of the Bush campaign, recalled that "we wanted NAFTA to be a Bush accomplishment, a defining issue. We wanted to make it hard for Clinton to walk away. This was also one issue where the press took Bush's side." NAFTA presented Clinton with a tough choice. It would be painful for him to support NAFTA, given the staunch opposition of labor and other traditionally Democratic groups. On the other hand, Candidate Clinton was vulnerable to the charge of "waffling"—he was on record in support of NAFTA, and if he now opposed the agreement, he could be accused of pandering to special interests.

Zoellick and other NAFTA supporters in the Bush camp also had another reason to push the negotiations to a conclusion: They wanted NAFTA. "I didn't want to lose NAFTA," he recalled. "I thought that the best way to get it though was to use the issue politically. I wanted to force Clinton to be ultimately positive. . . . I didn't think he could walk away." As Bush's numbers continued to drop in the polls, the stakes grew at the USTR as well. "At the end it was obvious that the administration was in bad shape," a USTR official recalled. "We felt, dammit we're going to get NAFTA finished at all cost. Bush is going to sign it."

On July 29 the negotiating teams took over three floors at the Watergate Hotel in Washington. They planned to stay until they finished. For eleven straight days negotiations were almost constantly in session. The ministers met; the chief negotiators met; the working groups met. In the U.S. delegation, Katz and Hills carpooled in every morning to go over what needed to be done that day. They would then meet with the staff, approximately ninety people, in the delegation office to issue instructions for the day. The Mexican and Canadian teams did the same.

Many issues remained unsettled; some of the toughest were about Mexican energy, Canadian culture, and the auto rule of origin.

Pressing the Limits: Mexican Oil   From the outset of the negotiations, energy had been a most difficult issue. Aside from an early decision by Mexico to allow opening in some petrochemicals, the energy talks had made little progress. Yet top U.S. officials remained unconvinced that the Mexicans wouldn't move. The United States now pressed for a "proportional sharing" provision that would prevent Mexico from cutting off oil supplies in the event of a shortfall. The Mexicans reacted angrily to the U.S. demand. This was a matter of national sovereignty, they argued. Jaime Serra threatened to walk away from the talks. With time running out, someone would have to blink. "What was required was a realization on our part that the Mexicans couldn't move," recalled Jules Katz. Bob Zoellick talked with Salinas's chief of staff, Jose "Pepe" Cordoba. "Cordoba said that the political impediment is real. His people weren't just negotiating. 'We are changing the *ejido* system and church and state relations, we can't also do energy,' " Zoellick recalled.

The message finally sank in. So U.S. negotiators shifted focus to contracting in the government procurement chapter. "After we realized we weren't going to get much on energy, then we wanted Pemex procurement," recalled Chip Roh. "The energy equipment people needed access to Pemex contracts. Otherwise they wouldn't get anything." In the end, Mexico refused to budge on proportional sharing, but it conceded ground on procurement, allowing foreign firms to bid on Pemex service contracts for the first time.

Finessing National Sensitivities: Canadian Cultural Industries   For Canadians, perhaps the most sensitive issue in the negotiations concerned the perceived threat to Canadian culture. Without limits on U.S.–produced television programming and magazines and without subsidies to Canadian artists, many (English-speaking) Canadians feared that Canadian culture would be completely overrun by U.S. culture, and much that was distinctively Canadian would be lost. Of course, stakeholders in these industries— magazine publishers, television producers, and the like—had considerable economic interest in maintaining protection as well. "It was a very emotional issue," recalled Canadian negotiator Weekes.

In the U.S.–Canada free trade negotiations, the Canadians had fought for and won a partial exemption. At the outset of the NAFTA talks, Canada's negotiators made clear that they intended to retain it. This position did not sit well with the U.S. entertainment industry, however, which not only wanted to sell more in Canada but also feared that allowing Canada this protection would set a poor precedent for the Uruguay Round of the GATT, where the Europeans were arguing for similar cultural exclusions. The entertainment lobby, through its allies in the administration and on the Hill, urged U.S. negotiators to push the Canadians.

Negotiators struggled to produce language that would be acceptable to both sides. (Mexico tended to side with the United States because it viewed the U.S. Spanish-speaking population as a potentially lucrative market.) The Canadians were willing to make some concessions at the margins, but U.S. negotiators, reflecting the views of the entertainment lobby, decided to cease negotiating, reasoning that no agreement created less of a negative precedent for the GATT than an unsatisfactory compromise in NAFTA. Both sides claimed victory. Canada's negotiators maintained that cultural industries were exempt. The U.S. negotiators argued that the United States retained the right to retaliate if Canada actually blocked U.S. products. The U.S. negotiators, with the Motion Picture Association of America and other interested parties watching closely, also made sure that Canada's partial exemption did not extend to Mexico.

Domestic Interests in the Driver's Seat: The Auto Rule of Origin
Numerous issues remained in the auto negotiations, including the final timetable for phasing out the Mexican Auto Decree, but perhaps the most contentious remaining issue was the rule of origin. Because stakes were so

high and there were such strong differences within each domestic arena, negotiators had resisted putting positions on paper. At the Watergate, the parties finally staked out positions, something the U.S. negotiators had found extremely difficult to do. The auto industry was split on the rule issue: Ford and Chrysler backed 70 percent, whereas GM pushed for 60 percent. The politically powerful autoparts makers wanted a percentage closer to 70 than to 60. The UAW pushed for 80 percent, which was out of the question, but U.S. negotiators felt some pressure to obtain a high enough percentage that they could say to the UAW that they would be better off with NAFTA than without it.

Forced to take a position, the USTR split the difference between the automakers and opted for 65 percent. Mexico and Canada had always wanted a lower rule than the United States, to make it easier for foreign operations to set up shop there. The Canadians, who would have been happiest with the 50 percent rule from the CUFTA, grudgingly inched up to 60 percent, but they were unwilling to go higher. The Mexicans joined the Canadians in committing to 60 percent.

Now that proposals were on the table, compromise was very difficult. For the United States, recalled Chip Roh, "getting over 60 percent on the rule of origin became a symbolic issue." For the Mexicans and the Canadians, going over 60 percent was equally difficult. The parties were at an impasse. No one wanted to make a move.

Bryan Samuel, Chip Roh's deputy recently brought over from the State Department, took the lead in trying to broker a compromise. Quietly, the Mexicans let Samuel know that they could live with 65 percent, but Canada still held firm, unwilling to jeopardize the status of their transplant auto makers. Said Canadian negotiator Weekes, "We didn't want to create a situation in which Japanese vehicles being manufactured in Canada wouldn't be open to free trade treatment. We were working very closely with the Japanese transplants."

With almost everything else settled, enormous pressure came to bear on these negotiations. The negotiators became testy. "Things were said that let it be known that there were tolerances that were not infinite," recalled Canada's Weekes. Finally, with time running down, the parties did what parties so often do: They split the difference at 62.5 percent. When informed of the U.S. concession, Ford CEO Harold "Red" Poling was furious. He called Jules Katz in a rage. Poling thought they had agreed on 65 percent. Trying to calm him down, Katz reminded him, "We're talking about a 2.5 percent difference on a 2.5 percent tariff."

Closing the Deal   On August 11, 1992, the end was in sight. The last tough issues were near resolution. The trade ministers and the chief negotiators met to review the day's progress and to iron out a few last details. The delegations, aware that the end was near, waited outside in the corridor. Finally, at 12:40 in the morning of August 12, the negotiators shook hands on a deal. Fourteen months to the day after they began, Carla Hills for the United States, Jaime Serra for Mexico, and Michael Wilson for Canada had reached a North American Free Trade Agreement.

As the negotiators walked out of the room and into the corridor, the delegations lining the corridor applauded. For the negotiators, it was a moment of euphoria. "The process," recalled Katz, "was all consuming." Now it was over, or so it seemed.

Reactions

President Bush's announcement in the White House Rose Garden reflected his personal feeling of accomplishment. "This historic trade agreement will . . . create jobs and generate economic growth in all three countries," he said. "[It] will level the North American playing field, allowing American companies to increase sales from Alaska to the Yucatan. . . . NAFTA will make our companies more competitive everywhere in the world." In Mexico, President Salinas was equally proud as he addressed his nation in a nationally televised speech that morning. The pact, he said, "will allow us to grow faster, create more and better-paid jobs." His negotiators had managed to spare Mexico's less competitive sectors from immediate competition, he argued. "Seventy percent of our exports will be freed immediately to enter their market, while we will free only around 40 percent of the products that they send us," he said. In Canada, Prime Minister Mulroney greeted the agreement with less fanfare. There was no formal announcement. Mulroney told reporters that the agreement was an "important step" toward a NAFTA.

Mulroney's approach may have reflected the unpopularity of NAFTA in Canada. Although business groups were predictably enthusiastic, unionists, environmentalists, Canadian nationalists, and a majority of the general public seemed solidly opposed. Bob White, president of the powerful Canadian Labour Congress, said that the government had shown "nothing but contempt" for Canadians by pursuing NAFTA.[32] White was joined in opposition by Action Canada, the coalition of 40 environmental, labor, and human rights groups, and by the Council of Canadians, whose president Maude Barlow wrote that it was fitting that the final "high-security talks were held at the infamous Watergate Hotel in Washington, which has come to symbolize political intrigue and dishonesty."[33] The opposition Liberal Party, now well ahead of the Conservatives in the polls, condemned the agreement and Mulroney's promises about its affects. "They are the same gang that botched up the [CU]FTA deal four years ago," a Liberal Party spokesperson said.[34] The Liberals warned that they intended to make NAFTA an issue in the next election. Liberal leader Jean Chretien asserted that he would renegotiate it if he became Prime Minister. Still, given the strong majority enjoyed by the Conservatives in Parliament, there was little question that Canada would ratify NAFTA.

Reactions to NAFTA in Mexico were generally more positive, with strong business and labor support and with much less visible and more fragmented opposition. Most Mexicans appeared proud to have been included as an equal partner with the United States. Unlike Prime Minister Mulroney, President Salinas continued to enjoy the confidence of a majority of Mexicans. Like Mulroney, Salinas also had a dominant majority in his legislature. No one predicted that he would encounter any significant problem in winning Senate ratification.

In the United States, however, the announcement immediately demonstrated the deep divisions that cleaved the polity. Business groups reacted positively. William Workman, head of the U.S. Chamber of Commerce, declared the agreement "clearly positive."[35] But opposition to NAFTA had not dissipated in the months since the fast track fight.

Labor unions blasted the agreement. The Tom Donahue of the AFL-CIO (American Federation of Labor and Congress of Industrial Organizations) declared that NAFTA is

> bad public policy. . . . Like trickle-down economics, our jobs will now trickle down to Mexico. . . . This agreement is not about free trade, nor is it about development in Mexico. It is about guaranteeing the ability of U.S. investors to move plants to Mexico to take advantage of

cheap wages and poor working conditions in producing goods for export to the U.S. market.[36]

Environmental reaction ranged from tepid to heated opposition. Moderate groups were not yet prepared to endorse the agreement, despite the changes that had been made at their request. "We must do more to link environmental protection with the economic integration of North America," said John Adams, president of the NRDC. More extreme groups blasted the accord. A Greenpeace spokesperson said that the agreement was "long on appearances to business interests whilst trying to 'greenwash' the rest of us," and a Sierra Club spokesperson said that the agreement was no more than saying "trust me and the polluters to clean up the environment."[37]

The Bush administration began considering more seriously the problem of winning support for NAFTA. For the rest of August and much of September, it attempted to wrap up the parallel track negotiations with Mexico on labor and environment and make good on the other promises of the Action Plan. It concluded a short agreement on labor, calling for periodic consultations, and nearly finished a similar deal on the environment. Carla Hills attempted to win support from the moderate environmental groups by responding to their request to create a North American Commission on the Environment. The World Wildlife Fund did endorse NAFTA, but the other groups held back, including the National Wildlife Federation, whose president, Jay Hair, had been working closely with Hills. Labor Secretary Lynn Martin announced the Bush administration's intention to expand labor adjustment assistance considerably as part of the NAFTA package, although the proposal was short on details and silent on how to pay for it.

By September, however, Bush's power was waning. He was running well behind Governor Clinton in the polls with time running out. Few were willing to cut deals with a president who might be a lame duck. Most obviously, the environmentalists recognized that they might be able to get an even more favorable deal with a President Clinton. Bill Clinton had been silent on NAFTA after its completion, saying only that he would wait until he saw the text to take a stand. There were no lack of opinions about what he should do, and Clinton was lobbied intensively by labor, by environmentalists, and by business. Now the real game shifted from national capitals to Little Rock, Arkansas, where the likely next president of the United States was deciding whether and on what terms he would ask Congress to implement the terms of NAFTA.

Interpreting International Negotiations:
Domestic Politics and International Bargaining

In this chapter we asked, Why *this* NAFTA? The question is interesting because there are many forms the agreement could have taken. The negotiation did not just involve whether or not the three countries would agree to free trade. Once they agreed to negotiate, it was likely they would reach agreement to liberalize trade. The issue was how far and how fast they would go and what new rules they would establish to govern commerce in the region. In the end, the most interesting features of the agreement have to do with deviations from free trade: some sectors exempted, long phase-outs of protection in others, high rules of origin, and a host of other carefully tailored provisions that make up the bulk of the several-thousand-page agreement. Also curious are the new rules to govern investment, intellectual property, government procurement, dispute settlement, and the relationship between trade and environment—all areas in which the decision to cooperate did little to dictate the form of cooperation.

Through what lens should we view the NAFTA negotiation? One possibility is to treat it as a purely international bargaining process among self-interested, strategic national players, essentially a realist approach. Such an analysis would specify the interests of each nation, consider the alternatives to agreement, identify the set of possible agreements, and trace the tactics employed by those parties to explain which of the possibilities was agreed to. This commentary will argue that such an approach can explain much given certain national preferences, but it cannot adequately explain those preferences and therefore is insufficient as a guide for predicting or for informing strategy. For these purposes, viewing NAFTA through the optic of two-level games, as described in chapter 2, brings the process into much sharper focus.

In trade negotiations, nations may be procedurally rational, but they often appear substantively irrational. If nations were unitary rational actors, then we would expect them to act in ways that are consistent with maximizing national welfare. Yet states consistently violate this tenet when they erect inefficient trade barriers and when they formulate objectives for trade negotiations. In trade negotiations, nations seek to maintain as many of their own barriers as possible and only agree to reduce them as a "concession" in exchange for similar "concessions" by other nations. From a welfare economics perspective, these objectives make little sense.

Much of what appears "irrational" at the international level can be explained by considering the way in which apparent national preferences reflect a contest of interests at the domestic level. We can better understand national bargaining behavior by recognizing that national negotiator preferences derive partly from a calculus of national (primarily economic) costs and benefits and partly from a calculus of political costs and benefits imposed in domestic bargaining.[38] The approach treats national negotiators as domestic politicians who not only consider what is good policy but also what is good politics. In the calculation of political consequences, negotiators are sensitive to the interests of powerful domestic factions, particularly concentrated producer interests.

The commentary here initially pays less attention to institutions or symbols. Although the NAFTA negotiations were partly structured by the pattern of the previously negotiated CUFTA, and the domestic bargaining within each country was affected by the nature of domestic political processes, negotiations are largely ad hoc institutions, whose structure is itself negotiated. Although symbolic politics mattered greatly at other points in the history of NAFTA, in the commercial negotiations, interests dominated, as we would expect. That said, however, an analysis based purely on interests, even for commercial negotiations, has its limitations. The end of the commentary will allude to these shortcomings.

A focus on domestic interests helps explain many of the peculiarities in national stance and international outcome we observe in NAFTA. Mexico fought to retain protection for oil not because oil was in Mexico's "national interest" but because Mexico's negotiators recognized that the political price they would pay for "giving it away" was too high. National stances in the talks on the auto rule of origin were not so much expressions of national interests but of politically powerful private interests. Mexican resistance to, and U.S. and Canadian insistence on, opening of the Mexican financial services market reflected not so much the policy preferences of three countries as much as the politically privileged role of financial service industries in all three countries. The perspective also solves the puzzle of why market opening requires a comprehensive free trade negotiation. For example, Mexico should unilaterally open its corn market and the United States should open its fruit and vegetable market if all that mattered were economic efficiency, but the political costs of such moves would be too high. By linking these issues in a free trade negotiation, the benefits of obtaining a concession on one issue can offset the political costs of giving in on the other.

The "Logic" of International Trade Negotiation: Tradeoffs in Agriculture

In NAFTA, as in other comprehensive trade negotiations, the core of the negotiation involved exchanging concessions on tariff and quota protection. As noted earlier, this phenomenon presents a puzzle: Why should nations need to negotiate to do what they "should" do anyway? Nowhere is this dynamic more puzzling from an economic efficiency perspective than in agriculture. Although there are credible arguments for protection under some circumstances—notably when a country enjoys considerable market power or when rapid technological change creates advantages for being first into a market—these conditions do not apply to agriculture. Agricultural protection is economically inefficient. Yet in Canada, Mexico, and the United States, agriculture remained one of the more protected sectors of the economy. Canada's extensive supply management programs for wheat and dairy products, Mexico's quotas on corn and other imports, and U.S. protection in several forms for sugar, fruit, and vegetables all raised prices for consumers, taxes for taxpayers, or both.

If the international negotiators' only goal was to maximize economic efficiency, there would not be much to negotiate in agriculture. The negotiators should fall all over each other in a race to give away protection as fast as possible. Yet this was not what happened in NAFTA. Canada found it so difficult to negotiate away its agricultural policies that it opted out of the deal altogether, whereas the United States and Mexico engaged in difficult and intense talks in which both sides drove hard bargains for each move toward market opening.

This behavior cannot be explained without reference to domestic politics. Market opening, no matter how "efficient" in aggregate, creates losers as well as winners within nations. In political competition, the losers—producers now subject to international competition—have the advantage of being a more cohesive group than the winners—consumers—who are much more diffuse. In all three countries of North America, as elsewhere around the world, concentrated agricultural interests are quite powerful in the domestic political arena. (Of course, not all agricultural interests were protectionist. U.S. grain companies, for example, saw in NAFTA an opportunity to increase their exports.)

The question then is how conflicting domestic interests translate into national behavior in international negotiations. One way to make the connection is to assume that national negotiators are simultaneously interested in (their conception of) good policy and good politics, that is, they are partly policy analysts and partly politicians. As politicians, they seek to maximize political support for the agreements they negotiate and must therefore respond to political forces operating in the domestic environment. This model of the international negotiator is consistent with the language negotiators use to describe what they do, the way in which they evaluate how well they are doing in terms of both policy and politics, and the often-expressed tension they feel between their policy beliefs and the political pressures they face. The model also provides a basis for explaining what it is that trade negotiators do when they negotiate.

The agricultural talks demonstrate the value of this approach. The essence of the bargaining problem was to trade Mexican "concessions" on corn for U.S. "concessions" on fruits and vegetables. (Recall that the agricultural negotiations were bilateral.) If both parties were only interested in economic efficiency, this would be an extremely simple problem, one that would not really require negotiation. Both countries would abandon protection unilaterally. But if we consider the political as well as the economic interests of the negotiators, the problem looks very different.

Consider the position of the U.S. negotiator. With respect to the level of fruit and vegetable protection, the U.S. negotiator's political and economic interests work against each other. Opening the market makes sense economically and conforms with negotiators' policy inclinations but is politically costly. Strong, focused grower interests in Florida, California, and Texas are politically much more potent that the diffuse consumer interest in cheaper produce. Offering unilateral opening is out of the question, because the political costs outweigh the economic benefits. Of course, the U.S. negotiator would receive both economic benefits and political benefits from a lowering of Mexican corn protection—the political benefits coming in the form of support from U.S. export interests, grain farmers and most notably the large grain companies such as Archer Daniels Midland.

The position of the Mexican negotiator is symmetric to that of the U.S. negotiator. For the Mexicans, opening corn involves economic benefits but greater political costs. Corn production engages an extraordinary fraction of the Mexican population. Opening the corn market, therefore, carries considerable political risk. Thus the Mexican negotiator will not offer to open Mexico's corn market unilaterally. Of course, U.S. opening of fruit and vegetables would provide both economic and political benefits to the Mexican negotiator.

This analysis is presented graphically in figure 5.1, which shows two "logics" of international trade negotiation: one in which nations pursue only

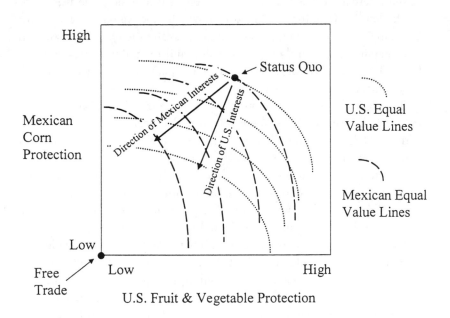

FIGURE 5.1 The Logics of Trade Negotiation: Economic and Political

(A) The economic logic. Mexican and U.S. economic interests in two issues, the level of Mexican corn protection and the level of U.S. fruit and vegetable protection, presented as an Edgeworth box. The direction of U.S. and Mexican interests is indicated by the arrows. Both prefer lower levels of protection for both issues. The zone of possible agreement (ZOPA) includes all points preferred by both to the status quo. The dominant outcome, however, is free trade, with or without negotiation.

their economic interests, the other in which national preferences reflect both international economic and domestic political considerations. The illustration is a highly stylized depiction of one piece of the U.S.–Mexican agricultural negotiation, the trade of reduced Mexican corn protection for reduced U.S. protection of warm weather fruit and vegetables.If the issues are considered separately, the political costs of opening will outweigh the economic benefits for both parties, and there is no possibility for agreement. If the issues are linked, however, making it possible for both countries to open simultaneously, national negotiators can gain sufficient political and economic benefits to offset the political costs by trading opening in fruit and

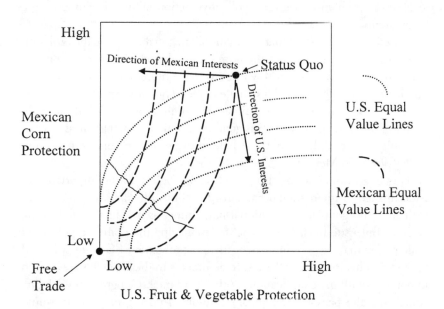

(B) The political logic. Apparent Mexican and U.S. interests in the level of Mexican corn protection and the level of U.S. fruit and vegetable protection, reflecting both international economic and domestic political concerns. The direction of U.S. and Mexican interests is indicated by the arrows. Unlike their interests as depicted in A, now both countries prefer higher levels of their own protection and lower levels of their counterpart's protection. The ZOPA again includes all points preferred to the status quo. This time, however, there is no dominant outcome, and negotiation is necessary to realize joint gains. Efficient solutions lie on the contract curve, close to free trade but not quite there.

vegetables for opening in corn. In the United States, southern fruit and vegetable growers will still impose political costs on the negotiator, but those costs will be outweighed by political support from midwestern grain producers and by the additional economic benefits of a more open Mexican corn market.

This depiction of a small subset of the NAFTA negotiations suggests a more general reinterpretation of the dynamics at work in international trade. The reason we observe inefficient levels of protection ultimately has less to do with international dynamics than with the disproportionate power of concentrated interests in domestic politics. To the extent that there are collective action problems in coordinating national trade policies at the international level, those problems arise from collective action failures in domestic political arenas.

Moreover, to the extent that international negotiations solve the problem, they do so by helping to solve the domestic problem. From the perspective of a national policy maker who wishes to make more rational national economic policy, a international free trade agreement is an opportunity to overcome domestic obstacles. The Salinas government believed that rationalization of Mexican agriculture was good economic policy regardless of what the United States did, but NAFTA helped make such rationalization politically feasible in Mexico.

Thinking in these terms also provides an insight into the importance of issue linkage in international bargains. Of course, linkage is important in realizing joint gains in international bargaining, as it is in any multi-issue bargain. But issue linkage is crucial for managing the domestic politics of trade policy making. Without such linkage, protectionist factions will tend to prevail. This is also why the fast track process in the United States was so important for ultimate ratification. Without fast track, Congress could delink issues, and the package of tradeoffs assembled during negotiation would unravel as concentrated interests mobilized to oppose the market-opening obligations undertaken by the United States in the international agreement.

Domestic Constraints on International Agreements: Mexican Oil

Although NAFTA eventually liberalizes trade and investment in most sectors of the economy, some notable exceptions include Mexican oil,

Canadian agriculture, and U.S. shipping. Why were these areas exempted from a comprehensive free trade agreement?

One possibility is that the exemptions reflected strong national interests in maintaining protection, so strong that nations were unwilling to negotiate them away, even in exchange for other concessions. In this interpretation, Mexico had such a strong interest in maintaining oil protection, Canada such a strong interest in maintaining agricultural protection, and the United States such a strong interest in maintaining shipping protection, that they were unwilling to trade them for other concessions. Certainly the outcomes can be squared with this description, but this interpretation is ultimately unsatisfactory. First, it does not explain and could not predict the form of these apparent national preferences. For all of these areas, protection was highly inefficient, imposing costs on the rest of the economy far in excess of any benefits. Second, it does not square with how the negotiators understood their problem. National negotiators did not believe that protection in these areas was in national interests; they simply felt too constrained to move away from protection.

Once again, what is unclear when viewed solely though an international-level lens comes into better focus if also examined through a domestic-level lens. As discussed in the context of the agricultural negotiations, powerful domestic interests in maintaining protection can impose political costs on national negotiators. In the case of agriculture, as with most other sectors of the economy, issue linkage in the context of a comprehensive trade negotiation enabled the negotiators to overcome the constraints imposed by domestic interests. For some issues, however, domestic politics impose such high costs that even creative linkage cannot solve the problem. In these circumstances, the interests of powerful factions place sharp constraints on national negotiators and bound the domain of what is possible in the international negotiation.

Mexican oil serves as an example. From the outset, the Mexican negotiators made clear the very tight constraints on what they could negotiate. One could argue that Mexican national interest demanded that its oil sector remain closed to international investment and competition. But this interpretation will not hold up long. Mexico's oil industry was hugely inefficient, which raised the cost of energy for the rest of the Mexican economy. Furthermore, Mexico's negotiators understood this reality and believed that the sector should be opened as far as possible, given constraints imposed by the Mexican political context.

This negotiation is better modeled, therefore, as a bargain in which the international negotiation was constrained by the power of domestic interests to block otherwise desirable outcomes. This analysis is illustrated in figure 5.2, which depicts the range of possible agreement with and without the Mexican domestic political constraint. Consider the bargain between Mexico and the United States. If all that mattered was national interest (or more specifically the negotiators' conceptions of those interests), the expected outcome of the bargain would be close to complete opening of the Mexican market. The United States would prefer maximum openness. Mexico would prefer considerable openness, although perhaps not complete openness for reasons of national security. Given these preferences, agreement would be

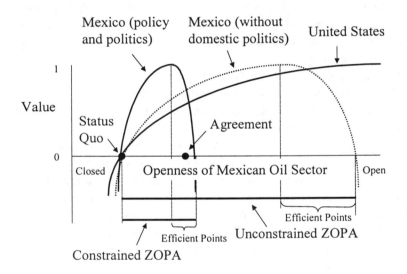

FIGURE 5.2 The Oil Negotiations

Preference curves for the United States and Mexico with respect to the degree of openness of the Mexican oil sector. (The dashed curve indicates Mexico's preferences in the absence of a domestic constraint.) The optimal point for each party has a value of 1, the status quo a value of 0. The solid horizontal lines beneath the x axis indicate the zone of possible agreement (ZOPA), with thicker lines indicating the most efficient outcomes. The constrained ZOPA (shorter horizontal line) leaves a very small set of efficient outcomes.

possible anywhere between the status quo and virtually complete openness, with agreement most likely somewhere close to complete openness.

However, given the power of Mexican oil interests in the domestic political arena, the Mexican negotiator's preference is better described as a small measure of market opening beyond which the political costs are prohibitive. U.S. interests remain in maximum openness. In this case, agreement would be possible only in the range between the status quo and the limit imposed by the domestic interest, with agreement most likely somewhere close to that limit.

This model corresponds quite well to the actual oil negotiations, where the essential bargaining dynamic was of the U.S. and Mexican negotiators exploring the limits beyond which the Mexican domestic politics would not allow the negotiations to go. Similar analyses could be conducted for other sectors in which the negotiations fell short of free trade. In Canadian agriculture, as well as in U.S. shipping and elsewhere, the outcome reflected less the pattern of preferences among the national negotiators than the limits of possibility imposed on them by domestic politics in one or more of the three countries.

The Interaction of Domestic Interests: The Auto Rule of Origin

Much of the NAFTA negotiation focused on the rules of origin that established how much of a good needed to be made in North America for it to be considered "North American," thus qualifying for preferential tariff treatment. For the same reasons as described above, but perhaps to an even greater extent, these negotiations are hard to explain in terms of an international-level bargain alone. In these negotiations, domestic politics does not so much constrain the national interest as actually define it.

The negotiations over the automobile rule of origin illustrates this dynamic. The issue was what percentage of a car would need to be North American before the car was declared North American. After long and tough bargaining, the negotiators finally settled on 62.5 percent. The content percentage actually started at a lower level before being stepped up to this percentage.)

We might interpret this result strictly as an international negotiation among three parties with differing interests. The evidence indicates that the United States's preference was for an agreement as close to 65 percent as possible. It was unwilling to agree to a rule as low as 60 percent (and probably as high as 70 percent, although that was moot given the location of Mexican and Canadian interests). Both Mexico and Canada wanted a somewhat lower percentage. Mexico's optimum was somewhere between 50 and 60 percent, but it was willing to agree to as much as 65 percent. Canada's optimum was close to Mexico's but it was more reluctant to go above 60 percent. Figure 5.3A illustrates this interpretation of the negotiation.

Given these interests, the outcome of 62.5 percent is not hard to explain. As described earlier, the bargaining proceeded with the United States committed strongly to 65 percent and Mexico and Canada starting lower but ultimately committing equally strongly to 60 percent. Near the end, Mexico expressed willingness to agree to 65 percent, but Canada continued to hold firm. Finally, under enormous pressure to complete the negotiations, the

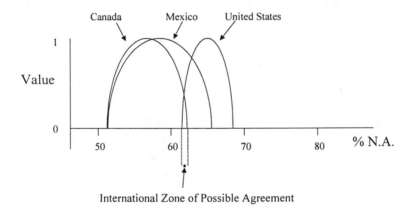

International Zone of Possible Agreement

FIGURE 5.3   The Auto Rule of Origin Negotiations

Preference curves correspond to the preferences as revealed by the parties in the negotiations. Optimal points are valued at 1. Resolutions less than 0 are unacceptable to the party (i.e., worse than agreement). (A) The preferences of the United States, Canada, and Mexico with respect to the percent of North American content required in a "North American" automobile. The United States, for example, has an optimal point at 65 percent and will not accept an agreement less than 62 percent or more than 68 percent. Together the preference curves define a very small three-way ZOPA.

United States and Canadian negotiators did what negotiators often do in such circumstances: They split the difference to settle at 62.5 percent.

This seems a satisfactory explanation in some regards. It certainly accounts for most of the observable facts. But on further reflection the explanation begs some interesting questions. The outcome is (more or less) predictable given national "preferences" and constraints. But why should these be the preferences of the parties? That 65 percent should be the apparent optimum for the United States is not the least bit obvious. Neoclassical trade theory would suggest, for instance, that the optimum should be 0 percent, since any protection at the borders of North American has efficiency costs. To the extent that the assumptions about perfect competition do not hold and the United States enjoyed some market power, strategic trade theory allows the optimal percentage to be positive, but there is no reason to believe it would have to be 65 percent, and in any event there is no good way to calculate the optimum. (There is also no evidence that anyone in the United States tried to do so.)

Similarly, little indicates that Canada's or Mexico's interests would be best served by something close to a 60 percent rule. Both Canada and Mexico had an incentive to make it easier for manufacturers to locate auto production within their borders and to ship assembled vehicles to the United States duty free. Hence, to the extent that strategic considerations were at work, one would expect these two countries to prefer a lower rule than the United States, but why it should be 60 percent and not 30 percent or 0 percent is unclear.

This deal, although murky when viewed strictly internationally, comes into sharper focus when viewed as a two-level bargain in which the preferences of powerful factions within the three domestic arenas largely determined the positions taken by negotiators in the international arena.

The United States's position can be explained as the outcome of a domestic-level bargain among strong domestic interests, most importantly the "Big Three" automakers—GM, Ford, and Chrysler—and the domestic autoparts makers. The UAW also certainly had an interest in the negotiations, but the very low probability that an agreement would secure the union's support meant that it had very little leverage in the domestic-level bargain. All three automakers had an interest in a reasonably high rule of origin to make it more difficult for European and Japanese competitors to locate assembly plants in Canada or Mexico and thereby ship finished automobiles to the United States duty free. But GM differed from Ford and Chrysler in an important regard. Because of GM's joint venture with Izuzu in Canada, GM favored a lower rule of origin, around 60 percent. For reasons that reflected their own patterns of production and competitive position, Ford and Chrysler preferred a higher rule, approximately 70 percent. Autoparts makers had every incentive to push for as high a percentage as possible, since high percentages protected them from foreign competitors.

In addition to preferences, each party in the domestic-level bargain had limits to what was acceptable. Ford and Chrysler appeared unwilling to accept anything below 60 percent. Autoparts makers had similar limits. GM, on the other hand, had limits on how high a percentage it would accept,

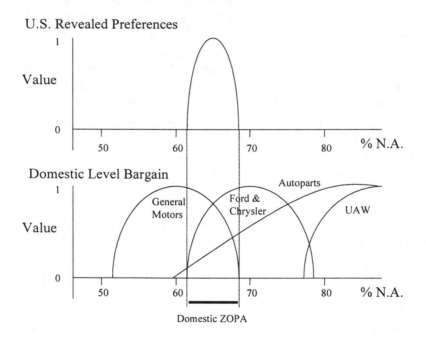

(B) Apparent U.S. preferences and the preferences of parties in the U.S. domestic-level bargain from which they are derived. The bargain is effectively among four parties: General Motors, Ford, Chrysler, and autoparts makers, here treated as a single entity. The intersection of outcomes acceptable to these parties defines the domestic ZOPA. United Auto Worker (UAW) preferences are largely irrelevant to the domestic bargaining process.

certainly below 70 percent. Figure 5.3B illustrates this interpretation of the U.S. domestic bargain.

Assuming these preferences and given that the rules of the game required something close to consensus, the only outcomes acceptable to the United States were somewhere above the 60 percent minimum acceptable to Ford, Chrysler, and the autoparts makers and below 70 percent, the maximum acceptable to GM. When these interests agreed to make 65 percent the U.S. bargaining position, the U.S. negotiators' flexibility was even further reduced. Any change from 65 percent would involve reopening a contentious internal debate.

The Canadian internal negotiation involved a slightly different cast of players than the U.S. negotiation and was conducted under different rules. It can be modeled as a game involving the Big Three again and Canadian autoparts makers, but joined by several European and Japanese transplants who assembled vehicles in Canada. (The Canadian UAW, like its American counterpart, urged a high rule of origin—perhaps 80 percent—but, with few ties to the Conservative party, had little relevance in the internal Canadian negotiation.) GM, Ford, and Chrysler had the same interests as in the U.S. negotiation. However, the transplants, with very different interests, wanted the rule of origin as close as possible to the 50 percent rule in the CUFTA so that they could continue to assemble vehicles in Canada from parts imported from Europe and Asia. (The percentages are not strictly comparable since the method for counting was different in the CUFTA.) They would strongly resist any rule above 60 percent, the point at which their Canadian assembled vehicles might not qualify as North American. Because Canadian negotiators were more insulated than their American counterparts from political pressures, agreement in Canada did not require complete consensus, but the Canadian negotiators were sensitive to the concerns of the transplants, giving them a near-veto over the Canadian position. As illustrated in Figure 5.3C the agreements acceptable to Canada, therefore, ranged roughly from close to the status quo to the limit imposed by the transplants, somewhere in the vicinity of 60 percent.

In Mexico, the constellation of players engaged in the internal negotiation included the Big Three, Mexican autoparts makers, foreign transplants, and the Mexican labor unions. As in Canada, negotiators' concerns about attracting transplants gave these interests considerable clout in the internal deliberations in Mexico, where they also pushed for lower rules of origin. GM, Ford, and Chrysler, while important, had relatively less clout. Mexican

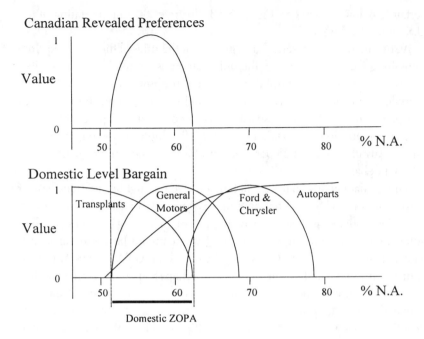

Canadian Revealed Preferences

Domestic Level Bargain

Domestic ZOPA

(C) Apparent Canadian preferences and the domestic bargain from which they are derived. The rules of the game in Canada do not require consensus; agreement between three out of the four players—GM, Ford and Chrysler (counted as one), Canadian autoparts makers, and Japanese and European transplants—is sufficient, provided one of them is the transplant interest. Canada's domestic ZOPA is bounded by the transplants' maximum on one end and GM's minimum on the other.

autoparts makers, the most significant indigenous economic interests, generally shared with their American and Canadian counterparts a desire for high rules of origin. The opinions of the labor unions mattered relatively more than in the United States or Canada because of their historically close ties to the PRI, but they were willing to live with lower rules of origin than their American and Canadian counterparts. Given the preferences of these players and the rules of the game, the set of outcomes acceptable to Mexico corresponded reasonably closely to those acceptable to Canada, although the Mexican negotiators had perhaps a bit more flexibility. Figure 5.3D illustrates the Mexican domestic-level negotiation.

From all these domestic negotiations put together emerges a picture of private interests, some national and some transnational, playing in domestic arenas to determine national positions and the international outcome. This way of thinking not only provides a richer and more satisfying interpretation of what we observe after the fact, it also provides a way of identifying the critical constraints at a level of specificity that might guide an actor in the moment. Thinking in these terms reveals that the central negotiation is likely to be between Canada and the United States, because Mexico's interests lie in between. Even more specifically, the essence of the problem lies in two specific interests, transplants in Canada and the Ford–Chrysler–autoparts maker alliance in the United States, whose preferences are the key con-

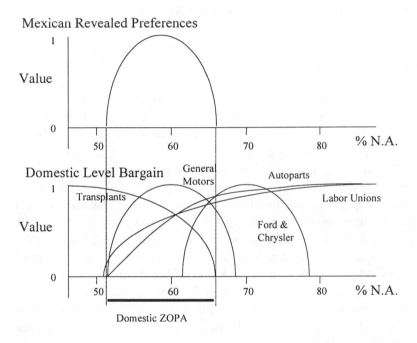

(D) Apparent Mexican preferences and the domestic bargain from which they are derived. Here the players are the Japanese and European transplants; GM, Ford, and Chrysler; Mexican autoparts makers, and the Mexican labor unions. Consensus is not required; a coalition of three that includes the transplants is sufficient. The Mexican domestic ZOPA is bounded by the transplants' maximum (higher in Mexico than in Canada) on one end and by GM's minimum on the other.

straints on national negotiators. Identifying the constraints on this level not only defines the realm of the possible, but also may point to where efforts should be concentrated should shifting constraints become necessary.

In this bargain, as with other parts of the NAFTA negotiations involving highly concentrated and powerful economic interests, the negotiation begins to look less like a deal among three nations than a deal among a collection of private interests, many of whom span national borders. That said, one cannot simply reduce the negotiation to these interests. National institutional structures matter in determining the rules of the domestic games, and hence the clout of the domestic players in determining national bargaining positions and international outcomes.

Nested Politics: Mexican Financial Services

Puzzles in the pattern of the financial services negotiations are also not easily explained without reference to domestic politics. Why did Mexico resist opening its markets so fiercely? Clearly, protecting one's banking, securities, and insurance markets, thereby imposing costs on the rest of the economy, is poor economic strategy. It is relatively easy to explain U.S. and Canadian interests in opening the Mexican market, but why the United States should have pushed so hard in this area is harder to explain.

The answers to these questions lie, at least partly, in the roles played by financial services in Mexico and the United States. Mexico's initial resistance to market opening had little to do with conceptions of Mexican national interest. Mexico's trade negotiators, left to their own impulses, would gladly have traded away much of the protection for financial services, but they were heavily constrained not simply because of the political clout of financial services in Mexico, but also because the NAFTA negotiations coincided with negotiations conducted by the Mexican Finance Ministry over the privatization of the banks. A market-opening move in NAFTA meant less value for the banks, so the Mexican trade negotiators were under enormous pressure to keep protection in place.

U.S. negotiators pushed hard for Mexican market opening, in part because they thought it good policy. But their efforts were reinforced by very strong pressure from the U.S. financial services industry, which saw opportunities in Mexico. These interests had considerable influence because of the prominent role they played in the business coalition supporting NAFTA.

As time passed, and the prospect of a significant political battle for ratification of NAFTA loomed larger, their clout only increased. When they threatened to withhold support, they got the attention not only of the U.S. negotiators, but also of the Mexicans, who were watching the American domestic politics of NAFTA with growing interest.

That the Mexicans relented, at least in some areas of financial services, reflected in part their assessment of the importance of keeping this key American interest supportive of the overall deal. But it also may have reflected a changed context in Mexico. By this time, the bank privatization was complete, and although there were commitments to uphold, Mexico was no longer playing two games at once and could afford to be a bit more flexible.

The financial services chapter demonstrates the intricate linkage between domestic politics and international negotiations. The broader political contexts in which domestic bargaining takes place can affect the powers of domestic interests in those bargains and thereby the way in which nations conduct international negotiations. As the context changes, clout in domestic arenas may grow or wane, thus creating a dynamic for changing national behavior. Changing domestic contexts decreased leverage for financial services interests in Mexico and increased them for financial services interests in the United States.

Conclusions

The preceding analysis demonstrates how a two-level analytic framework can provide insights that would be hard to obtain using only a one-level, international approach. In particular, the two-level framework provides a way to map from observable characteristics of domestic politics to international outcomes. National behaviors that are hard to square with notions of rational choice (and, therefore, hard to predict) when viewed solely from an international perspective can be explained as the outcome of bargaining processes among rational actors at the domestic level. The approach also provides a way of thinking about points of leverage in the system, in ways that not only help explain outcomes but also could provide useful guidance for a participant in such a negotiation.

To the question "Why this NAFTA?" there is now a better answer: This was the NAFTA that followed the contours of the possible as determined by the configuration of domestic interests in three political systems.

Nevertheless, the usefulness of a two-level games approach has its limits. The skeptical reader may have wondered about some issues brushed over in the preceding analysis. It is one thing to assert that a domestic constraint limited Mexican flexibility on oil; it is another to explain its existence. Negotiation analysis is a framework for working forward from assumptions about players, issues, interests, and alternatives to predictions about likely outcomes. Yet the parameters of the model must be established outside the model. The existence, shape, location, and mobility of the constraints that define what is possible may depend on deeper levels of negotiation, on the institutions that define the rules of the game, or on belief systems that generate conceptions of interest. For example, if we want to explain why the Mexicans were reluctant to open their oil market, it is helpful to recognize the existence of a domestic constraint, but if we want to know why the constraint is there, then we need to understand the institutional arrangements that gave Pemex power in the Mexican political system, and more importantly something about oil's unique historical importance as a symbol of Mexican independence and sovereignty. For that, we may need to step out of the rational choice framework entirely, a matter we consider in more depth in succeeding chapters.

6 Making Side Issues Central: The Labor and Environment Negotiations

With Bill Clinton's election in November, the side issues—environment and labor—became central. Candidate Clinton, pressed by George Bush to take a stand on NAFTA, had come down in favor of the agreement, but to soften the blow to Democratic supporters, he had promised to supplement it with additional agreements on labor and environment before he would submit it to Congress for approval. Now in office, he made good on his campaign pledge, demanding new negotiations with Mexico and Canada. The United States's international negotiating partners grudgingly acceded.

At the Office of the United States Trade Representative (USTR), the hope initially was to complete the talks in the spring, so that NAFTA could be submitted to Congress in the summer, but the task proved too difficult to complete so quickly. The United States took most of the spring to decide what it wanted, in part because this was new territory for international trade negotiators, in part because sharp internal differences made establishing a national negotiating position a matter of intense political conflict, and in part because the first months of the Clinton administration were so chaotic. Clinton's new trade representative, Mickey Kantor, found himself trying to navigate through the narrowest of openings, even before formally engaging with Mexico and Canada. In May, the United States tabled its first negotiating position, a position calculated to satisfy enough Democrats sympathetic to labor and environmental interests to win Congressional approval. But the U.S. position met with strong opposition from Mexico and Canada and at home from U.S. business interests and Republican members of Congress whose support would be needed.

As spring turned to summer, the broader political context became increasingly charged, further imperiling NAFTA. In contrast to the relatively insulated negotiations of the main agreement, the side negotiations were conducted in the spotlight of attention from interest groups, the public, and ever more, members of Congress. By summer's end, the vast majority of Democrats in Congress were ready to oppose the agreement, including the influential House majority leader, Richard Gephardt. Some of the president's political advisors urged him to use failure to reach agreement in the side negotiations as an excuse to pull the plug on NAFTA and avoid a bloody fight in Congress.

The president decided otherwise and directed Mickey Kantor to close the deal. Prodded by the prospects of failure, negotiators for all three countries found ways to make painful compromises. Finally, on August 13, 1993, a week after the U.S. Congress had recessed and well after they had originally intended to conclude the negotiations, the United States, Mexico, and Canada reached a final agreement. The accords established modest new international institutions, intended both to facilitate cooperation and to promote enforcement of national labor and environmental laws. The labor institutions had less independence and more limited powers than the environmental institutions. The United States and Mexico agreed that in extreme cases of failure to enforce national law, an international dispute panel could authorize trade sanctions. Canada, unwilling to allow the possibility, however remote, that international trade sanctions might be used against them (a sensitive matter in Canadian politics), agreed instead to make the decisions of the international dispute panel enforceable in Canadian courts.

Why side negotiations? Why did the United States, having agreed to terms in August 1992, change its mind and insist on additional talks in 1993? And why *these* side agreements? Why different institutions for labor and environment? Why did the United States demand, Mexico accept, and Canada reject the right to use trade sanctions to ensure enforcement of domestic environmental and labor laws?

Making Side Issues Central

At the Republican National Convention in August 1992, Carla Hills spoke to the gathered delegates. By then, Bill Clinton was well ahead in the polls, and there was a note of urgency in the Republican campaign. NAFTA was a good issue for Bush, his advisors thought. It showed Bush as decisive and effective, a leader on the international stage. Moreover, it put Bill Clinton in an awkward position, forced to decide whether to stick with his previously declared general support for NAFTA and go against the wishes of the Democrats' core constituency, particularly the labor unions, or to oppose NAFTA and risk being seen as caving to special interests.

For several weeks after the NAFTA talks concluded, Clinton delayed taking a stand, saying that he had not yet had a chance to read the agreement and would remain undecided until he did. The claim was plausible, since the text had not been made public and since, in truth, parts of it were still being drafted, but by mid September, Clinton felt pressure to announce a decision. In addition to being pressed by Bush, Clinton was hearing from Ross Perot, back in the race for president after a short hiatus, who had seized on opposition to NAFTA as a good vehicle for his populist candidacy. In one of the more memorable soundbites of the campaign, Perot had asserted that NAFTA would create a "sucking sound" as jobs went south to Mexico.

At campaign headquarters in Little Rock, establishing a stance on NAFTA became an important strategic issue for the Clinton campaign. Clinton and his advisors conferred with dozens of people. Most of the traditional Democratic party was opposed to the agreement. The labor unions and their friends on Capitol Hill strongly urged Clinton to reject the "Bush NAFTA" and promise to renegotiate the whole agreement. Elements of the centrist "New Democrat" coalition, particularly in the business community, urged him to support the agreement. Clinton's campaign advisors were split. On the one hand, supporting NAFTA might cost him votes in key states such as Michigan and California. On the other hand, given his earlier general support of NAFTA, opposing it now might look like he was capitulating to special interests, a charge that had dogged him on the campaign trail.

Several conferees pushed a middle course, in which Clinton would support NAFTA but promise to strengthen its labor and environmental provisions. In late September Bill Bradley talked with Clinton by phone. Bradley argued that NAFTA was a historic opportunity to transform U.S.–Mexican relations. Supporting NAFTA was good policy, but it was also good politics. It would take a campaign issue away from Bush. To deal with the labor and environmental issues, Bradley argued that Clinton should promise to negotiate supplemental agreements on labor and environmental issues. This middle course was supported by environmental groups and other centrist Democrats such as Lloyd Bentsen.

The "yes, but" position proved persuasive with Clinton's campaign strategists, many of whom were personally opposed to the agreement. Although there might be political costs, particularly in Michigan, a key primary state, backing NAFTA would signify that Clinton was tough enough to stand up to interest groups. To be perceived as backing away from his previous position in the face of political pressure — certainly the way that a stance in opposition would be interpreted — was to open himself to criticism on a dimension of character that was Clinton's greatest vulnerability. In a speech in Raleigh, North Carolina, given on October 4, 1992, Bill Clinton announced that he was supporting NAFTA. He said that the agreement Bush had negotiated had problems, but they could be fixed without starting over. If elected, however, he would not sign a bill implementing NAFTA unless it included additional agreements on labor and environment. The side issues were now central.

Initiating Negotiations

After his election, having promised in the campaign to negotiate the supplemental agreements, President-elect Clinton and his transition team now had to decide how serious they were about making good on that promise and had to persuade the Mexicans and the Canadians to talk. The Mexicans initially hoped that the proposed supplemental talks were an empty campaign pledge. They took the position that they had already concluded an agreement and that they had no intention of renegotiating its terms. However, they could also see that they would have to grant Clinton's request if legislation implementing NAFTA were to have any chance of passing in Congress. Grudgingly, the Mexicans agreed to negotiate, but laid down three "noes": no reopening of the NAFTA text, no hidden protectionism, and no compromise of Mexican sovereignty. The Canadians were a good deal more positive than the Mexicans about the prospect of supplemental negotiations. They well understood that Canada was not the object of concern. But like the Mexicans, they made clear that these must be *supplemental* negotiations, not a reopening of the NAFTA, and that they would oppose any measures that might be used to limit free trade.

The prospect of side agreements raised hope among some U.S. labor and environmental activists that Clinton might push for new international standards in these areas, something of a "social charter" along the lines of standards established by the European Union. The Clinton transition team for trade matters quickly squashed this hope. International standards could be used against the United States, they thought. Moreover, they were unnecessary. Mexico's environmental and labor laws were strong enough. What was needed, they decided, was a means to ensure "national enforcement of national laws," a phrase that would become a virtual mantra in the first months of the Clinton Administration.

Two weeks before his inauguration, Clinton met with Mexican President Carlos Salinas in San Antonio, Texas, Clinton's first meeting as president-elect with a foreign head of state. Clinton reaffirmed his insistence on new negotiations but agreed to the Mexican conditions, saying "I don't believe the negotiation needs to be reopened." He promised Salinas that he had no intention of using the supplemental negotiations to undermine free trade or Mexican sovereignty. Salinas agreed to negotiate.

A New Trade Representative

In late December, after much speculation in the Washington trade community, Bill Clinton announced Mickey Kantor as his nominee for the position of United States Trade Representative. The announcement caught most observers by surprise. Kantor had been Clinton's campaign manager and he was thought of as a tough negotiator, but he had no experience with trade issues. True, having a trade background had never been a prerequisite for the position. Carla Hills knew little about trade when she started, nor for that matter had the majority of U.S. Trade Representatives since the creation of the office. However, no trade representative had ever taken over with so many trade balls in the air. On its own, NAFTA would be a huge challenge, but Kantor would also have to close the enormously complicated the General Agreement on Tariffs and Trade (GATT) negotiations, something none of his predecessors had been able to do; tackle the increasingly acrimonious trade relationship with Japan; and decide on an approach to handling the U.S.–China trade relationship that balanced economic and human rights considerations.

On NAFTA, Kantor's first impressions were negative. He had gone along with the decision to support NAFTA during the campaign, and now that Clinton had decided in favor, Kantor's job would be to serve the president, but as he made his courtesy visits to Senators who would vote on his confirmation, he left little doubt that he was skeptical about the agreement. In his mind, the "Bush NAFTA" was deeply flawed and would need to be fixed with supplemental agreements before it could be pronounced good for the United States.

Kantor's political instincts meshed with his policy inclinations. NAFTA was very unpopular with key Democratic labor and environmental constituencies. But NAFTA couldn't pass without Democratic votes in the Congress. Congressional Democrats were understandably nervous about voting for the agreement. Strong side agreements might win them over, might even win union support. "Mickey had strong union ties, and he harbored the view that he could get unions to come along," recalled an official at the USTR.

The truth was that Kantor did not yet know how to proceed, nor had he grasped how difficult a task completing the NAFTA process would be. When he came before the Senate Finance Committee on January 19 for his confirmation hearing, his prepared statement barely addressed the side agreements. Most of the Senators offered questions on the trade conflict with Japan or narrow issues of particular concern to their constituents. Finance Committee member Bill Bradley, however, made what seemed a startling statement. "I believe [NAFTA] is the most important foreign policy decision that President Clinton will make in his first six to eight months," said Bradley. "I think it is enormously important for the future of this country. It offers a promise that might not come again. And I urge you to seize it, to conclude quickly any side agreements that you've obligated yourself to negotiate with Mexico, to quickly submit to us the Administration's adjustment package that will facilitate this agreement, and to push it forward with great energy."[1]

The Nature of the Problem

Whether he recognized it or not, the challenge facing Mickey Kantor was formidable. To negotiate side agreements with Mexico and Canada, the United States would first have to decide what it wanted. In some ways this was a more difficult policy design problem than crafting the NAFTA agreement itself, which followed the existing template, the Canada–U.S. Free Trade Agreement (CUFTA). Here there was no precedent, and Clinton's campaign promises gave very limited guidance. Kantor had to find solutions that were acceptable not only to the Mexicans and the Canadians, but also to enough domestic interests to make ultimate passage of NAFTA possible. Moreover, he had to do this quickly if he wanted Congress to consider

NAFTA before the end of the year, when the agreement was scheduled to go into effect.

A first obstacle was simply disorganization. The first months of the Clinton administration was extremely chaotic. For the first time in 12 years, the Democrats were in power, and the transition was moving very slowly. At the USTR, Kantor's top deputies did not even come on board until the second week of February. Moreover, many of the Clinton appointees were inexperienced and would need time to get up to speed. "We were asking guys in the fifth grade to perform brain surgery," recalled one career official at the USTR.

The new National Economic Council (NEC) in the White House, intended to streamline interagency economic policy making, was operating more as a bottleneck. "It was a crazy lifestyle," recalled an official at the NEC. "We would spend all day in meetings. Then we'd spend all night to do the work." And NAFTA was far from the only item on the agenda for the White House. "It was hard to get serious attention to NAFTA at high levels," the same official recalled. "Remember that the new Administration was dealing with gays in the military, the budget, and a lot of other stuff. We had to deal with China MFN [Most Favored Nation], with GATT, with our Japan policy. Everyone is saying you have to focus on one thing, but it should be my thing. The Administration was like a car starting from a dead stop. Once the car got going, and the Administration had been thinking about all these things, then we could take on more than one thing at a time."

The administrative confusion made it impossible for Kantor to move on the supplemental negotiations as quickly as first intended. When Kantor, Jaime Serra, and Michael Wilson met for the first time in mid February, Kantor could offer little more than generalities about U.S. intentions.

In February, Kantor finally assembled his new staff. Rufus Yerxa, a former Rostenkowski aide who had been negotiating the Uruguay Round of the GATT, took over from Jules Katz as deputy USTR and chief negotiator for the side negotiations. Tom Nides, a former Gephardt aide, would be chief of staff. Ira Shapiro, former top aide to Senator Jay Rockefeller (Democrat, W.V.), would be the new general counsel, and Nancy Leamond, president of the Congressional Economic Leadership Institute, would handle congressional relations.

In September, as part of its effort to secure support for NAFTA, the Bush Administration had tried to cut a deal with some of the mainstream environmental groups to secure their support. Over the opposition of the State Department, the USTR had agreed to support the creation of a trinational

North American Commission on the Environment (NACE), an idea pushed by a coalition of the World Wildlife Fund (WWF), the National Wildlife Federation (NWF), the Environmental Defense Fund (EDF), and the Natural Resources Defense Council (NRDC) in testimony before the Senate Finance Committee. The election had overtaken the negotiations, but the promise of a trinational commission, albeit with limited powers, established a base for negotiating the supplemental agreements in the Clinton Administration. Now the issue was what kind of commission, not whether there would be one.

No such template existed for the labor negotiations. What Bush had negotiated in parallel to NAFTA on labor issues amounted to little more than a promise to consult with Mexico annually on these issues. Clinton had promised something as substantial as the environmental accord, which meant starting from scratch.

For trade officials at the USTR, finding ways to accomplish environmental and labor objectives without undermining the goal of free trade was a paramount concern. Always for the USTR, however, the policy design challenge included an essentially political objective: to find a solution that would be simultaneously acceptable in the U.S. domestic arena and negotiable with the Mexicans and Canadians. This was a formidable political problem. First, it was unclear what, if anything, would win enough votes to pass NAFTA in the Congress. After the 1992 election, Democrats had large majorities in both houses. To win, therefore, NAFTA needed the support of a significant number of Democrats. But most Democrats had criticized the "Bush NAFTA" during the campaign, citing in particular their concerns about labor and the environment. The large incoming freshman class had been particularly critical. On the other hand, the agreements could not be so strong as to lose business backing and Republican votes. With a Democrat in the White House, Republican members of Congress, who had little reason to help a Democratic president, might find it politically attractive to use the side agreements as an excuse to back out of their earlier support.

Looming large in the strategic thinking of Kantor was the pursuit of Richard Gephardt. Based on the evidence of the fast track vote in 1991, NAFTA would probably have an easier time in the Senate than in the House. As House majority leader and perhaps the most outspoken member of Congress on trade issues, Gephardt was thought to have considerable influence over other House Democrats who might constitute the swing votes. On the other hand, Gephardt's strong ties to organized labor meant winning his support would probably not be easy and might be impossible without losing Republican support. At the USTR, there were strong differences of view about how far the Administration should go to accommodate Gephardt. Deputy USTR Rufus Yerxa, brought back from his labors on GATT to be chief negotiator for the supplemental talks, had seen Gephardt in action when Yerxa had worked for House Ways and Means Chairman Dan Rosten-kowski. Yerxa was skeptical about whether Gephardt would ever support NAFTA and worried that pursuing him risked losing Republican votes. Others at the USTR, most importantly Mickey Kantor, felt differently. "Mickey thought that we could get the lunchbucket Democrats epitomized by Gephardt," recalled one of his senior aides. For the next few months, the USTR would negotiate with Representative Gephardt almost as much as it did with the Mexicans and the Canadians.

At the beginning of the year, of course, Kantor could not know just how big a problem he really faced. He knew from the campaign that the labor unions were unhappy and many environmental groups were discontent. He did not know whether Ross Perot would continue to be a player on the national scene. Moreover, Kantor was on somewhat unfamiliar territory and could not see how his efforts to court NAFTA's critics might complicate his task. Early in the Clinton Administration, all things seemed possible, and it was difficult to imagine just how treacherous the political landscape for NAFTA would prove to be.

Defining the Negotiation: Issues and Players on Two Levels

By the end of February, two sets of core issues began to crystallize. The first concerned how much power the international environmental and labor commissions would have. How accountable would they be to national governments? Would they have single, permanent staffs? What investigatory powers would they have? The second concerned the mechanisms for ensuring national enforcement of national laws. Under what circumstances might a claim of failure to enforce national law be submitted to a panel for adjudication? What process and what standard would be used to judge the claim? And, perhaps the most sharply defined issue and one that would garner the most public attention, what penalties could be imposed if a country failed to respond to the findings of a dispute settlement panel?

As *demandeur* in the negotiations, the United States had first to decide what it wanted on these issues. Even more than in the commercial negotiations, this was not a matter of the trade negotiators' preferences. The U.S. negotiating position would need to be established through consultation and negotiation with interest groups—environmental, business, and labor—and, given the proximity of these negotiations to the eventual vote in Congress, with key members of Congress responsive to these interests. This process, more than in the commercial negotiations, would need to take place outside of the existing consultative structure, which was designed for trade issues, not for labor and environmental issues that engaged a much wider circle of actors. Before he could engage with Mexico and Canada, therefore, Kantor would need to navigate through the domestic political landscape.

Environmental Interests

Veteran trade officials at the USTR understood that they would need some environmental support for the side agreement. A supplemental agreement universally opposed by the environmental community would never make it through Congress. The lesson of the fast track fight, however, was that a split vote of environmental organizations would neutralize the issue. The Bush administration had been very close to gaining the blessing of several environmental organizations in the fall of 1992 when it promised to create a NACE—indeed the WWF had announced its support—but now the political context had changed and even the moderate groups were demanding more.

The number of environmental organizations involved in NAFTA had grown steadily. Now virtually the entire environmental community was plugged into the debate, including numerous smaller organizations that rarely played in the national policy arena. Officials of these organizations discovered that NAFTA was becoming a hot issue with their members. The groups shared some objectives: All wanted better enforcement of Mexican environmental laws, guarantees of the sanctity of U.S. environmental laws, greater environmental cooperation between Mexico and the United States, and more money for cleaning up the U.S.–Mexico border. But the community was far from homogenous, with organizations differing on how much they needed done on these issues to support NAFTA.

On one end of a spectrum were the large, well-financed Washington- or

New York–based institutions such as the World Wildlife Fund, the National Wildlife Federation, the Audubon Society, the Environmental Defense Fund, and the Natural Resources Defense Council. These organizations were generally more accepting of the coexistence of economic growth and environmental goals, more familiar with the corridors of power in Washington, and less alarmed about the environmental implications of NAFTA. To them NAFTA was more an opportunity to accomplish environmental objectives than a threat.

At the other end of the spectrum were more grassroots groups such as the Sierra Club, Friends of the Earth, Greenpeace, Defenders of Wildlife, and dozens of other smaller environmental and advocacy organizations. These groups were more skeptical about the relationship between economic growth and the environment, less comfortable with the Washington scene, and a good deal more critical of NAFTA. Joining them was Public Citizen, an advisory group founded by populist crusader Ralph Nader. To the leaders of these organizations, NAFTA represented a grave threat to the environment and to the ability of citizens to have a say in environmental policy decisions.[2]

The NWF had come close to announcing its support for NAFTA in the fall when Bush agreed to create a North American Commission on the Environment, but now it saw an opportunity to go well beyond the limited commission envisioned by Bush. The NWF expected it would support the agreement in the end, but it intended to bargain for more. "We felt at the end of the day we would get more if there is a *quid pro quo*," recalled the NWF's Stewart Hudson, the staffer who had been instrumental in organizing the environmental community during the fast track effort. In February, the NWF issued a report identifying "essential elements of the supplemental agreements": more funding for environmental cleanup, a package of "technical amendments" to the NAFTA, and "mechanisms for enhancing the adoption and more effective enforcement of national environmental laws. . . ." The report projected flexibility on the enforcement question, asking only that the commission "have the authority to make recommendations for fines and other trade remedies."[3] Importantly, it did not call for renegotiation of the NAFTA itself.

Shortly afterward, two other moderate groups—the NRDC and the EDF—joined with three groups generally more critical of NAFTA—the Border Ecology Project, the Texas Center for Policy Studies, and Arizona Toxics Information—to issue their recommendations. They took a harder line than the NWF on the enforcement question. "Enforcement failures that persist after full warnings and consultations could lead to NAFTA dispute proceedings and imposition of import restrictions, duties or other trade penalties," testified the NRDC's Justin Ward to the Senate Environment and Public Works Committee a few weeks later. For the NRDC and EDF, however, enforcement was not the top priority. "The primary rationale for a new commission is to provide a mechanism to enhance North American regional cooperation on environmental policies and programs," Ward testified.[4]

The Sierra Club report issued in February viewed NAFTA's environmental problems with more alarm and took an even harder line. Rather than urging clarification of ambiguities in the text, it stated that "[t]he United States must attempt to re-negotiate the words which give rise to these problems." Its called for a much stronger and more independent institution than that envisioned by the NWF, EDF, and NRDC "with the power to investigate claims of environmental wrong-doing." On enforcement the Sierra Club insisted that "citizens of each country should be provided the right to seek damages for lax environmental protection within courts of law of any party," and, even stronger, it called for amending U.S. trade law to make lax enforcement of environmental law "actionable," i.e., grounds for unilateral trade sanctions, and to require U.S. corporations operating outside the United States to adhere to U.S. regulations.[5]

Of these reports, that of the Sierra Club was least influential with the Clinton administration, since few at the USTR expected that this organization's support could be bought. Its new executive director, Carl Pope, was personally opposed NAFTA. Perhaps more significantly, with the majority of its grassroots membership strongly opposed to NAFTA, Sierra Club's elected leadership had an incentive to take a strong stance.

On Capitol Hill, Senator Max Baucus (Democrat, Mont.), new Chairman of the Committee on Environment and Public Works as well as Chairman of the Trade Subcommittee of the Finance Committee, saw an opportunity to seize leadership on the trade and environment issue. At a speech to the American Bar Association January 29, 1993, Baucus called for "something with teeth but which recognized national sensitivities."[6] He proposed making noncompliance with local environmental regulations a violation of NAFTA and thus subject to trade sanctions; giving the NACE authority to investigate complaints; and establishing a border fee to pay for the NACE, border cleanup, and worker retraining.

The cross-border fee was quickly rejected by the Canadians and Mexicans and was received coolly by the trade staff of the USTR, but Baucus's speech

influenced the thinking of Mickey Kantor. Kantor viewed Baucus as the key
to brokering a deal with the environmentalists. "Max's speech on how the
side agreements should be structured made a big difference," recalled
Mickey Kantor later. Others at the USTR were less sanguine at the time,
fearing that Baucus was pushing the United States into too confrontational
a negotiating position. Privately, some in the mainstream environmental
community felt the same way.

For the first few months of 1993, in meetings organized by the NWF's
Stewart Hudson, all segments of the environmental community attempted
to work together. They met as a group with the Administration officials
charged with putting together a negotiating position. The large group meetings, however, proved unsatisfactory for all concerned. For the USTR it was
hard to sort through the cacophony of voices to discern what the groups
really wanted and how their support could be won. Environmental groups
on both ends of the spectrum felt that their message was muddied by the
attempt to maintain consensus in the community.

In early March, a group of the critics, including Defenders of Wildlife,
the Center for International Environmental Law, Friends of the Earth, the
Sierra Club, Public Citizen, and sixteen other grassroots organizations, sent
Mickey Kantor a letter with a sharper point. "We support a NACE that will
possess investigative, monitoring, and enforcement powers . . . as well as
serve as a mechanism for meaningful public participation," it stated. "Enforcement is a crucial issue. We should not subject U.S. citizens to economic, health, safety, or environmental injury as a result of weak enforcement of standards elsewhere. . . . Sanctions, including both trade and
nontrade measures, must be available to ensure compliance."[7] Notably absent from the signatories were any of the moderates. "We thought the letter
was headed toward a cumbersome and contentious process," recalled the
NRDC's Justin Ward. "That letter focused on supernational enforcement
and dispute settlement, not on trinational cooperation." The environmental
community was beginning to split.

Labor Interests

Although the environment and labor issues were often lumped together,
the politics of labor differed widely from the politics of the environment.
Unlike environmental groups that were prepared to set a price for their
support, labor unions were not in a position to offer a deal. The unions

could never promise that particular side agreements would win them over. NAFTA's problems, in their view, were too profound to be handled with the kind of supplemental agreements that seemed plausible. In his testimony to the Senate Finance Committee in September, Tom Donahue, chair of the Labor Advisory Committee on International Trade, said,

> the North American Free Trade Agreement from start to finish is noth- ing more than the latest version of Reagan-Bush trickle-down econom- ics and an enlargement of the interests of U.S. and Canada-based multinational corporations, to the detriment of U.S. workers. The Congress should reject the agreement and send a new set of U.S. negotiators back to the table.[8]

Immediately after Clinton's election, some union strategists had hoped that the promised side agreements might create an opportunity for funda- mental changes in the nature of the agreement. The unions wanted a social charter for labor—common international rights and standards—enforceable through domestic courts and if needed through international sanctions. At the very top of the union list of rights was the right to free association. "For us, in any labor side agreement the major uncompromisable issue is freedom of association, the right to organize and bargain collectively," said the Mark Anderson of the AFL-CIO (American Federation of Labor and Congress of Industrial Organizations). "Without that, it is nothing." Other standards of interest covered workplace health and safety, child labor, and the minimum wage. Of course, even if the side agreements met these goals, there was no guarantee that the unions would support NAFTA.

Before Clinton even took office, however, it became evident that the side agreements would not come close to meeting union demands. When Clin- ton promised Salinas that there would be no reopening of the NAFTA and that the United States would respect Mexican sovereignty, the international standards were out, replaced by an emphasis on national enforcement of national laws. "It was fairly clear early on that the USTR was just going through the motions," recalled Bill Cunningham, the AFL-CIO's director of Congressional relations. "We were up front with the Administration, we didn't think this was a fixable agreement."

The recognition that no plausible resolution of the side agreements would win union support put union leaders in an awkward position as they tried to influence the content of the agreements. On the one hand, all the alternatives looked bad in union eyes; on the other hand, some outcomes were worse than others. Steve Beckman of the United Auto Workers (UAW) and Mark Anderson of the AFL-CIO continued to meet with USTR officials, and with Larry Katz, chief economist at the Labor Department, who was taking the lead on the side negotiation at the department. In contrast to the dialogue with the environmental community, the talks with Beckman and Anderson were quiet and largely invisible to the public and the union rank and file. Moreover, these were not negotiations in the same way as the talks between the USTR and the environmentalists. "There was never much give and take going on. It was more them listening to us, and later being presented with what they were doing," recalled Mark Anderson.

The key strategic decision facing the unions was how to position themselves publicly. Many in the union movement wanted to abandon all pretense of working with the Administration to fix the agreement, declare it beyond remedy, and take a firm stance in opposition. Others argued that they should wait until the side agreements were completed, so as to continue to influence their content, to give the president a chance to make good on his promises, and to do nothing to weaken the first Democratic president in 12 years. "We tried to hold off our more active sisters and brothers," recalled Mark Anderson. "Our argument to the Hill and to our affiliates was: It's only fair to wait and see what happens. President Clinton had promised to fix the agreement. We were trying to keep the door open. We were happy about the election of Clinton, and we were trying not to say 'welcome to Washington' and then kick him in the teeth."

The issue was debated within the Executive Council of the AFL-CIO in February at the annual meeting in Bal Harbour, Florida. The Council decided to wait to launch a political campaign against NAFTA. But the tensions were evident in the Executive Council's public statement: "[NAFTA] would be a disaster for millions of working people in the United States, Canada and Mexico. . . . As drafted, NAFTA is an agreement based solely on exploitation. . . . It should be rejected and renegotiated to advance the overall public interest."[9]

Some union leaders were not prepared to wait. William Bywater, president of the Electrical Workers Union, from the outset one of the more vociferous opponents of NAFTA, was clear about his intentions, "I am trying my best to fight NAFTA. We'll get out in the streets if we have to."[10]

If the labor unions were in a poor position to advocate a labor agenda in the side agreements, Richard Gephardt was not. As House majority leader and as perhaps the most vocal trade skeptic among Democrats, Gephardt's support could give other Democrats with strong union ties the political cover they needed to go along. Mickey Kantor viewed Gephardt as a crucial player, and he thought he could get him. As USTR General Counsel Ira Shapiro recalled, "there was a time when Mickey thought that the supplemental agreements would transform the NAFTA from a bad deal into a good deal, and that they would gain Democrats' support. If the supplemental agreements were strong enough we would get Gephardt, and that would be a signal to other Democrats that the deal was a good one."

Gephardt was sounding very moderate. In testimony before a House Foreign Affairs subcommittee in late February, Gephardt stated, "I'm prepared to vote for the agreement if these other matters are successfully concluded. . . . I intend to be a partner in this process and to work toward successfully concluding a NAFTA agreement this year."[11] Gephardt called for a strong labor side agreement that would improve Mexican labor standards, a "code of conduct" governing business practices in Mexico, strong worker retraining provisions in the implementing bill, and adequate funding for infrastructure improvements in the border region.

Yet despite these soothing words, some in the Administration were not so sure about what Gephardt was doing. On February 17, the first day the trade ministers met to begin discussions about the side agreements, Gephardt held a press conference to release information on an investment fund, partially financed by the Mexican government, whose purpose was to lure American businesses to Mexico. Gephardt accused Mexican officials of "stealing American jobs." The Mexicans were furious at what they viewed as an attempt to poison the atmosphere. The *Washington Post* quoted an unnamed senior Mexican official as saying "we don't believe in coincidences." President Salinas, clearly irked, urged Congress to conduct an "informed debate." "I hope that good faith will prevail, and that the aim is to improve relations between Mexico and the United States and not to wreck them," he said.[12]

At the USTR, reactions to the flap over the Mexican investment fund differed. Those sympathetic to Gephardt, including his former staff member Tom Nides and Kantor himself, were more angry with Mexico than with Gephardt. But for Rufus Yerxa and the trade veterans, the episode raised suspicions that Gephardt was doing little to position himself to support the agreement in the end. Suspicions might have been even greater had anyone known that the source of the material was actually Pat Choate, Ross Perot's principle advisor on NAFTA and other trade matters. Choate had received the "gift" by fax from a New York Perot supporter, but as he recalled later, he knew that "if it comes from us it only causes a ripple. But Gephardt was sitting on the fence." Whatever the reality of Gephardt's true intentions, over the next few months the Administration would spend more time with Gephardt than with any other member of Congress.

Business

At the beginning of the Clinton Administration, the concerns of the business community were not nearly as salient to Mickey Kantor as were the concerns of the unions and the environmentalists. Business support for NAFTA was without doubt necessary for eventual success, but Kantor could see little reason to believe there was any problem in getting it. In his mind, business had gotten a great deal in NAFTA, and nothing that the USTR was contemplating in the way of side agreements would change that.

The business community was not particularly attuned to the labor and environmental issues. Business was happy with things as they were. Bush's parallel negotiations in 1992 had not unduly worried them; they trusted a Republican administration to look after their interests. Clinton's election changed things, but until business knew where the new Administration was headed, they could not know how active they would need to be. Was Clinton serious about these side agreements or was he merely looking for political cover when he promised them?

Early in February, however, business leaders began to detect Kantor's receptivity to the proposals being advanced by the environmental community and championed by Baucus. The idea that trade sanctions might be connected to labor and environmental issues particularly caught their attention. Chuck Levy, a prominent Washington trade lawyer retained by the Business Roundtable, argued that business needed to get engaged. He and others created a "blue" and a "green" team to deal with the labor and environmental negotiations, respectively. The teams included representatives from the Business Roundtable, the Chamber of Commerce, the National Association of Manufacturers (NAM), the Emergency Committee on American Trade (ECAT), the U.S. Council of International Business, the Council of the Americas, and others. The idea, recalled Levy, "was to approach this in a totally unified fashion. . . . Otherwise we [would] get picked off one by one."

Business had not opposed the creation of consultative commissions composed of representatives of national governments. The idea of international organizations independent of national control, with investigative and enforcement powers, particularly if they might involve trade sanctions, was another matter. A March letter from the Chamber of Commerce to Mickey Kantor stated the common view. "Authority to impose sanctions against private interests in any of the signatory states should remain with the signatory states, and not reside in a supranational commission." The Chamber was "concerned that use of trade sanctions as a remedy for environmental violations could evolve into a new set of non-tariff barriers."[13] Moreover, business leaders not only disliked what was being proposed on policy grounds, they also feared that the more ambitious the U.S. negotiating position, the longer the talks would take, and the dimmer the prospects for NAFTA's passage would be.

Having heard from labor and environment's allies in Congress, in February Kantor began hearing quiet warnings from business's supporters on the Hill. Unlike the unions and the environmentalists, business's primary allies were Republicans, who had less access to the president. In the House, Jim Kolbe (Republican, Ariz.) emerged as the leading spokesperson. Kolbe worried that the Administration was taking Republicans for granted. He warned that Republican support was not automatic and that an agreement that made trade sanctions available for a labor or environmental dispute risked losing Republican votes. In the Senate, John Chafee (Republican, R.I.) and Jack Danforth (Republican, Mo.) sent Kantor the same message.

Bill Bradley had been closely monitoring the progress of the side negotiations, talking with environmental, labor, and business groups; with Kantor and other administration officials; and with contacts in Mexico and Canada. Bradley was sympathetic to the environmental and labor concerns, but he believed they would be best advanced in the long run by passing NAFTA. He worried that Kantor was risking the whole agreement by going too far in trying to meet the demands of labor and environmental groups. The way to lose NAFTA was to lose the Republicans, he warned Kantor.

Negotiating the U.S. Position

It was in this political context that the Clinton Administration moved to establish its negotiating position for the talks with Mexico and Canada. Central to the thinking at the USTR was the proposition that the environment and labor opening positions needed to be identical. "Clinton couldn't be accused of loving trees more than workers," recalled Chip Roh. "We thought, let's make the constituencies ask for differences." Because the dialogue about the provisions of the environmental side agreement was so much further advanced, environment became the template for labor.

At the Department of Labor, the strategy created frustration. As Larry Katz recalled,

> The USTR thought there was a political imperative for having identical side agreements. Given that the USTR knew environment, our position was more appropriate for environmental issues. There were provisions in there that didn't make sense for labor. Environmentalists cared about sunshine components, advisory groups, international organizations. Labor people don't care about international organizations. Their experience with the ILO [International Labor Organization] has left them skeptical about international institutions.

The USTR intended to lay out the basic U.S. position at talks scheduled for March 17 and 18. As the date approached, the Clinton Administration tried to decide what stance to take. Some pieces of the position were settled. The United States would not seek new North American standards, as advocated by the labor unions, but would instead encourage enforcement of national standards, which was the preference of many environmentalists who feared that North American standards might actually limit U.S. standards. The United States would also insist on single, permanent staffs for the commissions, not three national staffs, to give the commissions a measure of real independence. The remaining questions were what powers to grant the commissions and what sanctions to make available for ensuring enforcement should consultation fail.

In the early days of 1993, the dividing lines within the Administration were sharpest on the issue of sanctions, as they were on the Hill and in the communities of interest. The difference of position reflected differences in beliefs about NAFTA, judgments about what the Mexicans and Canadians could accept, and assessments of Congressional politics. One wing of the Administration, led by Treasury Secretary Lloyd Bentsen, the former Finance Committee chairman, viewed NAFTA as good on its own terms and the side agreements as bonuses. Bentsen worried that there were limits beyond which the Mexicans and Canadians would not go, and doubted the wisdom of a strategy aimed at winning Dick Gephardt's support. An insistence on trade sanctions in the side agreement, he felt, risked losing NAFTA.

The contending wing, led by Kantor, tended to think of the NAFTA as a flawed agreement and the side agreements as necessary fixes. Kantor was convinced that the Mexicans wanted NAFTA badly enough to accept whatever the United States demanded and that Congressional approval would require side agreements strong enough to sell to Democrats like Gephardt. Strong enough meant sanctions.

Bentsen won the first round. At an NEC meeting the first week of March, Bentsen spoke forcefully about the virtues of NAFTA and opposed the use of trade sanctions to enforce environment and labor laws. EPA Administrator Carol Browner, having been convinced in her conversations with the Mexicans that they would not accept sanctions, concurred with Bentsen. Despite his views, Kantor agreed to hold off on sanctions. Only Labor Secretary Reich openly questioned the approach. "He asked, 'What happens if they still don't enforce their laws, and after everything it [the agreement] doesn't work?' " recalled one participant.

In Washington, word gets out quickly. Within days, rumors of the meeting passed among the trade insiders. The rumored decision not to insist on trade sanctions was greeted with relief by the business community, by NAFTA's core supporters on the Hill, and by the Mexicans and Canadians. Many of the mainstream environmental groups were also satisfied; for them sanctions had never been the key issue. But the game was far from over. A vocal part of the environmental community and the unions fought back, and Kantor remained unconvinced.

Appearing before the Senate Finance Committee on March 9, Kantor's testimony reflected the NEC decision. The labor and environment commissions would be forums for discussion and analysis; their authority would be to "review," not to "investigate." The commissions "will not have power to enforce laws in the United States or enforce laws in Mexico or Canada,"[14] he said. Two days later, however, Dick Gephardt issued a public warning. "I can't bring myself to vote for a treaty or agreements that simply are setting up a commission to kind of review the bidding and to complain to somebody that's not going to be able to do anything if the problems aren't being resolved," he said. "I will not support NAFTA on a leap of faith."[15] Behind the scenes, Max Baucus pushed Kantor to take a more aggressive posture. Baucus sent Kantor a letter stating that "Congress will not accept an agreement in which NACE is a toothless tiger relegated to environmental research and education."[16] Baucus insisted that the commissions have investigative powers and that trade sanctions be available to deal with persistent problems.

On March 16, the day before the opening of negotiations, Kantor was

back on the Hill, this time testifying before Baucus's Environment and Public Works Committee. Kantor took pains to flatter the chairman, calling his
proposal for a NACE "very impressive." There was a sharper tone to his
testimony. The commissions "would be able to request information from
environmental enforcement agencies in the three countries and pursue effective follow-up actions to ensure compliance," Kantor told the committee.
"The process must result in decisions that have real teeth and meaningful
results."[17] The meaning of "teeth" seemed pretty clear to some committee
members. When questioned by Senator Barbara Boxer (Democrat, Calif.),
a NAFTA critic, Kantor tried not to commit himself. Boxer replied, "To me
that [teeth] equals trade sanctions. . . . Anything less than that isn't going to
work," she said. "We need to be tough." The staff at the USTR could see
where this was heading. A call went out to the Mexicans and Canadians
warning them not to lock themselves in on the sanctions question.

On March 17, the three delegations finally met. None of the parties
tabled a position. The U.S. team described its conception of the commissions, that they be independent entities with permanent staffs capable of
investigating complaints. It deferred the issue of sanctions but intimated that
the issue would be raised in subsequent meetings. The Mexicans and Canadians presented no positions; they had primarily come to hear what the
United States had in mind. The Mexicans, however, made clear that they
would resist independent labor commissions with inspection power. Both
the Mexicans and Canadians warned that they would oppose the use of trade
sanctions. To underscore the point, chief Canadian negotiator John Weekes
told reporters that Canada would view the use of trade sanctions to enforce
such agreements as a "mistake."[18]

Renegotiating the U.S. Position

The next international meeting was scheduled for April 15. By that time,
the U.S. negotiating team intended to table a written position. Time was
passing, and there was a new sense of urgency about the international negotiation. But the battle to decide on an opening position was not over.

With the issue of whether the United States should insist upon sanctions
still unresolved, NAFTA's critics redoubled their efforts to pressure the Administration. The Citizen's Trade Campaign (CTC), by now a coalition of
70 consumer, environmental, agriculture, labor, and citizens' groups critical
of NAFTA, rallied in the Capitol on March 25. Dick Gephardt addressed

the rally: "There's got to be ultimate teeth—teeth, teeth [Laughter]—at the end of the day that cause the laws to be enforced." He also clarified another demand—that there be a secure source of funding for enforcement, environmental cleanup, and worker retraining—saying there must be an

> adequate, guaranteed, constant—these are all important words, you should pay particular attention to them—adequate, guaranteed, constant stream of revenues that will allow us to carry out these activities, that is, enforcement and remediation of environmental problems; that is, the building of infrastructure on both sides of the border; that is, training and job placement programs that are adequate to dealing with the structural adjustment problems in all three countries.[19]

By this time, the environmental community had split into two camps, with the Sierra Club, Greenpeace, and Friends of the Earth now participating actively with Public Citizen in the CTC. These groups issued a statement April 13 that said "NAFTA needs a dramatic recasting by the Clinton Administration if it is to promote and protect the environment, workers, consumer health and safety, agricultural and rural communities, as well as reflect democratic decision-making."[20] Friends of the Earth spokesman Brent Blackwelder gave a sense of the general CTC outlook at the press conference: "Any trade agreement which does not embody these principles paves the way for social disruption and environmental decline."[21]

Meanwhile, the more moderate environmental groups began meeting separately to put together a coherent set of demands that would be the price for their support. In March, Kathryn Fuller, president of the World Wildlife Fund, hosted a meeting of the WWF, NWF, NRDC, Audubon Society, Nature Conservancy, and the EDF. As a strategist with this group recalled, the six groups "decided that what was needed was input into U.S. negotiating position. They decided it was imperative to play the game, put down what they wanted, and work to get it incorporated in the negotiating position." The two wings of the environmental community were now playing very different games.

The USTR had hoped to be in a position to table a written position at the April 15 meetings in Mexico, but the internal debate over what position to take made it impossible to meet the deadline. The United States could do little more than elaborate on the proposals it had made verbally at the first meeting and continue to duck the sanctions question. The U.S. delay worried the Mexicans. "The Mexicans were very nervous," recalled Chip

Roh. "There were two dominant notes for the Mexicans: When are you going to move this thing? And how much do you really need? It was always very puzzling for them what we needed to get this through."

A front-page *Washington Post* headline on April 27 heightened Mexican anxieties. It read "Panetta: President in Trouble on Hill; Agenda at Risk, Trade Pact Dead." Leon Panetta, Clinton's head of the Office of Management and Budget, and a former House member, had spoken candidly with reporters the day before about the status of the president's budget and of NAFTA. He said what insiders already knew, that NAFTA would not win a vote in the House if it were held then.

Senator Bill Bradley was in Mexico City that morning, conferring with the Mexican Trade Minster, Jaime Serra, and his chief negotiator, Herminio Blanco, as part of his effort to prevent miscalculations from derailing NAFTA. Serra was very upset about Panetta's comments: Was NAFTA really dead? he asked. Bradley attempted to put the comments into context: Panetta was only saying that NAFTA would lose if the vote were held today, but the vote wouldn't come until the late summer, at the earliest. Bradley assured Serra that NAFTA could pass if the president put his full effort into lobbying for its passage. But first the side negotiations needed to be completed.

The Panetta comment caused a stir in Washington as well. To some it appeared to signal that the Administration was preparing to throw in the towel on NAFTA, confirming a persistent rumor that the White House was not really committed to the agreement. The rumor, spread in part as a matter of strategy by NAFTA's opponents, frustrated Kantor. "There was never, never a serious discussion in this Administration where the question was whether or not to do NAFTA," he said later. "The only question was how to do NAFTA. The president was committed to it. The president was emotionally and politically committed to it. And intellectually committed to it." The White House mobilized to put out the Panetta fire. The president suggested at a press conference that Panetta had just had a bad day. He remained committed to NAFTA and expected to win. Labor Secretary Bob Reich wrote a ringing endorsement of NAFTA for the *Wall Street Journal*.

The Panetta flap shifted the balance of power in the supplemental negotiations, giving the upper hand to those who favored a stronger negotiating position in the talks with Mexico, particularly the use of trade sanctions. Congressional Republicans began to get nervous. The day after the Panetta article, Senator Danforth garnered 27 Republican signatures on a letter to the president warning the Administration not to go too far with the side agreements. The letter stated, "We are concerned that the supplemental

agreements may undermine the benefits of the NAFTA if they place significant new regulatory burdens on the U.S. economy. NAFTA is first and
foremost a trade agreement. It cannot and should not be viewed as a means
of solving all environmental and labor problems in North America."[22] The
same day, the two most powerful Republicans on the Ways and Means Committee, Bill Archer and Bob Crane, sent the president an even more pointed
letter, which said, "Unfortunately, the debate surrounding the side deals and
the options now being discussed [have] raised our concern that there are
possible outcomes in the side-deal negotiations that will render the main
text unsupportable."[23] In particular, Archer and Crane warned, the commissions should not be empowered to impose sanctions or conduct independent investigations. Minority leader Bob Michel, his chief whip Newt
Gingrich, and sixteen other Republicans echoed the Archer-Crane letter
with a letter of their own: "We believe the side agreements should neither
infringe on U.S. sovereignty nor create trade sanctions for supposed environmental or labor non-compliance."[24]

But the winds were blowing against the Republicans. On May 4, Mickey
Kantor received another letter, this one from the moderate environmental
organizations—WWF, EDF, NWF, Nature Conservancy, Audubon Society,
NRDC, and Defenders of Wildlife—who had taken to calling themselves
the "Group of Seven." These groups' support was critical for NAFTA's prospects, and both they and Kantor knew it. The letter established what it would
take for them to support NAFTA. It called for an independent environmental
commission with the power to self-initiate investigations and make recommendations regarding enforcement. The commission would not itself have
the power to impose sanctions, but should it find a "pattern of a signatory
failing to comply with NACE recommendations," governments could initiate dispute settlement proceedings, with the possibility of imposing trade
sanctions. The interposition of national governments in the dispute settlement process represented a softer position than the environmentalists had
previously demanded, but the Group of Seven was now committed to trade
sanctions.

The environmentalists' letter represented the culmination of a negotiation among themselves: a collective judgment both about what was desirable
and what was feasible. For nearly two months, these organizations had
worked to establish a common position to present to the Administration as
the price for their support. Their position was a compromise between those
groups such as the WWF, for whom sanctions were not necessary, and others,

such as the NRDC, who needed sanctions to support the agreement. For the NRDC, in particular, the decision to sign had not been easy. Its leadership prided itself on being an aggressive player in the environmental community, often working closely with the Sierra Club and Friends of the Earth. Moreover, its membership was strongly anti-NAFTA. To support NAFTA, therefore, NRDC's leadership needed to be able to point to teeth in the side agreement. However, NRDC's leadership recognized that there were limits to how much they could get. In the end, recalled the NRDC's Justin Ward, "We signed because it was consistent with our basic recommendation and because we agreed with the perceived need to make a clear statement and remove doubt that we might just be along for the ride." As an indication of how close the NRDC came to not signing, after the letter was printed a line had to be added at the bottom for NRDC president John Adams's signature.

The environmentalists' letter publicly committed them. Their cards were on the table: If we get this, we will support NAFTA. Max Baucus immediately endorsed their position: "The proposal is substantive but reasonable — it offers a good road map for American negotiators. . . . [If the position is adopted], I, and many environmental groups, will strongly support NAFTA."[25] Baucus's endorsement both gave more weight to the environmentalists' position and more firmly committed them.

The moderates' tactic infuriated the more critical groups in the environmental community, who felt that it was too soft a position. "The letter caused all hell to break loose," recalled one staffer involved with drafting of the letter. Greenpeace, Friends of the Earth, the Sierra Club, and Public Citizen questioned the legitimacy of environmentalists they derided as "Bush advisors." Privately, they felt betrayed. For public consumption, the Sierra Club would say only that it had declined to sign the letter because it "fell short" of what was needed.

The May 4 letter and the Baucus endorsement did not come as any surprise to Mickey Kantor. He and his staff had been in close consultation with the moderate environmental organizations and with Max Baucus for most of April. Not surprisingly, then, the position was very close to where Kantor wanted to be. Now Kantor had more ammunition in his dealings with the Bentsen wing. In early May the NEC met again to consider the U.S. negotiating position. Kantor described how his consultations on the Hill had led him to conclude that there had to be teeth in the agreement, and that teeth meant sanctions. As Kantor later recalled, it was clear what we had to do. We couldn't have credible labor and environmental side agreements without sanctions. It just wouldn't work. How far we could go, how far the Mexican government would allow us to go, we didn't know, but that was a part of the negotiation. We had to have something at the end of the day that both Congress and the American people and the press would see had some teeth in it.

This time, Kantor carried the day. Lloyd Bentsen could see that the Administration was now boxed in and reluctantly conceded the issue. Bentsen had the last word, though. At the end of the meeting, recalled one participant, Bentsen said to Kantor, "Just don't lose NAFTA, Mickey."

The U.S. positions for the labor and environment side negotiations, virtually identical, came very close to the stance advocated by the moderate environmentalists. The commissions were to be reasonably independent and powerful, capable of investigating allegations of nonenforcement made by governments, by individuals, or by the secretariat of the commission. The commissions would not have subpoena power (as the environmentalists had requested) but could request information from governments. Most important politically, if the commission found a "persistent and unjustifiable pattern" of nonenforcement, a national government could request an international dispute panel to adjudicate the matter, and should a majority of the panel concur with the commission finding, it could authorize the complaining country to impose trade sanctions.

The labor unions and their allies on the Hill were somewhat pleased with the tougher U.S. bargaining position. "[The position] tabled in May was not that terrible," conceded Steve Beckman later. The Executive Council of the AFL-CIO decided once again to hold off on its campaign against NAFTA, once again over the strong objections of some of its members. On the Hill, Sander Levin (Democrat, Mich.) one of the leading Democrats critical of NAFTA, sent a letter to his colleagues urging them to delay taking a position in opposition. Dick Gephardt said he was asking members to avoid taking sides.

Republicans on the Hill were a good deal less happy. In an executive session of the Finance Committee on May 11, Republican Senators Bob Packwood, Jack Danforth, and John Chafee—the core of the Senate Republican support for NAFTA—expressed grave concerns to Mickey Kantor. All left the strong impression that their support for NAFTA was imperiled by what they saw. House Republicans reacted the same way. A staffer to Jim

Kolbe, NAFTA's most vocal supporter in the House, recalled being "amazed" and "dumbfounded" by the text of the U.S. position. This was "social charter stuff," he said. Kolbe went to the floor of the House to deliver a public warning:

> I fear the new administration is about to make a major mistake on this vital trade agreement. . . . The administration is pursuing a side agreement strategy based on appeasing interest groups while sacrificing broad support of the agreement. If adopted, the President's side agreement position would infringe on U.S. sovereignty and create a large supranational bureaucracy with broad investigatory powers.[26]

On May 14, the day before the international meeting, the USTR faxed copies of the U.S. negotiating position to the Mexicans and Canadians. Now the question was whether the negotiating partners could accept what the U.S. demanded, and if not, whether the USTR had much room to compromise. NAFTA's supporters were worried. The internal negotiations to establish the U.S. negotiating position had been so intense that there was now little flexibility. As Chip Roh later said, the concern was whether in the "interagency process we had gotten ourselves in a position that left us insufficient room to maneuver on either side."

Gridlock

The chief negotiators—Yerxa, Blanco, and Weekes—met May 17 in Hull, Canada, just outside of Ottawa. All three tabled a written position. It was quickly evident that although there was some overlap—all three agreed there should be international commissions of some sort—there was sharp disagreement about how independent and how powerful they should be, and, of course, about the question of enforcement.

The Mexican negotiators most strongly opposed the U.S. labor position. "The Mexicans opposed trade sanctions and opposed independent secretariats on both labor and environment," recalled Chip Roh. " 'All of this is impossible,' they said. But it was obvious to us that the Mexicans had a much more serious problem on labor than on the environment." The issues at stake in the labor side agreement cut to the heart of the Mexican political system—the dominance of business interests in the ruling coalition and the cozy relationship between the national unions and the ruling Partido Revolucionario Institucional (PRI). The U.S. proposal would make such sensitive matters as the minimum wage, child labor regulations, and especially, the right to organize subject to international scrutiny and possibly even sanctions. The Mexican opening position on labor, therefore, was that they would only agree to consultation and only on issues involving health and safety standards.

The Canadian delegation was less strongly opposed to international institutions, but they wanted to make sure that those institutions were firmly under national government control. As chief negotiator John Weekes later described it, the principle was that "the secretariat of an international organization should be accountable to national governments. The political ministerial should manage the secretariat." Weekes also made clear Canada's strong opposition to trade sanctions. "By the time we got to this point in NAFTA, we had a constituency in Canada who strongly opposed giving another trade remedy to the Americans," he recalled. He was not moved by arguments that the standard the U.S. proposed of a "persistent and unjustifiable pattern" made it unlikely that trade sanctions would ever be used. "The feeling was that if something was there that could be tested and tried, people will try to use it."

At a press conference after the meeting, Weekes went public with his opposition. "We . . . have encountered some serious difficulties, particularly regarding the manner in which the secretariat might operate," Weekes said. "We have difficulties as well in the area of dispute settlement, including the use of trade sanctions."[27] Privately, Blanco shared Weekes's views and threatened to go public too, but U.S. chief negotiator Rufus Yerxa persuaded him not to voice his opposition. As one participant in the talks recalled, Yerxa said, "If you want to blow up the negotiations, go ahead." At the press conference Blanco merely observed that "differences are only natural" at this stage of negotiations. For his part, Yerxa defended the American approach as "practical, reasonable and prudent."[28]

Yerxa's assessment of the U.S. negotiating position was not shared by the U.S. business community. The proposal was "outrageous" said one advisor close to the business effort. "The business community decided that the Administration had been very disingenuous in terms of cooperation. We decided it was all out war." Up to that point, the business community had not put its position in writing. Now the strategy changed. On June 4, a coalition of every major business organization in the United States sent Mickey Kantor a letter. The letter was an unmistakable warning:

> We are concerned that the U.S. draft negotiating texts for the supplemental agreements have flaws that could undermine the agreements' potential to improve environmental and labor conditions. . . . The Secretariat is too independent of the Council and enjoys overly broad powers. . . . [The proposal] threatens to create a new, politically unaccountable bureaucracy. . . . [Trade sanctions are] unnecessary [and] counterproductive [and would] set a perilous precedent for imposition of trade sanctions by or against the United States to address such issues as human rights, civil rights, and any other type of disfavored noncommercial behavior.[29]

At the USTR, Mickey Kantor was livid. To him the debate over the U.S. negotiating position was over. The U.S. had a position. American business should get in line and support it. "[The letter] slapped us right in the face," he later recalled. "It undercut what we were trying to achieve. It gave aid and comfort to those who say you shouldn't have teeth in the side agreements, and it threatened the coalition we were building."

On the Hill, Max Baucus was equally furious. He had firmly staked himself to the USTR position on trade sanctions with a floor speech in late May. "Without trade sanctions as a last resort," he said, "NAFTA is not in this country's best interest. . . . Simply put: No teeth, no NAFTA. The threat of sanctions is a necessary deterrent." Baucus seemed to take the business letter personally. He issued an extraordinarily sharp press release charging that business "is more interested in its profits—and in embarrassing Clinton in the international sphere—than about the basic enforcement of laws that stand to better the lives of every person in the North America."[30] The pattern of increasingly definitive and public commitments on the sanctions issue— by Kantor, Baucus, and Gephardt on one side and by Danforth and Kolbe on the other; by the U.S. environmental and business communities; and by the Canadians and the Mexicans—left very little space for agreement. Less public, but equally difficult, was the fundamental incompatibility between the U.S. commitment to a labor agreement equivalent to the environmental accord and the Mexican refusal to consider anything of the kind. The negotiations were gridlocked. As Rufus Yerxa put it at the time, "We are between a rock and a hard place."

Breaking the Impasse

NAFTA's supporters were now in a state of high anxiety. With the talks stalled, NAFTA's political opponents in the United States had seized the upper hand. Ross Perot had now launched an all out assault on the agreement, beginning with a half-hour "infomercial" he paid CNN to broadcast on May 30. In response to Perot's appeal to stop NAFTA, opponents flooded Capitol Hill offices with thousands of "NAFTA NO!" postcards. It began to appear that NAFTA might be swept away by the rush of events. The negotiations are "not going well," conceded Kantor's chief of staff. Behind the scenes, in the Administration, on Capitol Hill, in the business and environment communities, in Mexico City and Ottawa, NAFTA supporters scrambled to find a way to unlock the negotiations. The goal was to calm things down and search for creative ways to break the impasse.

The United States took a new approach to the labor negotiations, which clearly were not going anywhere. The position tabled in May had mirrored the environmental position, much to the frustration of the U.S. Department of Labor. Now, the ball was handed back to that agency. Larry Katz, chief economist at the Labor Department, believed a different approach was necessary. "[The Mexicans] wouldn't play ball until we came up with a different structure," he recalled later. Katz took another approach. "We believed that the U.S. government should have more control over it," he recalled.

In the new U.S. proposal complaints by private citizens would go to "national administrative offices" instead of to the international institutions themselves. National governments could then decide whether the claims had sufficient merit to begin international consultation. Should consultation break down, a vote of two out of three countries could convene an "evaluation committee of experts" to look into the matter and report to the ministers. Should that leave the issue unsettled, a government could initiate dispute settlement procedures as in the environmental accord. Although the approach sacrificed independence, in Katz's view it "would be more effective and less likely to go off half-baked." U.S. labor unions, while still far from supporting NAFTA, were also more comfortable with an approach that gave political control to national political institutions rather than international entities.

On the issue of whether trade sanctions might serve as the ultimate tool for enforcement of labor and environmental laws, Kantor urged the business community to relent. He argued that the standard of "persistent and unjustifiable pattern" and the involved process leading up to trade sanctions made it highly unlikely that they would ever be used. Quietly, other officials at the USTR pointed out to business leaders that the powers and degree of independence of the commissions should be more important issues to the business community. The USTR also had similar conversations with business's Republican allies on the Hill, urging them not to stake out a position in absolute opposition to sanctions.

Several players began looking for a middle ground. Lobbyists for the business community quietly floated the idea of fines as an alternative to sanctions, sending this suggestion to officials at the USTR and friendly staffers on the Hill. On the other side of the conflict, Bill Bradley met with officials from the seven moderate environmental organizations that had signed the May 4 letter to Kantor to get a clearer idea of their priorities and to urge them not to lock themselves into a fixed position. The environmentalists were more interested in a strong and independent commission than trade sanctions, and they also wanted more progress on the parallel matter of funding for border cleanup. Bradley conveyed the groups' concerns to Kantor, along with his sense of what it would take to win their support. At the USTR, the idea of fines found some sympathy.

Despite the flexibility in both the environment and business communities that might have allowed some softening of the U.S. position, Kantor remained committed to trade sanctions. The hint of compromise in the air triggered an effort by Baucus and Gephardt to shore up the Administration's position on the issue. Both let it be known that they believed only trade sanctions were sufficiently strong to win their support.

The chief negotiators met July 8 in Cocoyoc, Mexico, to try to restart negotiations. The negotiators presented no new papers, but they each floated some new ideas. The United States described its new thinking for the labor negotiation. The Mexicans were considerably more receptive to the idea of administrative offices under firm national control. For environment, the Mexicans and Canadians both indicated that they could accept more autonomy for the international commissions than they had before. On the question of sanctions there was little progress, although Weekes indicated that Canada would soon propose an option involving fines instead of trade sanctions, a prospect that the United States did not reject outright.

The talks renewed optimism. "I think this has been a very good two days of meetings," said Rufus Yerxa. "I believe we are on a very clear path toward success."[31] Nevertheless, tough issues remained. On the enforcement question, although new ideas were in the air, the U.S. remained committed to trade sanctions, and the Mexicans and Canadians remained opposed. Rumors that the United States had backed away from the insistence on sanctions forced Kantor to reiterate his stance publicly, further cementing the U.S. position. "We have not changed our position at all. . . . We want real teeth, real enforcement," he told a press conference.[32] And on the labor negotiations, although agreement on structure constituted a breakthrough, the Mexicans were insisting on covering only worker health and safety—not minimum wage, child labor, or industrial relations—the other issues the United States and Canada wanted to include.

The chief negotiators met again two weeks later in Ottawa, this time with written positions spelling out the understandings of the previous meeting. The idea was to put together a bracketed single text for the first time. The parties were largely in agreement on the basic administrative structure and on several other points. But the exercise of combining texts also made clear that significant differences remained. The information gathering powers of the commissions remained in contention. The Mexican position on labor seemed to have hardened, with the positions still very far apart. And, of course, there remained the vexing enforcement issue.

The three negotiators decided they needed to draw attention to the difficulties they were encountering. Normally, they hid whatever differences they had when talking with the press. This time they decided to make public their differences. Said John Weekes later, "The three of us agreed we were at a serious impasse. We thought it was important for people in all three countries who had a stake in managing it to understand what was going on at the negotiating table." At the press conference, Yerxa acknowledged that "there are a number of areas in the agreement that seem . . . to be close to finalizing. But there are some other areas that, quite frankly, we're still at some odds [about]." Said Weekes, "Sometimes the . . . nuts that are the hardest to crack are the ones that are left to the end."[33]

Canada's situation was now complicated by changes on the home front. Prime Minister Brian Mulroney, deeply unpopular largely because of his handling of Canada's ongoing Constitutional crisis related to the status of Quebec, stepped down and handed over his office to Kim Campbell, a young and politically untried Conservative member of Parliament. Campbell faced a daunting political challenge of reviving her party in time for the general election, now scheduled for October 25. Campbell's political situation made compromise difficult. In an interview published shortly after taking office, Campbell let it be known that she was determined not to let the United States dominate Canada. She drew an analogy to the battle of the sexes. "I think the same thing holds between women and men because males' life experience, reality, tends to dominate society," she told the interviewer; this was hardly the language of someone laying the groundwork for compromise.[34]

When Mickey Kantor, Herminio Blanco, and Tom Hockin, Kim Campbell's new trade minister, met the last week of July in Washington, they hoped they might be able to wrap up the talks. But the two days of meetings were largely a chance to gauge how much progress had been made by their negotiators in Cocoyoc and Ottawa. The list of issues still to be decided was now considerably shorter, but they were tough issues. Time, too, was running short. If the talks did not conclude in the next two weeks, they would almost certainly spill over to the fall, making it all but impossible for the U.S. Congress to act in 1993. They agreed to meet again the next week, at the Madison Hotel in Washington, and continue meeting until they finished.

Endgame at the Madison

Now the pressure to reach agreement grew even greater. The Clinton Administration had intended that the side agreements be completed after the president's budget passed Congress but before the members left Washington for the traditional August recess. As the budget vote was pushed later and later in the summer, the window for completing the agreements got smaller and smaller. Congress was now scheduled to go into recess on Friday, August 6. That left one week to bridge the still considerable gaps between positions. By now the Mexicans were extremely nervous about NAFTA's prospects. Support for NAFTA was beginning to erode in Mexico. If the side agreements were not completed very soon, NAFTA would not pass Congress in the fall, with the likely consequence that it would begin to complicate the Mexican presidential election of 1994.

The negotiating teams met through the weekend and into the beginning of the week. Their charge was to clear away the lesser issues so that the trade ministers could resolve the final issues on Wednesday and Thursday. Canadian trade minister Tom Hockin, however, served notice that resolving the enforcement issues would not be easy. Before leaving Ottawa for Washington, he told reporters, "I am against trade sanctions and I will continue to carry that message to Washington. I am not changing my position. . . . We do not want the side agreements to be a back-door which allows protectionists to have a new game they can play to be protectionist," he added.[35] Lest this be misunderstood, at a formal dinner at Blair House on Wednesday, hosted by Mickey Kantor, he said Canada would "never, never agree to sanctions," a phrase he subsequently repeated for the press.

Meanwhile, on the U.S. side, Baucus and Gephardt moved to shore up what they perceived to be a faltering U.S. position. The week before, Baucus had sent Kantor a letter warning that fines alone would not be enough: "You have said many times that the administration will not send NAFTA to Congress for a vote unless these side agreements have teeth. Even dentures will not do. I urge you to remind Canada and Mexico this week of the importance of these side agreements to NAFTA's passage in the Congress."[36] On Tuesday, Gephardt joined Baucus in writing a letter urging Kantor not to bow to pressure from business and "our trading partners" on sanctions.[37]

On Wednesday, the ministerial talks appeared to be going well. Jaime Serra told the press that "we are working and we are making progress." The ministers settled the remaining issues concerning the structure and functions of the commissions. Most importantly, the Mexicans finally agreed to accept the U.S. proposal on enforcement, a scheme in which fines of up to $20 million could be assessed for failures to enforce national laws and in which trade sanctions would be used only if a country failed to pay the fines. This solution allowed the Mexicans to assert that sanctions would never be used, because each country could be counted on to pay any fines, and the Americans to say that the agreement allowed the use of trade sanctions. The word in Washington was that the talks would end Friday, Saturday at the latest. But the talks bogged down after all, dragging through Friday and into the weekend.

Mexico simply refused to accept the fines-sanctions enforcement scheme for anything other than environment and worker health and safety issues. On enforcement of minimum wage and child labor laws, they would accept only that disputes could be referred to a committee of experts for a recommendation. And for industrial relations laws—the right to organize and to strike—they refused anything other than consultations. U.S. labor leaders blamed the Mexican unions for Mexico's intransigence. Recalled the AFL-CIO's Mark Anderson, "Mexico tentatively agreed to keep industrial relations in, but our CTM [Confederacion de Trabajadores de Mexico, the

Confederation of Mexican Workers] brothers didn't want competition in Mexico." Even more problematic, the Canadians balked at even the remote possibility of trade sanctions for any disputes.

On Monday, August 9, Kantor decided he simply had to finish, and he agreed to the Mexican limitations on the labor agreement. Now the only remaining issue was Canadian acceptance of trade sanctions. If Canada agreed, they were done. If not, things might completely fall apart. Minister Hockin left for Canada to discuss the issue with Prime Minister Campbell and the cabinet. Although they had been warned otherwise, U.S. and Mexican officials believed that in the end Canada would swallow hard and agree. "We thought we had given enough," recalled USTR General Counsel Ira Shapiro. Kantor scheduled a press conference Tuesday morning to announce the agreement. Chief Negotiator Rufus Yerxa left with his family for a well-deserved vacation.

But on Tuesday morning, instead of announcing a deal, Kantor read a short written statement from Hockin, Serra, and himself that said that they had not reached agreement. To the consternation of the United States and Mexico, Kim Campbell and her cabinet had decided to say "no." Campbell issued a statement saying that she was "not satisfied that Canada would not ultimately be exposed to trade sanctions."

Canadian chief negotiation John Weekes later expressed puzzlement that the decision came as a surprise: "We said we weren't prepared to accept it. I don't know how our position could be misinterpreted. . . . It was clear from the position that [Hockin] was taking at the bargaining table that he wasn't going to recommend sanctions." Moreover, Campbell was down in the polls, facing an election in the fall and had made a public commitment on the issue. Standing up to the Americans was good politics. Caving in would not play well.

In Washington, the Canadian decision touched off a mad scramble. Kantor's first reaction to the news was that the USTR had lost the most important piece in terms of symbolism. As Kantor recalled later, "There was some disappointment in the Canadians' position because we all had agreed and they had backtracked. On the other hand, they had their own problems; they were going through an election, and you know, in Canada, trade is a major issue." (In fact, Canadian negotiators never actually agreed, although the U.S. and Mexican negotiators expected them to.) Kantor worried about the reaction on the Hill if he let Canada off the sanctions hook. In Mexico, officials did considerable soul searching. "The process came close to becoming unmanageable," recalled Weekes. The negotiators fell out of touch for a couple days.

The Clinton Administration now faced a choice. Having failed to complete the supplemental negotiations before Congress left town for the August recess, should they reach agreement as quickly as possible or should the negotiators take a break and aim to finish late in the month or early in September, when the White House would be better able to mount a campaign for it? A group at the NEC favored waiting, as did many of NAFTA's supporters on the Hill. But at the USTR, Ira Shapiro disagreed. "I was of the view that we had to finish," he recalled. "The Mexicans were saying that if we didn't finish, support would erode in Mexico. I knew the opposition was out there [in the United States] and that we would get beaten up in August, but . . . when Jaime was saying that support was eroding in Mexico I believed him. There was a limit beyond which the Mexicans could not be pushed." And they were running out of time. "There was no way for us to come back, finish the supplementals in September, and get legislation through in the fall," recalled Shapiro. Kantor agreed with Shapiro and decided to try to find a way to finish. Kantor had a long talk with the president. Kantor argued against delay. We should finish now while we have the momentum, he asserted. The president agreed. Now Kantor just had to find a way to do it.

Lurking behind the dispute over strategy was a question of Clinton Administration priorities. The budget battle had not only pushed NAFTA back, it had also delayed the centerpiece of the Clinton presidency, the health care reform effort run by First Lady Hillary Clinton. At a meeting in the White House solarium on Wednesday night, the president's cabinet and staff debated which issue should now come first, health care or NAFTA. The health care team argued that they had waited long enough. They should concentrate on pushing health care now. If NAFTA needed to wait until spring, so be it, they argued. The meeting resolved nothing.[38]

Kantor's problem was compounded by the fact that the Canadians were not the only ones unhappy with the terms of the proposal that had been nearly accepted on Monday. Officials at the Department of Labor were outraged that he had accepted the limitations demanded by the Mexicans. "We went berserk," recalled Larry Katz. The feeling at the Department of Labor was that Kantor had not pushed hard enough on the labor front and that he had stopped much too soon. Moreover, a labor agreement perceived as weaker than the environmental accord would create problems on the Hill.

Dick Gephardt stepped in to reinforce the point, asserting that this agreement was not acceptable to him and the Administration would need to get more concessions to gain his support.

The USTR tried to pin Gephardt down. What did he need? Gephardt's trade assistant, Mike Wessell, represented his boss. Wessell gave a list of demands: Trade sanctions needed to apply to the full range of environment and labor issues. There needed to be a secure source of funding for border cleanup. And there needed to be a guarantee that Mexican wages would rise with productivity. None of these were altogether new demands, but it wasn't clear how much was enough. Recalled Larry Katz later, "Mike Wessell and Gephardt set out so many conditions. . . . It was never clear which one mattered most. They never said, if you do these three things then we will support [NAFTA]."

Some at the USTR also felt that Gephardt was raising the bar. "For example, Gephardt and Wessell always said there had to be dedicated funding," recalled a senior official at the USTR. "At first, this meant we had to find ways to pay for it. Then it meant that it couldn't be paid for out of existing revenues. Then it meant not out of appropriated revenues. By the end it had to be a cross-border fee." On the issue of linking wages with productivity, the Mexicans were prepared to promise a link to minimum wage, but Gephardt insisted that average wage be linked to productivity gains, an idea being pushed by political economist Harley Shaiken, but a kind of government intervention in the market that few economists endorse. Recalled Katz, "There was no way we could do what Harley Shaiken wanted, but there was no way we could pull Gephardt away from this."

Whatever the suspicions at the USTR, Kantor decided that he needed to make one more effort to get Gephardt's support. "We were counting Democratic votes, potential votes, and kept going back to those who were critical, including the majority leader," he recalled. "[We were] trying to satisfy them that there was enough there." On Wednesday, he reopened the talks with the Mexicans on the labor issues. No one at the USTR was too pleased with this development. "It is a miserable experience when you have to go back to the well," recalled Chip Roh.

The Mexicans were furious. They thought they had an agreement. Now the Americans were back for more. The sense was, if we agree to this now, what will the United States want next? On Thursday morning, Jaime Serra called Bill Bradley at home in New Jersey. Serra explained the situation. The United States now was insisting that enforcement of minimum wage, child labor, and industrial relations laws be subject to the same dispute settlement procedures as worker health and safety. The United States also wanted some promise that wages would be linked to productivity. Serra was very reluctant to reopen negotiations, but he wanted to know what the United States really needed and wanted some assurance that if Mexico made additional concessions, the United States would not come back for more. Could Bradley find out for him? Bradley agreed to talk to Kantor.

Kantor confirmed Serra's story and explained to Bradley that it was political necessity. Unless he could get more from the Mexicans, Gephardt and other Democrats would not support the agreement. Bradley called Serra back. Kantor really did have to get more, he explained. Where can you give? he asked. Serra intimated that he might be able to broaden the scope of the dispute settlement procedures to cover minimum wage and child labor laws, but that industrial relations was politically impossible for him. Mexico could also promise a link between minimum wage and productivity, but not between average wage and productivity, as Gephardt demanded. Bradley conveyed the information back to Kantor. Over the course of the day, Bradley played the role of mediator, carrying information back and forth between Kantor and Serra, and eventually between the two chiefs of staff, Mack McLarty and Pepe Cordoba.

Kantor and Gephardt spoke during the morning. Kantor sketched out where things were heading and what he thought he could get from the Mexicans. Gephardt was noncommittal. At that point Kantor recognized that Gephardt would probably never accede. Now he had to decide whether to conclude the agreements without Gephardt's support. Kantor called President Clinton, who was aboard Air Force One en route to Denver, and explained the situation. They agreed that they had to finish the talks, even without Gephardt's support. There was no more time to negotiate. Clinton tried to reach Gephardt by phone in the St. Louis airport, but they missed each other.

At days end, a conversation between Clinton and Salinas sealed the deal. Mexico would accept the full dispute resolution process on enforcement of child labor and minimum wage laws. Salinas promised a letter guaranteeing that the minimum wage would be pegged to manufacturing productivity. Clinton agreed to exempt industrial relations from dispute settlement and promised Salinas that there would be no further demands.

Kantor recognized later the importance of Bradley's role in brokering the endgame with Mexico. "He really understood that we had to get this done, and even though he didn't like some of what we were trying to do because he thought it was going too far, he understood the political necessity. Senator Bradley was an incredible help."

The Mexican problem, however, was not the only holdup; there was still the matter of how to handle Canada's refusal to accept trade sanctions. Canada was proposing to allow dispute settlement discussions to be enforced in Canadian courts, a concession the trade negotiators understood to be more effective than trade sanctions. For the United States, the issue was whether lack of sanctions for Canada affected how the agreements would be perceived on the Hill. After the initial moment of near panic, consultations with Congress members revealed that handling Canada differently did very little political damage. NAFTA's critics weren't worried about Canada. For the Mexicans, the issue was whether by accepting something that the Canadians had refused they would be vulnerable to charges that Mexico had sold out. Late Thursday the Mexicans decided it was a risk they would have to take. Recalled Canadian negotiator Weekes, "the Mexicans were the most eager to have the impasse unblocked."

Mexican negotiator Herminio Blanco called John Weekes around 6 o'clock Thursday evening and told him he was faxing a Mexican proposal, already cleared with the United States. Mexico could accept a different process for Canada. Weekes called his staff back into the office. Over the next few hours, the details were worked out in conference calls and faxes. Canada would not be subject to any trade sanctions. At around 3:00 A.M. Friday, August 13, 1993, the supplemental negotiations were over.

Reactions

On the morning of Friday, August 13, an exhausted Mickey Kantor announced the completion of the supplemental negotiations. He depicted the agreement as a promise fulfilled. "[President Clinton] made a promise to the American people which he has now kept, that he would make sure economic growth of Mexico and Canada does not come at the expense of the environment, and that the trade agreement addresses issues of basic worker rights, protection against child labor, health and safety, minimum wage, and industrial relation concerns."[39] The agreements, said Kantor, fixed the "major flaws" in the NAFTA that Clinton had inherited from Bush.

Not everyone in the United States agreed. Dick Gephardt issued a statement. "The agreements fall short in important aspects," he said. "I cannot support the agreement as it stands."[40] Kantor was later philosophical about Gephardt's decision to oppose. "He was *serious*, and studied, and he understood every detail of this, and he worked with it, and finally just couldn't bring himself to do it," Kantor said. The Mexicans were less philosophical. "We got the additional concessions because Serra was led to believe we would get Gephardt," recalled Ira Shapiro. "The Mexicans were frustrated and bitter."

At the National Press Club, the Citizen's Trade Campaign put its own spin on the agreements. Flanking CTC chair Jim Jontz at the conference were officials Willie Baker of the United Food and Commercial Workers Union, Bill Bywater of the International Union of Electronic, Electrical Salaried Machine and Furniture Workers (IUE), Ron Carey of the Teamsters Union, Evie Dubros of the International Ladies Garment Workers Union, and Bill Lucy of the American Federation of State, County, and Municipal Employees (AFSCME), along with Lori Wallach of Public Citizen, Jane Perkins of Friends of the Earth, and Mike Dunn of the National Farmers Union. Jontz summarized the coalition's views on the supplemental accords:

> These side deals aren't half a loaf. In fact, they aren't even half a slice. NAFTA is fundamentally an agreement to protect investors, to encourage them to go to Mexico to take advantage of low wages and lax environmental standards and enforcement. And nothing in the side agreements announced this morning will fundamentally change that. NAFTA is still a bad agreement for workers. It's still a bad agreement for the environment, it's still a bad agreement for family farmers, it's still a bad agreement for consumers.[41]

Bywater was even more blunt. "It's a sellout, and we're not going to stand for it," he said.[42] Lest there be any mistaking his meaning, Bywater made it even clearer later, when he spoke on CNN, "Anybody who votes for this agreement, we're going to defeat."[43]

Mickey Kantor left for a vacation in Europe. The next evening, while watching a fireworks display from the roof of a building in Geneva, Kantor stepped into an open airshaft, fell 12 feet and broke several vertebrae in his back. The accident seemed an omen of what was in store for NAFTA during August. Around Washington, there was talk of the curse of NAFTA.

Interpreting the Side Negotiations:
Issue Linkage, Deep Nesting, and
the Political Context

This chapter began with two basic questions. First, why side negotiations? Why did the United States, having agreed to terms in August 1992, change its mind and insist on reopening negotiations in January 1993? Second, why *these* side agreements? Why did the United States demand, Mexico accept, and Canada reject the use of international trade sanctions to ensure enforcement of domestic environmental and labor laws? Why did these countries create different institutions for labor and environment?

Through what analytic lens should we view these questions? For the question of why side negotiations, international-level theory is unlikely to be satisfactory. Nothing much changed in the international arena between August 1992 and January 1993. Rather, the demand for side negotiations arose out of the need to solve a domestic political problem in the heat of a U.S. presidential campaign. For the question of why these particular agreements, the stances taken in the negotiations and the pattern of international bargaining are difficult to explain as manifestations of national interests interacting in the international arena. The bargaining positions of the United States in these talks was quite obviously established only through an intense internal negotiation. Thus, these questions can be more usefully interpreted in terms of a two-level bargain in which contending interests at the domestic level determine the behavior of national negotiators at the international level, as was the case in interpreting the NAFTA negotiations themselves.

The two-level approach, however, has its limitations. First, by treating interest groups (or other aggregates) as the basic units in the model, two-level theory ignores any intragroup dynamics, much as international-level theories ignore domestic politics. This flattening may cost little in analytic precision when the groups in question have relatively homogeneous members and few internal collective-action problems, as is likely to be the case with a large business, such as GM. For other groups, however, particularly voluntary membership associations, trade unions, and political parties, intragroup dynamics may play important roles in determining the behavior of the group.

Second, by abstracting away the broader political context in which domestic-level bargains take place, two-level bargaining theory cannot explain who gets to play and who doesn't and why the rules of the game are as they are. As with any bargaining model, these characteristics are exogenously determined. In some cases this information may not be a significant problem, when, for instance, the puzzle is why a certain configuration of players and rules led to a particular outcome. But in other circumstances, it may be important to understand the focus that determines these parameters.

In the case of the NAFTA negotiations, a two-level bargaining approach can help explain why the side negotiations became necessary and much about the conduct and conclusion of those negotiations. However, it fails to explain adequately the bargaining behavior of key groups in the U.S. domestic negotiation, in particular why and how the mainstream environmental groups committed to trade sanctions and why the more politically powerful labor unions committed to positions that weakened their ability to influence the course of the international negotiations.

To explain these stances, we must extend negotiation theory in two ways. First, the two-level approach must be deepened to a third level, that of intragroup bargaining among individuals. In the side negotiations, bargaining processes were *deeply nested*, that is, bargaining among individuals within groups affected the bargaining behavior of groups at the domestic level and, therefore, ultimately of the nation at the international level. Second, we must widen the approach to consider the broader political landscape in which the domestic-level bargaining was *embedded*, which in the United States was determined largely by anticipation of the upcoming Congressional implementation process.

Issue Linkage: Adding the Side Negotiations

The U.S. decision to demand side agreements on environment and labor cannot easily be explained on the basis of national interests. If it was in the U.S. interest in 1993, why wasn't it before? The decision is better understood in terms of both the configuration of interests and the operation of political institutions in the U.S. domestic arena.

The Bush parallel accords on environment and labor, and the promise of an expanded labor-retraining program, was judged by the Bush administration to be an adequate side payment to win Congressional approval of NAFTA. This may have been a miscalculation, but the evidence suggests that the mainstream environmental groups were prepared to accept the deal in September 1992. (Labor unions were not, of course, but labor support was not judged to be politically necessary.) Less than a month later, the deal was off.

The reason for the change is obvious in one sense: Candidate Clinton promised labor and the environmentalists more. As the likelihood increased that Clinton would win the presidency, environmental groups saw that it was to their advantage to wait. Then the question becomes, why did Clinton make this promise? To understand this, we must understand how the context in which Clinton formulated his position gave the environmental and labor groups greater leverage.

In the campaign context, the political problem had less to do with assembling a coalition to win eventual approval of NAFTA than it did with assembling a coalition to win the election in November. This gave both labor and environmental groups much greater leverage than they had enjoyed throughout the Bush administration (and for labor, a good deal more leverage than it had later, when passing NAFTA was the issue). Clinton needed their support. Business interests, on the other hand, had somewhat less leverage than before (or after the election), because the game was more public and because many business interests were more closely aligned with the Republicans anyway. Clinton's stance as announced in early October represented a compromise among these contending interests. Clinton would stick with NAFTA, but to mollify labor and to solidify environmental support, he promised to deliver more for them.

Once publicly committed, no way was left open for Clinton to back down after he won election. Moreover, the problem of Congressional ratification became more salient in 1993, and with a Democrat in the White House, the coalition needed to pass NAFTA had to include more Democrats than it would with a Republican president. This meant that side agreements were now a political imperative for Congressional approval. Mexico and Canada, recognizing that Clinton was committed and that Congress would insist, agreed to talk.

The decision to negotiate side agreements reflects both institutions and interests. The institution of the Bush Action Plan established the dimensions along which the side negotiations would be conducted. The balance of interests for and against NAFTA kept the issues alive and compelled Bush to try to make good on his pledges in the fall of 1992. That might have been the end of the matter, but the domestic institutional context changed: The

United States held a presidential election. That context empowered labor and environmental interests, weakened business interests, and compelled a commitment from candidate Clinton that would endure beyond the election and into his presidency.

Deep Nesting: Multilevel Bargaining in the Side Negotiations

Why did the side agreements take the form they did? For instance, why did the mechanism for ensuring enforcement of national laws allow the possibility that trade sanctions could be imposed on the United States and Mexico but not on Canada? Why did the labor agreement exempt some key issues from sanctions altogether and establish a less independent international institution than the environmental agreement?

An international-level interpretation of the side negotiations would explain the international outcome on the basis of national preferences. On the question of enforcement mechanism, the United States strongly favored a particular approach, one that involved trade sanctions but placed numerous procedural obstacles in the way of actually ever using them. Mexico preferred nothing and wanted enforcement as weak as possible, but it was willing to move toward the U.S. position because it was so eager to enter into the NAFTA. Canada was happy with some degree of enforcement on labor and environment, but it was less willing than Mexico to accept trade sanctions as the mechanism for enforcement. Given the strong U.S. attachment to trade sanctions and Canada's unwillingness to accept them, a three-way agreement was impossible. Mexico and the United States had a very small zone of possible agreement close to the U.S. optimum and agreed to a point in that zone. Canada opted out and settled separately with the United States and Mexico.

The differences between the environmental and labor accords, viewed through this lens, reflected national interests as well. In the labor talks, Mexico wanted as weak an agreement as possible and strongly resisted establishing an independent international institution and subjecting domestic labor relations practices to international review. The United States also wanted a weaker international institution and was more willing to exempt labor relations practices from the enforcement provisions because it was concerned they might be used against the United States. Canada had interests similar to those of the United States (but balked at trade sanctions).

This interpretation describes what happened, but it does not really explain it. In particular, it provides little basis for understanding the apparent U.S. preferences: for trade sanctions as the ultimate enforcement mechanism and for stronger, more independent institutions for the environment than for labor. Nor does the international-level analysis explain why Canada should be so adamant about trade sanctions or Mexico more willing to concede on environment than on labor.

Here a consideration of domestic-level bargaining among contending interests in all three countries is more helpful. With respect to the enforcement issue, the apparent U.S. interest in a particular enforcement mechanism can be explained as the outcome of a fiercely contested battle between two factions crucial to NAFTA's ultimate success: business and mainstream environment. The mainstream environmental groups committed in May to a position that included trade sanctions, thus compelling the United States to adopt them in the international negotiation. The business community, while opposed to sanctions, could not so credibly commit to abandoning NAFTA and conceded on sanctions. So did Mexico, but Canada, reflecting the opposition from domestic constituencies to the prospects of trade sanctions, refused to accept them and had to be exempted from the provision. (Canada's constraint had less to do with opposition by particular groups than with the symbolic significance of trade sanctions in the Canadian political context, a point discussed later in this chapter.)

With respect to the question of why the environmental accord was stronger than the labor accord, consideration of domestic-level bargaining can help explain both the U.S. and Mexican stance. The United States did not push as strongly on labor because labor interests had less leverage in the domestic-level bargain. Usually labor unions are a potent political force, but because labor had committed so firmly to a position that was nonnegotiable, either domestically with U.S. business interests (which were more opposed to a strong labor agreement than a strong environmental one) or internationally with the Mexicans, they lost much of the their ability to influence the international negotiation. In contrast, Mexican business interests, with the complicity of the unions, were considerably more resistant to concessions on labor than on environment, particularly on the critical issues of workplace governance.

Thinking on two levels goes a long way toward explaining the outcome of the negotiations. Some questions remain, however. First, why and how did the mainstream environmental organizations commit to a position on sanctions in May upon which their leaders had not previously insisted? Second, why did labor unions commit so firmly to a position that limited their ability to influence the course of the side negotiations? To answer these questions, we must examine a yet deeper level of negotiation, that within these groups at the individual level.

We have seen how bargaining processes among groups in the domestic arena can constrain the behavior of nations in international negotiations. By the same logic, bargaining processes within groups can constrain the behavior of those groups in domestic negotiations and, by extension, the behavior of nations in international negotiations.[44]

Consider the enforcement issue in the context of the environmental side negotiation. The commitment to trade sanctions by the mainstream environmentalists is better explained if we recognize that environmental groups are membership organizations, with their own internal bargaining processes. Representatives of these groups in the domestic-level bargain must balance personal policy preferences with the political imperative of attending to their members' concerns. Like the national negotiator at the next higher level, interest-group negotiators must be partly politicians. Under some circumstances, they may have considerable slack before encountering political constraints, particularly if group membership is inattentive, presumably the norm on many issues. On high-profile issues such as NAFTA, however, member preferences may be quite constraining. In this case, the evidence indicates that rank-and-file environmentalists were much more attached to enforcement mechanisms with "teeth" than were the professional staff members who represented them. As a result, the leadership of the mainstream groups had difficulty accepting anything less than trade sanctions.

Business interests, although themselves complex consortia of firms and trade associations, did not really have the same constituency problem as the environmental (or other membership) groups. Stockholders are too far removed from firm policy making to have much of an impact. Thus the absence of an individual layer of bargaining may actually have made it more difficult for business to credibly oppose sanctions.

Figure 6.1 provides a highly stylized graphical treatment of this interpretation. It depicts the negotiation over the enforcement mechanism in the environmental side negotiation as a three-level bargain in which intragroup bargaining defines the preferences of the group, which in turn defines the preferences of the nation in international bargaining. The issue is simplified to "teeth," a measure of the toughness of the enforcement mechanism, and ranges from "gums" to "fangs," in the language that defined the debate in Washington. As already discussed, at the international level, Mexico preferred no enforcement, but was willing to move part of the way toward fangs; Canada preferred some enforcement, but was unwilling to go as far as Mexico; and the United States had a distinct preference for moderately sharp teeth. These preferences leave no three-way zone of possible agreement (ZOPA), and the two-way ZOPA between the United States and Mexico is quite small and very close to the U.S. optimum.

As illustrated, the U.S. preferences revealed in the international-level bargain reflect the domestic-level bargain between the two factions whose support is crucial for NAFTA—business and the mainstream environmental

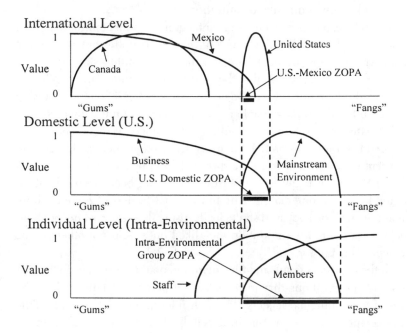

FIGURE 6.1 The negotiation over the strength of sanctions as a three-level bargain. Top: the international-level negotiation among the United States, Mexico, and Canada. Middle: the U.S. domestic-level negotiation between business and environment. Bottom: the individual-level negotiation between staff and rank-and-file members of a mainstream environmental group. The horizontal axis depicts the strength of possible sanctions from weak to strong using the dental metaphor so prominent in the debate. The thick line indicates the zone of possible agreement (ZOPA).

groups. Business interests are similar to those of Mexico's in the international-level bargain—minimal sanctions. The mainstream environmental groups have a fairly narrow set of acceptable agreements that range between sharp teeth and fangs. The ZOPA between the two is quite small and effectively defines the U.S. negotiating stance at the international level.

Mainstream environment's preferences at the domestic level reflect the individual-level bargain between members and staff. Staff are willing to accept more moderate sanctions while members insist that sanctions be as strong as possible. The ZOPA between the two defines the range of outcomes acceptable to the organization in the domestic-level bargain. Note that in this interpretation of the bargain, the ultimate constraint on the U.S. position in the international negotiation is imposed by the preferences of the memberships of key environmental organizations.

This model explains how environmental groups could commit to a point that staff would in all likelihood not have insisted upon, but it does not explain why the environmental organizations committed strongly in the summer of 1993 to a position that they did not insist upon earlier. Why did the leaders think they could agree to no sanctions earlier if their membership felt differently? The three possible explanations are not mutually exclusive. The first is that the position of the rank and file changed as members became convinced that there was problem that needed strong remedies. The second is that staff were constrained in the spring of 1993 by a third level of negotiation that did not really exist until the side issues became so salient for rank-and-file environmentalists. The third is that leaders of these environmental organizations behaved strategically, using their internal negotiations to help them commit to a position they liked but would not otherwise be able to credibly put forward.

Both the decision of rank-and-file environmentalists to engage on the side issues and the positions that they took were partially determined by the tactics of environmental leaders. Through internal newsletters and public pronouncements, environmental leaders helped to mobilize interest among their members and helped define what should be acceptable to them. Through this effort, environmental leaders could commit credibly to positions they might otherwise have had to abandon. Having told their members that NAFTA created environmental problems that could only be fixed by a side agreement with teeth, environmental leaders were implicitly contracted to pursue that end on their members' behalf and thus could not back down.

A three-level approach can also explain why labor unions adopted what seems a counterproductive strategy of committing to a nonnegotiable position. Labor unions are democratic institutions in which the positions of union members count. Union leaders who represent their constituencies in negotiations must cater to the preferences of union members. In the NAFTA side negotiation on labor, the very strong feelings of union members made it all but impossible for labor leaders to engage in a meaningful negotiation without paying a severe political penalty. Whether any side deal would have been acceptable to labor leaders on policy grounds is unknown, but in any event the leaders were far too constrained by internal union politics to explore the possibility.

The deeply nested nature of international negotiations raises the issue of how deeply the analyst needs to probe. One is tempted to answer: deep enough. In some circumstances, strong institutions, charismatic leadership, or internal consensus may make it unnecessary to consider intragroup dynamics to explain international outcomes. In other circumstances, however, the solution to puzzles about the behavior of nations in international bargaining may lie several levels below the international.

Embeddedness: The Side Negotiations in Political Context

Complex as it is, the multilevel bargaining approach abstracts negotiations away from much of the context in which they take place. Every negotiation is embedded in a broader political context of interests, institutions, and symbolic constructs that determine in large measure the overall structure of the negotiation: the configuration of levels, the key players at each level, and the rules by which they play. To the extent one is interested in the factors that determine these parameters and, therefore, the existence, location, and shape of constraints, one needs to consider the larger political context.

For example, implicit in the model of the environmental supplemental negotiation illustrated in Figure 6.1 was a decision rule in the U.S. domestic bargaining that required the support of certain "mainstream" environmental organizations. This rule gave those organizations considerable power. To explain why they had that power, however, one needs to consider the larger political context in which the environmental side negotiation was embedded.

Environmental groups had leverage in the NAFTA supplemental negotiations because of their location in the political landscape confronting the

Clinton administration, a landscape that included key opinion leaders such as Max Baucus, grassroots environmental organizations, the press, the general public, and ultimately and most importantly a group of Democratic representatives sensitive to voters' concerns about the environmental effects of NAFTA. Because the side negotiations were conducted in the shadow of the eventual vote in the United States Congress, whatever the policy problem, the USTR's political problem was to win a majority in both houses of Congress. Already it was clear that the House of Representatives posed the greater difficulty. One group of swing voters was composed of House Democrats who would otherwise be disposed to support NAFTA but who needed "cover" in dealing with constituents concerned that NAFTA was bad for the environment. Mickey Kantor and others in the administration could talk directly to these Congress members, but that approach would and did have little effect on the negotiation of greatest concern to the members, i.e., the negotiation with their constituents. Kantor, therefore, needed an indirect approach to influence House Democrats. The strategy was to map backward from the swing votes in the House to identify a path to them. As it happened, the mainstream environmentalists lay squarely on the only available path.

The problem for these Democrats was the widespread belief among voters with environmental concerns that NAFTA would be bad for the environment: that it would cause an environmental disaster on the border, that it would make Mexico a pollution haven, that it would undermine U.S. environmental laws, and the like. These beliefs had been fueled by press accounts of the horrors of the border region, by the Clinton campaign rhetoric, and by the tactical acquiescence of the mainstream groups who did not share these beliefs but who were in no hurry to refute the ideas. Members of Congress needed the press to say that the problems had been fixed by the supplemental agreements or at least to report that the environmental community was divided on the subject, thereby neutralizing the issue. The press would tell this story if and only if the mainstream groups blessed the supplemental agreement.

The grassroots environmental organizations played an important role in enhancing the leverage of the mainstream groups. In coordination with their union allies, grassroots environmentalists had been instrumental in creating the negative public impressions of the relationship between NAFTA and the environment. Without these attitudes, there would have been no problem that could only be solved by the support of the mainstream groups. Moreover, the grassroots organizations, directly and through the press, had an influence on the membership (and potential membership) of the mainstream groups, which in turn affected what members of those groups were willing to accept, thus constraining the domestic-level ZOPA in ways that worked to the mainstream groups' advantage (see Figure 6.1).

Thinking in these terms helps explain the surprisingly significant role played by Max Baucus in the environmental side negotiation. His vote did not matter directly; NAFTA appeared to have a comfortable margin in the Senate. Yet he emerged a player because of his standing with the press and with the mainstream environmentalists (and also because he was aggressive about using this position). As a consequence, a triangular negotiation among Mickey Kantor, the mainstream environmentalists, and Max Baucus ensued in which each party needed something from the other. Kantor needed the support of the environmentalists to help give House members political cover. The environmentalists needed Baucus because he helped them sell their position in their internal negotiations with members. Baucus wanted credit with his constituents and with the environmental community for advancing the environmental agenda. In this triangular negotiation, Baucus's insistence that trade sanctions be a central part of the U.S. negotiating position helped force both Kantor and the mainstream organizations into taking the same position.

This network of negotiations is only a subset of the still larger landscape in which it, too, was embedded. House Democrats, for instance, were obviously a subset of the whole House body and would not be a swing group but for the balance of support and opposition among other subsets of that body. Without the opposition of Congress members with strong labor ties, there would not have been such a large core of Democratic opponents in the House, and the environmentalists would have had less leverage. Similarly, without the opposition of a smaller group of conservative Republicans, the environmentalists' support would have been less critical.

The political analyst must exercise much judgment in deciding how broad the field of vision should be. There is no logical limit to the horizon: Every negotiation is embedded in a network of other negotiations, each of which is embedded in others, and so on. Deciding where to draw the boundary depends on the relative benefits of broadening compared with the costs of greater complexity. Sometimes much of the broader landscape can be safely suppressed, as in the commercial negotiations conducted largely out of the glare of public scrutiny and relatively far from the prospects of legislative action. In other circumstances—such as the side negotiations—elections, legislative processes, public opinion, and other features of the political landscape may need to be more explicitly considered.

Conclusions

This analytic commentary has built upon approaches developed in previous chapters. To explain why the United States demanded the side negotiations requires an examination of both domestic interests and institutions, in particular how the operation of a purely domestic institution—a presidential election—shifted power in the contest of domestic interests. To explain why the side agreements took the form they did requires extending the two-level bargaining approach developed in the previous chapter to include deeper-level bargaining processes and the larger political context in which the negotiations were embedded.

These extensions yield a rich understanding of the history of the side negotiations. That they were demanded by the United States reflects the confluence of a national election and opportunistic behavior by interest groups empowered by that context. That the negotiators concluded with these agreements reflects the complex interplay of interests at multiple levels, which together constrained the domain of the possible to the particular and peculiar outcomes observed. Some puzzles, however, remain to be explained. The nature of public attitudes that required a campaign commitment from candidate Clinton, the beliefs of individual members of environmental groups and labor unions that constrained the behavior of those institutions, and more generally the nature of the larger political environment in which the side negotiations took place all require thinking in terms other than interests and institutions. As the politics of NAFTA became more public in the United States, spilling out of the traditional institutions and beyond the normal trade interests to engage the larger polity, what the side agreements *were* became less important than what they *meant*, and symbolic constructions became more central. To fully understand this we will need a theory of the politics of meaning, to which we will turn in the next chapter.

Section III

The Politics of Ratification

7 Symbolic Politics: Growing Grassroots Opposition

With international agreement in the supplemental negotiations, NAFTA once again became largely a matter for U.S. domestic politics. It would become the biggest issue of the fall of 1993. Yet in Washington the debate started quietly. In August, official Washington becomes a ghost town. Everyone who can heads for the beaches of Maryland or Delaware. This year was no different, although the sense of exhaustion was perhaps even greater after the breakneck pace of the young Clinton administration and especially after the cliff-hanging drama of a narrow budget victory for the president.

If members of Congress were expecting a break when they left Washington for their home districts and states, however, they were soon disappointed. For months, a remarkably diverse collection of opponents had been targeting August as the month to kill NAFTA. They were ready. Across the country, union locals, chapters of Ross Perot's United We Stand, and an extraordinary network of grassroots environmental, human rights, and other groups packed town meetings, tied up phone lines to local Congressional offices, held rallies, and generally vented their fury at this thing called NAFTA.

As the politics of NAFTA moved outside the Washington Beltway—the freeway that circles the city and serves as a symbolic boundary between Washington "insiders" and "outsiders"—it also spilled out of the usual confined trade circles and into the public domain. In this arena, the opponents had the upper hand. Members of Congress home for the recess heard almost nothing from NAFTA's supporters and a furious earful from its opponents.

The August recess was "three weeks of Nirvana," recalled one of the opponents. For supporters, it was agony. By the end of the month, NAFTA appeared all but dead.

This chapter begins with a puzzle: Why, given the likely small effects of NAFTA—economic, environmental, and other—in the United States, did the agreement become such an enormous political issue? What accounts for the remarkable breadth of the opposition? How could Ralph Nader, Jesse Jackson, Ross Perot, Pat Buchanan, and Lane Kirkland find themselves on the same side of an issue? And, not least, what accounts for the extraordinary passion with which so many opposed an agreement that seemed likely to have so little immediate impact on their lives?

NAFTA's Effects

The public debate over NAFTA in the United States would revolve around several issues. First and foremost was the issue of jobs: Would NAFTA create or destroy jobs in the United States? Following closely in prominence were NAFTA's effects on the environment, public health and safety, and immigration. Other issues of concern were drug smuggling and human rights in Mexico. The public conversation on these issues would be only loosely connected to the likely real effects of the agreement.

Projecting the effects of an agreement as complex as NAFTA on phenomena as complex as jobs, the environment, immigration, drug smuggling, and Mexican human rights is extremely difficult. Numerous analyses, of varying quality, on all of these issues appeared throughout the effort to pass NAFTA. A sober critique of these studies, however, suggests that on balance, NAFTA's net effects on U.S. interests—whether jobs, environment, immigration, drugs, or human rights—was likely to be positive, although disagreement was reasonable. Regardless, almost every credible analysis concluded that whatever the direction of effect, the magnitude would likely be very small.

On the most politically important issue, the effect on jobs in the United States, the best estimates of NAFTA's impact predicted it would create over a ten year period somewhere between near zero and two hundred thousand new jobs, net.[1] (A study sponsored by the AFL-CIO [American Federation of Labor and Congress of Industrial Organizations] predicted losses of five hundred fifty thousand jobs, but to get that number required an assumption about investment diversion that few economists thought credible.) These are very small numbers. To put them in perspective, the U.S. economy typically expands by two hundred thousand jobs in a good month. There were two basic reasons for the small projections. First, NAFTA would have only a slight effect on how open the United States was to Mexican goods. The United States, with a few notable exceptions, was already quite open to trade. Moreover, given the existence of the maquiladora program, corporations that wished to manufacture in Mexico for export to the United States were already quite free to do so. Second, Mexico's economy was very small, less than 5 percent of the U.S. economy. Even large changes in the Mexican economy would, therefore, have only small effects on the economy in the United States. Of course, the likely magnitude of the economic impacts on Mexico were not so small.

The issue of NAFTA's effect on the environment had three faces: the effect on border pollution, the possibility that Mexico would become a "pollution haven" for firms seeking to avoid U.S. regulations, and the effect on U.S. environmental laws. On the question of border pollution, it was hard to conclude that NAFTA would have anything but positive effects. To the extent that the very real problems of the border were manifestations of concentrated rapid industrialization coupled with lax environmental regulation, NAFTA would help matters by eliminating the incentive to locate only on the border, by providing the catalyst for greater environmental cooperation between the United States and Mexico, and eventually (and predictably) providing an infusion of funds to remedy some of the worst of the region's problems.[2] NAFTA's effects on the overall environment of Mexico were harder to project and were dependent on, among other things, what one assumed about the relationship of economic development to environmental protection and about the future regulatory intentions of the Mexican government.[3]

There was also very little reason to believe that NAFTA would make Mexico a pollution haven. On the one hand, lower regulatory costs in Mexico already provided an incentive to relocate production, as several firms had already done. On the other hand, little evidence pointed to systematic relocation to Mexico for this reason. For few industries is regulatory cost more than a tiny fraction of the overall cost of doing business.[4] Most important, the likely marginal effect of NAFTA would be to reduce these incentives. Although NAFTA was intended to make investment in Mexico easier, the combination of Mexico's strong environmental laws and the existence of a watchdog international commission would likely narrow the gap in regulatory differences between Mexico and the United States.

On the question of whether NAFTA might erode U.S. environmental, health, and safety laws, it was highly unlikely that there would be significant effects. Because of environmental outcry on this issue, NAFTA contained language intended to protect against this possibility. Moreover, given the imbalances in political power, Mexico was not likely to challenge a U.S. environmental law. Corporations could use the threat of moving to Mexico as leverage to induce less stringent regulation, but NAFTA, as noted above, did little to make the threat of moving more credible.

NAFTA's likely impacts on immigration from Mexico to the United States were extremely difficult to project, as they depended on estimates of NAFTA's effects on the Mexican economy and particularly on the adjustment difficulties that Mexico might encounter. Most economic analyses suggested that NAFTA would contribute to growth in the Mexican economy over time, resulting in fewer incentives for Mexican workers to migrate. (Note that this is the implication of the strong anti-NAFTA analyses that foresaw jobs going to Mexico and wages being depressed in the United States.) On the other hand, NAFTA might cause significant dislocations in the Mexican economy in the more immediate future, as previously protected small businesses and, most importantly, farmers encountered foreign competition.[5] To a great extent, though, the estimated effects of NAFTA depended on whether or not one considered Mexican agricultural reform an independent initiative that would have proceeded without NAFTA, in which case the marginal contribution of NAFTA would be quite small. Whatever the direction of NAFTA's effects on migration, however, underlying economic and demographic factors in Mexico would continue to be much more important.

As the public debate heated up, NAFTA also stood accused of making it easier for the drug cartels to transport contraband across the border, thereby contributing to the U.S. drug problem. The reasoned case for this proposition rested on the presumption that a greater flow of goods from Mexico would make it more difficult for customs agents to carry out their duties. This argument presumed that current interdiction efforts were effective deterrents that would be significantly impaired by NAFTA. Customs officials countered that increased numbers of inspectors and greater cooperation with Mexican authorities would more than compensate for the dangers posed by increased flow of goods. (They did not argue that their current efforts were ineffective anyway.) Although the drug issue could not be completely dismissed, the likely effects of NAFTA on U.S. drug consumption were minimal.

On the issue of Mexican human rights, the key question was NAFTA's likely effect on the Mexican political system. Opponents charged that by rewarding the Salinas government the United States would further entrench a repressive political system. The United States was missing an opportunity to pressure Mexico to reform, they maintained. Some opponents simply stood on principle: "How can we have free trade with a country that isn't free?" asked Daniel Patrick Moynihan. NAFTA's supporters countered that rejecting NAFTA would empower the old guard in Mexico, the real enemies of political reform, and that economic reform would lay the groundwork for political change. Both arguments had some merit, but whatever NAFTA's real effects, they would almost certainly be much smaller that the effects of internal dynamics within Mexico, a point sometimes lost on both sides of the debate in the United States.

For all the issues that dominated the U.S. public debate about NAFTA, the likely effects were quite small relative to the effects of larger forces at work in the economy, the environment, and the society. Still, however small the real effects of NAFTA, the political apprehension of them was anything but. What NAFTA was to the experts and what NAFTA meant to the antagonists in the political struggle were two very different things. For the experts, evaluating NAFTA was a complicated matter, requiring distinctions between the marginal effects of NAFTA and underlying trends; understandings of complicated economic, environmental, and social systems; and processing of large amounts of information. For most participants in the political process, apprehending NAFTA was more a matter of deciding which story fit best. For the first part of 1993, the dominant story was told by NAFTA's opponents.

Organizing the Opposition

The opposition to NAFTA that boiled over in August did not arise spontaneously. It built on the 1991 efforts to deny fast track authority, on the protests lodged during the course of the negotiation, and on the opposition stirred by the presidential candidacies of Democrat Jerry Brown, Republican

Pat Buchanan, and especially, independent candidate Ross Perot in 1992. But the campaign to stop NAFTA took on greater urgency in the spring of 1993, as opponents looked toward the vote in Congress that would most likely take place later in the year.

Opposition strategists recognized the challenge that faced them. If the contest over NAFTA turned out to be trade politics as usual they stood little chance. Their strength did not lie in the inside game of trade lobbyists and trade experts. To win, they would need to change the rules of the trade policy making game. They would need to mount an outside campaign, mobilizing members of unions, environmental organizations, citizen groups, Ross Perot's followers, conservative and religious groups, and others in the general public to pressure Washington from the grassroots.

The Unions

There was never any real doubt whether unions would oppose NAFTA, the question was how aggressive and how effective the opposition would be. Unions had blasted the "Bush NAFTA," and they saw little chance that Clinton's side agreements would change it fundamentally. To the unions, NAFTA symbolized lost jobs and lower wages. It was designed to make it easier for big business to escape unions, as well as environmental and safety regulations, by moving production to Mexico. It was one more chapter of the antiunion, probusiness Reagan-Bush agenda that was making the rich richer and working Americans poorer. At the annual AFL-CIO meeting in Bal Harbour, Florida, in February 1993, the Executive Council stated that

> the proposed North American Free Trade Agreement, signed by President Bush but not approved by Congress, would be a disaster for millions of working people in the United States, Canada, and Mexico. It should be rejected and renegotiated to advance the overall public interest. As drafted, NAFTA is an agreement based solely on exploitation. It would destroy jobs and depress wages in the U.S. and Canada. . . .[6]

But union leaders were in a strategic quandary. Notwithstanding their antipathy to NAFTA, they had little incentive to attack the first Democratic president in twelve years, and every reason to give Clinton time to make good on his campaign promise to fix the agreement, or better yet, to abandon it altogether. Willingness to give Clinton time was not shared by more activist union officials, nor was it universal among the rank and file. The Teamsters, the textile and garment unions, the electrical workers union, the glass union, and others within the movement took a more aggressive stance. State and local union chapters pressed forward largely independent of the national effort with their anti-NAFTA campaign. In many states, unionists mounted campaigns against NAFTA that included rallies, phone calls, and personal visits during the Easter recess, when Congress members were back in the their districts. Still, the official rallying cry of the AFL-CIO in the spring of 1993 was "Not This NAFTA," a motto that seemed to leave open the possibility that they would support it with the right side agreements. The consequence of the differences within the unions was a somewhat disjointed strategy.

The AFL-CIO continued its efforts to focus attention on the problems of the border as tangible evidence of what free trade with Mexico would mean. The union organized tours of the border for members of Congress and the press, intended both to educate members and to generate negative publicity regarding border problems. The trips involved visits to the *colonias* to talk with poor residents and to factory plants to talk with workers, as well as meetings with local activists. These trips had been going on since 1991, when a leadership group that included Dick Gephardt first went down to the border.

After Clinton's election, Gephardt decided he wanted to do a series of additional trips. "Gephardt was really impressed with the advantages of having a first-hand look at the practices of the companies in the *maquiladoras* and about how hard it was for U.S. companies to be able to compete with workers being paid $1 an hour," recalled Ed Feigen, the union organizer of these trips. He led several groups to the border in 1993, including a group of new Congress members. In April, Representative Marcy Kaptur (Democrat, Ohio) led a group of women Representatives on a similar tour. Senator Paul Wellstone (Democrat, Minn.) led yet another group.

Union publications covered the trips for their members. For instance, the *AFL-CIO News* reported that "after a grueling tour of the festering toxic dumps and poverty-ridden worker villages south of the border," the House members "agreed that Congress should dump the North American Free Trade Agreement as negotiated by the Bush administration." Studies have shown, it continued, that "500,000 U.S. jobs had been lost to the maquila-doras during the 1980s and another half-million jobs would be wiped out in the 1990s under the flawed NAFTA."[7]

In early May, the AFL-CIO officially launched its "Not This NAFTA" campaign, using billboards, radio ads, posters, and other media. Neverthe-less, at the highest levels, union officials continued to debate whether to launch an all-out campaign against the agreement. The ambiguity of this stance resulted in fewer resources being devoted to the campaign. Although many events were taking place locally around the country, at AFL-CIO headquarters in Washington, the "Not this NAFTA" effort operated with only a tiny staff. At the United Auto Workers (UAW) offices in Washington, only two people were working on NAFTA. For others in the coalition against NAFTA, including many unions, the AFL-CIO's less than total commitment became a source of frustration.

The Citizen's Trade Campaign

More activist unions gravitated toward the Citizen's Trade Campaign (CTC), the coalition of grassroots organizations opposed to NAFTA. CTC succeeded the Citizen's Trade Watch coalition that had first formed during the fast track fight and had continued to monitor the course of the NAFTA negotiations. The CTC brought together a remarkably broad collection of organizations under one tent. The CTC described itself in on its letterhead as "a coalition of environmental, consumer, labor, family farm, religious, and civic organizations promoting environmental and social justice in trade policy." The executive committee included John Audley of the Sierra Club; Brent Blackwelder of Friends of the Earth; Evelyn Dubrow of the Interna-tional Ladies Garment Workers Union; Michael Dunn of the National Farmers Union; Mark Ritchie of the Institute for Agriculture and Trade Policy; Lauren Rothfarb of the International Union of Electronic, Technical, Salaried Machine and Furniture Workers Union; Liz Smith of the Amal-gamated Clothing and Textile Workers Union; and Lori Wallach of Public Citizen. Other members of the coalition included Jesse Jackson's National Rainbow Coalition, the United Methodists General Board of Church and Society, the Humane Society, Greenpeace, and Americans for Democratic Action.

At a March press conference announcing its campaign against NAFTA,

Jim Jontz, a former Indiana Congressman serving as the campaign's chair, stated the common view of the groups: "This agreement is fundamentally flawed. It would serve the interests of multinational corporations and not average citizens."[8] The CTC's position statement elaborated the point:

Coalition members are united in the position that the North American Free Trade Agreement (NAFTA) is fundamentally flawed, and therefore, unacceptable. It will encourage companies to move operations and factories to areas of cheap labor and lax environmental and worker safety regulation. It will result in a lower standard of living, disruption of our communities, and irreparable harm to our environment. NAFTA undermines the gains we have achieved over the years in food safety, labor standards and environmental protection.[9]

The CTC also worked closely with the Alliance for Responsible Trade (ART), successor to the MODTLE (Mobilization on Development, Trade, Labor, and the Environment) coalition that had organized during the fast track fight. Like MODTLE, ART was organized by Pharis Harvey, head of the International Labor Rights Education and Research Fund (ILRERF). An ILRERF book of 1982 entitled *Unions and Free Trade* captured many of the beliefs about NAFTA shared by the entire grassroots opposition:

The North American Free Trade Agreement is not about the commerce of nations. This treaty that binds the United States, Canada, and Mexico in economic union is more about corporate profit than about trade. It is about letting private businesses reorganize the North American economy without the checks and balances once provided by unions, social movements, or governments. The North American Free Trade Agreement (NAFTA) would roll back a hundred years of controls and restrictions that were placed on private business in the interests of the majority of the people.[10]

The members of CTC and ART were considerably less ambivalent than the leadership of the AFL-CIO about their position on NAFTA. They had opposed fast track, had protested the negotiations as they proceeded, and now stood ready to fight the agreement. Few members of the coalition held out hope that the supplemental agreements would fix what they believed to be NAFTA's fatal flaws, although as an internal coalition memo explained to members,

> For some CTC member groups, being willing to discuss side agreements is a tactic that they find necessary in Washington in order to be at the table and be a credible part of the political debate over the NAFTA. In talking to the administration now, these groups are laying markers by which the finished agreement can later be judged.[11]

The CTC's strategy was to build grassroots opposition to pressure members of Congress, particularly when they were home on recess. At a "grassroots conference" in Washington March 25–27, activists from around the country went through a program of education about NAFTA, training for organizing local communities, motivational talks, and strategic planning. The group met with several members of Congress, including Richard Gephardt. Ralph Nader gave a pep talk. There was some discussion about reaching out to United We Stand America, although many were uncomfortable about aligning with Ross Perot. A union leader who was also a member of United We Stand advised the group that they could get United We Stand troops without involving Ross Perot. He offered to put the group in touch with United We Stand state coordinators.

A first target was the April 1993 recess. In a letter to activists April 5, Jontz urged them to set up meetings with Representatives when they were back in their districts and to appear at town meetings to "remind members [of Congress] that this is an important issue to a growing number of citizens." Jontz suggested that activists urge members to write to President Clinton outlining their concerns about NAFTA. "Many members are taking a 'wait and see' attitude," he wrote, "but by asking them to weigh in at this point we can help set the 'markers,' by which the NAFTA should be judged."[12] The intent was to get members on record with demands that would be unlikely to be met by the side agreements.

CTC next organized a "National Week of Action for Fair Trade," May 1–9 (extended to include May Day). Events included rallies in New York City led by Jim Hightower, the colorful liberal Texas politician; in St. Louis led by Jesse Jackson; and in Seattle, demonstrating the new alliance of environmentalists and unions, led by Jane Perkins, president of Friends of the Earth, and George Korplus, president of the Machinists Union. In Colorado, local organizers set up a "tractorcade/truck convoy" between Colorado

Springs and Denver. In Minnesota they held a car caravan and tractorcade. Throughout the country, organizers held rallies, conferences, chili dinners, and other events to publicize their opposition to NAFTA.

The CTC and the unions together began working closely with a core of Democratic members of Congress opposed to NAFTA. In March, several House members had joined David Bonior (Democrat, Mich.), the chief Democratic whip, the third-ranking Democrat in the House, in forming an anti-NAFTA caucus. Bonior quietly made available his whip offices for opposition strategy meetings. For the duration of the NAFTA fight, Bonior's offices would be the meeting ground for NAFTA's liberal opponents.

Ross Perot and United We Stand America

In the third presidential debate with George Bush and Bill Clinton in 1992, Ross Perot described his views on NAFTA.

> Let's go to the center of the bull's eye—the core problem. And believe me, everybody on the factory floor all over this country knows it. You implement that NAFTA—the Mexican trade agreement where they pay people $1 an hour, have no health care, no retirement, no pollution controls, etc., etc., etc.—and you are going to hear a *giant sucking sound* of jobs being pulled out of this country.

The phrase "giant sucking sound" became the most memorable phrase of the campaign.

For Perot, though, NAFTA was more than lost jobs; it was emblematic of much that he thought was wrong with America. Perot's views on trade had been heavily influenced by Pat Choate, an author who had written a scathing attack on the politics of U.S. trade policy entitled *Agents of Influence*. Choate's thesis was that high-powered lobbyists bought by the multinationals and by foreign governments were corrupting American trade policy. Perot found the argument appealing. Big corporations, hired agents of the Mexican government, and insiders in the U.S. government had conspired to negotiate an agreement in secret that served their interests and hurt the American people. Perot saw NAFTA as an "agreement to lure businesses to Mexico," recalled Choate. "Perot saw a bunch of sleazy people paid to argue that the world is flat or round for a buck."

In 1993, Perot decided to make opposition to NAFTA his top issue and made Pat Choate his chief advisor. However deeply felt, Perot's personal views about NAFTA were not the only reason for this decision. After the presidential campaign, during which he had assembled a nationwide organization called United We Stand America, the challenge was to keep the organization afloat. "My idea was to use NAFTA as a pedagogical device on trade," recalled Pat Choate. "Perot's people were using it as an organizing device. NAFTA was a great organizing device for all the opponents," he noted.

Perot's strategic decision was not complicated by loyalty to Bill Clinton, and side agreements were not going to change his views. The only question was how active he and his organization, United We Stand America, would be in opposition to the agreement. The answer was very active. Perot and Choate planned an all-out campaign against NAFTA. They recognized that they had to attack from outside the usual trade circles. "We knew we could never win inside the Beltway. The only way to win it was outside the Beltway," recalled Choate. And they saw that their best chance to defeat NAFTA was to hit it early. "February to June was the critical moment," Choate said. "Once the president clicked it on and the PR machine clicked in we would be at a disadvantage. . . . The whole objective was to kill the deal early."

Choate tried to find ways to generate negative media coverage of NAFTA and Mexico. The idea was to come up with something new every two weeks, on the theory that was about all the trade reporters would handle until the issue heated up. The first issue had been handed to Choate in February when a supporter faxed him the advertisement for Amerimex, the outfit trying to recruit U.S. businesses to Mexico, and Choate passed it on to Richard Gephardt, knowing that the ad would make more news coming from him. Gephardt's release of the ad the day before the first meeting of trade ministers on the supplemental negotiations had created a distraction from the negotiations.

The next big splash also centered around an ad. In April, appearing at a Senate Banking Committee hearing organized by Donald Riegle (Democrat, Mich.), the most outspoken critic of NAFTA in the Senate, Perot produced a series of advertisements that had been running in *World Trade Magazine*, a magazine for American business people. The ads, purchased by the Mexican state of Yucatan, were intended to attract business to the region."Here's a headline, here's an ad in one of them," Perot told the committee, holding up an ad. " 'I can't keep my labor costs down, my turnover rates low and my standard of living high.' That's *my* standard of living, this guy is talking about his standard of living, okay, not his workers' standard of living. 'Yes you can, in Yucatan.' "

Senator Riegle interrupted: "Say that again. Let's hear that again, how was that?"

Perot continued, " 'Yes you can, in Yucatan.' Yuck-a-tan, I guess I ought to say.

"Now, it gets better," Perot promised. He held up a second advertisement and read the headline. " 'I can't find good, loyal workers'—this is a U.S. executive here scratching behind his ear—'for a dollar an hour, within a thousand miles of here.' You can't live on a dollar an hour in this country. 'Yes you can, in Yucatan. We're only 460 miles.' "[13]

For Perot, and for many others during the subsequent course of the NAFTA fight, the Yucatan ads said it all. At every opportunity, an appearance on NBC's Sunday morning "Meet the Press" program later that month, for instance, Perot produced the Amerimex and Yucatan ads as exhibits to demonstrate the essence of what he maintained NAFTA was about.

Notwithstanding their occasional success in getting media coverage, Perot and Choate felt that they were at a disadvantage in the mainstream press where the vast majority of producers and editors were NAFTA supporters. An important element of Perot's media strategy, therefore, centered on talk show appearances, particularly radio talk shows. The talk shows catered to a conservative public, many of whom were disaffected with government and mainstream media. Perot and Choate found the shows an excellent vehicle to reach the segment of the public that had responded to Perot's presidential candidacy. Choate built a radio studio in his offices on Capitol Hill. Beginning in February, every Friday he was the guest on the "Chuck Harder Show," a popular nationally syndicated talk show. For Choate this was an opportunity to educate listeners about trade, to tell the story of foreign agents, corruption, bad deals, and lost jobs.

The talk shows seemed to Choate to strike a chord with listeners. "NAFTA became a Rorschach," he recalled. "It was a symbolic issue as much as anything." Listeners to the Harder show began calling other talk shows, including those featuring members of Congress on C-SPAN. Other listeners organized opposition groups in their communities. A nurse in Houston heard Choate claiming that NAFTA that would allow less qualified professionals to come into the United States. She organized a group of nurses against NAFTA.

Perot himself appeared numerous times on other talk shows, including the most prominent program on CNN, "Larry King Live." Still, Perot was frustrated with his attempts to get his message across through the mass media. He decided, therefore, to adopt the tactic that had worked well for him in the presidential campaign: the paid "infomercial." Perot purchased half an hour of air time from NBC for the end of May.

Pat Buchanan and the Republican Right

Further right on the political spectrum, Pat Buchanan, having returned to his role as television commentator and columnist after his bid for the presidency in 1992, resumed his harsh rhetoric about NAFTA. During the primary season in 1992, Buchanan had run in the Republican primaries on an "America first" platform that included opposition to NAFTA. Buchanan, the former Nixon speech writer, was never at a loss for colorful words to convey his message. On April 22nd, 1992, Buchanan made clear his world-view in a speech in Washington, D.C., to the Daughters of the American Revolution:

> It is time Americans took their country back. Before we lose her for-ever, let us take America back from the global parasites of the World Bank and the IMF [International Monetary Fund], who siphon off America's wealth for Third World socialists and incompetents. And, let us take her back from the agents of influence who occupy this city and do the bidding of foreign powers.
>
> Now that the Cold War is over, we need a new foreign policy, of Americans, by Americans, and for Americans. Time to set aside all this geo-babble about a New World Order, and begin restoring the Old American Republic. Time to set aside the temptation to empire, time to put America first.

Buchanan also tapped into a growing anxiety about immigrants. "Our own country is undergoing the greatest invasion in history, a mass immigra-tion of millions of illegal aliens yearly from Mexico," Buchanan asserted to an audience of conservative political activists that February. "This invasion is eroding our tax base, swamping social services, undermining the social cohesion of the Republic."[14] For Buchanan, NAFTA was more than a threat to America's standard of living: it was a threat to the society.

Buchanan had backed away from criticism of NAFTA once Bush's re-nomination was assured, but with Clinton in office, Buchanan was free to resume his attack. On CNN's "Crossfire" in May 1993, Buchanan explained his opposition to NAFTA.

> I used to be a 100-percent free trader in Ronald Reagan's White House, but you go around this country, and you see the average wage of work-ing Americans is falling. There are more people working in govern-ment now than in manufacturing. From 1865 to, say, 1910, the two leading protectionists in this country were the two Republicans up on Mount Rushmore, Teddy Roosevelt and Abraham Lincoln, and the standard of living of American workers rose higher in that period than any other period of our history, whereas it's been holding or falling in the last 20 years. Why not look at free trade as a reason?[15]

As an indication of how complicated the politics of NAFTA was becoming, an amused Michael Kinsley, Buchanan's liberal counterpoint on the show, noted:

> I've got Republican Senator John Chafee of Rhode Island over here on the left with me supporting free market capitalism, and over there on the right with Pat, defending burdensome government regulation, is [Democratic] Senator Fritz Hollings of South Carolina.[16]

In comparison to the unions, the grassroots environmentalists, or United We Stand America, Buchanan and others on the Republican right were not nearly as organized in the spring, although the talk show circuit provided an important forum for their views. Unless one was listening carefully, it was still easy to miss the rumblings from the right that would eventually pose problems for NAFTA.

The Supporters' Dilemma

The forces of support were much less organized than the opposition in early 1993. The main dilemma was that likely elements of a supportive coalition—the Clinton administration, the business community, and moderate environmental groups—were all engaged in the supplemental negotiations on labor and environment and, therefore, not in a position to advocate for NAFTA. The Mexican lobby was in place, as Perot noted, but Mexico could do little directly to influence the public debate on NAFTA. This predicament created a vacuum for the opposition to fill, and it would nearly spell the death of NAFTA.

The Business Community

Shortly after the conclusion of the NAFTA negotiations in 1992, Jim Robinson, the chair of the Business Roundtable's trade task force, was forced out as CEO of American Express, thereby losing his seat at the Roundtable. Kay Whitmore, CEO of Kodak, took over for Robinson as task force chair. Robinson and Whitmore called a meeting of top players in the United States and Mexico to discuss the upcoming efforts to pass NAFTA. Among those attending were Jim Jones, former Congressman from Oklahoma and then chair of the New York Stock Exchange; Rodman Rockefeller, head of the U.S.–Mexican Businessman's Association; Jerry Jaznowski of the National Association of Manufacturers; Juan Gallardo, head of Coordinadora de Organismos Empresariales de Comercio Exterior (COECE), the Mexican Business lobby; and Carlos Salinas, the president of Mexico.

To coordinate U.S. business efforts on NAFTA's behalf, the group agreed to create a new organization: USA*NAFTA. Whitmore and Robinson decided on a budget of $2 million and made the rounds of the Business Roundtable to collect the money. Sandy Masur, Whitmore's advisor on international trade, was charged with putting together the new organization and planning a strategy. For Masur, the problem was getting businesses to do something beyond adding their name to the USA*NAFTA membership list. The $2 million budget was too small to do more than basic public relations and lobbying. Without real commitments from CEOs, the campaign would go nowhere. But in the early spring, she recalled, "It was hard for business to focus on NAFTA."

Many factors contributed to business's lethargy. First and foremost, the business community was concerned about the direction of the supplemental negotiations on labor and environment. To retain leverage in these talks, they could not firmly commit to supporting NAFTA. Second, the business community did not have as good a working relationship with the new Democratic president as they had had with his Republican predecessors. The Clinton administration compounded suspicions by urging business to take the lead while it appeared ambivalent about the agreement. As one trade insider put it, "for forty-five years on international trade issues, the president led and the business community provided support." Third, business attention was focused elsewhere, on the tax bill and on the early stages of health care, issues of much more immediate financial concern. Finally, and more generally, few in the business community recognized the potency of the opposition forces that NAFTA was engendering and the nature of the political problem they were about to face. Trade had always been an inside game. It was hard to imagine it becoming the public issue that it would soon become.

Masur and a small group of trade lobbyists and consultants began meeting weekly to plan and coordinate strategy. The strategy looked much the same as the effort they had put together to pass fast track two years before: traditional lobbying of Congress members and staff by business representatives; public relations, primarily involving the generation of favorable editorials; and a modest "grassroots" effort to get local businesses to demonstrate their support to their members of Congress. The Washington strategy relied on the community of company lobbyists, the "Washington Reps," who made the rounds on Capitol Hill to talk with members and staffers. The Washington Reps began meeting once a week to compare notes and to get a pep talk. The meetings had little energy.

Gail Harrison of the Wexler Group, a grassroots lobbying firm, was in charge of the grassroots effort. The original effort consisted of designating a state "captain" to organize business support in the state. As the spring wore on, however, Harrison and Sandy Masur realized that the approach was not working. Most captains had never run a grassroots campaign. They thought that if they set up one meeting with thirty people and the Congressperson, they had done their job. "We were looking to company people in the states to manage what was a bigger battle than they could handle," recalled Masur. Moreover, state captains were not getting signals from their CEOs that NAFTA was a priority. Without the committed support of CEOs, the grassroots efforts fizzled.

The Mexican Lobby

The Mexicans had set up a NAFTA office in Washington during the fast track effort and assembled a team of U.S. lawyers, lobbyists, and public relations firms to advise them. The Mexican team included some of the best (and highest priced) Washington talent, including several former U.S. trade officials, among them former United States Trade Representative (USTR) Bill Brock. By the spring of 1993, the Mexicans had already spent more than $25 million on the effort, and by the time the NAFTA effort was over the tab would be well over $30 million.

For all the high-powered help they employed, the Mexican lobbyists were limited in the activities they could engage in. They recognized that the same message coming from a U.S. CEO would be more effective than if it was coming from them. Nonetheless, their lobbyists had access and could get and give information; their public relations firms could attempt to improve Mexico's image in the United States; and their technical staff could provide quick analyses to counter charges leveled by the opposition. These capabilities would later quietly serve to bolster efforts by business and the Clinton administration.

Inside the Administration

In the spring, the Clinton administration was not focused on making a case for NAFTA. At the USTR, Mickey Kantor and his staff were fully engaged in negotiating the supplemental agreements. Worse, early in the year, Kantor's message was a continuation of the campaign theme: Bush's NAFTA is flawed and needs to be fixed with supplemental agreements. This position, useful for the election campaign, prevented Kantor from making a case for NAFTA.

The problem was that passing NAFTA was the central concern nowhere else in the administration. At the newly created National Economic Council (NEC) in the Old Executive Office Building next to the White House, more pressing issues pushed NAFTA off the agenda. Bob Kyle, a deputy at the NEC and formerly chief trade council for the Finance Committee and a veteran of the fast track fight in 1991, began holding a once-a-week meeting of other deputies in the White House, but he, like everyone else at the NEC, was stretched too thin to do more than monitor the progress of the supplemental agreements.

NAFTA was also not a priority at the White House. The president had his hands full with other issues. Moreover, support for NAFTA was far from unanimous in the president's inner circle, as had also been the case during the election campaign. In one camp were internationalists like Lloyd Bentsen and National Economic Advisor Robert Rubin, who viewed NAFTA as an important part of the centrist Democratic agenda. On the other side, however, many of the president's top political advisors continued to harbor doubts; among them was George Stephanopoulos, the former Gephardt aide who served as White House communications director. They advised the president to at least keep open the option of backing out. The president seemed to support the principle of the agreement. In a foreign policy speech at American University in February, he used strong language crafted for him by NAFTA's advocates for the purpose of forestalling NAFTA's opponents in the administration and sending a strong public message of his commitment to NAFTA. But there was enough ambiguity in the message coming from the White House to encourage NAFTA opponents to believe that the president was not yet fully committed.

At the end of April, Jeff Faux, a Clinton confidant and president of the Economic Policy Institute, a union-funded Washington think tank, wrote a memo to his friends on the White House political team. The memo was a carefully constructed and well-argued bombshell that began, "The international trade people in the administration are steering the president off a political cliff." Faux went on to make a compelling political case against NAFTA:

> NAFTA makes no sense to most people and *undercuts the imagery of a president concerned about jobs for Americans.* Everything we know about politics over the last twenty years tells us that a Democratic president must have the populist advantage on jobs and growth issues to offset the discomfort that many ordinary people feel with a social agenda that to them seems to emphasize gay rights and political correctness.
>
> Right now, no one is "responsible" for jobs lost because of investment that moves across the border. But the president is making NAFTA his program. And after it passes, Bill Clinton will be blamed

for every factory that closes down, *whether NAFTA was the cause or not.* That is exactly what happened to Mulroney in Canada.

This will be a very tough fight . . . with Democrats! It will divide the party and leave scars. If the president pushes this and wins, *there will be Democratic districts where he will not be welcome.*

Perot could do real damage on NAFTA. . . . As a Democratic Congressman said to me last week: people in my district are beginning to say that he's giving away our tax money to the Russians and now he wants to give our jobs to the Mexicans. Imagine hearing that one a few million times on talk radio.

When the debate gets going, the issue of Mexican money buying access and influence in Washington will resurface. . . . This could hand Perot his third issue: corruption in Washington.

You can't trust your allies on this. You can't control Salinas. And there is some evidence that some of the big business community will not go to the mat on this. These people do not like controversy.

The absence of a Republican resistance to NAFTA is deceptive. Some Republicans will peel off on the NAFTA vote now that Bush is gone. More important, at the local level, right wing populist Republicans (helped by the Christian right) will be shameless about exploiting NAFTA to portray the president as the friend of everyone but the average American.[17]

Faux recommended having someone in the White House be responsible for "a plan to back out of NAFTA." Faux's memo touched all the right buttons. It was read with great interest by its recipients.

The View from the Hill

Eventually, all the outside efforts would be focused on the Congress. In the spring of 1993, the situation did not look good for NAFTA's supporters, particularly in the House. Most House Democrats were opposed to the agreement; only a handful supported. Majority Leader Gephardt had not yet announced his opposition to NAFTA, but the betting was that he would eventually oppose. The chief whip, David Bonior, was holding two sets of weekly meetings for opponents, one of the anti-NAFTA House caucus, the other with the outside groups mobilizing against the agreement. Moreover, the majority of committee chairs were opposed to NAFTA.

Dan Rostenkowski, chairman of the Ways and Means Committee, was supportive, but he was by now deeply wounded by the House post office scandal that would eventually cost him reelection. The business community and the White House seemed to be looking toward Bill Richardson (Democrat, N.M.), the energetic deputy whip, as their point man in the House, but Rostenkowski wanted to keep things in the Ways and Means Committee. Rostenkowski designated Bob Matsui, a soft-spoken but respected member from California, to lead the effort. Matsui's aide, Diane Sullivan, would become the center of the pro-NAFTA effort in the House. The designation created some tension between Richardson and Matsui, and between their staffs, both of whom felt better equipped to run the show.

On the Republican side of the aisle, leadership was nominally supportive but unwilling to commit until the side agreements were complete. Moreover, Minority Leader Bob Michel and Republican Whip Newt Gingrich were locked in battle with the president over the budget and other issues and in no mood to help him on NAFTA.

In the Senate, the situation was more favorable. In 1991, fast track had passed there with a more comfortable margin than in the House. Certain Senators were quite vocal in their opposition, notably Fritz Hollings of South Carolina and the two Michigan Senators, Carl Levin and Donald Riegle, but the opposition was not as organized as it was in the House. However, it was uncertain who would lead the effort to pass NAFTA in the Senate. Normally, the chair of the Finance Committee assumes this role. With Lloyd Bentsen's move to the administration, this position had passed to New York Senator Daniel Patrick Moynihan, but Moynihan had voted against fast track and continued to be critical of NAFTA. He was not going to take the lead. Max Baucus was second ranking on Finance and chaired the Trade Subcommittee, but his efforts to influence the outcome of the side agreements kept him from committing his support.

Bill Bradley was only the fourth-ranking Democrat on the Finance Committee, but he had no ambivalence about supporting NAFTA. Bradley believed deeply in its historic significance and was prepared to work hard for its passage. In March, Bradley, sensing the leadership vacuum, decided to set up a bipartisan whip group. From the outset maintaining bipartisanship was a central objective, since the one way NAFTA could be defeated in the Senate was if Republicans bolted. Bradley spoke with John Chafee of Rhode Island, a moderate Republican with whom he had a good relationship, about jointly chairing the effort. Chafee agreed, and he and Bradley quietly began talking with other Senators to feel out their positions. The author, then serving as Bradley's chief aide for foreign policy, worked with Chafee aide Amy Dunathan, to staff the working group.

Bradley was frustrated with the lack of strategy coming from either the administration or the business community. Both were leaving the field to the opponents, letting them frame the public debate. Bradley urged the administration to designate a point person to coordinate strategy and to begin making the public case for NAFTA. Bradley also met on a regular basis with the business strategists. "This isn't going to be trade politics as usual," he told them. "You need to think of this as an election." He urged USA*NAFTA to hire a campaign strategist, someone skilled in developing and testing messages. He felt that opponents were being more effective because they could use specific stories to paint a negative portrait—plant closings, toxic dumps, and the like—whereas supporters were relying on generalities about free trade. Bradley sent a letter to USA*NAFTA members asking for specifics about what they planned to do if NAFTA passed. Their responses would later provide important ammunition for the pro-NAFTA forces.

In late February, at a speech to a sparse breakfast audience of a few Congress members and staffers, Bradley laid out his message for NAFTA. As always, Bradley took a long view. He argued that the agreement would create jobs by making America more competitive with Europe and Asia in the international economy of the twenty-first century. Even more important, NAFTA was a historic opportunity to break from the history of suspicion and animosity that had for so long characterized U.S.–Mexican relations. NAFTA meant one more thing to Bradley: It was an expression of something fundamentally American, the ability to embrace people of a different culture and to be enriched by pluralism. Although few heard the speech, Bradley's talking points were distributed widely, first in raw form to the business strategy group and then in a more polished version in letters distributed to every member of Congress. As Bradley campaigned for NAFTA, with the president and others in the administration, with fellow members of Congress, with the media, and in dozens of talks to public groups, these were the themes to which Bradley returned.

Is NAFTA Dead?

On April 27, Washington was greeted by a front page headline in the *Washington Post* declaring that OMB (Office of Management and Budget)

Director Leon Panetta had declared NAFTA "dead."[18] A gloomy Panetta had talked with reporters the day before about his frustrations with progress on Clinton's entire agenda and let slip that NAFTA was dead for now in the Congress. The administration scrambled to repair the damage, but most insiders thought that Panetta was simply telling the truth about where things stood. Matsui's whip counts in the House, while very soft, were showing fewer than forty Democrats supportive, far from the hundred he thought they needed (and that the Republican leadership would later insist upon as the price for delivering the remaining votes).

In the month that followed Panetta's gloomy musings, the prospects for NAFTA grew even dimmer. Two days after the Panetta story, Citizen's Trade Campaign and its union allies launched a "National Week of Action for Fair Trade" at a rally on Capitol Hill. For the next week the campaign staged more than thirty events around the country to dramatize opposition to NAFTA. In the words of William Bywater, president of the International Union of Electronic Workers (IUE), "It is our goal to open the eyes of the American public so they understand that the real supporters of this trade agreement are rich corporations who will make massive profits by exploiting low wage Mexican workers and lax environmental regulation. The opponents of this agreement are working people whose families and communities will be devastated by plant closings and U.S. job loss." He promised "to wage an all-out campaign to defeat this agreement."[19]

In mid May, leaks of the U.S. negotiating position on the side agreement prompted attacks from opponents on both ends of the political spectrum. On the left, the Citizen's Trade Campaign blasted the administration for not going far enough. On the right, conservatives attacked the administration for going too far. Then, as Jeff Faux's memo had predicted, the issue of foreign lobbyists came to the fore. An outfit called the Center for Public Integrity released a study entitled *The Trading Game: Inside Lobbying for the North American Free Trade Agreement.* "Mexico has mounted the most expensive, elaborate campaign ever conducted in the United States by a foreign government," said Charles Lewis, the Center's director. "The decision-making process for this historic legislation has been distorted by the recent infusion of tens of millions of dollars." The report documented that Mexico had hired thirty-three former U.S. government officials, including Bill Brock, the former USTR, and numerous people close to President Clinton. "Short of moving into the Lincoln bedroom," said *The Trading Game*, "Mexico could not have positioned itself closer to Bill Clinton."[20]

Charles Lewis and his effort would likely have remained inside the Washington Beltway, however, were it not for Ross Perot and Pat Choate. Here was additional evidence and ammunition for their speeches, talk show appearances, and the infomercial that Perot had purchased for the end of May.

The prospect of the Perot infomercial alarmed the business strategists. They urged the administration to take on Perot. Yet the White House was wary of confronting Perot directly, recognizing that Perot supporters represented the swing constituency in the national electorate. The administration chose to respond quietly, with a no-cameras-allowed background briefing for reporters, given by Labor Secretary Bob Reich, Economic Advisor Laura Tyson, and Mickey Kantor, at which they largely focused on rebutting Perot's assertions about NAFTA's effects on jobs.

Perot's infomercial on NBC was a rambling exposition with several themes. First, NAFTA would cost jobs, Perot asserted. "Automobile workers in the United States earn $16 an hour plus benefits. Mexican automobile workers make one-ninth the salary of a U.S. automobile worker," said Perot. "Benefits such as retirement, health care, and so on, which we take for granted in the U.S., in the automobile industry in Mexico are virtually nonexistent." Corporations wanted NAFTA so they could move to Mexico. Moreover, Mexico was actively seeking to lure away American jobs. Perot held up the "Yes You Can, in Yucatan" ad as evidence.

Second, NAFTA was being pushed on the American people by paid foreign agents. Here Perot picked up on *The Trading Game*. "Sad to report, a former chief U.S. trade negotiator has been retained by the Mexican government, is being paid several hundred thousand dollars a year to direct this effort," said Perot. "People in key positions on the 1992 presidential campaigns have been retained as Mexican lobbyists. . . . Once again we've been out-traded and out-negotiated with a great deal of help from former American trade officials who are now working for foreign agents."

Third, NAFTA was negotiated in secret to serve the special interests in Washington. "Our country went to extraordinary efforts to keep the details of the NAFTA negotiations from the American people. The negotiations were conducted in secret. Members of Congress had to go to a secret room to read the agreement as it was being negotiated."

Finally, Perot emphasized the differences between Mexico and the United States. "How does Mexico treat its workers, compared to our country?" he asked. "The typical worker in Mexico lives in a one-room shack with no plumbing or electricity. His counterpart in the U.S. is a middle class citizen who can afford to send his children to college, who lives in a nice home. Many Mexican workers with U.S. companies cannot afford a low income house and must scavenge cardboard and trash to build their homes." Perot held up photographs of impoverished and poorly housed Mexicans.

At the end of the half-hour, Perot urged viewers to write or phone their Representatives and Senators and say "No" to NAFTA. Many did. An orchestrated postcard campaign flooded Congressional offices with preprinted "NAFTA NO!" postcards. Mail in most offices ran twenty to one against the agreement.

The Summer of '93

The Perot infomercial marked the beginning of the public phase of the NAFTA battle. This was not going to be trade politics as usual—NAFTA was going to be a public issue. In the public arena, NAFTA's opponents temporarily held the upper hand. Public opinion, while on the surface equally divided on NAFTA, appeared to be susceptible to the anti-NAFTA message. With the administration on the sidelines because of the delay in completion of the side negotiations, negative images and messages dominated through the summer. Outside of Washington, opponents were much more active and visible than proponents. A few pro-NAFTA political strategists began to see that without a countervailing public campaign for NAFTA, the political pressure on Congress would be too great to overcome.

Public Opinion

Although NAFTA had long been a hot issue among activists, until the summer of 1993 it had not really become a major issue for the general public. That was now beginning to change. The opposition publicity efforts, the travails of the side negotiations, and news about Mexico through the summer of 1993 would raise the salience of NAFTA in public opinion. Strategists on both sides began attending more closely to public opinion, and pollsters began sampling it with more regularity and in greater depth.

At the beginning of the summer, the American public was evenly divided on NAFTA, although not yet particularly attuned to the issue. The April NBC–*Wall Street Journal* poll showed 27 percent favored NAFTA and 25 percent opposed, with 44 percent undecided. In July the same poll found

31 percent in favor and 29 percent opposed, with 36 percent undecided. A poll conducted for the White House by Stan Greenberg found 39 percent favoring and 34 percent opposing it, with 27 percent undecided. These results appeared generally encouraging for NAFTA, but beneath this surface lurked some problems.

The Greenberg poll began and ended with the basic question about support for NAFTA. Between the two questions, the survey asked respondents to say whether they agreed or disagreed with a series of statements about NAFTA, half favorable and half unfavorable. Not only did respondents agree more often with the negative messages (agreeing overwhelming that NAFTA would cost jobs, for instance), at the end of the poll they were significantly more negative about NAFTA than they had been before exposure to the messages. After hearing both pro and con messages, only 36 percent said they favored NAFTA while 48 percent opposed it. One other finding also boded poorly for NAFTA. Respondents had a very negative image of Mexico, considering it poor, dirty, and corrupt.

Illegal Drugs and Immigrants: The NAFTA Connection

The news about Mexico did little to help Mexico's image. On May 24, a front-page headline in the New York Times read "Free-Trade Treaty May Widen Traffic in Drugs, U.S. Says." The article reported "Cocaine smugglers working with Colombian drug cartels are starting to set up factories, warehouses, and trucking companies in Mexico to exploit the flood of cross-border commerce expected under the North American Free Trade Agreement, United States intelligence and law-enforcement officials say."[21] This was good copy. Papers across the country picked up the story.

The same day, the shooting of Guadalajara's Catholic Cardinal Juan Jesus Posadas Ocampo in an apparent drug shoot-out at that city's international airport made front page news.[22] The Mexican government claimed that Posadas was caught in the crossfire between rival drug dealers and that this was a case of mistaken identity. Within days, doubts began to surface about the account. The cardinal had been wearing clerical attire and had been shot repeatedly at close range. A survey of the Mexican public "found that 83 percent of those questioned did not believe the government's account of Posadas' slaying," American papers reported.[23] The story provided another opportunity for newspapers to discuss the Mexican drug connection and to link the story to NAFTA.

The assassination came just as President Salinas was embarking on a long-planned speaking tour in the United States intended to project an image of modern Mexico. Salinas sought to make the best of the situation by promising to avenge the killings and to crack down on Mexican drug traffickers, but his two-day visit to the United States merely provided another hook for damaging stories about Mexico. As the *Washington Post* reported, "A diplomat here described Posadas's death as 'an embarrassing moment for Salinas' as he enters the final months of an intense campaign to win U.S. congressional approval for the proposed North American Free Trade Agreement. 'This doesn't help,' the diplomat said."[24]

Then, on June 3, less than a week later, U.S. drug agents discovered a nearly completed tunnel under the U.S.–Mexican border, apparently intended for drug smuggling. "It's pretty mind-boggling," said Jack Hook of the Drug Enforcement Administration (DEA) office in San Diego. "Law enforcement is lucky that it was caught at this point. They could have gotten tons through there without us knowing anything about it."[25] This was a great story, complete with visuals for television. The networks showed pictures of the nearly complete, lighted, air-conditioned tunnel. ABC News speculated that if authorities were lucky to have found this tunnel, there were probably other undetected tunnels.[26]

In addition to drugs, a second issue captured the attention of the media and its consumers that summer: illegal immigration. A steady drumbeat of news stories kept immigration on the front burner. Most dramatic were a series of stories about Chinese aliens, who were being crammed into dangerous boats and landed on U.S. shores. Two boatloads of Chinese were arrested in California in early June, three more were intercepted in July, and a freighter carrying hundreds of aliens ran aground in New York. The stories created a hook for other stories about immigration, many of them noting that the real immigration problem was on the border with Mexico.

Particularly in California, mired in recession, it was easy for some to believe that America was being overrun by illegal immigrants. Representative Dana Rohrbacher (Republican, Calif.), an Orange County conservative, said immigration is becoming

a decisive political issue in California. . . . People in California are feeling under attack and overrun, and a lot of people feel cheated. . . .

They feel as if they're paying for services and an educational system and . . . all of a sudden, they look around and the people who've come here illegally and been here for a few months are siphoning thousands of dollars out of that system.[27]

Calls for action to stem the imagined flood came from across the political spectrum. California Senator Dianne Feinstein, the liberal former mayor of San Francisco, a year away from a reelection campaign, wrote a searing opinion column in the *Los Angeles Times*. "Today, there are 1.3 million Californians out of work," it began. "Families throughout our state face overcrowded schools and a scarcity of affordable homes. Meanwhile, there are an estimated 1.3 million undocumented immigrants in California."[28] Drawing a causal connection did not take much imagination. Conservative Republican Duncan Hunter gathered thirty-seven signatures from the California House delegation on a letter calling for three thousand new border patrol agents. At the California statehouse in Sacramento, legislators called for the National Guard to patrol California's borders and considered such measures as denying welfare, health, and educational services to aliens.

A few voices opposed the rising sentiment against immigrants. When the Immigration and Naturalization Service (INS) proposed building a steel wall on the Arizona-Mexico border, the *Arizona Republic* worried about the symbolic message it would send.

Besides being an ugly eyesore that would undermine the strides being achieved on social, political, economic and environmental fronts between the two nations, the steel curtain is sure to have one demonstrable impact this nation can do without: that of reinforcing the racist stereotype of Mexican immigrants as criminals.[29]

Still, so strong was the sense that something needed to be done that at the end of July President Clinton proposed a new, tougher immigration policy.

Although NAFTA's proponents attempted to argue that the agreement would help stem the flow of drugs and immigrants, NAFTA's opponents had the easier story to tell. Surely a more "open border" for trade was a more open border for other things as well. Economists were projecting that California would enjoy the largest economic gains in the nation from NAFTA. Yet in that state, popular sentiment ran strongly against NAFTA. Both of

California's Democratic Senators announced their opposition, as did a clear majority of its House delegation.

Growing Opposition

With the side negotiations dragging on through June and July, and with Clinton's budget still hanging in the balance, the administration continued to leave the political field to NAFTA's opponents, and the opposition continued to grow. The union "Not This NAFTA" campaign continued. The opposition environmental groups, aware now that the side agreements would not go as far as they liked, stepped up their organizing efforts. The Perot campaign was gathering steam, as United We Stand chapters around the country organized speeches, rallies, letter-writing campaigns, and other activities. On the right, the trajectory of the side negotiations inspired louder assertions about loss of sovereignty.

New voices now joined this confederation. In testimony before the Congressional Black Caucus in June, William Lucy, Secretary-Treasurer of the American Federation of State, County, and Municipal Employees (AFSCME) and President of the Coalition of Black Trade Unionists, gave voice to widely shared sentiments:

NAFTA just doesn't make sense for the African-American community. NAFTA will fail to deliver benefits to the African Americans for many of the same reasons that it is a bad deal for the overwhelming majority of all Americans. First, the African-American worker is more likely than his/her white counterpart to be employed in a non-managerial capacity in those industries most likely to be affected by NAFTA. And, second, the unemployed African American worker will find it more difficult to find a new job once his/her existing job is lost. . . .

[NAFTA] would permit more drugs to come into the U.S. from Mexico than comes across at the present time. Sadly, we know that much of these drug shipments are headed into our inner cities where unemployment is high and opportunities for a better life are poor.[30]

Lucy's views were widely shared by prominent African-American leaders such as Jesse Jackson and Ben Chavis, the executive director of the NAACP

(National Association for the Advancement of Colored People). In June, the Congressional Black Caucus took a formal stand in opposition to NAFTA.

Religious and human rights organizations added their voices to the chorus. The Evangelical Lutheran Church in America, the Mennonites, the Friends, the Mary Knoll Fathers and Brothers, Catholic lay organizations, and other religious groups all expressed concerns about NAFTA.

Reassessing the Pro-NAFTA Strategy

In May, USA*NAFTA had hired political strategist Francis O'Brien to help with them with their public relations campaign. O'Brien could see that things were not going well. As he later recalled,

> there was a terrific misunderstanding of the issue, the public issue. All the trade people say it is a very closed undertaking. An arcane matter for the lawyers. They never leave Washington D.C. I felt that this was not the case. I didn't understand in May that this would be front page news in October, but I knew it would be more [than the trade people thought].

O'Brien hired Page Gardner, a young campaign strategist who had been in the Clinton campaign war room in Little Rock. Gardner shared O'Brien's view of the problem. "The business community . . . didn't understand the operating environment they were in," recalled Gardner. The "opposition was heartfelt. This was not political posturing on David Bonior's part."

At an all day meeting of the USA*NAFTA brain trust in early July, O'Brien and Gardner insisted that they had to have a media campaign. One participant in the meeting remembered that O'Brien told the group, "you are doing everything right but you are still going to lose unless you reframe the debate. . . . He pushed and pushed that we had to have a media campaign. [He said,] 'This was a political war.' We had to refocus the debate. We had to seize the message. We had to neutralize the opposition and shape the message." There was no way to do what needed to be done on a $2 million budget. At the end of the day, the group decided to seek an additional $5 million from the Business Roundtable for advertising and to hire an advertiser skilled in campaign commercials.

The pro-NAFTA forces in the administration were also increasingly nervous. This was shaping up to be a much bigger issue than anyone had anticipated. In June, Bentsen, Rubin, and Reich met to discuss the situation. They worried that with Kantor tied up with the supplemental negotiations, the political situation was not receiving sufficient attention. They decided that the effort to pass NAFTA needed a overall strategist and a campaign-style war room, an idea that Bradley had urged on the administration since early in the year. Clinton agreed.

Still, the administration was not yet ready to move. Until the budget passed, the NAFTA side negotiations could not conclude. Until there were side agreements, the administration could not sell the agreement. As Mickey Kantor explained later,

> The president understood from the very first that [NAFTA] was con-
> troversial within the Democratic party, and he needed every Demo-
> cratic vote to get his economic package through. He could not engage
> the NAFTA situation until after his economic package passed. We
> made a decision in the administration [to] slow walk the negotiations
> over labor and environment until the situation was finished on the
> Hill on the economic package. It was the president's idea that we wait,
> and we did.

As the budget battle continued through July and into August, however, the window closed for finishing the side negotiations before Congress went on recess.

There was one other problem for NAFTA: Some in the administration viewed it as a competitor to the health care reform effort.

Health Care or NAFTA?

On Thursday, August 5, the House finally passed the budget bill by one vote. Not one Republican voted with the president. The next day in the Senate, a last-second change of heart by Bob Kerrey (Democrat, Neb.) left a tie, enabling Vice President Al Gore to cast the deciding vote. Again, not one Republican voted with the president. The mood at the White House was near euphoria.[31] The crisis over, it was now time to turn to the next item on the agenda. The question was what that item would be.

At the White House, the health reform task force had been getting more and more restless. All year, more immediately pressing events had forced delay. Now Hillary Clinton and task force chair Ira Magaziner thought it was finally their turn. The health care team was joined by most of the White House political operatives, who questioned the wisdom of doing NAFTA at all and who feared that a battle over NAFTA would detract from the more important effort to pass health care reform. On the Hill, David Bonior sensed that health care made NAFTA vulnerable. He gathered 102 signatures on a letter to the president urging him to delay NAFTA until after Congress had voted on health care reform. "The debate over NAFTA will be difficult and divisive," the letter said. "It will detract from our efforts to build a broad coalition of support for health care reform."[32]

On the evening of August 11, cabinet officers and senior staff met with the president, the vice president, and the first lady to discuss priorities. Hillary Clinton and the health care team wanted six full weeks for launching the health care initiative. They had been waiting patiently in line. One participant recalled that Mrs. Clinton argued that "we were not elected to balance the budget or to pass NAFTA. We were elected to do health care. Why risk health care for NAFTA?"

Some of the president's political advisors continued to argue for abandoning NAFTA altogether. Top presidential advisor George Stephanopoulos made the political case against the agreement. NAFTA was bad politics. It would split the Democratic party when Clinton needed every bit of support he could muster for the health care effort. The president risked the credibility of the Presidency if he were to lose. As Howard Paster, director of Congressional relations, recalled, "Some were saying get out. 'Why not just get out now?' they asked. 'Don't finish the side negotiations.'"

Vice President Gore, Secretary Bentsen, Secretary Warren Christopher, and National Security Advisor Tony Lake argued the other side. As presidential counselor David Gergen recalled:

It was a situation one could turn around. First, we have found that when the public is provided with arguments, support for protectionism goes down. That's what happened to Gephardt and Buchanan [in their presidential campaigns]. Second, opinion on foreign affairs is mushy. Go back to the Panama Canal Treaty. Jimmy Carter started with public opinion against the treaty and turned it around.

Gore argued strongly for going ahead, asserting "If you stand for something you don't give it up."

Political advisor James Carville came into the meeting opposed to

NAFTA, but the more he listened the more he felt that it made better political sense not to abandon it. If Clinton backed away from NAFTA, he would be perceived as caving in to political pressure, creating a credibility problem. Carville broke ranks with the other political advisors, arguing that the president should conclude the side agreements and throw himself into the NAFTA campaign.

In the end, the decision was to finish NAFTA and fight for it in the fall. But health care remained the top priority. NAFTA would get only two days of the president's time before the focus turned to health care.[33] Kantor reassured the health care team that the president could do both NAFTA and health care. NAFTA, he said, would be an inside-the-Beltway effort, not requiring the president to travel outside of Washington. Two days after the meeting, on August 13, Kantor reached a deal with Mexico and Canada on the labor and environment supplemental agreements.

From the perspective of NAFTA's Hill supporters, the middle of August was the worst possible time to finish the side negotiations, with members of Congress far outside the Beltway, back in their districts for the traditional recess. "We pleaded with them not to announce the side agreements in the middle of an August recess," recalled Matsui aide Dianne Sullivan. "Because the thing that was so key was to be able to have all of your soldiers debriefed on the contents of the agreements, why they were good, that we achieved what we were looking to." A "white paper" making the administration case for NAFTA was printed, but it had not yet been distributed. "The administration was afraid that with the budget vote pending and so close, a wavering member might see the NAFTA piece and panic," recalled Nancy Leamond, the head of Congressional Relations at the USTR, soon to be at the center of events. "We never had a chance to distribute it before recess, to work the issue. There were no briefings, no ground work laid before recess."

The president was headed for a much needed vacation. Mickey Kantor was on his way to Europe for vacation. (A week later, in Geneva, he would break his back in a fall.) Bill Daley of Chicago, son of the late mayor Richard Daley and younger brother of the current Mayor Richie Daley, had been identified in the press as the president's choice to head the NAFTA campaign, but he had not yet accepted the job. As a key administration strategist later conceded, "we had no strategy for August. We knew we needed one, but . . ."

The business community was no more prepared for August than the administration. For months, some members of the business strategy team had been urging that business have a grassroots strategy for the recess, but all the talk came to little. USA*NAFTA had negligible grassroots capacity, had not yet hired a media firm, and still was fumbling for a message. Moreover, USA*NAFTA chair Kay Whitmore was mired in troubles at Eastman Kodak. By mid August he had lost his job, which meant that by the rules of the Business Roundtable, the effective parent of USA*NAFTA, he could no longer serve as chair. Uncertainty over the business leadership complicated the effort to mount any campaign. With nothing in place, all the business advocates could do was watch and hope that the opposition wouldn't do too much damage. Many went on vacation.

August

Washington in August was the eye of a hurricane. Inside the Beltway, all was eerily calm. With Congress out on recess and the president on vacation, half of the rest of Washington was out of town too. It was hard to find a cab on Capitol Hill. But outside, the storm over NAFTA had begun to rage.

NAFTA's opponents had been targeting August since the spring. The recess played to their strength. "We weren't going to win this inside the Beltway," recalled the AFL-CIO's Mark Anderson. "We had to use our strength: people. We were not going to outspend the government of Mexico or the business community. Our tactic was to bring this back to the districts and make it a matter of concern to the constituents back home." Perot strategist Pat Choate echoed the sentiment, "We knew we could never win inside the Beltway. The only way to win it was outside the Beltway." The administration felt helpless. "If Barbara Kennelly [Democrat, Conn.] went home," recalled a White House strategist, "we couldn't get to her, but she was naturally with them [labor] at breakfasts, etc. back in the district. We didn't have a grassroots capacity."

Also, there was a sense that NAFTA was on the ropes. With the side agreements completed, members of Congress could no longer take cover by saying that they wanted to wait to see them before making up their minds. For the first time, even the more jaded of the opposition strategists began to smell victory. Their knew that if the president ever threw the full weight of his office behind NAFTA, he would be very difficult to beat, but if they could raise the price high enough, they might just deter him. The time to kill NAFTA was at hand.

Around the country, unions, the CTC, opposition environmental groups (most notably the Sierra Club), chapters of Perot's United We Stand America, and other organizations planned media events and primed their membership for encounters with Representatives at town hall meetings, union breakfasts, and church potlucks. When the text of the supplementary agreements was leaked a week after they were completed, the opposition network quickly distributed a critique and talking points. As a result, citizens at town meetings had more ammunition than the members, who had not yet received the text or been briefed on it. Members of Congress met an angry citizenry armed with assertions to which the members had few ready answers.

The effort was only loosely coordinated from Washington; union leadership wanted nothing to do with Ross Perot, for instance. "I kept us away from the SOB," recalled Mark Anderson. There was more cooperation out in the communities, and the result was some unusual coalitions. In San Francisco, the Teamsters Union and a group of grassroots religious, citizen, and environmental groups called the Coalition for Justice in the Maquiladoras held an anti-NAFTA press conference at the headquarters of Greenpeace.[34] In Washington, Jesse Jackson and Ross Perot appeared together at the annual convention of the Southern Christian Leadership Conference to denounce NAFTA. Perot told the audience that "the first jobs that will go to Mexico" will be those that otherwise might be funneled into inner-city economic development in this country. Jackson described NAFTA as "a slippery slope southward" for American jobs that would lead to the closing of U.S. factories. "NAFTA," he said, "is a shafta, shifting our jobs out of the country."[35] The next day, before a throng gathered on the steps of the Lincoln Memorial to commemorate the thirtieth anniversary of Martin Luther King's "I Have a Dream" speech, AFL-CIO president Lane Kirkland drew his biggest applause for a spirited attack on NAFTA.

At the other end of the political spectrum, Pat Buchanan railed against NAFTA as a threat to American sovereignty:

> NAFTA is about America's sovereignty, liberty and destiny. It is about whether we hand down to the next generation the same free and independent country handed down to us; or whether 21st-century America becomes but a subsidiary of the New International Economic Order.

Buchanan sounded a populist theme.

And all the power elite embrace NAFTA: The *Washington Post, Wall Street Journal* and *New York Times*; Big Business, Big Media, the Big Banks; the Trilateral Commission and the Council on Foreign Relations.

Buchanan ended with a flourish.

From a distance out in the harbor, NAFTA appears a fetching little vessel, flying a proud pennant of "Free Trade." But it is a ship that carries in its cargo the virus of globalism, and the bacillus of statism. Populists and conservatives ought to tow it out beyond the 12-mile limit, with a long rope, and blow it out of the water. Sink NAFTA, and save the old republic.[36]

Whether hand in hand or at arms length, the strange bedfellows in opposition to NAFTA drew attention. Ralph Nader explained to National Public Radio listeners that "the conservative can oppose it because ... U.S. sovereignty is being unduly compromised. Liberals can oppose it because it represents more control of global corporations over our economy. Perot types can oppose it because it represents a sense of loss of control over our society that many people are feeling."[37]

Perot's Surprise

At the end of August, Ross Perot launched another salvo. For months he and Pat Choate had secretly planned and written a book on NAFTA. Remarkably, there had been no leaks. Suddenly, *Save Your Job, Save Our Country: Why NAFTA Must be Stopped—Now!* appeared in bookstores. Washington was abuzz. Congressional aides rushed out to Trover Books, on Pennsylvania Avenue a couple blocks from the Capitol, to get their copies. When Trover sold out, photocopies quickly got around the Hill. More importantly, though, Perot's troops had copies of the book. People started appearing at town meetings with the book in hand, quoting from it as they asked their questions.

The Perot-Choate book had a simple thesis: NAFTA was a conspiracy by big business, big government, and foreign agents intent on enriching themselves at the expense of ordinary Americans. The book's chapter titles give a sense of the argument: "Out Traded—Again," "A Secret Deal," "A Giant Sucking Sound." Page after page, the book leveled charges at NAFTA. "Mexico's strategy depends on taking jobs from the United States." NAFTA will endanger "millions of jobs." NAFTA would allow unsafe Mexican trucks on American highways. "Under NAFTA, smuggling drugs into the United States will become much easier." "Florida's citrus industry will be devastated." Moreover, the agreement had been negotiated in "wartime-like secrecy," and it was the "ultimate insider deal." An appendix listed "Former U.S. Government Officials Working for NAFTA's Passage."[38] Phone and fax numbers of U.S. Senators and Representatives and handy "NAFTA Ballot Cards" ready to mail to Congress members were included. (A United We Stand America membership form was also conveniently appended as well.) To maximize the impact of the book, Perot made the rounds of the radio and television talk shows and bought time for another infomercial to be aired the last weekend of the month.

Perot's book triggered a frenzy of activity at the USTR. Under Rufus Yerxa's supervision, Chip Roh, Ken Freiberg (the deputy general counsel), and Bryan Samuel—the people who knew what was really in the NAFTA agreement—carefully culled through the Perot missive. Within a week they had produced a seventy-three-page, point-by-point rebuttal and distributed it around the Hill. As General Counsel Ira Shapiro recalled, "We took the Perot book very seriously. We made an intense effort to respond to the book. The book was a piece of trash but we didn't underestimate its potential appeal." The administration rebuttal was a most effective critique for anyone not already persuaded by Perot. In the coming months it would provide useful ammunition for NAFTA's defenders.

Assessing the Damage

The opposition strategy seemed to be having its intended effect. Public opinion, for a long time equally divided on NAFTA, turned sharply negative. The NBC–*Wall Street Journal* poll taken September 10–13 found that the percentage favoring NAFTA had fallen from 31 percent in July to 25 percent, whereas the percentage of those opposing NAFTA had shot up from 29 percent to 36 percent, a statistically (and politically) significant difference. Other polls confirmed the finding. A CBS–*New York Times* poll taken September 16–19 showed 33 percent for the agreement and 40 percent against.

On the Hill, David Bonior was increasingly confident. He was now beginning to get close to enough commitments from Representatives to make NAFTA impossible. An AFL-CIO–compiled vote count dated August 20 showed 166 members as "No" and 63 as "Lean No," a total of 229, already well over the 218 needed to defeat NAFTA. With 119 listed as "Undecided," the opposition vote seemed sure to climb. Only 58 members were listed as "Yes" and 29 as "Lean Yes." The numbers corresponded closely with Bonior's own estimates.

Most of those opposed were Democrats, and Bonior thought he might be able to get close to two hundred Democrats in the end, but he would also need conservative Republican votes. Bonior and his staff were getting assurances from California Republican Duncan Hunter, the leader of Republican opposition to NAFTA, that as many as fifty or even sixty Republicans might oppose the agreement. The Republican assurances, however, made Bonior and his staff nervous. The relationship between Hunter and Bonior was uneasy at best. Hunter had campaigned for Bonior's opponent in 1992, and the two men did not like each other. Bonior also kept at arm's length from Ross Perot (they never met during 1993), who was working closely with Hunter and the Republicans. As a result, the conservative Republican vote was a bit of wild card for Bonior and his staff. Still, there appeared to be enough of a cushion.

Hoping to deter the president from making a push for NAFTA, Bonior began to show the strength of his hand. Appearing on NBC's "Meet the Press," Bonior stated, "The fact of the matter is that up to two-thirds and maybe 75 percent of the Democratic caucus in the House is opposed to this treaty."[39] The press could do its math. Two-thirds of the Democrats' two hundred fifty-nine meant that NAFTA was in deep trouble.

Interpreting Grassroots Opposition:
The Market for Meaning

This chapter began with the question of how to explain the unprecedented depth and breadth of opposition to NAFTA in the United States. How can we explain how NAFTA became the focus of such intense opposition for a coalition of such diversity that it could include labor unions and Pat Buchanan, Greenpeace and Ross Perot?

Through which analytical lens should we view this question? In previous chapters, this book has primarily relied on rational choice approaches, arguing in particular that multilevel models can explain apparently irrational behaviors. The opposition to NAFTA, however, would appear to pose a formidable challenge to even multilevel rational choice approaches. Given the small direct effects of NAFTA on the U.S. economy, on the environment, on immigration, on drug smuggling, and the like, and the minuscule impact of any particular individual's opposition, why an average citizen would join United We Stand America, carry a banner at a union rally, write his or her Representative, or even bother to inform him or herself about the issue is hard to understand through a rational choice lens. The scale of political mobilization is simply incompatible with the likely tiny real effects of NAFTA on the issues ostensibly motivating opponents. The domestic grassroots opposition to NAFTA was based less on what NAFTA *was* and more on what it *symbolized*.

The nature of the opposition to NAFTA bears upon an important theoretical issue in political science: the extent to which political phenomena can be explained by strategic interaction among rational actors. Contemporary political science is increasingly dominated by rational choice approaches, which have successfully enlarged the domain of phenomena (many apparently "irrational") explicable by economic, game theoretic, or other formal rational choice models. Among such expansions, two notable thrusts are, first, the concept of ideological consumption as a way of reconciling observed collective action—including voting and political joining—with a logic of collective action in which it is rational for individuals to free ride and, second, the concept of entertainment consumption as a way of reconciling observed demand for policy information with a logic of rational ignorance in which it is rational not to attend to policy issues.

Rational choice theory predicts a demand for and a supply of both ideology and entertainment, in short, a market for symbols. The existence of such a market, therefore, is no threat to rational choice theory. However, rational choice cannot predict the form of the exchange: what symbols will be demanded, and therefore what will be supplied. An understanding of these choices requires a different theoretical lens that considers the form of the symbolism and the way in which symbolic constructs can motivate political action. The section will argue in particular for a theory of narrative politics, in which understandings of politics, and interests in them, are structured by the stories of politics told by and to communities of individuals.

Arguing for the importance of symbolic constructs is not incompatible with rational choice. The behavior of anti-NAFTA activists is consistent with the hypothesis that individuals maximize ideological and entertainment consumption and, in this case, behaved quite rationally given their interests and beliefs. However, to say that the facts do not contradict rational choice is not to say that rational choice adequately explains the facts. Rational choice models can explain much given certain interests and beliefs, but they cannot explain and are not designed to explain the sources of either. Why, in NAFTA, did some individuals care passionately about human rights in Mexico or environmental conditions on the border? Why did they believe that NAFTA would be devastating to these interests? Nor are rational choice theories well suited for fully explaining the mechanism through which constructed interests and beliefs actually translate into political action. Why, even if one cared deeply about Mexico's environment and believed that NAFTA would harm it, would one have an "interest" in acting when such action would have so little effect? On these questions rational choice is silent.

To answer them we need to understand how NAFTA was constructed and what it meant to partisans in the NAFTA battle. We need consider NAFTA not as the 2000-page legal document it was to the technical experts but as a symbol standing for much larger issues to union members, environmentalists, and followers of Ross Perot and Pat Buchanan. That construction was established through the stories told about NAFTA, which not only defined what it meant, but also created an imperative to act.

Collective Action and Ideological Consumption in NAFTA

Rational choice theories—whether the actor is the individual, the group, or the nation—share basic assumptions. Actors are presumed to recognize the options available to them, to predict the likely consequences of those options, to evaluate those consequences in terms of interests, and to choose the option that maximizes expected value. Strong forms of rational choice insist that actors consider all available options, that they correctly predict the consequences of each, that they completely evaluate the impact of those consequences on their interests, and that they always choose the outcome with the highest expected value. Usually, such theories also posit a very limited set of interests, most commonly personal wealth or power. The great virtue of these models is that they allow us to map directly from observable conditions—economic circumstances, for instance—to predicted behaviors, without requiring us to consider such intervening factors as the market for information and the capacities of humans to process it.

The strong version of rational choice is vulnerable to both empirical and theoretical challenge, however, particularly in dealing with mass political phenomena. In *The Logic of Collective Action*, Mancur Olson explicated the problem faced by the collective in the procurement of public goods.[40] Individuals given the choice between acting or not acting have an incentive to free ride on the actions of others, since the actors must bear the full marginal costs of acting but enjoy only a fraction of the marginal benefits. The tendency to free ride becomes more acute as the size of the group increases. The theory nicely explains many collective action failures. But in some sense it overpredicts such failures. Notwithstanding a tendency toward free riding, individuals do not always free ride. People vote, although it appears illogical to do so; people give money to charity; and people join and participate in political advocacy organizations.

To resolve this apparent contradiction, rational choice theorists have broadened the scope of interests to include the possibility that individuals derive utility from altruism or from ideological consumption.[41] We vote not only because we care about the outcome but because we gain satisfaction from doing our civic duty. We participate in organizations not because we will gain if the policy goals are realized but because we gain by participating in the process of attempting to realize them. (Some incentives, of course, have nothing to do with altruism or ideology. Organizations often give their members such perks as breaks on car rentals, magazine subscriptions, and discounts on merchandise.)

The idea of ideological consumption applied to NAFTA provides a way of understanding how interested communities—environmentalists, human rights activists, and the like—overcame the logic of collective action to mobilize in opposition to NAFTA. If individuals concerned about the environment derived utility only from the expected incremental change in policy resulting from the decision to join an organization, write a letter, or attend a rally, the marginal benefits of such action would be so small that the rational choice would be not to act and to free ride on the actions of others. Instead, if individuals receive satisfaction from the act of joining, writing, or attending because of some form of ideological consumption—they feel good about themselves, for instance—then acting might be entirely rational, even when the individual correctly understands the expected effects of action on policy outcome and the effects of policy outcome on his or her policy interests. However, the question remains as to why individuals have particular ideological interests of this kind.

Rational Ignorance and the Market for "Entertainment" in NAFTA

The theoretical challenge posed by Anthony Downs in *An Economic Theory of Democracy* is similar in form but even more formidable than the logic of free riding. As Downs demonstrates, it is not often rational to be rational. More specifically, it is irrational for most individuals in a society to inform themselves enough about political issues to make the kind of judgments strong forms of rational choice require. By its own logic, rational choice theory is, therefore, self-limiting.

Downs demonstrates that when acquiring political information is costly and the marginal benefit of its acquisition is low there is no incentive to acquire it. The marginal benefit of learning more about a political candidate's views on a particular issue, for instance, depends on the probability that additional information would change one's vote, the probability that the changed vote would change the electoral outcome, and the probability a changed electoral outcome would result in a change of policy: in short, a vanishingly small number. Citizens may have greater influence on policy decision making between elections because of the smaller number of people who will attempt to influence policy, but this relatively greater incentive to acquire information is offset by the additional problem of acquiring information about the decision making processes in which the citizen might intervene. Taken together, these conditions imply, as Downs put it:

In general, it is irrational to be politically well-informed because the low returns from data simply do not justify their cost in time and other scarce resources. Therefore, many voters do not bother to discover their true views before voting, and most citizens are not well enough informed to influence directly the formulation of those policies that affect them.[42]

The logic of rational ignorance can be extended to the entire rational choice process: the identification of options, mapping from option to outcome, and evaluating outcomes. To the extent that any of these steps are costly, individuals should, logically, not incur the costs for those policy matters on which their actions will have little appreciable effect. Thus even when acquiring information is virtually costless (available free and at the touch of a few keystrokes via the Internet, for example), one may opt to remain ignorant because processing the information remains costly.

One might predict on the basis of the theory that individuals with little political power would simply ignore the political process and hold no views on policy matters (in much the same way that they would, by the logic of collective action, not involve themselves). Empirically, however, people do acquire information above the levels one might predict based on a calculus of its marginal value. For Downs, all such information is acquired for its "entertainment" value.

> Some citizens find exhilaration in arguing about politics or following campaigns; others pin social prestige at cocktail parties from appearing well-versed in current affairs. We classify information obtained for all such purposes as entertainment information, no matter how political its contents may seem.[43]

The concepts of rational ignorance and of entertainment information can explain why there might not be congruence between the reality of NAFTA and the beliefs held about it. The problem of analyzing the likely effects of NAFTA on one's future job prospects, or on the environment, or on any other dimension of concern was extremely difficult. Consider assessing the marginal impact of NAFTA on the environment. To do this, one needs information about the status quo, about the terms of the agreement, about the nature of plant location decisions, and a host of other factors. For a citizen with little ability to influence the policy outcome, the marginal ben-

efit of acquiring such information is absolutely dwarfed by the cost of acquiring and processing it. In short, it would be irrational not only to acquire
such costly information but also to use it to derive beliefs about the relationship between NAFTA and desired policy outcomes.

Nevertheless, many citizens with little prospect of influencing the policy
outcome did acquire information about NAFTA and formed strongly held
beliefs about its likely effects. The questions are: Why did they acquire such
information? and How did they form such beliefs? To the first question, the
answer has a supply side and a demand side. On the supply side, a small
number of parties provided relatively costless information to union members
and Sierra Club members (and USA*NAFTA members, for that matter).
On the demand side, the information was consumed because it was "entertainment" in Downs's terms, or more generally because it had value independent of its utility for furthering individuals' policy interests.

Beyond Entertainment: The Market for Symbols
and the Politics of Meaning

Downs's concept of entertainment information works as a residual category when the subject of interest is political information, but the concept is
insufficiently developed if we wish to understand what it is that is "enter-
taining" about politics. What made information about NAFTA so "enter-
taining" when other trade agreements of equal or greater policy import were
apparently so dull? (For instance, the author once received the following
comment on a student evaluation of his trade policy course: "I learned that
trade policy is not funny.") To answer this question, we need to understand
more about what it is we really consume when we are entertained by politics.
For that, we need to consider the importance of symbols and stories in
serving a fundamental human interest: the desire to make sense of the world
and one's place in it—the desire for meaning.

To make sense of the form of symbolic communication requires a sociological and social psychological perspective. In recent decades, this perspective has been largely ignored by political scientists, although there is now a
renewed interest in the role of ideas, myths, and other socially constructed
forms of ideation.[44] A theory of socially constructed knowledge that emphasizes the importance of dramatic narrative is most useful to the present discussion.[45]

A first assumption of the theory is that humans apprehend the world through symbol systems. Humans are "symbol-using animals" writes the sociologist Kenneth Burke.

> But can we bring ourselves to realize just what that formula implies, just how overwhelmingly much of what we mean by "reality" has been built up for us through nothing but our symbol systems? Take away our books, and what little do we know about history, biography, even something so "down to earth" as the relative position of seas and continents? What is our "reality" for today (beyond the paper-thin line of our own particular lives) but all this clutter of symbols about the past combined with whatever things we know mainly through maps, magazines, newspapers, and the like about the present?[46]

This perspective implies a gap between reality and our apprehension of it.

Second, humans tend to organize symbols into narrative constructions, i.e., stories. Through stories we apprehend our world, we place ourselves in it, and we remember. Stories are central to identity formation of people and groups. Humans are story tellers and story consumers.

Third, our consumption interest in stories is a function of both the form of the story and the content. We consume stories for their own sake. We enjoy stories that are dramatic, that have sympathetic protagonists, rising and falling plot lines, and the possibility of heroism and villainy, triumph or disaster. Thomas Schelling, erstwhile economist, contemplates what interest is being met when we consume fiction:

> Lassie died one night. Millions of viewers, not all of them children, grieved. At least, they shed tears. Except for the youngest, the mourners knew that Lassie didn't really exist. Whatever that means. Perhaps with their left hemispheres they could articulate that they had been watching a trained dog and that *that* dog was still alive, healthy and rich; meanwhile in their right hemispheres, or some such place (if these phenomena have a place), the real Lassie had died.
>
> Did they enjoy the episode?
>
> We know they would not have enjoyed the death of the dog that played Lassie. Did the adults and older children wish their children hadn't watched? Do the dry-eyed parents of a moist-eyed teenager wish their children hadn't watched? If he hadn't watched, what would have

been his grief at breakfast, reading the news that Lassie was dead? And would he regret missing the final episode?[47]

Schelling notes that stories such as Lassie "capture the mind" and ponders what that means.

> The characteristic that interests me is the engrossment—not merely the surrender of attention but the participation, the sense of being in the story or part of it, caring, and wanting to know.[48]

What is being consumed is the *engrossment*, the abandonment of self in the story.

Fourth, communities of people share a stock of socially constructed symbols, stories, and myths.[49] These stories not only entertain, they also define identity and interest. The stock of these stories taken together constitute what Burke calls a "folk psychology."[50] They define a worldview, create a sense of communal identity, give meaning to experience, and resolve psychological conflicts.

Fifth, new stories, stories of NAFTA for example, will resonate in a community to the extent that they confirm existing worldviews, reinforce communal sense of identity, give meaning to new events, and limit the psychological dissonance of those events. Resonance depends on their fit with the folk psychology.

Sixth, stories can create interests as well as understandings. This is not news to advertisers. Of course, some advertising is intended to convey information to help consumers make rational choices: Medication X lasts longer than medication Y. But most advertising is about telling stories to capture the mind, to trigger certain associations, and thereby to shape demand. Take, for example, the demand for diamond engagement rings. What is it that a man purchases when he nervously approaches the counter at the jewelry store? Is it a densely compacted, precisely cut, extremely hard lump of carbon? Unlikely. More likely, he is purchasing not the stone, but what the stone signifies—love, commitment, affluence—just what the Ayer company hoped he would purchase when it created the demand for large diamond engagement rings with its "A Diamond Is Forever" advertising campaign for the DeBeers company in the late 1940s.[51]

Stories do more than inform interests, they are also a vehicle for internalizing values, norms, and mores. We learn how to conduct ourselves in life, how to relate to others, what is right and wrong through stories. This is obvious in religious teaching, where the parable is the primary approach to teaching morals. It is also obvious in the stories we tell our children. *The Little Engine That Could* is more than entertainment; it is a way of teaching about the virtue of charity, the importance of persistence, and the perils of pride.

Seventh, public stories can create an imperative for social action by connecting events to personal and group identity. In the same way that we participate in the story of Lassie, public stories invite us to participate in them, to become engrossed, and in so doing to lose the distinction between private and public. The dramatic imperative of the story becomes a matter of personal identity.[52] To take arms against oppression is a civic duty, to march together against injustice an expression of who we are. We "couldn't live with ourselves" if we didn't act. In this way, symbolic communication can overcome the problem of collective action, by creating a private interest in the maintenance of identity.

A narrative theory of politics consistent with these assumptions would suggest that our understandings of politics are mediated by symbols, that we have a predilection for symbols organized into simple dramatic narratives, that we particularly like stories that confirm our worldviews, resolve psychological conflicts, and maintain our sense of personal and collective identity. The essence of this mode of politics, then, is the contest of possible meanings, the way in which different stories, dramatizations, and gestures orient us to political events. To analyze this politics requires careful attention to the content of rhetoric, gesture, and symbol. It requires attention to the symbolic meaning of texts.

The Meaning of NAFTA

The theory of the politics of meaning suggests that political events such as NAFTA are apprehended through simple symbol systems and that those symbols give meaning through dramatic interpretation. We understand in terms of simple stories that not only make sense of the world, but also locate us in it. To understand the political response to NAFTA, therefore, requires that we pay close attention to what people said it meant to them, to the story as they told it.

We can treat the rhetoric of the protagonists as text to be interpreted. The rhetoric, of course, was instrumental and may or may not reveal the speaker's true beliefs. But these texts reveal what the speaker believes to be effective with an audience.[53] For a skilled politician such as Pat Buchanan, we will assume that the rhetoric is not without effect.[54]

What was the story of NAFTA for labor unions? Take as an example this letter written by a union worker opposing NAFTA and published in the UAW magazine *Solidarity* in July 1993.

> I see the destruction of America's working class. The destruction is not only the loss of financial security and physical property gained through years of hard work, it is the destruction of the dreams, the expectations of each of us that our children will have a better life. Millions of Americans have already begun the descent down the ladder, and as pay levels of every class continue a downward spiral, there is nowhere else to go but further down. And those at the top are pushing the ones at the bottom right off the ladder.[55]

The story is a tragedy, a tale of a lost golden age. In the beginning (before Reagan, at least), all was well. But the corporations got greedy. With their friends in power they used the weapons of free trade and deregulation to ship American jobs overseas, dismantle social regulation, and destroy unions. The victims are workers, unions, and the American dream. The villains are the faceless corporations, driven by greed, remorseless, relentless. Their accomplices are the friends of corporations in government, corrupted by the big money.

"NAFTA is killing us," said more than one angry union spokesperson to the author during the NAFTA campaign. Note the present tense. NAFTA was not some marginal change of rules that might or might not be implemented next year. It was all that was happening now, all that had happened in the past, all that might happen in the future. It was shuttered factories in the Midwest. It was trickle-down economics, deregulation, and cheap foreign labor. It was two million jobs lost in the 1980s. It was cardboard shacks, toxic dumps, and babies with no brains. It was the corporate executive contemplating a move to Mexico in the "Yes You Can, Yucatan" ad. It was America gone wrong.

Logically, of course, NAFTA was not to blame for what had already happened or for underlying trends that would continue with or without the agreement. But symbolically, NAFTA stood for all that had happened to American workers in the 1980s and all they feared for the future.

What was the story of NAFTA for the grassroots environmental organizations? Take as example the rhetoric in a full-page advertisement entitled "8 Fatal Flaws of NAFTA: Environmental Catastrophe, Canada to Mexico" purchased by Public Citizen, Sierra Club, Friends of the Earth, Earth Island Institute, the Humane Society of the United States, the American Society for the Prevention of Cruelty to Animals, Community Nutrition Institute, Southwest Network on Environmental Racism, and seventeen other groups. The ad ran in both the *Washington Post* and the *New York Times* in September 1993.

1. Don't Call it "Free Trade": it's Corporate Aid. . . . The true purpose of NAFTA is to help large corporations increase their profits. . . . NAFTA was a major part of George Bush's "trickle down economics" scheme.
2. NAFTA Prevents Public Participation. . . . The corporate world is spending more than $5 million, and Mexico is spending more than $30 million, on public relations campaigns to obscure the truth.
3. NAFTA Suppresses Democracy. . . . NAFTA will seriously stifle representative democracy by making local, state or national laws *subject to an unelected NAFTA bureaucracy that citizens cannot control.*
4. NAFTA Can Kill Environmental Laws. . . . "Good-bye" dolphin protection.
5. Ravaging Natural Resources. . . . NAFTA could devastate the resources of *all three* NAFTA countries. *That is its intention:* To help corporations seize resources, wherever they hide.
6. Creating Toxic Hell. . . . Corporations can freely dump their toxic wastes without the interventions of an EPA [Environmental Protection Agency]. We have seen the results in the toxic hell on the Mexican border, where the mess makes Love Canal look like Yellowstone Park. Under NAFTA, the situation will get worse.
7. Side Agreements Fiasco. . . . The public is still kept from any true role. There are still not enough funds for clean-up. Corporations can still flee across borders to freely pollute.
8. NAFTA's Big Bucks Backers. . . . IF NAFTA succeeds, multinational corporations stand to reap huge windfall profits. *That is why the agreement was created in the first place.* The lobbying is underway. Eastman Kodak and American Express have spearheaded a pro-NAFTA coalition of 2,000 of the largest corporations in the

country, including such stellar environmentalists as Exxon, Dupont, General Electric, Dow Chemical and Union Carbide.

The story told here is, like the union story, a tragedy, but with different protagonists. In the beginning, the environment was clean, pure, uncorrupted. Citizen environmentalists sought to protect it, but international corporations and their accomplices in the (Reagan-Bush) government were bent on dismantling the protection and despoiling nature for profit. The villain is again corporations but somewhat more abstractly development itself, the accomplices the agents of business in government, and the victims now are the environment and democracy.

NAFTA stood for toxic waste and brain-damaged babies. It was dolphins drowned in tuna nets. It meant destruction and death. It was about greed, corruption, and irresponsibility. Logically, NAFTA could not be responsible for what had happened. But symbolically, it stood for all that had enraged the environmental community.

What was the story of NAFTA to Ross Perot? Consider this transcript from Larry King Live on CNN. Perot begins by holding up a picture.

MR. PEROT: There in the shadow of the plant there. There's dirt floor, cardboard shacks, no plumbing, no electricity.

MR. KING: This where Mexicans live who work in American plants?

MR. PEROT: In the American plants now that are in Mexico. If we could go to the second picture. That's a close-up of one of the houses. See, these people have none of the standard of living that, say, and automobile worker in Detroit would have, lives a middle class life. Go to the third picture if you will. Here's a man building a cardboard shack. Those are—

MR. KING: But what does that have to do—what does that say about NAFTA?

MR. PEROT: That says these are the working conditions under which the people live because they make so little.

MR. KING: But that's now. Wouldn't NAFTA improve that?

MR. PEROT: No. Now is the maquiladora program that has been going on for years and the whole reason people go to Mexico is for the low cost labor. If you can cut your labor cost to one-seventh of U.S. labor, that's an overwhelming reason to go.

MR. KING: But if you can do that anyway—

MR. PEROT: No, but—now wait just a minute. We're $4 trillion in debt; we're going a billion dollars in debt every other day. We've got everybody west of the Mississippi working all year long just to pay interest on the debt. If we implode the middle class in our country—now here's why we're so much against it. We're destroying good, decent, hard-working people. They will not be paying taxes any more. We won't have a chance to balance a budget and their lives will be devastated, Larry. That's why it's so wrong. They will have to give up their homes. You see? . . . People haven't thought through how this interrelates. Corporate America likes this deal, Wall Street likes this deal. . . .

MR. KING: And they have bought both parties?

MR. PEROT: No, no, no, I'm not saying that. But these are the people they're associated with and these are the people they talk to and inside the Beltway a who's who of the lobbying industry loves this deal because it's making them rich.[56]

Perot's story was yet another tragedy, but with a slightly different cast and a sharper edge. In the beginning (before trade deficits and the global economy), America was healthy and strong. But the short-sighted corporations, corrupt government, and foreign agents conspired to weaken America and make us vulnerable to international competitors. NAFTA was about the evisceration of America, a sucking from the south that was leeching the lifeblood from the American economy. The victims are Americans: good, honest, hardworking. The villains, co-conspirators, are big international corporations, big government, and agents of Mexico (metaphorically Mexico itself).

NAFTA was "a sucking sound" of jobs bleeding out of America. It was "Yes You Can, Yucatan." It was disgusting cesspools and cardboard shacks. It was former government officials gone bad, corrupt, traitorous. It was secrecy and conspiracy. Logically, the United States and Mexico would share a border with or without NAFTA. Metaphorically, NAFTA was about contamination by the poverty, filth, and corruption of Mexico.

What was NAFTA to Pat Buchanan? Consider as text Buchanan's August 1993 editorial against the agreement.

NAFTA is about America's sovereignty, liberty and destiny. It is about whether we hand down to the next generation the same free and independent country handed down to us; or whether 21st-century America becomes but a subsidiary of the New International Economic Order. . . . And all the power elite embrace NAFTA: The *Washington Post, Wall Street Journal* and *New York Times*; Big Business, Big Media, the Big Banks; the Trilateral Commission and the Council on Foreign Relations. . . . [NAFTA is] a ship that carries in its cargo the virus of globalism, and the bacillus of statism.[57]

The Buchanan story was again a tragedy. America was once healthy, free, strong, independent. Foreign contamination, spread by the international elite, was entangling us, sapping our strength, eviscerating our culture, corrupting our health. The victim here is America itself, the villains the corrupt international elite, big business, and big government.

What is obvious by now is the remarkably similar form of all the stories told by players across a wide political spectrum. All are variants of populism, a staple of American political culture, a perennial tale of bad big government and big business against the little people. Considered as variants of the central populist mythology, it should not be so surprising to hear virtually the same story from both ends of the political spectrum. Tom Watson, for example, a dynamic populist leader of the late nineteenth century, began a liberal on the question of race and ended a virulent racist, and never abandoned his populism.[58]

Meaning and Motivation: The Dramatic Imperative

If the meaning of NAFTA to members of unions and opposition environmental groups, and to followers of Ross Perot and Pat Buchanan, was defined by the heated rhetoric, then it is a good deal easier to explain grassroots political mobilization. A belief that NAFTA would destroy hundreds of thousands of jobs, devastate the environment, undermine democracy, or threaten American society certainly is more compelling than a belief that NAFTA would have only modest effects. Opposition political leaders, by exaggerating the likely effects of NAFTA as they constructed it for their followers, changed the incentives for action.

This interpretation of the role of symbolic construction begins to explain how symbolic construction operates to overcome the natural tendency toward collective inaction. It is not, however, completely satisfactory. Even if individuals believed the worst about NAFTA, they still faced a temptation to free ride when deciding whether or not to take action. That a failure to act collectively will have devastating consequences does not ensure that the collective will act. In order to explain collective action, we need to posit that individuals benefit not only from the goals of action, but also from the action itself.

The theory of symbolic politics developed earlier suggests two related interpretations. First, taking action against NAFTA was not so much an act in pursuit of some policy interest as it was an act of identity assertion. If one identifies oneself as an environmentalist and believes that NAFTA will devastate the environment, then one is compelled to act in order to maintain that identification. If one is a unionist and believes that NAFTA will destroy jobs, then opposing NAFTA is an expression of solidarity. Not to act in the face of these beliefs would threaten one's sense of identity.

A second closely related way of interpreting action has to do with the relationship between narrative and action. To the extent that stories of NAFTA were engrossing, in the sense of participation in the dramatic narrative, those stories both served to mediate between private and public identity and to create a dramatic imperative for action. If NAFTA was a story about the destruction of the working class by the forces of big business, and one identified with the victims, opposition to NAFTA would become an act of heroism, and failure to act one of villainy. If NAFTA engaged its audiences as potentially tragic narratives about despoliation of the environment, corruption of democracy, or treasonous betrayal of America, then opposition would become the right thing to do.

A Note on Public Opinion

It is difficult to establish just how these narrative framings affected attitudes about NAFTA, either among followers of particular leaders or among the general public. The evidence, however, suggests that the framings did make some difference in public opinion. During the period in which public messages about NAFTA were largely dominated by its opponents, public attitudes turned sharply worse. Even more suggestively, the dimensions that underlay this negative attitude corresponded reasonably well to the ways in which opponents sought to frame NAFTA. At the beginning of September 1993, a large segment of the American public apparently imagined NAFTA as a conspiracy that aimed to enrich corporate America by allowing it to exploit cheap labor and lax environmental standards in Mexico, that risked American jobs and the environment, and that opened America to the twin dangers of illegal drugs and illegal immigrants.

Conclusions

This commentary has argued that to interpret the grassroots politics of opposition to NAFTA requires a theory of symbolic politics. Although the tenets of constructivist theory differ markedly from rational choice (and institutional process) approaches, they are not incompatible. Indeed, by its own self-limiting logic, rational choice predicts a market for symbols when the costs of information acquisition and processing are high and the potential benefits of using symbols to reinforce identities or worldviews are also high.

A symbolic lens applied to the domestic politics of NAFTA can explain why NAFTA evoked such a disproportionate political response. As apprehended by union members, grassroots environmentalists, disaffected citizens supporting Ross Perot, conservative followers of Pat Buchanan, and members of the general public, NAFTA had come to stand for stories of greedy corporations, corrupt politicians, and foreign interests in league against workers, family farmers, communities, and the environment. NAFTA was cast as the villain in a drama whose symbolic imperative was opposition. Opposition to NAFTA wasn't a calculated choice to maximize one's interests, it was a matter of honor, a matter of moral imperative, and an affirmation of identity.

8 Diagnosis and Strategy: The Campaign for NAFTA

As Washington returned to work in September, strategists at the White House, in the business community, and on Capitol Hill surveyed the situation. What they saw was not encouraging. August had been a disaster. Members of Congress had been pummeled by angry opponents back in their home districts. They had heard nothing from NAFTA's supporters. Public opinion was now running against the agreement. The vote counts looked terrible. If the vote were held then, NAFTA would lose.

The strategists recognized that this was not trade politics as usual. To solve their problem in Congress, they would need more than lobbying pressure, they would need to change the political context outside of Congress. There was little time to waste. From a near standstill, the administration, the business community, and a host of other allies sprang into action. Over the next two months they would conduct the most extensive campaign ever waged for a trade agreement, complete with grassroots organizing, paid television commercials, and the spectacle of a nationally televised debate between Vice President Al Gore and Ross Perot. NAFTA's opponents, of course, did not stand still, but rather redoubled their efforts. The resulting battle made great news, and as NAFTA became the most covered issue of the fall, the stakes rose ever higher.

This chapter recounts the tumultuous battle of the fall of 1993, focusing particularly on the campaign for NAFTA. It seeks to answer three questions: What was the nature of the political problem confronting NAFTA's supporters as the campaign began? How did their diagnosis of the problem translate into strategy? and How did strategy contribute to NAFTA's ultimate victory?

Planning the Campaign for NAFTA

Advocacy for NAFTA had been plagued for most of the year by the lack of a coherent strategy. The Clinton administration had been preoccupied with other matters, the business community unequipped to take the lead, and NAFTA's advocates on the Hill limited in what they could do alone. In August, President Clinton had announced the appointment of Bill Daley, youngest son of former Chicago mayor Richard Daley and brother of the current mayor, Richie Daley, to head up the administration's NAFTA effort. Now, at the beginning of September, with Daley on board and the White House finally paying attention to NAFTA, with new leadership in the business community, and with the Hill whip groups in place, the campaign for NAFTA could begin in earnest.

The Strategists

The administration team came together quickly in early September. Bill Daley had been brought on to head a new NAFTA task force with as much fanfare as could be mustered at the time. President Clinton issued a statement saying that Daley's appointment "should be viewed as a signal of my personal commitment." The press quickly dubbed Daley the "NAFTA czar." As deputies, Daley brought in Rahm Emmanuel from the White House political operation and Lloyd Bentsen's aide Kurt Campbell from the Treasury Department. After a couple weeks camped out in Mickey Kantor's office at the USTR (Office of the United States Trade Representative), Daley's staff began to assemble in temporary quarters in the Old Executive Office Building next to the White House.

Also joining Daley was Bill Frenzel, a former Republican Congressman well-versed in trade from his days on the Ways and Means Committee. Frenzel's appointment had been urged by House of Representatives Whip Newt Gingrich, who wanted a Republican to work with Daley. "Republicans were nervous that the inside stuff would go over their heads or pass them over," recalled Frenzel later. "They wanted an in-house friend."

Daley's shop worked closely with Howard Paster, head of White House Congressional Relations and his deputy Susan Brophy, both now freed from the budget battle to focus on NAFTA, and with Mickey Kantor and his Chief of Staff Tom Nides, General Counsel Ira Shapiro, and Assistant USTR for Congressional Relations Nancy Leamond. For the next two and a half months, this group would be consumed with the effort to pass NAFTA.

Before the business community would really commit to a serious campaign, it needed reassurance that the administration was equally committed. In August, David Rockefeller, scion of the Rockefeller family and a long-time advocate of free trade with Mexico, organized a meeting between the leadership of the business community and key players in the Clinton administration. With Rockefeller were John Ong, new chair of the Business Roundtable; Hank Greenberg, CEO of the insurance company American International Group (AIG); Kay Whitmore, outgoing CEO of Eastman Kodak; and Larry Bossidy, CEO of Allied Signal and soon-to-be chair of USA*NAFTA. The administration was represented by National Economic Advisor Robert Rubin, Treasury Secretary Lloyd Bentsen, Commerce Secretary Ron Brown, White House chief of staff Mack McLarty, and USTR Mickey Kantor.

As one observer recalls, "There was real skepticism on both sides of the table." The business leaders came in suspicious that Clinton was going to take a walk; the administration was not impressed with the business effort. The discussion was frank. Both sides laid out what the other needed to do, and each told the other that nothing short of total commitment would be sufficient. The administration show of strength did its job. The business leaders left convinced that the White House was prepared to fight for NAFTA.

In early September, leadership of USA*NAFTA formally passed to Larry Bossidy when Kay Whitmore was ousted from the top spot at Eastman Kodak. The change energized the business effort. Whitmore had been a low-key leader, distracted by his troubles at Kodak. "Bossidy," recalled one member of the business strategy team, made "a light-year's difference. He is a focused, take no prisoners, take charge guy." With the switch at the top, too, the day-to-day leadership of USA*NAFTA was transferred from Whitmore aide Sandy Masur to Ken Cole, director of legislative affairs for Allied Signal. Joining Cole in the inner circle of business strategists were Francis O'Brien and Paige Gardner of the Fratelli Group, Business Roundtable lawyer Chuck Levy, and Gail Harrison of the Wexler Group.

Other business groups joined the effort, including the U.S. Chamber of Commerce, the National Association of Manufacturers, and the Emergency Committee for Action on Trade (ECAT). Paralleling the USA*NAFTA effort, viewed by Republicans as too dominated by Democratic strategists and too close to the White House, a smaller Republican business lobbying effort took form. Nick Calio, former head of Congressional Relations in the Bush White House, coordinated a group of Republican lobbyists.

In the House, the pro-NAFTA effort was divided along partisan lines. On the Democratic side, Bill Richardson and Bob Matsui continued to share responsibilities for the pro-NAFTA efforts, with Matsui aide Diane Sullivan being the key liaison with the White House and business strategy efforts. For the Republicans, Minority Leader Bob Michel and his chief whip Newt Gingrich were the lead players, with Michel aide Billy Pitts serving as chief liaison with Bill Frenzel and Nick Calio. In the Senate, Bill Bradley and John Chafee jointly chaired an informal whip group staffed by the author and Chafee aide Amy Dunathan.

Assessing the Situation

For all the NAFTA strategists, a first task was to assess the situation on the Hill after the August recess. Daley, Paster, Brophy, Leamond, and other strategists made the rounds on the Hill, conferring in the House with Bob Matsui, Bill Richardson, and Dan Rostenkowski and in the Senate with Bill Bradley. USA*NAFTA did the same. What they learned was that, although the Senate looked OK, the votes simply weren't there in the House.

Through the summer the administration and the business community had been reasonably confident of winning. The USTR vote count of June 30 showed 196 in the "yes" and "lean yes" columns and 169 in the "no" and "lean no" columns, with 71 undecided. USA*NAFTA's numbers were about the same, Matsui's a bit more pessimistic. The expectation had been that completion of the side agreements would enable many undecided members to announce their support. Instead, exactly the opposite happened. In September the numbers plummeted. USA*NAFTA's numbers of "yes" and "lean yes" went from 186 in August to only 161 in mid-September, and then to 139 by the end of the month. Its numbers of "no" and "lean no" jumped from 168 to 191 to 203. "We were in worse shape than we imagined," recalled Susan Brophy. "We were shocked at the number of people who announced their opposition around Labor Day. We looked at the numbers, kept looking at the spreadsheet. It wasn't impossible, but we had so little maneuverability."

To further complicate matters, the Republican House leadership intended to force the White House to deliver as many Democratic votes as possible. Republicans were in no mood to risk political damage to deliver a victory to Bill Clinton. They were feeling political pressure from Ross Perot, whose supporters had been the margin of victory in many of their elections. Minority Leader Michel and Whip Gingrich insisted on 100 Democrats. To keep the pressure on, they refused to share whip lists with the White House. "The Republican votes were kept quiet," recalled Nick Calio. "We were going to make sure they provided us as many votes as possible. We didn't want to give them any passes."

In September, getting 100 Democratic votes looked nearly impossible. By Matsui's count, no more than 60 Democrats were in the "yes" or "lean yes" column. To get to 100 would require winning the support of every member listed in the undecided column. Furthermore, the momentum was in the wrong direction. Indeed, the opponents appeared close to getting the necessary 218 locked up. "My fear was always that they would be able to stand there with 218 bodies and it would be numerically impossible," recalled Bill Daley.

In the Senate, the vote looked to be less of a problem. The Bradley and Chafee head count in September showed 47 "yes" or "lean yes," with 20 undecided. But in the Senate, there was a significant procedural obstacle. Senator Daniel Patrick Moynihan, chairman of the all-important Finance Committee, was not tipping his hand about where he stood. His staff warned that he might well oppose NAFTA. Fritz Hollings, chairman of the Commerce Committee, which would also have to act on the bill, was squarely opposed. Under fast track rules, either Senator, if he wanted, could hold the bill in committee for up to fifteen legislative days after the House acted, which might make it impossible to bring the bill to a vote in 1993 if the House did not act quickly enough.

NAFTA's strategists recognized that the ultimate problem was not really on the Hill. It was with the tremendous pressure Congress members were feeling from outside political forces. The opposition had been very effective during the recess. "People came back to Washington saying they had been pretty well beaten up on this," said Representative David L. Hobson (Republican, Ohio).[1] Mail in every Congressional office ran strongly against the agreement. The labor unions, for many Democrats their largest campaign contributor, were angrily opposed. Members of the large freshman class, many of whom had run on an anti-NAFTA platform the year before, were particularly vulnerable. The forty-member Black Caucus had taken a formal stand against NAFTA. Other Democrats had problems with strong agricultural constituencies, especially in Florida, Louisiana, and California, where sugar, citrus, and vegetable growers were likely to face competition from Mexican imports.

Moreover, general public opinion appeared to have swung solidly against NAFTA. The September NBC–*Wall Street Journal* poll showed that now only 25 percent of the American public favored NAFTA whereas 36 percent opposed it.[2] The opposition message that NAFTA was a job loser appeared to have done the most damage, as the Greenberg survey in the summer warned that it might (see chapter 7). Fully 74 percent of the American public agreed with the proposition "American jobs will move to Mexico," whereas only 20 percent disagreed. And "jobs" appeared to be the most important determinant of stance on NAFTA. Of those who opposed NAFTA, a startling 66 percent volunteered "lost jobs" when asked why, no other answer being offered more than 6 percent of the time. Of those opposed to NAFTA, 79 percent disagreed with the statement "Some jobs would be lost in the U.S., but even more jobs would be created." Interestingly, NAFTA supporters held almost opposite views, with 77 percent agreeing that more jobs would be created than lost.

Opinions about NAFTA did have some silver linings, however. When asked what might happen if NAFTA were *not* passed, 34 percent of Americans thought that immigration from Mexico would go up and only 3 percent thought it would go down (the rest saying it would not be affected); 54 percent agreed that the United States "would have to give more foreign aid and loans to Mexico in order to support their economy"; and 53 percent thought that "Japan and Europe will take advantage of economic opportunities in Mexico, and we would lose the chance to export our goods to Mexico." Perhaps most hopeful was the finding that 69 percent of Americans would support NAFTA, and only 21 percent oppose it, if it "resulted in some U.S. industries being hurt and some jobs being lost, but more new jobs were created than were lost."

An Initial Strategy

First, supporters of NAFTA had to stop the bleeding, i.e., halt the flow of commitments to the opposition. "The whole thrust of our message after

Labor Day was, 'Don't make a decision. Give us time,' " recalled Bill Daley. "I thought if we could get to October 1, and we could get action by committees started that it would be hard to stop." Administration officials and business lobbyists took the message to the Hill: "Wait. Don't get locked in. Keep your powder dry." The bleeding slowed.

Howard Paster and Speaker of the House Tom Foley agreed to set a date for the House vote. Senate Majority Leader George Mitchell had announced his intention to adjourn the Senate before Thanksgiving. That meant that the House vote would need to be in November. Bill Daley urged that the vote be as late as possible, to give him as much time as possible, but the president was going to Seattle for a meeting of APEC (Asia-Pacific Economic Cooperation) member heads of state on November 18. Howard Paster did not want the vote while the president was away. "The only issue of any significance I lost all year was the economic stimulus bill," he explained. "The president was in Vancouver for the timber summit, and then meeting with [Russian Prime Minister Boris] Yeltsin. The president is the best lobbyist in town. If he had been here, we would have won. We had to vote before he left." Paster and Foley agreed on Wednesday, November 17, for the vote.

The administration strategists planned a two-pronged approach. "We had an inside strategy and an outside strategy," recalled Daley. The inside strategy would focus solely on undecided members in the House. "We took it as a given that if we got it out of the House, the Senate would be all right," Daley recalled. Howard Paster and Susan Brophy in the White House and Nancy Leamond at the USTR took the lead in organizing the Hill effort. The president was their best lobbyist, but his time would be limited at first. In his stead, however, all cabinet officers would be available to talk with members. Every contact would be logged, providing the strategists with increasingly elaborate profiles of every undecided member's concerns. Staffers at the Departments of State, Treasury, and Agriculture, and, of course, those at the USTR and in Daley's war room, geared up to answer questions and provide information.

The administration's outside campaign was designed to help members of Congress with their political problem. "We were developing a cover to let members vote the way they substantively and intellectually wanted to vote," recalled Bill Daley. With the president's time limited, the cabinet officers would again need to step in, appearing on the television talk shows and writing opinion columns for the major newspapers. Much of the effort, how-

ever, went into working with the business community in its efforts to mobilize support for NAFTA.

Until September, the business community had not really focused on
NAFTA. Now, reassured of the administration's commitment, USA*-
NAFTA's Ken Cole set out to mount an effective business campaign. To
Cole, as to the White House strategists, the task looked formidable. "We
were digging out of an enormous hole here," recalled Cole. "My thinking
was, we'll put our best effort and try as hard as we can, but at the time I
didn't think it would work." In Cole's mind, the first task was to "change the
conventional wisdom in Washington from 'dead on arrival' to 'watch out,
they have their act together.'" To do that, he needed to do three things:
"make NAFTA a first tier issue in Washington offices, start winning the
grassroots back home, and compete on the airwaves around the country."

Cole later explained, "NAFTA was in every Washington office a third-
tier issue. First-tier issues are issues that have an immediate company significance. Second-tier issues are issues that affect the industry. But third-tier
issues are issues where you have a functional person monitoring it but aren't
doing anything." Cole and his boss Larry Bossidy set out to change that. At
a meeting of the Business Roundtable in early September, Bossidy gave a
rousing speech to the hundred CEOs gathered there. Bossidy asked them
to make NAFTA their top priority. He asked them for their money and for
their personal time and followed up his request with phone calls.

The business grassroots effort had accomplished little to date. "Every time
members would go back home we would lose a dozen members," recalled
Cole. "They were beating us in the grassroots." Business couldn't compete
everywhere, but it didn't have to. The challenge was to match the opposition
in the key swing districts. USA*NAFTA hired two sets of field organizers,
one for Democrats and one for Republicans. The Dewey Square Group, an
outfit run by the field coordinators for the Clinton and Dukakis campaigns,
and Bond-Donatelli, Republicans experienced in campaign mass-mail techniques, brought new capacity to generate pro-NAFTA mail and phone calls.

But Cole and the other business strategists recognized that the problem
went deeper than generating lobbying visits, or phone calls and letters from
constituents: The problem was with opinion about NAFTA. And to change
that, they felt a paid media campaign was needed. The battle to convince
CEOs that they needed to think about public messages had not been easy.
Finally in August, Francis O'Brien had convinced the Business Roundtable
to foot the bill for a $5 million advertising campaign. USA*NAFTA selected

election commercial producers Grunwald, Eskew and Donilon, the firm that had done Clinton's presidential campaign commercials.

The Campaign for NAFTA

From slow beginnings the campaign for NAFTA moved into high gear. The administration worked closely with the business community and other outside groups, including notably the mainstream environmental organizations, to mount a direct lobbying, grassroots lobbying, and mass media effort, all targeted, directly and indirectly, at the critical swing votes in the U.S. House of Representatives. By the end of October, the full weight of the campaign would press on those members. Now, in September, the campaign needed an event to announce what was coming.

A Presidential Kickoff

Given only two days of the president's time, squeezed between the reinventing government initiative and health care reform, the NAFTA strategists searched for a big event to kickoff the campaign. One idea was to find a way to highlight the fact that every living U.S. president—Richard Nixon, Gerald Ford, Jimmy Carter, Ronald Reagan, George Bush, and Bill Clinton—supported NAFTA. Opportunity knocked. A breakthrough in the Middle East peace talks meant that there would be a signing ceremony at the White House on September 13. President Carter would certainly be there. Why not hold a ceremony to sign the NAFTA side agreements at the White House the next day and invite Bush, Ford, and Carter? (Reagan was judged to be too ill, Nixon too controversial.)

On September 14, in the East Room of the White House, four presidents stood side-by-side for the first time in American history. The atmosphere was electric. For Bush, in particular, the moment was poignant, his first return to the White House since leaving office. Each president spoke. Ford emphasized NAFTA's economic benefits and warned that without it immigration would increase. Bush focused on the foreign policy implications of the agreement. Carter, speaking without notes, made the biggest stir. "We have a demagogue who has unlimited financial resources and who is extremely careless with the truth, who is preying on the fears and the uncertainties of the American public," he said, not naming Ross Perot. "And this must be met." The room erupted in applause.

Clinton gave a ringing speech that ended any doubt of his commitment and sounded out the themes on which he would campaign.

> I want to say to my fellow Americans, when you live in a time of change, the only way to recover your security and to broaden your horizons is to adapt to the change, to embrace it, to move forward. . . . In a fundamental sense, this debate about NAFTA is a debate about whether we will embrace these changes and create the jobs of tomorrow or try to resist these changes, hoping we can preserve the economic structures of yesterday.

The NAFTA strategists were exhilarated by the event. "It raised the issue to a higher level," recalled Bill Daley. "We were trying to raise the importance of NAFTA. Never had three former presidents been in the White House. We were getting people to think about it as more than a petty political fight with Ross Perot and the unions." As Mickey Kantor recalls, the event did three things. "One is bipartisanship. Two, it had support from people the American people admire. Three, it let you control the center of the debate and let the left and right go off on their own and become a fringe argument." For Cole, Carter's remarks were particularly important. "All of a sudden it was legitimate to criticize Perot. Carter changed the whole dynamic." Finally, the event conclusively demonstrated the president's commitment. "I loved that event," recalled David Gergen. "At that point we were in it to win."

The Administration Campaign for NAFTA

The day after the excitement of four presidents at the White House, the administration campaign seemed to fizzle. The president traveled to Louisiana to talk about the benefits of NAFTA for that state. It rained. Few people came to the scheduled events. The press gave only limited coverage. Worse, several weeks would pass before the next scheduled presidential time to promote NAFTA. Nevertheless, the campaign for NAFTA began to gather speed in terms of lobbying on the Hill and attempting to influence public opinion.

Lobbying   Every day, Howard Paster, Susan Brophy, and Nancy Leamond met to go over the latest whip lists, identify swing members, discuss
the nature of their concerns, and deploy the administration's assets. The
NAFTA team began inviting Representatives to the White House to meet
with the president. At first, the meetings were in groups: Hill leaders, undecided Democrats, undecided Republicans. Rahm Emmanuel, Daley's
deputy detailed over from the White House, fought aggressively for more
presidential time. As the campaign gathered steam, Emmanuel succeeded,
and the size of the groups began to shrink. Eventually, the president would
meet one-on-one with undecided members. In mid October, he began to
take a call list with him at night when he retired to the residence.

In these meetings, Clinton would give his pitch for NAFTA: It was good
for jobs, good for the environment, important for American leadership in
the world, a test of whether of America would embrace change or retreat
from it—much the same pitch that he gave in public speeches. Vice President Gore would add his remarks. Together, the two of them made a formidable presentation. Few members were prepared to debate the substance.
Some expressed concerns about jobs or the environment, but more often
they talked about problems specific to their district. Most commonly, they
told the president that what they really needed was "political cover."

A significant part of the lobbying effort involved providing information
to address concerns expressed by undecided members of Congress or requested by the Hill whip groups. The purpose was not only to reassure
members on points of information, it was also to arm them for interactions
with their constituents. Often, the administration would provide "talking
points" on the subject, such as NAFTA's effects on immigration. Daley and
Paster also had virtually unlimited call on cabinet officers. A member who
had expressed a concern about drug smuggling would receive a phone call
from Attorney General Janet Reno. If that conversation revealed that the
member seemed receptive to the arguments about the foreign policy rami-
fications of rejecting NAFTA, the member could expect a call from Secretary of State Warren Christopher. With every contact, the White House
updated its member profiles.

The relationship between the White House and Republicans on the Hill
was more complicated. Given the partisan nature of the summer budget
fights, there was a pervasive atmosphere of distrust. Bill Frenzel worked hard
to dispel this, but much of the lobbying of Republicans was left in the hands
of Republicans outside the White House. Nick Calio coordinated calls from

former President Bush and from such other influential Republicans as Jim Baker and Carla Hills.

The Public Message   Although it had been slow in developing, the administration's public message on NAFTA gradually emerged. The message reflected a distillation from many sources and from experience, although it bore a strong resemblance to the message Bill Bradley had been articulating since the beginning of the year. Bradley's message reframed the jobs issue as a matter of long-term competitiveness and recast the debate as both a matter of U.S. foreign policy and as a referendum on America's future. In essence, the administration message now also had three parts, although the themes varied and not everyone stayed on message:

First, NAFTA is good for American jobs because it will allow more U.S. exports to Mexico and help the United States to compete with Europe and Japan. Here the goal was to neutralize the jobs issue, not necessarily to win it. Specific examples of products that the United States could sell to Mexico and jobs that would be created as a consequence would counteract the specific examples offered by opponents of jobs lost to Mexico and make concrete the usually abstract arguments for free trade. Redefining "us" and "them" from the United States versus Mexico to the United States versus the world provided a way to think about the long-term benefits of NAFTA and to disentangle NAFTA from anxieties about competition from Europe and Asia.

Second, NAFTA is part of the solution to environmental, immigration, drug, and other problems with Mexico, not part of those problems. In essence, this was a foreign policy argument. It sought not to change attitudes about Mexico but to put those negatives in a context that made NAFTA the hero rather than the villain. Often, this message was delivered in the negative: If NAFTA is *not* passed, these problems will only get worse. In addition, by making this a matter of U.S. national interest, the message sought to raise the debate above the level of who would win and lose at home.

Third, the choice is between hope and fear, between going forward and going backward, between embracing change or shrinking from it, between competing or retreating. As much as anything, this message was intended to wrap NAFTA in essentially American values and to cast opposition to NAFTA in negative terms, an approach made easier by the increasingly negative image of Ross Perot and others opposed to the agreement.

Delivering these messages presented a challenge, however. With the president largely unavailable for public appearances after the September 14 kick-off, the administration team had to rely at first on appearances by cabinet secretaries on the Sunday talk shows as well as on opinion articles in leading newspapers. To a great extent, the administration had to rely on others to deliver the message.

The Business Campaign for NAFTA

With an energetic new leadership and encouraged by the commitment coming from the White House, the business community mounted a three-pronged attack. First was a massive, coordinated direct lobbying effort at a level unprecedented for a trade issue. Second was a public relations campaign that including for the first time television commercials for a trade issue. Third, was a grassroots effort of a kind business groups had never before attempted.

Lobbying   Usually business lobbying is a largely uncoordinated affair, as individual companies or trade associations lobby for specific items of concern to them. This had been the case during the negotiation of NAFTA. But with the agreement finished and no possibility of amending it in Congress, business interests had nothing specific for which to lobby. Virtually the entire business community, therefore, could unite around the single objective of passing NAFTA. The campaign was also unusual in another regard. It was conducted in close coordination with a Democratic White House.

Larry Bossidy and Ken Cole set out to get the personal involvement of CEOs. They both knew that in Washington, unless the CEO personally calls, members of Congress judge the issue to be of low importance. Bossidy worked the business community, every day phoning CEOs he knew and asking them to make personal calls. The CEOs were receptive. As Ken Cole recalls, CEOs got involved for three reasons:

> First, fundamentally, they though it was the right policy, the right thing to do. Second, they were offended by Perot. . . . He wanted to present [NAFTA] as inappropriate policy, created behind closed doors for the benefit of a few and to the detriment of the American work force. They were categorically angry at Perot. . . . Third, President Clinton

was persuasive. Do not underestimate the importance of the president of the United States asking CEOs for their help.

Cole aimed to mobilize the "heavy-hitters," the top business lobbyists in Washington. "We wanted to change the cocktail circuit chatter, to show that NAFTA was the number one issue for every company [the lobbyists] represented, that we had a strategy, that there was a financial commitment, that we were going to compete in every forum," he recalled. An elite group of Washington lobbyists began meeting every Monday at AlliedSignal's Washington headquarters to plot strategy. Almost always, Bill Daley or another administration official was on hand to describe what the administration was doing. Another, larger weekly meeting was held at the U.S. Chamber of Commerce. A group of lobbyists organized by Bob Barrie, General Electric's Washington "rep," met weekly with Bob Matsui and aide Dianne Sullivan to coordinate efforts targeted at the House. More quietly, a group of forty Republican lobbyists organized by Nick Calio met regularly with House Minority Leader Bob Michel and aide Billy Pitts.

Together, the direct lobbying conveyed a clear message to members of Congress: "NAFTA is important to business." But Cole and the other business strategists understood that CEOs and inside heavy hitters alone were not enough. Unless they could demonstrate ability to change the grassroots politics of NAFTA, they would not change votes on Capitol Hill.

The Media Campaign   Although television talk shows and newspaper opinion pages provided a limited forum for business to reach the public, the heart of the business media strategy was a paid media campaign with election-type television commercials. The goal was to reframe the debate. As Paige Gardner recalled, "People did not know how to be for [NAFTA]. We had to give them tools to talk about it. We had to construct a way to be for it. There was not a conceptual framework that resonated with constituents."

Ken Cole, Francis O'Brien, and Page Gardner worked with the advertising firm Grunwald, Eskew and Donilon to produce the commercials. Normally, television commercials reflect careful research involving testing of various messages with focus groups. In this case, however, the only research available was the earlier Greenberg poll, a quick survey by Mike Donilon, and the publicly available surveys such as the NBC–*Wall Street Journal* poll. The media team had to rely largely on instinct, testing the ads on themselves in Ken Cole's office.

In total, there would be eight commercials. The first, quickly put together and aired in early September, focused on jobs. Its purpose, as much as anything, was to get people's attention. Perhaps the most important commercials involved Lee Iacocca, the former CEO of Chrysler who had served as a very effective pitchman not only for his company but also for the renovation of the Statue of Liberty. In the eyes of the business strategists, Iacocca was perfect. He had very high name recognition and "unbelievable positives," recalled Page Gardner. When he agreed to do the commercials in late September, that alone was news. Iococca had a clear idea of what he wanted to do. He insisted on his own scriptwriter and his own camera crew. The result were commercials with the familiar look and feel of the ads he had made for Chrysler over the years.

Iococca stressed competition with Japan and Europe: "The Japanese and Europeans think NAFTA is a bad deal. Why? Because it's good for us and bad for them. It puts them on the outside looking in on the biggest market in the world. It's a no brainer. If we say 'yes' to NAFTA, we say yes to jobs." Another version of the ad had Iococca making the points even more strongly. "And believe me, if we say 'no' to NAFTA, the champagne corks will be popping all over Japan and Europe, and we'll be crying in our beer. 'Cause if we don't take the deal, they will."

Other USA*NAFTA commercials took different tacks. One compared the cast of characters in favor of NAFTA with those against it: Every living president and every living Nobel Prize–winning economist was for NAFTA; Ross Perot, Pat Buchanan, Jesse Jackson, and Jerry Brown were against it. Another began with the image of a chain link gate closing, while a voice said, "Some people want to put a fence around America. It's called protectionism. The last time we tried it, we had a Depression." The commercial showed an image of hungry children in rags.

Because USA*NAFTA had a limited budget for purchasing television air time, the commercials were carefully targeted. Once a week, a small group of strategists would meet in Ken Cole's office to decide on the media buy for the week. In deciding where to run ads, the group weighed information from the Hill whips, from the lobbyists, and from their own lists. They also considered requests coming in from the grassroots efforts. "There is no reason to put up media without active grassroots," recalled Cole. "We were running a national campaign directed locally."

Much of the effort was to influence opinion leaders and to create the impression that there were more ads running than there actually were. Every ad ran in Washington. Some ads ran on CNN, targeted expressly at opinion leaders. One ad featuring Microsoft Chairman Bill Gates ran only in Denver, but videotapes of it were distributed to staffers on the Hill. The ad was terrible television, but "I only cared that people talked about the ad," recalled Francis O'Brien. "The offices up there [on the Hill] are made up of young people. The whole point was in creating conversations." Most media buys, however, were targeted at the undecided members. "We didn't have to convince two hundred million people," recalled Page Gardner. "We had 'X' number of people to convince. We never lost our focus on that. We were really targeting resources at the swing votes."

Business Grows Grassroots   In contrast to the grassroots techniques often employed by public interest organizations, business efforts to influence legislation generally involve traditional, behind-the-scenes lobbying by top business officials and professional lobbyists. For NAFTA, however, business decided that it needed a genuine grassroots effort, one that would demonstrate to members of Congress that more than a few CEOs cared about the outcome of the NAFTA battle.

USA*NAFTA's pair of grassroots lobbying firms began organizing a grassroots campaign. For the Democrats, the Dewey Square group put together a network in fifty districts. For the Republicans, Bond-Donatelli focused on around thirty districts. Both efforts targeted people who might be influential with members. "We would identify people who could make a difference and went and sold NAFTA to them. . . . At the end of the decision process, when the member is sitting with his staff, he's going to ask, 'What does X say,' " recalled Ken Cole. The organizers also sought to generate favorable mail for NAFTA to match the torrent of negative mail members had been receiving. In late September, USA*NAFTA distributed 1.2 million four-part postcards, one part for the Representative, two for the Senators, and one to return to USA*NAFTA. By mid October, significant numbers of pro-NAFTA postcards began appearing in key members' offices on Capitol Hill.

Whenever possible, company CEOs were urged to participate in the grassroots efforts. Bossidy's message to CEOs was not just to make personal calls, but to work in their communities. Recalled Ken Cole,

> He told them three things: "First, educate your own employees. Second, get your people active in the communities where you have facilities. You don't have to explain how to do this. These people are members of the Rotary Club, the Lions Club; they run the Little

League. They can change the conventional wisdom in that town. Third, target the member's district office. . . . Get the [member's] district manager out to your plant. District managers are good filters for the member."

The grassroots effort was contagious. Companies started running their own radio commercials and buying billboard space. Some companies developed extensive educational materials for their employees. One company in South Carolina installed phone lines so that workers could call their district office during their break to urge NAFTA's passage. In Washington, Cole encouraged the grassroots efforts by disseminating information through an increasingly extensive fax network. The network served as a vehicle for disseminating the latest rebuttal of Ross Perot, the scripts of upcoming television ads, the weekly message. The materials helped arm people for local radio and provided the basis for letters to the editor in the local paper. The network also provided a way to publicize creative efforts around the country.

Part of the business grassroots campaign was coordinated with White House personnel. Kurt Campbell of Bill Daley's office worked with USA*NAFTA to organize trips to Washington for CEOs and other business executives. Groups of these business leaders would typically meet with administration officials at the White House and then go to the Hill to talk with members of Congress. To highlight business support for NAFTA, the administration and the business community put together a "products fair" on the White House lawn, at which were displayed hundreds of products from around the country that were sold to Mexico. The assembled business leaders heard from President Clinton and Lee Iococca. In addition, administration officials spoke to business groups in Washington and around the country.

On the Hill

Crucial to the whole campaign were the whip groups on Capitol Hill. Although they lacked the resources of the administration or the business community, members of Congress and their staffs were in a better position to gather information about the positions and concerns of their colleagues and to communicate directly with them. Because members are more candid with other members, the inside vote counts were more reliable. Moreover, information that came with a "Dear Colleague" letter from one member to another was much more likely to be read.

The hottest action was in the House. There, the offices of Democrats Bob Matsui and Bill Richardson and Republicans Bob Michel, Newt Gingrich, and Jim Kolbe became the nerve center of the campaign. Staffers in these offices now went into overdrive, desperately trying to manage the stunning volume of information coming at them, assessing the ever changing political landscape, and attempting to direct resources where they were needed. Although, as a matter of courtesy to other members, even the Democrats kept their actual whip lists confidential, both Democrats and Republicans used the lists to direct the lobbying resources of the White House, the business community, and other outside groups.

In the Senate, things were a bit quieter. Moynihan's continued ambivalence about supporting NAFTA and Baucus's interest in pushing for additional concessions from the administration meant that Bill Bradley remained the de facto Democratic whip. The author, working with Chafee aide Amy Dunathan, maintained the whip lists, communicated with the White House and the business community, and distributed information to members. Bradley's Senate strategy was designed with the House in mind. The goal was to persuade Democrats who might have influence with Representatives to announce their support. Bradley spent hours talking with Carol Moseley-Braun, the newly elected African-American Senator from Illinois. Moseley-Braun's announcement of support on October 21, the day after that of Paul Simon, the senior Senator from Illinois, all but guaranteed that NAFTA would prevail in the Senate and eased the pressure on some Representatives.

But Bradley was not content with indirection. He took the unusual step of organizing Senators to lobby the House directly. In meetings in his "hideaway" in the Capitol, Matsui and Richardson shared their lists with Bradley and a small group of other Democratic Senators supporting NAFTA. In October, members of the House began receiving notes and phone calls from these Senators, as well as visits from Bradley himself.

Other Efforts for NAFTA

Other groups and individuals also come forward to promote the trade agreement, representing much of the nation's economic and political elite.

Some of this was at the urging of the administration or business leadership, but much was spontaneous, as NAFTA became something of a litmus test.

The mainstream environmental organizations that had worked closely with the administration during the side negotiations were particularly important. On September 15, at a Capitol Hill press conference organized by Max Baucus and attended by Al Gore, six major groups—the National Wildlife Federation, the World Wildlife Fund, the Audubon Society, the Environmental Defense Fund, the Natural Resources Defense Council, and Conservation International—announced their support. Said the World Wildlife Fund's Katherine Fuller: "The environment in North America, the global environment, for that matter, will be better off with NAFTA than without it." The National Wildlife Federation's Jay Hair commented that "the environmental community in the United States is split over support for NAFTA, but it is not split down the middle. The nation's leading environmental organizations, which represent the overwhelming majority of the nation's grassroots environmental network, those who join with me and us here today, support its passage."[3] These groups would lobby environmentally sensitive members of Congress, explaining the merits of the agreement; provide information and arguments to Hill staffers; and rebut NAFTA's environmental critics in the media. But most importantly, the simple fact of their support effectively eliminated environment as a political problem for NAFTA.

Former presidents Carter and Bush remained active in the campaign. Carter visited with and telephoned dozens of Democratic members of Congress to reiterate the points that he had made in his White House talk in September. Bush called dozens of wavering Republicans, urging members not to let partisanship stand in the way of what he considered sound policy. Bush's USTR, Carla Hills, also made numerous calls, usually when members had technical questions and wanted reassurance.

Other national opinion leaders weighed in with op-ed articles and letters to the editor. Republicans such as former Secretaries of State Henry Kissinger and Jim Baker, and former Baker aide Bob Zoellick, were joined by Democrats such as former USTR and Democratic Party Chairman Bob Strauss as well as current cabinet secretaries Lloyd Bentsen, Robert Reich, and Ron Brown. Other party figures such as Lee Hamilton and Bill Bradley also wrote opinion articles for leading newspapers. MIT economist Rudiger Dornbush organized a large group of economists to endorse NAFTA, including all of America's Nobel Prize winners. Finally, the editorial boards of the majority of America's major newspapers wrote favorable editorials. Although news coverage of NAFTA continued to be mixed, and most papers made some attempt to balance opinion articles, the editorial pages were predominantly positive toward NAFTA.

The Opposition Campaigns

As the fall began, the anti-NAFTA campaigns were in full swing. The successes of August and early September gave members of the coalition increased confidence that NAFTA could be defeated. They were winning the battle in the grassroots and gaining votes. However, problems lurked. The extraordinary diversity of the opposition coalition made coordination difficult. The unions wanted nothing to do with Ross Perot. Liberal environmental groups found it embarrassing to be on the same side as Pat Buchanan. On the Hill, Democrat David Bonior and Republican Duncan Hunter, the chief anti-NAFTA vote counters, were not even on speaking terms. The result was that the campaigns against NAFTA lacked the coherence of tactic and message that increasingly characterized the pro-NAFTA effort. Time had begun to work against the opposition.

Unions

By the end of August, Mark Anderson, in charge of the AFL-CIO effort, thought he had a chance to win. A union vote count listed 166 Representatives as "no" and another 63 as "lean no," a total of 229, already over the 218 needed to defeat NAFTA. With another 119 members listed as "undecided," the opposition total seemed almost certain to climb. Yet, for Anderson, there was also a sense of urgency. "We felt that the longer people stayed in the undecided column the more money power and the power of the president would erode it," recalled Anderson. Reliance on Republican votes also made Anderson nervous. "We could win if we had conservative Republicans," he recalled. "But I was never too comfortable with that."

The AFL-CIO campaign got a slow start. Although individual unions had been working on NAFTA's defeat for some time, the AFL-CIO had not begun an all-out effort until after the side negotiations were complete. Until August, Mark Anderson was working only part-time on NAFTA. Not until

October 4 was the campaign formally launched, at the AFL-CIO convention in San Francisco. In his keynote address to the convention, AFL-CIO president Lane Kirkland denounced the "unholy matrimony" between the United States and Mexico and promised vigorous campaign to defeat it. Kirkland received thunderous applause, in stark contrast to the stony silence that later met President Clinton when he attempted to explain his reasons for supporting NAFTA.

The union delegates watched a six-minute video on NAFTA. The agreement, it explained to the convention, is

> a relic of the Reagan-Bush era that would benefit wealthy corporations in the United States, Canada, and Mexico. . . . In the end NAFTA is about one thing: cheap labor and the opportunity of the wealthy few to exploit it.

With stirring music in the background, the video described the movement to stop NAFTA. Workers at town meetings, labor leaders appearing on television to set the record straight, Labor Day marches around the country, a national petition drive, and a major media campaign. Union members were called to action:

> Congress's vote on NAFTA will determine the future for all working Americans. . . . In the end, this issue will not be decided by Washington insiders, it will be decided by men and women who work hard, serve their communities, and vote on election day. And when we are heard, NAFTA will be defeated.

After the convention, Anderson and his staff finally set up a Washington war room to provide resources, information, and encouragement to the campaigners around the country. But the campaign was highly decentralized. "I didn't know more than a fraction of what went on, particularly as the campaign developed," recalled Anderson. "As time went on, the level of spontaneity was growing. This was a bottom up campaign, . . . a rank-and-file driven exercise." The result was much creativity. In Cincinnati, union members carried coffins in a Halloween parade. Unions held "No NAFTA!" pig roasts. Unionists linked hands "across America" to demonstrate their solidarity in opposition.

Decentralization, however, also created some problems, among them consistency of strategy. For the top leadership, winning was important, but not everything. "We were trying to defeat it but also to set the stage for the future," recalled Anderson. Top AFL-CIO officials avoided threatening members of Congress. But in the field, local union organizers were often not so restrained. In California, state AFL-CIO officials pressed first-term Congresswoman Anna Eshoo. "They laid down the gauntlet and said essentially to me this is total divorce," she said. "You don't vote with us, we are not with you."[4] As the recipient of the largest union campaign contributions of any freshman in Congress, Eshoo felt intensely pressured. Said Rick Sawyer, a top AFL-CIO official in her district, "I would expect a lot of that money to dry up. She needs it."[5] In Ohio, first-term Congressman David Mann also received a warning. "Unless David can start representing the people who put him in office in a better manner, he'd probably have opposition," said Cincinnati AFL-CIO official Dan Radford.[6] The strong tactics put pressure on Democrats in Congress, but they also annoyed their targets.

To supplement the grassroots efforts, the AFL-CIO planned a media campaign with both unpaid and paid components. The heart of the unpaid media strategy was the program to bring journalists to the Mexican border, a continuation of the effort that had been going on for some time. As the vote got closer, the war room coordinated a nationwide campaign of plant gate demonstrations, around one hundred fifty in all. The demonstrations attracted some local coverage. Union officials made themselves available for television interviews and continued to write opinion articles in newspapers.

Originally, the AFL-CIO had planned only a modest paid media strategy: billboards on the sides of buses, print ads in major papers, and a few radio spots. "We had no notion it would get so big," recalled Anderson. When USA*NAFTA went on the air with its first television commercial in September, however, the union decided it needed to respond in kind. It hired its own advertising firm and budgeted $3 million for television commercials. The union's major commercial was a thirty-second spot entitled "Bad Deal." The ad focused on jobs:

> In Washington, big corporations and lobbyists are spending millions making false claims about the NAFTA trade deal. . . . But people going to factories, to farms, to offices know NAFTA means jobs going South. Economists . . . say we could lose up to 500,000 jobs. . . . NAFTA: It's a bad deal for America, and Americans know it.

The Citizen's Trade Campaign

The second army of opposition was the community of nonprofit public interest groups, coordinated through the Citizen's Trade Campaign (CTC). Lori Wallach of Public Citizen directed the strategy. Different groups brought different strengths to the coalition. The Sierra Club's extensive membership provided a grassroots organizing capacity. Other groups, Public Citizen among them, were more adept at working the media for news coverage. Although lobbying was not the coalition's strong suit, the CTC also testified at Congressional hearings, wrote letters to members, and provided information to their staffs. They had no money for television commercials.

On September 13, the CTC announced the beginning of its fall campaign to defeat NAFTA. The group now included three hundred environmental, community, human rights, and other grassroots organizations claiming membership of more than five million members. But the announcement received almost no press coverage. The little attention the group got came in the form of articles noting that environmentalists were split on NAFTA.

Because the CTC had little funding for a national campaign, its media efforts were largely confined to placing opinion articles in newspapers and attracting coverage of its views. The group did, however, twice purchase full pages in the *New York Times* and the *Washington Post* to run an ad entitled "NAFTA's Eight Fatal Flaws" (the themes of this ad were described in detail in chapter 7). The stridency of the ad's message about NAFTA's effects on the environment, national sovereignty, and democracy was so great, however, that it immediately drew a strong rebuttal from the National Wildlife Federation. The ad also caused some tension within the coalition, many of whose members believed that the rhetoric was overblown.

Perot's Fall Campaign

As the fall began, Ross Perot's anti-NAFTA campaign had considerable momentum. He had unlimited funds, a national organization, and an ability to command public attention unmatched by anyone other than the president. *Time* magazine estimated that United We Stand America's membership topped two million, making it the largest citizen-action group in American history. Yet as the fall progressed Perot's ability to influence events would begin to wane.

The main thrust of Perot's fall campaign was a series of rallies around the country. The campaign began September 18 on the steps of the Michigan state capital in Lansing. There, flanked by Senator Don Riegle (Democrat, Mich.) and Representatives Marcy Kaptur (Democrat, Ohio) and Helen Bentley (Republican, Md.), Perot addressed a crowd estimated by the *Washington Post* at 3500. Notably absent was Michigan Representative David Bonior, who refused to appear with Perot.

The crowd roared its approval of Perot's message. "Do you think it's right for your job to go to Mexico?" he asked. "No!" they shouted back. Perot dismissed the support of former presidents for the pact. "They don't think you have any sense. Those are the very presidents who enacted all these trade agreements with Japan, Asia and everybody else that cost us 2 million jobs."[7] A local Lansing paper described Perot as the "human equivalent of an air raid siren."[8]

Every weekend throughout the fall, Perot would address rallies of this kind. "Perot was holding five or six rallies a weekend," recalled Pat Choate. "He was going full bore. He was totally committed." Perot's staff advanced the rally. "Local politicians, both Republicans and Democrats would be part of the event," Choate recalled. "Usually, local chapters of the AFL were coordinating with local Perot supporters" to set up the event. Perot would then do local radio interviews two days before, fly in on his own Gulfstream jet, address the crowd, and fly out again to the next location.

Always, Perot found an enthusiastic audience as he spoke to the converted in high school gyms and town halls. But for all his effectiveness in the hall, Perot's impact outside was diluted by the media coverage the rallies received. Local newspapers and television usually covered the event, but the articles and reports typically treated them as spectacles, and the journalists usually felt compelled to balance whatever Perot had to say with some criticism of him. Typical of this coverage was the treatment of a rally in Rosemont, Illinois, by the *Chicago Sun-Times*. Under the headline, "Perot Criticized for Trade Stand," the story began

Ross Perot brings his campaign against the North American Free Trade Agreement here today while under fire for hypocrisy because a Perot family business supports the treaty. . . . Rep. Robert T. Matsui (D-Cal.), a strong backer of the controversial trade pact, wrote Perot a letter Friday saying, "You can't have it both ways. You cannot use the merits of NAFTA to privately support your investments, while publicly denouncing NAFTA . . . to further your political agenda."[9]

To add injury to insult, the location of the event was incorrectly reported. The headline for the next day's story read "Perot Crowd Disappoints Organizers."[10] Even when the local coverage was more favorable, after the Lansing kickoff the national media began to ignore the Perot rallies. In Washington, they were old news.

The Rosemont coverage reflected a more general problem for Perot: His press coverage was turning increasingly negative. Several factors appear to have been at work. First, the publication of *Save Your Job, Save Our Country* had provided a useful target for NAFTA's supporters. A detailed 73-page, point-by-point rebuttal put out by the USTR in early September provided ammunition for politicians prepared to take on Perot. Second, former president Carter's reference to Perot as a "demagogue" opened the floodgates of criticism. Virtually no article about Perot was published without some strong denunciation of him by NAFTA supporters. Third, Perot was having a difficult time getting his message across through the national media. Not only was the media largely ignoring his rallies, but also the networks were rejecting his requests to purchase time for his thirty-minute "infomercials." Meanwhile, Perot chose not to make short television commercials. His standing in public opinion polls began to fall. A CNN-*Time* poll conducted in early October showed Perot's approval rating falling below 50 percent for the first time all year.[11]

Between weekend rallies Perot made the rounds on Capitol Hill, talking exclusively to Republicans. "Perot didn't go in to see any Democrats," recalled Pat Choate. "We kept him away because we knew the White House would use this as a party loyalty issue." Perot's visits to Republicans were coordinated by California Republican Duncan Hunter. Most Republicans gave Perot a respectful hearing, in part because Perot voters made the difference in their last campaigns, but this was not familiar terrain for him. As Choate recalls, "The Hill was all new territory for Perot. He had never met most of the members before. But the meetings went well. Perot was able to establish personal relations with these guys." But Perot's presence on the Hill was not welcomed by all Republicans. Senator Thad Cochran (Republican, Miss.) attacked Perot as a "shrill demagogue" and warned that "he's not interested in helping Republicans. Getting too close to him is like getting on the back of a tiger."[12]

The Conservative Right

Largely hidden from the national media, a network of conservatives opposed to NAFTA intensified their efforts after the signing of the side agreements. Through newsletters and talk shows, Pat Buchanan, South Carolina textile magnate Roger Millican, former Utah Republican Senator Paul Laxalt, future Senatorial candidate and Iran-Contra hearings star Oliver North, and other conservatives spread the message that NAFTA was a threat to American sovereignty and that it would increase immigration and the flow of drugs coming from Mexico. Until the fall, right-wing opposition among Republicans did not seem a serious threat, but NAFTA's supporters were shocked by an announcement from freshman Representative James Talent (Republican, Mo.), originally counted as a supporter of NAFTA, that he was opposing NAFTA because of its effects on American sovereignty.

But conservatives were far from united in their opposition. Pat Robertson, president of the increasingly influential Christian Coalition, and popular talk show host Rush Limbaugh both announced support for NAFTA, as did the Heritage Foundation and the Cato Institute, the two most prominent conservative think tanks. The Cato Institute even issued a rebuttal of the sovereignty argument, concluding that "charges that NAFTA poses an unprecedented threat to American sovereignty are specious and unsupported by the facts."[13] A letter from Ronald Reagan to conservative Republicans further reassured them.

Opposition on the Hill

In the House, the headquarters for the Democratic opposition was the suite of offices David Bonior commanded as chief majority whip, where the anti-NAFTA whip group of Representatives and their staffs as well as the coalition of liberal outside groups met regularly. Now the effort intensified. The strategy was to lock up the vote quickly by getting members to take a public position against NAFTA. The closer the vote count came to a majority against the agreement, the more likely it was the administration might back away from the fight. Bonior still hoped that the administration might focus most of its attention on health care and would not put the full resources of the presidency on the line for NAFTA. Bonior focused on liberal Democrats with strong union and environmental ties, as well as on freshmen members and the Congressional Black Caucus.

On the Republican side, the opposition was much less well-organized. Whereas the Democratic leadership was largely opposed to NAFTA, the Republican leadership supported it. As a consequence, it fell to Duncan Hunter, chair of the Republican Research Committee, a minor leadership position, to organize the opposition. Hunter helped Ross Perot set up meetings and distributed articles by Pat Buchanan and other opponents, but he never really put together a whip organization and had at best a very soft vote count. Hunter and Bonior did not share their whip lists; indeed, as mentioned earlier, they were not on speaking terms.

In the Senate, there was little organized opposition. Michigan Senators Donald Riegle and Carl Levin and South Carolina Senator Fritz Hollings spoke out against NAFTA, held hearings at which NAFTA opponents could testify, and distributed anti-NAFTA articles, but they recognized that the real game was in the House and never really mounted a serious anti-NAFTA effort in the Senate.

Last Chance to Exit

By the end of October, NAFTA still trailed badly on all scorecards. Bill Richardson's Democratic whip count for October 26, for instance, showed only 49 in the "yes" column and 18 in "lean yes," a total of 67, well short of the 100 that NAFTA supporters believed they needed. To win they would have to convert virtually every one of the 37 Democrats still listed as undecided, a daunting prospect. But the pro-NAFTA campaign had stabilized the vote counts. The media campaigns were in full swing and seemed to be changing public opinion. Members were reporting that pro-NAFTA mail was picking up. And Ross Perot was increasingly marginalized.

The anti-NAFTA forces could sense that time was now working against them. They had close to a firm majority but getting the last few commitments was proving maddeningly difficult. The media seemed increasingly stacked against them, as newspaper editorial after editorial supported NAFTA. Articles about the opposition now seemed always to include the phrase "strange bedfellows" and to focus on their internal divisions. Although the union commercials had started running, the campaign was not nearly as sophisticated or as extensive as the business effort. Still, the vote count seemed to include a comfortable cushion. If the opposition held onto their votes, it was hard to see how NAFTA could win. Bonior now publicly asserted that the opponents were "up to 208. We have an additional 31 or 32 leaning our way. The best case that they can put on it—solid votes for and leaning for—is about 150. . . . We're picking up a few each day, and we expect we'll have the number that we need some time within the next week."[14] In the administration, the numbers seemed high, but no one was sure enough to dispute Bonior publicly.

Into this mix, another potential obstacle to NAFTA caught both sides largely by surprise. Following American habit, few in the United States paid attention to the fact that Canada was holding a national election. However, the Canadian election spelled potential trouble for NAFTA. Since her installation as Brian Mulroney's successor in mid summer, Prime Minister Kim Campbell's political stock had fallen precipitously. The beneficiary was Jean Chretien and his Liberal Party, which by mid October looked to be the sure winners of the election. Although NAFTA was not the central issue in the campaign in the way that the Canada–U.S. Free Trade Agreement (CUFTA) had been in the previous national election, Chretien had staked out a position critical of NAFTA, promising to renegotiate the treaty to better protect Canada from misuse of U.S. trade remedy laws and to ensure labor and environmental protection.

The Liberal triumph in the election October 25 exceeded even the most extreme predictions. Chretien and his party won a clear majority of seats in the House of Commons, 179 out of 295, up from 79. Campbell and the Conservatives were crushed, falling from 153 seats to 2, the most dramatic defeat of a ruling party in Canadian history.

In Washington, the question of the moment was what the election might mean for NAFTA. Bonior claimed that NAFTA was doomed and that the administration should seize the moment to back out. At a Hill press conference he emphasized the political hazards of association with NAFTA:

> The people of Canada sent a clear and a powerful message yesterday: this NAFTA won't work, it's fatally flawed and it's time to go back to the drawing board. . . . As a result of this election, the party that negotiated this NAFTA has nearly ceased to exist. They won two seats where they used to hold over 150 seats in the parliament. By this time

next year, the three presidents who negotiated the original NAFTA will all be private citizens.[15]

Bonior's message found a receptive audience with some of the president's political advisors, who wondered whether the Canadian election didn't provide the administration with a last chance to exit without suffering a defeat in Congress. For twenty-four hours, the White House was in turmoil, trying to assess what, if anything, the election really meant about Canada's intentions. Administration officials, however, quickly ascertained that Chretien had no real interest in renegotiating the agreement and that the magnitude of the landslide actually reduced the political pressure on him to do so. The idea of backing out was quickly squelched. The next morning President Clinton spoke with the new Canadian Prime Minister. Afterward he told reporters the Canadian election "will have no impact at all. I see no reason to renegotiate the agreement or any grounds or basis for it, and I think we should just go ahead."[16]

Now, there appeared to be no obstacle to a vote. But first, the administration had to put together a bill.

Putting the Pieces Together

Nearly forgotten in the midst of the political fray was the more mundane problem of putting together the implementing bill and getting it to a vote in Congress. Although the fast track powers basically ensured that the vote in Congress would be up or down on the agreement as negotiated, the bill would need to specify just what changes in U.S. law would be required to implement the agreement. Moreover, U.S. trade law also allowed the inclusion of other provisions that might be "necessary and appropriate." These provisions would almost certainly need to include a labor adjustment package, a mechanism to fund border environmental cleanup, and some means to pay for all of this. Putting the bill together was a true insiders' game, orchestrated by the professional staffs in the administration and on the Hill, particularly Marsha Miller, chief trade counsel for the Finance Committee, and Bruce Wilson, Miller's counterpart with Ways and Means. Although few took part in these inner workings, those on the inside knew this would not be an easy matter.

First, however, the administration had to make sure a vote would take place. The earliest the bill could actually be introduced was around November 1. To get a vote in the House on November 17 and in the Senate before Thanksgiving would require moving faster than the fast track required, not an easy matter.

Fast track rules gave House committees with jurisdiction up to forty-five working days before it compelled them to discharge the bill to the floor. The House then had up to fifteen days before it needed to act. Speaker Foley could cut short the fifteen-day period, but he could not compel a determined chair to act faster than the rules required. If the House was to vote on November 17, therefore, the implementing bill would need to be kept out of committees where the chair was likely to be uncooperative. That meant crafting it to avoid the Labor and Public Works Committee chaired by staunch NAFTA opponent William Ford (Democrat, Mich.).

The administration hoped that the Senate would vote almost immediately after the House, but fast track rules did not compel Senate committees to act on the bill until fifteen working days after the House vote and the full Senate to act for another fifteen days. Majority Leader George Mitchell would not only need cooperation from committee chairs, he would also need consent from the full Senate to proceed this fast. The implementing bill could be tailored so that it did not need to go through Riegle's Banking Committee, but there was no way to avoid Moynihan's Finance Committee or Hollings's Commerce Committee. If either wanted, he could hold things up. Mitchell discussed the situation with senior Democrats who favored NAFTA. He was determined to adjourn the Senate before Thanksgiving, but he was prepared to bring the Senate back and keep it in continuous session for the rest of the year if Hollings or other opponents held up the NAFTA bill. Mitchell then talked with Moynihan and Hollings. Moynihan had never had any intention to delay a vote. Hollings, convinced that NAFTA had the votes in the Senate and that Mitchell meant what he said, agreed not to delay.[17] Now, Congress just needed a bill.

Beginning in mid October, the Clinton administration had been working with the key Congressional committees to draft an implementing bill. Although fast track turned the normal legislative process on its head, allowing the president to present Congress with an unamendable bill, historically Congress had gone through a "mock mark-up" process to draft the bill that the president would eventually support. The plan was to follow this process once more. The problem was that several key provisions of the implementing bill were still being debated, and time was running short.

Labor Adjustment

From the beginning, even NAFTA's strongest supporters acknowledged that a free trade agreement with Mexico would cost some workers their jobs. President Bush had assured Congress in 1991 that a worker assistance and retraining program would accompany NAFTA, and in 1992 he had proposed a comprehensive, $2 billion per year program. When Clinton took office, the expectation was that he would do even more. His new Secretary of Labor, Robert Reich, a champion of retraining and lifetime learning, hoped to make a comprehensive overhaul of the hodgepodge of existing programs.

Testifying before the House Ways and Means committee in March 1993, Mickey Kantor promised "a comprehensive program to deal with those who lose their jobs whether the cause is this trade agreement, defense cutbacks, or corporate downsizing. We know that NAFTA will be judged in part by the effectiveness of that program, as it should be."[18] Reich's team at the Labor Department set out to design a comprehensive new set of training programs. Reich avoided mentioning a price tag, but numbers on the order of $3 billion a year floated around Washington. Reich promised a proposal in time to go along with NAFTA.

As the summer progressed, however, and the Labor Department still had not briefed the Hill on its intentions, NAFTA's advocates began to get nervous. To pass a comprehensive worker retraining bill would be no simple task under any circumstances. Many powerful members of Congress had their own ideas about what the bill should look like and wanted to be consulted. They would not take kindly to being handed a "take it or leave it" offer on an unamendable trade bill.

Not until early September did Labor Department officials begin to brief the Hill about their intentions. They intended to propose a comprehensive program for which workers who lost their jobs for any reason, not just NAFTA, would be eligible. All existing programs would be folded into the new program, including Trade Adjustment Assistance (TAA), the largest and most popular of the existing trade-related programs. To pay for the additional costs of the program, they hoped to increase employer contributions. They were unclear about whether they expected the program to actually be on the NAFTA implementing bill or to travel through Congress alongside it.

The proposal immediately ran into difficulties. Republicans balked at raising taxes to pay for worker retraining. Democrats worried about eliminating the popular TAA program. Most importantly, Hill strategists insisted that worker retraining had to be part of the NAFTA implementing bill. The vote had to be "bundled" if the labor legislation was to help NAFTA. But a comprehensive program could not avoid the Labor committees, and that meant dealing with Representative William Ford (Democrat, Mich.), a staunch NAFTA opponent. The first week in September, Reich paid a visit to Ford to finally discuss whether he would let NAFTA out of committee if it included a strong labor-retraining component. Ford flatly refused. As late as September 21, in an appearance before the Senate Finance Committee, Reich was still advocating a comprehensive program, but the die was cast. At a meeting of the National Economic Council (NEC) shortly thereafter, the comprehensive proposal was shot down and the Labor Department charged with coming up with a less ambitious program.

Two weeks later, Larry Katz, a Harvard economics professor serving as the Labor Department's chief economist, was back on the Hill. The comprehensive program would wait. In the interim, the Labor Department proposed simply to expand an existing program whose features were closer to what the department hoped to do later, an approach that would not require any new authorizing legislation and only a small supplemental appropriation, less than $100 million.

On the Hill, NAFTA's advocates immediately recognized that the new proposal was all wrong from a political standpoint. Without legislation authorizing a new program to help displaced workers, members in need of this kind of political cover would not have anything to point to. A request for a new discretionary appropriation would provoke a fight over whether it was large enough, and that would likely bid up the cost. Strategy called for a new entitlement program, the cost of which need not be specified as it would automatically expand as needed. Entitlement programs also had the advantage of falling within the jurisdictions of the Senate Finance and House Ways and Means Committees.

Calls went out to officials at the Labor Department and elsewhere in the administration, urging a different approach. At Labor, Andrew Samet, a former legislative director under Senator Moynihan, immediately grasped the situation. Samet explained the problem to Secretary Reich. Within two days, the Labor Department had settled on a new proposal, a NAFTA-specific expansion of TAA, an entitlement program. In the end, the Congressional Budget Office estimated the ten-year cost of the program to be only $90 million, a far cry from the $2–3 billion annual figure initially envisioned.

The Labor Department still hoped to introduce the comprehensive overhaul at a later date, but it would never happen.

Inventing a "NADBank"

The implementing bill would also need to include funds for cleaning up the environment along the U.S.–Mexican border, a commitment first made in 1991 by President Bush as part of the Action Plan. But what form the plan might take, how much it would cost, and how it would be funded remained unclear.

Richard Gephardt had insisted that cleanup would take at least $30 billion and urged a cross-border tax to pay for it. As long as Gephardt's support of NAFTA remained a possibility, the administration had been careful not to rule anything out, but by mid summer it was clear that financial constraints in both Mexico and the United States required the two governments to think creatively about leveraging smaller amounts of money.

Creating this program, unlike worker retraining, would require international negotiations, with Mexico and with international lending agencies. The Treasury Department took lead responsibility. The original intent was to complete these talks at the same time the side negotiations concluded, but that proved impossible. Not until early September did Treasury officials begin briefing the Hill on the outlines of the plan they were negotiating. The United States and Mexico proposed to create a Border Environmental Finance Facility (BEFF), which might lend $2 billion or more for environmental cleanup projects.[19] The BEFF could be financed with very small outlays from the U.S. and Mexican governments.

This plan was sufficient to win the support of the mainstream environmental groups on September 15. It did not, however, satisfy a coalition of environmental and Mexican-American groups or, importantly, their champion, Representative Esteban Torres (Democrat, Calif.). Torres's undecided status gave him considerable leverage. His support might bring along others in the Hispanic Caucus; his opposition would be costly. Torres had introduced a bill to create a North American Development Bank (NADBank). The NADBank would be larger and capable of financing a broader array of development projects along the border.

Given the importance of every vote, the administration decided that it needed to satisfy Torres's demands and went back to the Mexicans to negotiate for more. Finally, on October 27, days before the implementing bill was to be introduced, the administration announced agreement to create a NADBank along the lines of the Torres bill. The bank would underwrite $8 billion over ten years for environmental projects. To finance the bank, each government would put up $225 million, supplemented with funds from the World Bank, the Inter-America Development Bank, and private lenders.

Torres announced his support of NAFTA. "This is not an easy decision for me. I have spent most of my professional career fighting for economic and social justice for all workers, the poor and disenfranchised," said Torres, a former assembly-line welder and UAW official.[20] Torres was joined by several Latino groups, including the National Council of La Raza, the nation's largest, but not by any other members of Congress that day. Privately, administration officials were disappointed. They had hoped to get as many as seven votes from the deal. "One bank, one vote," they quipped. Nonetheless, the NADBank further solidified environmental support for NAFTA and gave the administration more ammunition for selling the agreement. Said Secretary Bentsen, "Pass NAFTA and we make progress on cleaning up that environment. Fail to pass it and it's business and polluting as usual."[21]

Paying for Free Trade

Congressional budget rules required that the NAFTA implementing bill be "paid for," i.e., the costs of lost tariff revenues, working retraining, border cleanup, and administration of the agreement be offset by cuts elsewhere in the budget or by new revenues. The effort to find a way to fund NAFTA got off to a very slow start. The Office and Management and Budget (OMB) could pay little attention until after the budget vote in early August. Even then, uncertainty about the worker retraining and border cleanup items made estimating how much money would be needed difficult and further slowed the effort. One thing, however, was clear: Little money was to be found after the summer budget fight. The funding problem contributed to the decision to scale back worker retraining and to limit the amount of new money going into border cleanup, so that by mid October the amount needed to fund NAFTA looked to be only in the range of $2–3 billion over five years. Still, the administration struggled to find the money.

On Tuesday, October 19, Mickey Kantor revealed the administration's plan during the mock markup in the Ways and Means Committee. The administration intended to ask Congress to double fees on trucks, railroad cars, and sea and air passengers crossing the borders. "This was the best option we could find . . . in a range of very bad options," a defensive Kantor told the Committee.[22] The negative response was immediate. Transportation interest groups sprang into action. More ominously, twenty-seven House Republicans, all of whom were counted as likely "yes" votes on NAFTA, fired off a letter to President Clinton threatening to oppose NAFTA rather than raise taxes to pay for it. Within hours, Clinton was telling reporters that the administration was rethinking how to pay for NAFTA.

In the Senate two days later, the Finance Committee was continuing its own mock markup, having deferred consideration of the funding package the day before. The members waited that morning for Budget Director Leon Panetta to appear and make the administration proposal. After some time, a message came from Panetta; he apologized to the Committee, but he would be unable to make an administration proposal that day. A disgusted Moynihan abruptly adjourned the session, setting no date for its resumption. In the anteroom, the administration team huddled with Marsha Miller, Chief Trade Council for the Finance Committee, dumbfounded by what had just happened and uncertain about what it meant.

Over the weekend, the administration frantically tried to resolve the funding impasse. On Monday evening, Panetta sent a letter to Chairman Moynihan outlining a new proposal. The administration had scaled back the transportation fees. Most of the money would come from speeding up the electronic deposit of tax payments from businesses and banks, a change that would put the money in the Treasury a day quicker, and which the Congressional Budget Office (CBO) generously scored as worth $1.4 billion. The administration pressed Moynihan to resume the Senate markup. Moynihan agreed, and on Thursday, October 28, the Finance Committee completed its work.

Now, however, there was no time at all for a conference committee to reconcile the minor differences that had crept into the two bills, the procedure employed for every previous trade bill. The USTR staff scrambled to iron out the differences, consulting with the Hill trade staffs as needed. At the USTR, General Counsel Ira Shapiro, Ken Freiberg, and the rest of the team worked around the clock to get the bill together. The workload was crushing. The USTR lawyers were putting together sections previously drafted by other agencies, drafting new language, redrafting as inconsistencies were discovered, checking the text with members of Congress and their staffs, madly racing to meet the November 1 deadline, but still not getting closure on critical issues such as funding. As Shapiro recalls,

> The last week in October was incredible. We had promised that the implementing bill was going to the Hill on November 1. I said to Mickey, "This is not going to be there on Nov. 1." He said, "It's got to be there." I said, "What it's got to be is perfect.". . . There were a million things to do.

In the end, the bill was not transmitted to the Hill until the evening of November 3, precisely two weeks before the House was scheduled to vote.

Full Court Press

In the last two weeks, the politics of NAFTA reached a fevered pitch. To be an undecided member of the House was to be in a maelstrom, postcards flooding your mailroom, phone lines tied up continuously, lobbyists lining up outside the door. NAFTA had became a media obsession, culminating in the extraordinary spectacle of a vice president of the United States debating a wealthy ex-presidential candidate on a cable television talk show. Out of the limelight, on the inside, politics turned retail, as the administration worked a strategy for each undecided member.

The Deluge

President Clinton now threw himself totally into the NAFTA fight. There was no more question about priorities. The prestige of his presidency was on the line.

Clinton played the cheerleader for NAFTA's troops. On November 1, he spoke at the Chamber of Commerce, directly to hundreds of business representatives, and indirectly via satellite to hundreds of groups around the country. Clinton, clearly warming to his subject, departed from his prepared text to give an impassioned speech about the importance of passing NAFTA. He understood the concerns of Americans about jobs, but "I would never knowingly do anything that would cost an American a job," he said. A new theme took prominence. "If we walk away from this and Mexico decides to pursue its development strategy, what must it do?" asked the president. "It must make this deal with Europe or with Japan." Clinton acknowledged that the meaning of NAFTA had changed for its proponents, saying "When we started, NAFTA had a significance for those who were fighting against it, all out of proportion to the impact it could have. . . . It has now acquired a symbolic significance for those of us who are for it, too." Then he urged the business leaders to redouble their efforts. "I know I am preaching to the saved," the president said. "But you all have to be missionaries."

The next day, the president was at another pep rally for NAFTA, this time a remarkable gathering of prominent Americans in the East Room of the White House. Former president Jimmy Carter was back, joined by former secretaries of state Jim Baker and Henry Kissinger, former USTR Carla Hills, former U.N. Ambassador Andrew Young, a collection of Nobel Prize–winning economists, Lee Iococca and other leaders of the business community, and of course, undecided Representatives.

The talks emphasized foreign policy. Baker gave the most compelling speech, one that seemed to define the meaning of NAFTA for the gathering:

> How we decide this issue and how we vote on NAFTA is really going to reveal a lot about what this nation is going to be in the future. Even more importantly, I think it's going to tell us what sort of people we are. I think this agreement marks a defining moment in American history, a moment that ranks with America's entry on to the world stage in the 1940s, first to defeat Fascism and then to lead the great alliance of democracies that fought and won the Cold War. Then, as now, America faced a new era, an era full of opportunities, but also full of risks and perils. Then, as now, America had to choose between engagement on the one hand and isolationism on the other. And fifty years ago, the United States of America chose to lead.

The group was clearly moved by Baker's speech.

Carter and Clinton called the group to action. Carter said he had made twelve phone calls that morning, and challenged them to do the same. Clinton urged them to "make three calls, make twelve calls, make two dozen calls. For goodness sakes, make however many you can. But remember this is a test of our confidence. Every one of you can give confidence to someone else by the life you have lived, the experiences you have had, the things that you know." For the next two weeks, wavering members of Congress, many of them freshman, would receive calls from former presidents, Nobel Prize winners, and powerful CEOs. It was a heady experience.

But most importantly, perhaps, they would receive phone calls and invitations to the White House from the president of the United States. Clinton was now meeting one-on-one with members, giving his pitch for NAFTA, sounding out their concerns, gently twisting their arms. "I'm going to get an artificial socket for my arm," joked Representative David Mann (Democrat, Ohio) after his meeting with Clinton on the November 8.[23] Recalled Mickey Kantor later,

> The President spent an *enormous* amount of time individually with members. . . . Even those who finally ended up voting against him walked away shaking their heads in amazement with what he knew and his commitment to it, how clearly he understood the rationale for it, and how it fit in with where he wanted to take the country.

In Congress, Bill Bradley was now devoting much of his day to the push for NAFTA. Every day, he would take the shuttle from his Senate office, stride through the Capitol, and take the train to the House office buildings, to call on wavering Representatives. He carried a card in his pocket listing undecided members and their concerns, information gathered in part in meetings he was holding in his Senate hideaway office with Matsui and Richardson. Bradley's presence in the House caused a minor stir. The last time he had done this was in 1986, when he played such a pivotal role in the tax reform effort. Said Susan Brophy later, "Bradley in the House was very effective. A lot of people really respect Bradley. People talked about the fact that he did it. Also, Bradley really knew the arguments."

NAFTA's opponents did not have the firepower to match its supporters. Letters opposing NAFTA continued to pour in, although in targeted districts, letters of support now more than matched letters of opposition. Ross Perot, Ralph Nader, Pat Buchanan, Lane Kirkland, and many others opposed to NAFTA redoubled their efforts, but they had nothing comparable to the setting of a state dinner in the White House in which to make their pitch. An increasingly shrill tone entered their denunciation of NAFTA as they struggled to be heard above the cacophony of voices. The secretary-treasurer of the San Francisco Labor Council of the AFL-CIO wrote to Democrat Nancy Pelosi: "Even though you are considered a safe district, we will not forget."[24]

On November 7, President Clinton made a rare appearance on NBC's Sunday morning program "Meet the Press." Clinton made his usual pitch for NAFTA but went on to complain about the unions' "roughshod, muscle-bound tactics." Clinton's comments enraged union leaders. Teamsters president Ron Carey called on the president to apologize:

> The president's use of the words "muscle-bound" and "roughshod" were an insult to every working man and woman in America. If he had used similar code words to attack civil rights groups, women's groups, or environmental organizations who oppose NAFTA, he would be strongly condemned by every member of Congress.[25]

The fracas made a great story: the president fighting with his core constituency. It would be pushed off the headlines, however, by the biggest drama of the season: a nationally televised, live "debate" between Vice President Gore and Ross Perot.

The Gore-Perot "Debate"

The idea came from Jack Quinn, Vice President Gore's chief of staff. What if Gore challenged Perot to a debate? Gore jumped at the suggestion. He had been debating NAFTA for months with members of Congress and others. He felt he knew the facts inside and out, and he felt Perot was vulnerable. He was sure he could best him. Gore called CNN talk show host Larry King to see if he would moderate a debate. King agreed. The vice president then took the idea to the president on the morning of November 4, when Clinton gave Gore the go-ahead.

Later that day, the president was in Lexington, Kentucky, for a NAFTA event. A reporter asked him a question about Ross Perot. Clinton responded that the vice president had challenged Perot to a debate. "Let's see if he takes it," Clinton said. Bill Daley, Press Secretary Dee Dee Myers, and White House Communications Director Michael Waldman, standing next to the president, looked at each other in surprise. None of them knew anything about it.

Ross Perot was on Capitol Hill making the rounds of Republican Representatives when the wire services reported Gore's challenge. "Of course you accept," recalled Pat Choate of Perot's reaction. At a hastily convened press conference, Perot told reporters, "They've issued the challenge and I've accepted it."

Few in the pro-NAFTA camp thought debating Perot was a good idea. At the White House, Howard Paster recalled, "I was aghast. Why are we giving Perot this platform? I frankly thought it was demeaning to the vice president to be debating Ross Perot." Many insiders didn't think it was necessary. Mickey Kantor's chief of staff Tom Nides thought "Perot was fading into the woodwork. . . . If you take Perot on, you only build him up." USA*NAFTA's Ken Cole recalled, "I thought the Gore debate was a mistake. I wouldn't have recommended it. I thought we were winning."

The conventional wisdom in Washington was that Gore's challenge reflected NAFTA's desperate situation. Gore had a reputation as a wooden speaker. The contest against Perot, the master of the sound bite, seemed a mismatch. Republican political consultant Ed Rollins opined that

> Ross Perot will kill them. . . . You have now given a guy who's been blanked by the TV networks, has been complaining that there's a conspiracy to keep him off the air—you've now made him the most significant player in this whole debate one more time. They'll have a tremendous viewership, and I promise you, Ross Perot in these arenas is as tough as anybody.[26]

But on reflection, some of the president's political advisors recognized the potential advantages of the debate. "I thought it was a good idea," Gergen recalled. "I also thought it was worth taking a risk." Perot's popularity had been falling all year long. In March, 42 percent of the American public had a favorable impression of Perot and only 30 percent had a negative impression. By mid September his numbers had slipped to 36 percent positive and 35 percent negative. A poll released a week before Gore issued the challenge showed only 30 percent positive and 42 percent negative. Perhaps there wasn't such a risk to raising Perot's salience if Gore could just hold his own.

On Tuesday, November 9, eight days before the House vote, the vice president of the United States debated former presidential candidate and private citizen Ross Perot on "Larry King Live," a cable television talk show. If any citizens tuned in for a reasoned discussion of NAFTA, they were quickly disappointed. Almost immediately, the encounter became a contest of competing images and sound bites.

Perot held up a photograph of cardboard shacks.

Livestock in this country, and animals, have a better life than good, decent, hardworking Mexicans working for major U.S. companies. Now, here's a good, decent man working his heart out, making his cardboard shack. And the cardboard came from boxes that were used to ship the goods down there.

NAFTA will make this worse, Perot implied.

Gore was prepared. He had studied Perot's performance on "Meet the Press" in August when Perot got flustered when pressed by reporters for specifics,[27] and he wanted to challenge Perot's credibility. Perot did not like being challenged. Gore thought he had a strategy to rattle Perot. "I brought some pictures too," Gore said.

This is a picture of Mr. Smoot and Mr. Hawley. They look like pretty good fellas. They sounded reasonable at the time. A lot of people believed them. The Congress passed the Smoot-Hawley Protection Bill. [Looking at Perot] He wants to raise tariffs on Mexico. They raised tariffs, and it was one of the principal causes—many economists say the principal cause—of the Great Depression in this country and around the world. Now, [to Perot] I framed this so you can put it on your wall if you want to.

A surprised Perot could only mumble. "Thanks. Thanks." Gore pressed the attack, emphasizing who was supporting NAFTA:

Every living former president of the United States, in both parties. The two-termers and the one-termers. Every former secretary of state, every former secretary of defense, secretary of treasury. Every living Nobel Prize winner in economics, conservatives, liberals, every one in between. They'd never agreed on anything. And distinguished Americans from Colin Powell to Tip O'Neil to Rush Limbaugh.

And then the list got closer to home as Gore continued,

Ross Perot, Jr., the head of his business, Mort Meyerson, Orville Swindle, the head of United We Stand, the last time, and Ross Perot, Sr., supported it until he started running for president and attempting to bring out the politics of fear.

Perot countered with:

Now, a good deal will sell itself, folks, just plain talk. Four former presidents came out for it and couldn't sell it. All the secretaries of state came out for it and couldn't sell it. We had satellite going across two hundred auditoriums across the country. That didn't sell it. Got Lee Iococca for it. That didn't sell it. Thirty million dollars coming out of Mexico, and that is rotten and that is wrong, and that didn't sell it. Thirty, thirty-five million dollars coming out of corporate America to try to get out of this country, go south of the border and hire that cheap labor, and that didn't sell it. This dog just didn't hunt.[28]

But Perot was now on the defensive and having a hard time making a coherent case against NAFTA.

Gore pointed to an investment that Perot and his son had in a Texas international transport park, which would stand to gain from NAFTA. Perot, clearly irritated by the reference to his personal stake in NAFTA, gave a confusing response. Gore seemed to imply that Perot was hiding his involvement in the park. Finally, Perot snapped at Gore, "Would you even know the truth if you saw it?" Gore had gotten under Perot's skin, and Perot was sounding more and more shrill.

The pro-NAFTA forces were ecstatic with the debate. Said USA*NAFTA's Ken Cole, "When I saw the debate, I knew we were going to win. This is ours. They were going to start running [away from Perot]." Howard Paster and Newt Gingrich spoke during the debate to exult over what was happening. Another Congressman called Paster to surrender. Afterward, Perot knew it hadn't gone well. Explained Pat Choate later, "Perot has mastered a lot of formats. Town hall, talk show, but he hadn't been on 'Crossfire.' He will never be unprepared again."

A quick poll taken during and immediately after the debate showed that of those watching, 47 percent thought Gore had won, 33 percent thought Perot had won.[29] But since only a fraction of the electorate actually watched, what mattered more was the popular verdict that Gore had won. Insiders in Washington all scored the debate a knockout for the vice president. The media swiftly reached the same conclusion. The next day's coverage was dominated by assertions that Gore had trounced Perot. On ABC's "Nightline" two days later, Ted Koppel announced the topic as "How the White House Ambushed Perot." He reported a Nightline poll conducted that day showed 46 percent of the American public thought Gore had won, and only 13 percent thought Perot had won. Political advisor Paul Begala said, "The fact that Mr. Perot has emerged as the discredited embodiment of opposition to NAFTA certainly helps the pro-NAFTA cause."[30] "This gave some political cover that people could use as an excuse in their district," recalled Susan Brophy. "[They could say] I was undecided and listened to the debate and the vice president won."

Euphoria in the pro-NAFTA camp was matched by despair and more than a measure of embarrassment in the anti-NAFTA camp. Andrea Durbin, a grassroots organizer for Friends of the Earth, recalled being "very embarrassed with Perot." The labor unions were sick that Perot had been made their champion. The real damage, however, was done among the Republicans Perot had been courting. Suddenly, they had much less to fear from Ross Perot. An aide to Duncan Hunter said "the Perot-Gore debate was a disaster."

Public Opinion

Ross Perot's increasingly negative image corresponded with a marked improvement in NAFTA's popular standing. In September, the NBC–*Wall Street Journal* poll had found that only 25 percent of the American public favored NAFTA whereas 36 percent opposed it. By the third week in October, NAFTA's numbers had improved slightly, to 29 percent favoring and 33 percent opposed, as the pro-NAFTA public relations effort began to offset the opposition. In the last couple weeks of the campaign, though, there were unmistakable signs that public opinion was shifting even more strongly in NAFTA's favor. The NBC–*Wall Street Journal* poll taken November 14 and 15, and released the day before the House vote, picked up the change. A plurality now *favored* NAFTA, 36 percent to 31 percent.

The pro-NAFTA public relations strategy seemed to have worked. The jobs issue had been largely neutralized. Now only 49 percent of the American public agreed with the statement "American jobs will move to Mexico," down from 74 percent in September. And 42 percent now disagreed. Even more significant, 50 percent now agreed and only 38 percent disagreed that "some jobs will be lost in the U.S., but even more jobs will be created," a reversal of the September numbers. The foreign policy arguments appeared also to have had an effect. A remarkable 85 percent of those polled believed that if NAFTA was defeated it would affect "President Clinton's standing as a world leader dealing with other countries." Ross Perot's numbers fell even further. Now only 28 percent of Americans had a positive view of him, while 47 percent had a negative view.[31]

Retail Politics

While public attention was on Gore and Perot, the inside game was now retail politics. The number of undecided members continued to shrink. The White House whip count for Wednesday, November 10, the day after the debate and a week before the vote, now showed 61 Democrats for NAFTA and 131 opposed. Only 64 members had not yet announced a position. Of these, 24 were leaning yes, 20 leaning no, and 22 undecided. NAFTA was still behind, but the undecideds were now mostly breaking for NAFTA.

The administration redoubled its lobbying efforts. Clinton met one-on-one with undecided members and made phone calls late into the night. Business lobbyists clogged the corridors of the House. Bradley's Senate whip group went over the House list and divided the undecideds among themselves. Bradley spent hours in the House, talking at length with members such as Anna Eshoo and others.

A few members tried to make deals for unrelated items. In one of his visits to the House, Bradley discovered that Floyd Flake (Democrat, N.Y.), who had already announced his opposition to NAFTA, might be willing to change his mind if he could get some help on an urban program of interest to him. Flake met with President Clinton, got what he wanted, and announced his support on the White House steps. Other members wanted promises of political support. The president promised some that Hillary Clinton would campaign for them in the next election. But the biggest block of remaining undecided legislators were from Florida and Louisiana. Ten Democrats and roughly an equal number of Republicans were holding out for changes in the terms of NAFTA on three agricultural issues: sugar, citrus fruits, and winter vegetables (notably tomatoes).

U.S. sugar producers had never been happy with NAFTA's sugar provisions. In response to their complaints, Mickey Kantor had all but promised to take care of the sugar "problem" during his confirmation hearings in January. Now, as the vote neared, he would need to make good on that pledge. The United States reopened talks on the terms of the sugar agreement in late October and also began talking about citrus and winter vegetables. Said Louisiana sugar producer Charles Melancon, "Without sugar's problem fixed, I think we can kill NAFTA."[32] Most observers agreed. Louisiana Democrats William Jefferson and Billy Tauzin were claiming 15–17 votes in House depended on the sugar deal. Publicly, the Mexicans said they would not renegotiate, but they could see the political necessity. "It was a hard call," said one advisor to the Mexican government. "But we looked at the votes."

On November 3, Mexico and the United States reached tentative agreement on modest changes in the sugar, citrus, and vegetable deals. The sugar changes included corn sweeteners in the calculation of Mexican sugar consumption, thus making it less likely that Mexico could become a net exporter of sugar and thus eligible to export more sugar to the United States. The citrus and winter vegetable deals allowed the United States to provide price supports for domestic growers should imports cause prices to fall.

Two Louisiana Representatives joined Louisiana's Democratic Senators John Breaux and J. Bennett Johnston at a press conference to announce their support. But the Florida delegation remained unmoved. The administration then lobbied the Florida trade associations. On November 4, Florida Citrus Mutual, a growers group, dropped its opposition. On the 12th, the Florida Fruit and Vegetable Association and the Gulf Citrus Growers Association followed suit. The Florida delegation started to break for NAFTA. Democrat Harry Johnson announced his support. Republican Tom Lewis called a delegation meeting for the 16th, the day before the vote.

Mickey Kantor later attributed great importance to the deals. "[Because of] the willingness of the Mexican government to make some changes on the sugar and the vegetable issues, we picked up probably 26 votes out of that." But it was not clear how many of these members would actually have voted against the agreement.

Opponents claimed that NAFTA was for sale. "No votes were changing until the pork started flowing," said Perot.[33] His advisor Choate later described their strategy:

> The problem for Members was how to vote for it without committing political suicide. They were looking for a way to do it. Some needed sugar or citrus deals. The [administration] strategy was to use trade associations to give [members] cover. On the Perot talk shows, we called it flat bribery. We tried to poison the tactic.

Administration officials disputed the charge. Mickey Kantor later asserted, "Frankly, substantively, it [the deals] didn't cost the U.S. one penny. That's what's so silly. We didn't give away anything. What we did is strengthen the agreement in terms of our industries." Said the USTR's Chip Roh, "We have never paid so little [for a trade agreement]."

The Vote

With the House votes scheduled for Wednesday, November 17, the NAFTA strategists were still nervous going into the last weekend. Things were breaking their way, but all fall, whenever members went home for a weekend, NAFTA had lost votes. This was going to be another long weekend–Veterans Day weekend–and they held their breath. David Bonior sounded confident. "We have about 222 votes going into this weekend and we think we are going to hold our votes," he told reporters.[34]

But this time, the weekend was different. Many members went home to announce their decision to support NAFTA. On Monday evening, the House whip count looked much better. Of the Democrats, 87 were now "yes," 6 more were "lean yes," and 13 more were undecided. With the sugar, fruit, and vegetable deals working their way through the Florida delegation, Howard Paster and Bill Daley could now see 100 Democratic votes. Moreover, for the first time they had seen the real Republican numbers. Gingrich had more than enough votes to put NAFTA over the top.

The next day, Tuesday, the insiders knew the game was over. Florida Republican Tom Lewis held a press conference to announce his support for NAFTA, along with that of others in the delegation. While the lobbyists lined the halls of Congress (literally–it was difficult to walk through the corridors) the NAFTA strategists were over in the Senate, meeting with the author in Senator Bradley's office. "OK, what do you want us to do over here?" they asked. "Nothing," they were told. "We've got the votes." The fiftieth Senator publicly announced his support for NAFTA the next day.

The vote itself was anticlimactic for the insiders, but for the outside world it still appeared to hang in the balance. The formal House debate raged most of the day. There was little middle ground. But when the vote began that evening, the only question was when the one-hundredth Democrat would vote for NAFTA. The Republicans held back, and then when they saw the vote, the yes votes flooded in. The final tally, 234 to 200, surpassed all public expectations and even most private ones. One hundred and two Democrats had joined with 132 Republicans in favor.

NAFTA was not yet law, of course. The Senate would not act for four more days, but by then the president was in Seattle basking in the glow of victory and a strong surge of public confidence in his administration. With him were most of the administration officials who had worked so hard to pass NAFTA. Bill Daley was back in Chicago. Only a skeletal staff remained to monitor the Senate vote. The author double-checked his vote counts. On Saturday, November 20, the Senate voted 61 to 38 for NAFTA and the implementing legislation went to the president for his signature. On January 1, 1994, the North American Free Trade Agreement entered into force.

Interpreting the Victory: Political Diagnosis
and Political Strategy

This chapter began with three questions: What was the nature of the political problem facing NAFTA in the fall of 1993? What strategies did that problem demand? How did the strategies adopted by NAFTA's
supporters affect the outcome of the vote in Congress?

The first question is diagnostic. At one level the problem was located in
Congress, where NAFTA clearly faced an uphill battle. Yet an exclusive
focus on the game within Congress is clearly insufficient, although the interests of members and rules by which they played certainly mattered. Congress does not operate in a political vacuum; it is by design highly responsive
to pressures from outside. For NAFTA, the biggest political problem was in
the outside environment. Part of the outside pressure came from the usual
trade interests, but this was not trade politics as usual. Instead most of the
pressure came from normally inattentive publics, some organized into advocacy groups. To diagnose this problem requires a theory of Congressional
decision making that considers simultaneously processes within Congress
and those in the general public—some rational choice, some institutional,
and some symbolic—and that can explicate the relationship among them.
To evaluate that relationship, the commentary develops a theoretical approach that draws on a multilevel rational choice approach developed by
Arnold and modifies it to account for the limits of rational choice and the
operation of symbolic politics for explaining voter attitudes.

The second question is prescriptive. The dimensions of appropriate strategy depend on the diagnosis of the problem. NAFTA's political problem
demanded a multifaceted strategy, one that took into account the need to
manage Congressional processes, to deal with traditional pressure groups,
and most importantly to transform the interaction among members and
voters.

The third question is evaluative. Although the evidence is somewhat in-
conclusive, NAFTA's advocates, after a slow start, appear to have done reasonably well in diagnosing the problem they faced and in devising appropriate strategies. Furthermore, these strategies likely made the difference
between defeat and victory for NAFTA.

Theories of Congressional Action

To understand the nature of the problem faced by NAFTA's advocates as they entered the fall campaign requires a theory about Congressional voting, about how characteristics of Congress and the external political environment determine how Congress acts.

One possibility is to focus exclusively on the game within Congress, perhaps as a rational choice process among members playing by the elaborate rules that govern that institution. These factors were elements of the problem faced by NAFTA supporters—strategists needed to maneuver a bill through committees to get it to a vote—but this was ultimately not that hard a problem under the fast track rules. Moreover, a consensus of observers on both sides of the issue agreed that NAFTA would easily win a vote were it not for outside political pressures. Clearly, then, much of the problem lay in the way in which outside pressures affected members.

As discussed in Chapter 4, the dominant trade politics literature focuses on the role of concentrated commercial interests in influencing the actions of Congress. Scholars in the tradition of E.E. Schattschneider have identified the pervasive asymmetry between concentrated economic interests of producers and the diffuse economic interests of consumers. Historically, producers have sought and obtained protection for their interests, with the net effect being economically inefficient high levels of protection. But this was not NAFTA's problem in the fall of 1993.

First, concentrated protectionist interests were more than offset by concentrated free trade interests. A quick scan of the forces aligned for and against NAFTA reveals just how one-sided this lineup was. Against NAFTA were producers of a few agricultural commodities, some glass manufacturers, some small garment firms, a subset of the textile industry, ceramic tile makers, and a smattering of other smaller firms. For NAFTA were the Big Three automakers, the nation's biggest banks and insurance companies, the major pharmaceutical companies, big agribusiness, and all of the major business associations. The vast weight of concentrated economic interest was focused not just on "resisting protectionism" but in dismantling it.[35] Second, to the extent that powerful concentrated losers, who had strong incentives to change the agreement or block it altogether, had allies in Congress willing to fight for them, the rules of fast track prevented them from doing either.

If concentrated economic interests were the only political forces that mattered, this would have been no contest.

But this was not trade politics as usual. The strongest opposition was coming not from trade interests but from more general advocacy groups and, to a remarkable extent for a trade agreement, from the general public. To understand this problem, therefore, requires a theory that connects members of Congress to nontraditional advocacy groups, and ultimately most importantly, to the voters.

Connecting Voters to Congress: Arnold's Logic of Congressional Action

The question of the extent to which members of Congress concern themselves with the preferences of their constituents has occupied many scholars of Congress.[36] Logically we would expect members to be most concerned with voter preferences when those preferences are likely to affect their prospects for reelection. Most of the time, however, the majority of voters are unaware of the issues, let alone how their member votes. Nevertheless, strong anecdotal evidence indicates that members *do* concern themselves with voters, even when current voter interest is small.[37]

It is possible to view both legislators and voters through a rational choice lens. In *The Logic of Congressional Action*, Douglas Arnold offers an elegant framework for connecting voter preferences to legislative decisions. His approach is quite similar to the multilevel negotiation framework developed in previous chapters of this book: Rational choices on one level of politics—in this case, the electorate—constrain the actions of actors on another level—here, members of Congress. Arnold's logic is quite straightforward:

1. Citizens establish policy preferences by evaluating both policy proposals and policy effects.
2. Citizens choose among congressional candidates by evaluating both the candidates' policy positions and their connections with policy effects.
3. Legislators choose among policy proposals by estimating citizens' potential policy preferences and by estimating the likelihood that citizens might incorporate these policy preferences into their choices among candidates in subsequent congressional elections.

4. Coalition leaders adopt strategies for enacting their policy proposals by anticipating legislators' electoral calculations, which in turn requires that they estimate both citizens' potential policy preferences and the likelihood that citizens might incorporate these policy preferences into their choices among congressional candidates.[38]

In Arnold's formulation, members care primarily about reelection. Only when the political consequences balance are members free to vote their policy preferences. They are extremely attentive to the preferences of their constituents, but the public's opinion at the moment of decision does not matter so much as the views of the "potential public" in the next election. Even when only a small circle of "attentive" publics seem to care, members need to worry that elements of the normally "inattentive" public could be stirred to action.[39]

Arnold's model assumes a tight connection between the actual effects of policy on voters' *outcome* preferences and their *policy* preferences. Each citizen "performs a miniature cost-benefit analysis for a policy proposal, incorporating all costs and benefits that might affect his or her own personal welfare."[40] Arnold acknowledges that most citizens don't pay enough attention to notice policy proposals as they come along, particularly when the likely costs or benefits are quite low. He proposes, therefore, the idea of an *instigator*. Instigators alert potentially affected publics to the effects of a policy proposal even when the stakes are low. As an example, he suggests Ralph Nader.

> Ralph Nader helps to identify the effects of proposed bills and regulations on consumers' interests. . . . Nader's contribution was not to organize consumers—a nearly impossible task—but rather to label legislative votes as pro- or anti-consumer. The media then disseminated these messages, challengers helped citizens reach the proper political conclusions, and suddenly a formerly inattentive public was alive.[41]

Taken together, the portrait of a self-interested electorate and of instigators eager to help the public recognize its latent interests suggests that members need to ask themselves two questions as they decide to vote:

> First, if I were on the other side, could I figure out how to incite inattentive publics against legislators like me who voted on the wrong

side? Second, are there, in fact, potential instigators who might mobilize inattentive publics against me?[42]

This way of thinking provides a very useful framing for the problem of
legislators in the case of NAFTA. Members were quite worried about normally inattentive publics and about the possibility that instigators might in-
cite them. Indeed, much of the guesswork about this possibility had been
taken out the problem by the fact that during the August recess, when members were lobbied heavily by anti-NAFTA constituents, they experienced
something of the way in which the issue might be used against them in their
next campaign.

However, a model that relies purely on self-interested calculation on all
levels presents problems. First, the portrait of how voters establish their policy
positions does not conform either to the logic of rational ignorance or to
observation. Even with instigators to identify categories of cost and benefits,
actually conducting a cost-benefit analysis for most policy issues—certainly
for something as complex as NAFTA—is itself prohibitively costly for most
citizens (and for most legislators—more on this later). As Downs has shown,
citizens have very little incentive to acquire information or to conduct the
analysis needed to estimate the effects of most policies on their interests. As
the previous chapter demonstrated, in these circumstances, the market, if it
forms, will not be for policy information, but for symbols. To the extent that
a third party, Ralph Nader for instance, helps citizens map from interests to
policy preferences, the way in which he does so bears little resemblance to
the logic of a cost-benefit analysis. Nader does not simply reveal the costs
and benefits of a policy to consumers, he tells the public (or at least that
segment with whom he has credibility) what a policy means. Nader is not
just an "instigator," he is an "interpreter."

Second, it is unlikely that members of Congress perform the kind of
calculated assessment of public opinion that Arnold describes. As he puts it
the task is straightforward, although complex.

To reach a decision, then, a legislator needs to (1) identify all the
attentive and inattentive publics who might care about a policy issue,
(2) estimate the direction and intensity of their preferences and potential preferences, (3) estimate the probability that the potential preferences will be transformed into real preferences, (4) weight all these
preferences according to the size of the various attentive and inatten-

tive publics, and (5) give special weight to the preferences of the legislator's consistent supporters.[43]

Members are assumed to have a clear picture of where attentive publics
stand, so the question is one of predicting whether (normally) inattentive
publics will develop policy preferences. For Arnold, this task is made easier
by the close connection between the actual effects of policy and the stance
taken by constituents. Indeed, the political problem can almost be reduced
to an economic assessment of costs and benefits, with the caveat that one
needs to survey the landscape for potential instigators.

There are two problems with this model of how politicians evaluate the
potential preferences of citizens. The first is theoretical and relates to the
source of those preferences. If citizens' preferences are not solely, or even
primarily, a function of the real outcomes of policy, but are rather related
to the way in which policy is interpreted by and for them, then the method
for anticipating potential opinion cannot be a calculus of the incidence of
costs and benefits. The second objection is empirical. Little indicates that
members of Congress assume that their constituents engage in miniature
cost-benefit analyses and might discern the impact of policies on their interests. Members certainly worry about how an issue will be used to oppose
them, but they fear how the issue might be framed by potential interpreters
with an interest in spinning the story against them, not that their constituents
will discover how their own interests are affected.

Arnold's two key questions for a legislator might be reformulated as: First,
if I were on the other side, could I figure out ways of interpreting my vote
that could hurt me in the next campaign? Second, are there interpreters out
there (including most obviously my opponent) interested and capable of
framing the issue to my disadvantage?

Answering these questions is more an act of imagination than of calculation, which introduces the possibility that members of Congress may be
deluded in their apprehension of either current or potential public opinion.
The proposition that politicians' estimates and projections of public opinion
can be manipulated is supported by the obvious effort policy entrepreneurs
make to do just that, for example when they flood Congressional offices with
prepaid postcards, orchestrate phone calls, or publicize the results of carefully slanted polls.

Finally, there is the issue of the extent to which political calculations
determine how legislators vote. For Arnold, only when the politics is a wash

do members vote their own preferences. What precisely constitutes a wash is another question, given the uncertainty of political calculations, but there is considerable evidence that members do not simply vote to maximize their chances for reelection. The large number of members who have recently resigned from Congress should be sufficient to demonstrate the point. Ideology and altruism do play roles in legislative decision making.[44]

Amending the Logic: A Multilevel, Multimode Theory of Congressional Action

The preceding discussion has demonstrated both the strengths and the shortcomings of a theory of Congressional decision making based solely on interests. A modification of the theory is needed to account for the limited demand for policy information and for the use of symbolic shortcuts in the electorate, to allow for the possibility that members of Congress may misperceive public opinion given the difficulty of estimating it and the opportunity for manipulations of the signals on which they rely, and to acknowledge a larger role for members' policy preferences in determining how they vote.

As in the negotiator model applied in previous chapters, members of Congress have two arguments in their utility function, one for political consequences and one for policy preferences. Political calculations relate to the possible use of an issue in the member's next election. Since the position of attentive, organized interests is relatively well known, the problem is to estimate the likely stance of normally inattentive, unorganized publics. So far, the theory is largely consistent with Arnold. The theory departs from Arnold in five ways, however.

First, public opinion, current or potential, is only loosely connected to real policy effects. When the policy stakes are relatively low for individuals and policy effects are difficult to predict, policy preferences, if any, are less likely to be driven by cost-benefit calculations. To the extent that the general public forms preferences in these circumstances, those preferences will depend primarily on symbolically constructed understandings. Interpreters can shape opinion for publics with whom they have credibility.

Second, members of Congress estimate potential political impacts on (normally) inattentive publics based on ad hoc sampling of current opinion and on imagining the symbolic potential in the hands of a political opponent. Members ask whether the vote might be used to paint them as, for example, "soft on crime," to demonstrate "flip-flopping," to allege a "sellout to special interests," or other such damaging framings. The task is to estimate the potential for a negative story.

Third, members' conceptions of current and potential public opinion can be and are manipulated by interpreters. Because members must rely on imperfect measures of current opinion—who shows up at the town hall meeting, the volume of mail for and against, the number of phone calls— and because of the inherent difficulty of anticipating how a story might play in the future, members are susceptible to plausible trial runs of the negative story.

Fourth, members care about the effects of policy at all times, not just when the political forces are balanced against each other. The greater the perceived policy stakes, the less important political considerations become. Members can and do vote against their political interests, even when those are reasonably clear to them. The relative mix of policy and politics varies considerably by member.

Fifth, members' estimates of policy consequences, which inform both their policy preferences and (to some degree at least) their calculation of political consequence, may or may not be accurate, and will reflect, in part, the way in which the issue is framed for them, not just for their constituents. Interpreters, therefore, may influence member preferences directly by influencing the meaning of an issue for members and indirectly by shaping meanings for constituents.

Diagnosis and Strategy

The theoretical framework developed above can be used to diagnose the problem faced by NAFTA's advocates in September 1993. That diagnosis suggests possible points of leverage for influencing members of Congress, which in turn suggests possible strategies.

Part of the problem did reside in Congress, particularly with the arcane institutions and processes that had to be followed for the NAFTA bill to become law. Part of the problem did have to do with concentrated economic interests opposed to NAFTA. But to a great extent NAFTA's real problem lay outside the traditional domain of trade politics, in the normally inattentive publics now attending quite closely to this unusual trade event.

At its core the problem for members of Congress was the perceived electoral consequence of a vote for NAFTA. Members did not have a hard time imagining how the issue might be used against them. Their encounters at town hall meetings in August and earlier in the year had demonstrated the form of the story that would be spun. In the next election, NAFTA would be associated with each job lost in the member's district, as well as with all that had already been lost. Members would be accused of selling out to corporate interests and foreign agents, of selling American sovereignty, of undermining environmental laws, and other charges. From what they could sense from their sampling of mail, phone calls, and personal contacts back in the district, their constituents were willing to believe these stories.

The theory sketched out earlier suggests some of the factors underlying this situation (and the potential points of strategic leverage for solving the problem). First, public opinion was not based on the real effects of NAFTA but on how it was being interpreted by normally inattentive publics, in large measure in response to the way in which its negative interpreters—Ross Perot, Ralph Nader, Pat Buchanan, et al.—had spun the story. Second, members of Congress understood the state of public opinion and estimated the future shape of it very imperfectly. Their interpretations had been successfully manipulated by the packed town hall meetings, the flood of anti-NAFTA postcards, the volume of phone calls, and the absence of countervailing manipulation from the other side. Third, members' policy assessments were themselves only loosely connected to facts and analysis and had been strongly influenced by the negative framings provided by various interpreters (and by constituents with whom they communicated).

This diagnosis suggests the dimensions of a possible strategy. One dimension would involve managing the institutions of Congress, keeping the implementing bill out of unfavorable committees, working it through the trade committees, and using the rules of Congress to compel a vote. A second would involve dealing with particularly strong special interests, assessing the magnitude of the threat they posed, identifying what they wanted, and bargaining for their support. In the case of the sugar and citrus deals, this meant renegotiating parts of the international agreement. Another aspect of the strategy would require mobilization of those concentrated interests with a stake in supporting NAFTA. Most of the strategy, however, would need to address the larger public opinion problem.

First, if public opinion was not a direct manifestation of the actual policy implications of NAFTA but rather of its symbolic meaning as interpreted by NAFTA's opponents, public opinion could be changed. Change would require that NAFTA be reframed by a positive message, one that told a story about why NAFTA was good and why it was the right thing to do, and it would also demand a plan for communicating that message to the public through credible interpreters.

Second, to the extent that members' understandings of actual and potential public attitudes had been distorted by opposition tactics, what was needed was a grassroots campaign to alter members' perceptions. The campaign would need to generate postcards and phone calls, as well as persuade supporters to go to town hall meetings and drop by members' offices. Even more importantly, supporters would need to ease members' apprehension about future public opinion by providing them with language to defuse the opposition.

Third, to the extent that members' policy views did matter, what was needed was a campaign of persuasion that both changed the direction of views and raised the perceived policy stakes. Many members were concerned about the real consequences of NAFTA. As the results of the political calculus approached a draw, policy concerns might matter more. The bigger the perceived policy stakes, too, the less important political considerations would become in members' calculations. A strategy to change members' views would involve both provision of information and argument by individuals whose policy judgment the member trusted.

If the diagnosis was correct, these were the strategic levers available to NAFTA's advocates. The question is how well they actually understood the problem and devised strategies appropriate to it.

Diagnosis and Strategy in the Event

To what extent did NAFTA's advocates diagnose their problem in ways similar to that suggested by the theory? To what extent did the strategies used correspond the diagnosis? The record suggests that although the diagnosis was slow in coming, a critical core of strategists ultimately evaluated the situation with reasonable accuracy, and although the strategy was never totally coherent, the campaign put together by NAFTA's advocates was generally consistent with the diagnosis.

NAFTA's proponents only gradually came to realize the nature of the political problem they faced. The realization came earlier for some than for others, and an important part of the story concerns the efforts by individuals to persuade the key decision makers in the Clinton administration and the business lobby of what they were up against. From the beginning of the year, Senator Bradley, for instance, was counseling that this was not trade politics as usual, that instead this was a political campaign that needed a public message and a grassroots strategy. Media consultants Frances O'Brien and Paige Gardner fought hard to convince the business community that this was a different kind of problem requiring a different kind of solution. Inside the administration, Bill Daley urged the president to take the case for NAFTA to the public, convinced that this step was necessary and that public opinion could be turned around if the right themes were struck.

By September, the network of strategists in and out of the administration had come to a near consensus about their situation. Of course they would undertake traditional lobbying, and take care of particular interests wherever they could, as they would in a usual trade politics situation. Moreover, the trade experts would have to make sure that the institutional obstacles were overcome. But the real problem was in the apprehension felt by members of Congress about the political danger of a vote for NAFTA. The challenge was to convince members that a vote for NAFTA was not political suicide, perhaps even to raise the possibility that a vote against NAFTA could have political costs. Then, having neutralized the political problem, the strategists had to persuade members that NAFTA was the right thing to do.

The strategy they adopted conformed with this assessment. It was a strategy conducted on many fronts, loosely coordinated through the daily meetings of the core strategy group in the White House and through constant communication with business, other pro-NAFTA groups, and the pro-NAFTA strategists on Capitol Hill. It involved managing the policy making process of putting together an implementing bill. It involved striking deals with members and the interests they represented. But mostly it involved reducing the political pressure on members by changing public opinion, members' perceptions of public opinion (particularly how opinion might affect the next election), and members' beliefs about NAFTA.

To change public perceptions, NAFTA's advocates sought to tell a different story about the meaning of NAFTA. First, the story sought to combat the jobs issue by making it a matter of international competitiveness, thus reconfiguring the "us" and "them" in the economic parable. This was not the United States versus Mexico, it was North America versus Japan and Europe. Second, NAFTA was a foreign policy matter of overriding national interest, a historic opportunity to serve our interests by strengthening our neighbor. If we miss this opportunity, the problems in Mexico will get worse.

Third, an attempt to spin the opposition, the vote on NAFTA was a test of the American character. If we defeat NAFTA we show that we are afraid to compete, afraid to embrace change. These messages were conveyed by credible interpreters—Bill Clinton, Lee Iococca, Jimmy Carter, and Bill Bradley among them—in television commercials, public speeches, talk show appearances, and op ed articles.

Altering members' perceptions of public opinion entailed designing a business-funded, targeted grassroots campaign to demonstrate political support for NAFTA in key districts. Here the object was not so much to change public opinion as it was to change members' perceptions of public opinion in their districts. The business consultants worked with local businesses to generate phone calls and postcards and to persuade people to go to town meetings. To help members anticipate how NAFTA might play in the future, the business community ran many commercials primarily in the Washington area. The purpose was to create the illusion that these commercials were running back in the home district so that members might imagine how their constituents were reacting to the messages and how they might react in the future. Of course, the significance of the Gore-Perot debate was not that so many people watched it and changed their minds but that it demonstrated to members how they might combat Perot on this issue in the future. The debate dramatically reduced the estimate of the threat from Perot on this issue in the next election.

The campaign for NAFTA was not only intended to alter the political calculus of members, however. It also attempted to alter their policy beliefs. Some members had firmly fixed views about NAFTA, either positive or negative, and some undecided members were almost exclusively concerned about politics. But a substantial number of legislators cared about the policy consequences and were struggling to make sense of this bewildering issue.

To persuade these members, the strategists first needed intelligence: How was the member thinking about the issue? With assessment in hand, NAFTA's proponents could then devise a strategy to change those policy perceptions. In some cases, the focus was simply on providing information. If a member had an incorrect understanding of the phaseout period for certain tariffs, or of the status of U.S. environmental laws, or of the procedure for invoking trade sanctions in a labor dispute, or any other aspect of the agreement, the administration would assemble and dispatch a brief rebutting the misconceptions. In other cases, the essence of communication was less factual rebuttal than signaling by credible individuals. If a member displayed a general concern about NAFTA's effects on jobs, the environment, immigration, drug trafficking, or other broad issues, individuals with credibility on those issues were detailed to convey the message. On jobs, Secretary of Labor Reich and President Clinton himself had considerable personal credibility (at least with Democrats). On the environment, the message might be conveyed by Vice President Gore or by a representative of one of the pro-NAFTA environmental organizations. On drugs, Attorney General Janet Reno or "drug czar" Lee Brown might meet with the member. If the concern was with human rights in Mexico, former president Jimmy Carter might call.

Much of the persuasion effort, however, entailed reframing the story of NAFTA for members in much the same way as for citizens. What the president said to undecided members in private did not differ substantially from his public rhetoric. The arguments that Al Gore used with such great effect against Ross Perot in their debate were the same arguments he would make to members when they were in the Oval Office. When Bill Bradley spoke to other members about NAFTA, he spoke about its strategic importance and its historic significance.

The Effectiveness of Strategy

Did the strategies work? This is not an easy question to answer. True, NAFTA won, but to the extent that any of these strategies were effective, the outcome was multiply determined. Moreover, statements by members about what influenced their vote should be taken with a grain of salt, since members have an incentive to downplay the importance of political calculation in their decisions. We must rely, therefore, on the insights of the experienced insiders who saw the process up close. The evidence, admittedly, is imperfect, but it suggests that the strategies worked.

The administration and the Hill strategists managed to cobble together a bill and navigate it through committees to a vote, although the process was ragged at times. The accommodations for sugar, citrus, and vegetable interests appeared to have secured a few needed votes, although some of those members may have been posturing to extract as much as possible from the administration. And the campaign to change the broader political climate for NAFTA appears to have accomplished its goal.

Public attitudes changed dramatically in the last few weeks of the campaign. This can be seen not only in the percentages favoring NAFTA in the polls, but in attitudes about the key dimensions of opinion that the public campaign sought to influence. By November, the jobs issue had been transformed to the point that a majority of Americans believed more jobs would be created than lost. The foreign policy implications of NAFTA were much more salient in voters' minds, with a majority believing that defeat of NAFTA would hurt the president's ability to conduct foreign policy. Moreover, Perot's stock had fallen precipitously. What exactly caused these swings is impossible to know, but it is certainly plausible to assume that the barrage of positive messages had their effect.

Did members' perceptions of public opinion change? Certainly, members' experience of public sentiment changed dramatically, almost certainly more dramatically than the actual change in public opinion. Mail that once ran 20 to 1 against NAFTA was almost evenly balanced by November. Delegations of supporters came by the office. NAFTA advocates started appearing at town hall meetings. How did members read this change? The best evidence here is what members were saying at the time, in private, to other members and others with whom they had contact. According to the whip organizations, members felt considerably less pressure by the end of the fall than they had at the beginning, or more accurately they felt countervailing pressure from the pro-NAFTA forces.

Did members' anticipation of future public opinion change? This question is hard to answer, but one suggestive fact is the hunger members demonstrated for pro-NAFTA messages that would work in their encounters with constituents, and another is the way in which effective messages seemed to buoy their confidence. The close connection between the Perot-Gore debate and the flurry of announcements in favor of NAFTA is also noteworthy. Many, perhaps most, who announced support for NAFTA in the next week would have done so anyway, but Washington insiders watching the debate knew instinctively that the game was up, not because public opinion would change or because members' assessments of public opinion would change, but fundamentally because the debate transformed how members imagined NAFTA playing in their next campaign. Now they knew how to combat Perot.

Did members change their policy views? Most did not, of course, but many appeared to have been persuaded. The extraordinary market for information stands as evidence here: This was not just a matter of the administration pressing information on members; many policy-oriented members actively demanded information from the administration and from their staffs. Members spent hours in discussion with each other, with trusted advisors, and with advocates. All this consumption might, of course, have amounted to little, but the insider judgment was that many members really did not know what they thought of NAFTA at the beginning of the fall, and their policy decisions were affected by information and persuasive argumentation. In the rhetoric that members used to describe their reasons for supporting NAFTA, one could hear echoes of the framings provided to them by the campaign for NAFTA. We should not be so quick to dismiss the statements of members that they voted for, or against, NAFTA because of what they believed it would do.

Conclusions

To diagnose NAFTA's problems in the fall of 1993 requires thinking across levels and modes of politics. What is needed is a framework that allows us to assess the nature of Congressional institutions, interest group politics, and symbolic constructions in the broader public; understand the complex interrelationships among them; and most importantly, identify the possible points of leverage in this system.

In the event, of course, the challenge was not just to diagnose the problem but also to devise strategy. Political analysts, thinking in ways similar to the framework developed in this chapter, diagnosed the problem with reasonable accuracy and devised strategies that made a difference.

9 Conclusions

This book has moved back and forth between narrative and analysis. It has been a dialogue between fact and theory. The structure reflected the two goals of the book. The first was to understand the history of NAFTA: why the nations of North America decided to negotiate, why they negotiated what they did, and why they ultimately accepted what they negotiated. To understand this history required the application of different theoretical lenses, each of which brought different aspects of the history into focus. The second goal was to evaluate theory in light of evidence, to identify the uses and limitations of existing theories, and to modify and extend them when necessary. As the book moved through the chronology of NAFTA, it also developed an argument about the nature of theory for political analysis.

Political Analysis

Throughout, the book has used the term *political analysis* rather than *political science* to describe the task at hand. The distinction is between the problem of understanding a particular event and the problem of discovering universal tendencies in politics. Understandings of tendencies are useful as a guide to analysis. Yet general statements of the form "if X, then on average Y," are at best a first cut for establishing a particular Y rather than an average one. The question for the political analyst is not whether, for instance, totalitarian governments are more aggressive on average than democratic ones, but whether a particular totalitarian government is likely to act aggressively in a particular circumstance. The object of (much) political science is probabilistic generalities; the goal of political analysis is accurate diagnosis.[1] Indeed, the ultimate purpose of political analysis is to inform strategy; it is diagnosis for prescription.

The medical metaphor is apt. When confronted with a patient complaining of discomfort, the physician cannot be satisfied with an analysis of the form, "medical research has shown that for your gender and age group you have a 0.3 chance of colon cancer." That knowledge may inform an examination, but it cannot substitute for the careful dialogue between particular manifestations and general knowledge that is at the heart of good diagnosis. Without such probing inquiry, the physician cannot know what actually ails the patient and may do more harm than good.

Diagnosing NAFTA requires an analytic framework of some complexity. The politics of NAFTA operated at several levels: across the international bargaining table, in the corridors of Congress, in corporate boardrooms and union halls, and over dinner tables. At every level, the politics involved strategic interaction among contending interests; the operation of institutional rules, norms, and routines; and the contest of symbolic meanings. To understand NAFTA, therefore, requires an understanding of these different levels and modes of politics.

In the preceding chapters we have seen how different analytic lenses, focused on different levels and modes of politics, illuminated different aspects of NAFTA. In the course of the book, we have considered and applied theories concerned with bargaining among nations, interest groups, and individuals within interest groups; with institutional structures at the international level, the national level (constitutional structures), and the subnational level (within the U.S. Congress); and with constructed meanings held by international, national, and subnational communities.

The approach taken here for NAFTA is in some regards similar to that of Allison's use of alternative conceptual models for explaining the Cuban missile crisis. In *Essence of Decision*, a book which has served as something of a model for this book, Allison describes three broad models—the "rational actor" model, essentially realism; an "organizational process" model, a domestic-level institution approach; and a "bureaucratic politics" model, a domestic-level intragovernmental bargaining model.[2] This book expands Allison's typology in two ways: first, to consider the possibility of political processes operating at several levels of aggregation and, second, to add the politics of symbols to that of interests and institutions. In addition, more explicitly than in Allison, these approaches are treated less as alternatives than as complements in a comprehensive framework.

The political processes at work in the history of NAFTA, however, do not respect the boundaries of the cells of this matrix. The multiple levels of NAFTA politics were nested, not layered. They were *simultaneously* international, intergroup, and interpersonal. The behavior of Mexico, Canada, and the United States in the international arena is an artifact not only of international processes but also of domestic processes operating at the next level, which in turn often reflected processes at still lower levels. One cannot make sense of the U.S. insistence on labor and environmental side negotiations (or the U.S. stance in those talks) without understanding the interaction between Congress and the president, as well as the role of labor and environmental groups in U.S. politics.

Similarly, the politics of NAFTA were often *simultaneously* about interests, institutions, and ideas. In our discussion of the relationship between members of Congress and constituents, for example, we saw how constructed understandings of NAFTA by constituents defined real interests by members.

To understand the interaction of processes at one level with those at another and of one mode with that of another requires theory that crosses boundaries. Where possible, the book has drawn on theories that do that, most notably the two-level games literature. Most theory, however, is not designed for this purpose. Realism, for instance, concerns only the operation of interests at the international level. Pluralist theory concerns the interaction of interest groups at the domestic level. Contemporary interest group theory concerns the internal dynamics of interest groups. Most of the literature on Congress concerns either bargaining in Congress, often in committees, or the relationship between members and constituents, but rarely both. Some scholars have crossed boundaries between theories of interests and theories of organizations, but few attempt to incorporate rational choice and constructivist approaches. More energy has been expended defending the borders than in building bridges across them.

Political scientists focus on one level or one mode of politics for good reasons, but the tendency has led to insufficient attention to the linkages among these approaches and to the ways in which theories are complementary. Most notably, the effort to reduce all political phenomena to rational choice is misguided. A self-limiting logic to rational choice requires other approaches. First, except in unusual circumstances, it is not possible for political systems to be simultaneously rational on more than one level, as we saw in our analysis of bargaining in NAFTA. Second, all rational choice models require the prior specification of parameters to work forward to prediction of outcomes. Some of those parameters can be derived from other rational choice processes, but they cannot all be reduced to rational choice. Third, the logic of rational choice creates a demand for institutions and for symbols. If they did not exist, it would be rational to construct them.

The question then is not which theory is right, but which theoretical approach is most appropriate for the problem at hand. The political analyst must decide what matters most and what can be safely ignored. To some extent this is a matter of judgment. But this judgment can be informed by theory, too. If national policy making processes are highly centralized and there is little domestic conflict over objectives, one would expect the international dynamic to be more important than domestic bargaining among interest groups. When national policy making processes are more consensual and there are factional differences of interests, domestic bargaining may take precedence over international circumstance. In policy areas for which there are repeated transactions, there is likely to be a greater demand for institutions. The less direct economic or other interest individuals have in policy outcomes and the less influence they exert over them, the greater the likelihood that their demand for information, if any, will be for symbolic communications. We could expect, therefore, to find symbolic politics playing a larger role among the rank-and-file membership of organizations and among the general public.

To understand an event as complex as NAFTA—at a depth sufficient not only to explain what happened after the fact, but to predict outcomes from observable circumstances and to have an informed strategy in the event— requires many analytic tools and the skill to use them. Admittedly, without firm guidelines about when to apply what tool, there is much art to this approach. The approach is not simple eclecticism, however. It is judicious use of appropriate technology.

NAFTA Interpreted

The story of the decision to negotiate NAFTA is a story about elite decision making in a particular historical circumstance. Although the international environment was an important factor in defining the circumstance, it was by no means the only factor.

For the critical decision by Carlos Salinas, both international and domestic conditions mattered. Among them were Mexico's need for international capital and its standing with potential international investors, the legacy of earlier partial opening of the economy that helped to create economic forces in Mexico favorable to further opening, a Mexican political system that suppressed populist pressures and allowed for bold presidential action, and the historic accident of a president and a cabinet trained in U.S. universities and steeped in free trade theory. The appeal of NAFTA lay in the way in which it fit with the larger domestic agenda of Mexico, the way it facilitated and locked in economic transformations that Salinas and his cabinet sought for Mexico, and the way in which it signaled those changes to the outside world.

For the United States, domestic considerations played a lesser role in the initial decision to agree to negotiate. Indeed, had they been more prominent, Bush might have been more hesitant to engage. For Bush and his key advisors, particularly Jim Baker, NAFTA was about foreign policy. In part, a regional free trade agreement was perceived as a counterbalance to trade competition from Asia and, particularly, Europe. Arguably we would not have a NAFTA (and before that a Canada–U.S. Free Trade Agreement [CUFTA]) had the Europeans not moved to create the European Union (EU). In part, NAFTA was a hedge against the failure of the Uruguay Round of the GATT. But the primary attraction of NAFTA was its predicted consequence for relations with Mexico. Like Salinas, Bush viewed a free trade agreement as a way of encouraging economic transformation in Mexico and believed those transformations would serve U.S. interests.

For Canada, Mulroney's request to join the talks, despite his initial visceral reaction to keep out, reflected a more considered view of Canada's trade interests, pressed upon him by business interests and by his trade officials. It also reflected a reconsideration of the domestic politics of NAFTA, a realization that opposition to NAFTA would be nothing like the populist backlash that accompanied free trade negotiations with the United States alone.

The fast track fight in the United States is a story of the intersection of institutions and interests. The conspicuous absence of a similar process in both Mexico and Canada points to the importance of the peculiarities of the U.S. trade policy making process. For interests opposed to NAFTA, the vote in 1991 not only created a moment to stop NAFTA, it was the last best chance to stop the process, given the nature of the fast track process. For other interests, most notably the mainstream environmental organizations, the vote on fast track provided an opportunity not so much to stop NAFTA, but to hold it hostage in exchange for the concession that environmental issues would subsequently be on the agenda.

Important to the story is the realization that sophisticated interest groups understood quite well the way in which a vote on procedure would affect their interests in the subsequent negotiations. In hindsight, though, the political forces mobilized during the fast track fight clearly reflected not only cool calculations of interest, but hot reactions to the symbolic content of NAFTA. Already, in 1991, among union members and social activists, NAFTA had come to stand for corporate greed at the expense of workers, communities, and the environment.

The story of the commercial negotiations is a story about the interaction not only of three states, but also of three political systems and three societies. Domestic interests, empowered by their relative ability to bring political pressure to bear on negotiators, constrained and sometimes determined what was possible in international negotiations. To understand the particular rule of origin for autos, or the long phase-out of tariffs for U.S. fruits and vegetables, or the refusal of the Canadians to negotiate on agriculture, or any of the myriad other ways in which the agreement deviated from the ideals of free trade, one must think not about national interest, but about the interests of powerful domestic factions.

The relationship between domestic interests and international bargaining did not all flow in one direction. In a very important sense, NAFTA provided an opportunity for all three countries to redefine the rules of the trade policy making game in ways that made possible policies otherwise politically infeasible. The clearest example comes from Mexico. The opening of financial services and the reform of agriculture (Salinas believed) were in Mexico's interest on their own terms, but were politically infeasible unless negotiated as part of a comprehensive free trade agreement. The same dynamic operated in the United States, although to a lesser extent. NAFTA made possible modest reductions in agricultural and manufacturing protection that would not have been politically feasible without being linked to other issues.

The decision to enter into side negotiations on labor and environment is a story about a changing domestic context compelling adjustment in an international agreement. The side negotiations began with a commitment in the heat of a presidential campaign, a decision that split the difference between positioning candidate Clinton with key interest groups and signaling his steadfastness in the face of interest group pressure.

Whereas in the commercial negotiations, economic interests determined national negotiating positions, in the side negotiations symbolic meaning played a significant role in determining negotiating positions. Once framed as the solution to the problems with "Bush's NAFTA," side agreements became a matter of political necessity for Democratic members of Congress as well as potential deal breakers for Republicans. To establish a negotiating position, U.S. Trade Representative Mickey Kantor not only had to navigate between business and environmental interests, he also had to find a formulation that would satisfy the symbolic need of Democrats for agreements with "teeth" and of Republicans for agreements with "gums."

Although the agreements reached were significantly affected by the United States's debate with itself, their form also reflected Canadian and Mexican politics. The Canadian exemption from trade sanctions as an enforcement mechanism of last resort reflected the symbolic importance of sanctions to the Canadians and the symbolic unimportance of Canada to the Americans. The limits in scope and independence of the labor institution reflected the power of Mexican business interests.

The story of the rising tide of opposition in the United States is partly a story about national institutional arrangements, in that no comparable event occurred in Canada and Mexico, where constitutional arrangements made ratification largely a formality. This story is also partly about the mobilization of economic interests threatened by NAFTA, the kind of interests typically associated with support for protection. But to explain how NAFTA became the subject of the most intense public battle over a trade issue in the twentieth century requires an understanding not of how NAFTA impinged on interests, but of what it came to stand for. To a very great degree, the opposition to NAFTA had less to do with what NAFTA was than with what it meant. As constructed by NAFTA's opponents, NAFTA meant a "sucking sound" of jobs going to Mexico; a betrayal by government, corporate interests, and foreign agents; a license to pollute; a border more open to drugs and illegal immigration.

The campaign for NAFTA and its eventual victory in the fall of 1993 is a story about many things. It is about the power of corporate interests to

influence members of Congress. It is about the ability of the president to
bargain with members of Congress. But ultimately it is about political diagnosis, and political strategy.

In August and early September, the strategists in the Clinton administration, on the Hill, and in the business community, working together, began
to understand that this was not trade politics as usual. NAFTA's problem
had little to do with narrow protectionist interests, although pockets of opposition would need to be accommodated. At its core, the problem was with
the constructed understandings of NAFTA, which not only created intense
popular opposition in the moment but instilled fear in members of Congress
that a vote for NAFTA would become a damaging campaign issue in the
next election.

This diagnosis led to a strategy consisting of several parts. One part was
an intense traditional lobbying effort in Washington, as the president, his
cabinet, and corporate CEOs let members of Congress know the intensity
of their interest. A second part was an untraditional effort by the business
community to mount a countervailing grassroots campaign in targeted districts. But perhaps the most significant element of the campaign was an
effort to reconstruct the meaning of NAFTA.

The public campaign for NAFTA was a story about the use of symbolic
politics to reframe meaning. The campaign began with four presidents in
the East Room of the White House, an image that wrapped NAFTA with
living symbols of the American national interest. Television commercials
starring Lee Iococca, the popular former CEO of Chrysler and symbol of
American competitiveness, reframed the economic story from competition
with Mexico to competition with Japan. A cable television "debate" between
Vice President Al Gore and billionaire and ex-presidential candidate Ross
Perot cast Perot as the villain and Gore as the conquering hero.

The campaign of interests and symbols altered the political calculus for
members of Congress. Now a "no" vote seemed to carry significant political
risk, whereas the risks of a "yes" vote looked less ominous. For House Republicans, in particular, the combination of business pressure for NAFTA
and the apparent evaporation of the threat from Ross Perot made supporting
NAFTA much easier. Wavering Democrats dined at the White House and
were wooed by their president. Last minute efforts to change the sugar and
citrus deals won support from the powerful agricultural lobbies in Florida
and in turn from undecided members of the Florida delegation. In the end,
NAFTA passed in the House by a surprisingly wide margin of 31 votes.

Passage, however, did not end the politics of NAFTA. NAFTA's legacy was a changed political landscape in the United States: a different presidency, a different Congress, a different public. The experience of negotiating NAFTA with the United States reverberated in the politics of Canada and, especially, Mexico. Although NAFTA was an economic event, its ultimate significance may have less to do with changes in the economic trajectory of North America than with its effect on the political, social, and cultural relationships among Mexico, Canada, and the United States. The process of negotiating—the engagement of three governments, three societies, three cultures—changed those relationships, and it changed the face of North America.

Notes

Headnote

Unless otherwise indicated, all quotations are from interviews conducted personally by the author.

Chapter 2

1. Waltz, *The Man, the State, and War: A Theoretical Analysis* (New York: Columbia University Press, 1959). For an overview of the level of analysis problem, see Andrew Moravchek, "Introduction," in Peter E. Evans, Harold K. Jacobson, and Robert D. Putnam, eds., *Double-Edged Diplomacy: International Bargaining and Domestic Politics*, 1–42 (Berkeley: University of California Press, 1993).
2. There is an immense literature in the realist tradition. Classics include Hans J. Morgenthau, *Politics Among Nations*; Kenneth Waltz, *Theories of International Politics*; and Robert O. Keohane, ed., *Neorealism and Its Critics*.
3. See especially, Stephen D. Krasner, ed., *International Regimes*.
4. See, for example, Alexander Wendt, "Collective Identity Formation," and Peter M. Haas, "Introduction."
5. For an analysis based on class, see Ronald Rogatsky, *Commerce and Coalitions*. For an analysis based on industry, see Helen V. Milner, *Resisting Protectionism*.
6. See especially Robert D. Putnam, "Diplomacy and Domestic Politics"; Frederick W. Mayer, "Managing Domestic Differences"; and Peter B. Evans, Harold K. Jacobson, and Robert D. Putnam, eds., *Double-Edged Diplomacy*.
7. See, for example, Alexander L. George, *Presidential Decisionmaking*; Graham T. Allison, *Essence of Decision*; and Robert Jervis, *Perception and Misperception*.
8. There is an immense literature in this field. Of particular interest here are James M. Buchanan and Gordon Tullock, *The Calculus of Consent*; Kenneth Arrow, *Social Choice*; Mancur Olson, *The Logic of Collective Action*; and Terry M. Moe, *The Organization of Interests*.

9. The distinction is from William Riker, "Political Science and Rational Choice," in James E. Alt and Kenneth A. Shepsle, eds., *Perspectives on Positive Political Economy*, 163–181.

10. Kenneth N. Waltz, *Man, the State, and War.*

11. The classic in the field is James March and Herbert Simon, *Organizations.* For applications to foreign policy see Allison, *Essence of Decision*, and John D. Steinbruner, *The Cybernetic Theory of Decision.*

12. John D. Steinbruner, *The Cybernetic Theory of Decision*, falls in this category.

13. This is the stance adopted in Judith Goldstein and Robert O. Keohane, "Ideas and Foreign Policy: An Applied Framework," in Judith Goldstein and Robert O. Keohane, eds., *Ideas and Foreign Policy*, 3–30.

14. See especially Stephen Krasner, ed., *International Regimes.*

15. See for example Peter J. Katzenstein, ed., *Between Power and Plenty.*

16. See in particular Robert Jervis, *Perception and Misperception.*

17. Major works in this school included George Herbert Mead, *The Philosophy of the Act*; Peter L. Berger and Thomas Luckmann, *The Social Construction of Reality*; Clifford Geertz, *The Interpretation of Cultures*; Victor W. Turner, *Dramas, Fields, and Metaphors*; Kenneth Burke, *On Symbols and Society*; and Jerome S. Bruner, *Acts of Meaning.*

18. Notable exceptions include the work of Harold Lasswell and Murray Edelman. See for instance, Harold D. Lasswell, *World Politics and Personal Insecurity*; Murray Edelman, *The Symbolic Uses of Politics.*

19. See, for example, John Gerard Ruggie, "International Regimes, Transactions and Change." See also Alexander Wendt, "Collective Identity Formation."

20. Judith Goldstein, *Ideas, Interests and American Trade Policy.*

21. See, for example, Peter M. Haas, "Introduction."

22. Many have made this point. For a clear exposition see Jon Elster, *The Cement of Society.*

23. Ronald Coase, "The Problem of Social Cost," 1–44.

24. Anthony Downs, *An Economic Theory of Democracy*, 207–219.

25. This possibility suggests another interpretation of the common distinction between substantive and procedural rationality. Actors may be procedurally rational even when the process of establishing interests is far from rational.

Chapter 3

1. Robert A. Pastor and Jorge G. Castenada, *Limits to Friendship*, 36.

2. The Mexican Constitution limits presidents to one six-year term in office.

3. Nora Lustig, *Mexico*, p. 115, table 5-1.

4. United States International Trade Commission, Investigation No. 332-282, 3–7.

5. Nora Lustig, *Mexico*, p. 15, table 1-1; 22, table 1-5.

6. Nora Lustig, *Mexico*, p. 32, table 2-2.

7. For an excellent account of the role of the Mexican financial community in Mexican politics, see Sylvia Maxwell, *Governing Capital*.

8. United Press International, "Leftist Blasts Austerity Plan," 23 December 1982.

9. See Luis Rubio, Cristina Rodriguez, and Roberto Blum, "The Making of Mexico's Trade Policy and the Uruguay Round," in Henry Nau, ed., *Domestic Trade Politics*, 167–185.

10. Nora Lustig, *Mexico*, pp. 117–120.

11. For an account of the alliance of interests in support of de la Madrid's economic policies, see Robert R. Kaufman, Carlos Bazdresch, and Blanca Heredia, "Mexico."

12. Socioeconomic Time-Series Data and Retrieval System, World Data 95 (Washington, D.C.: World Bank, 1996).

13. United States International Trade Commission, Investigation No. 332-282, 5-1.

14. Ibid., 5–14.

15. Sidney Weintraub, *Free Trade Between Mexico and the United States?* (Washington, D.C.: Brookings, 1984).

16. Indeed, when de la Madrid was first informed by Salinas in 1990 that he intended both to privatize the banks and to negotiate a free trade agreement with the United States, de la Madrid responded, "Privatizing the banks is a good idea." A free trade agreement, de la Madrid felt, was "too precipitous."

17. For a critical account of the politics of "solidarity," see Denise Dresser, "Bringing the Poor Back In."

18. Joel Kurtzman, "Prospects; Free Trade with Mexico," *New York Times*, 22 October 1989, sec. 3, p. 1.

19. Ibid.

20. Ross Laver, "Continental Murmurings," *Maclean's*, 16 April 1990, 16.

21. William Branigin, "Quayle Hears Criticism of Kidnapping; Mexican President Seeks 'New Rules,' " *Washington Post*, 27 April 1990, A33.

22. "Mexican President Calls for Free Trade with U.S.," Reuters, 22 May 1990.

23. Bruce Stokes, "Trade Talks with Mexico Face Hurdles," *The National Journal*, 16 June 1990, 1486.

24. NBC Nightly News, 11 June 1990.

25. "International Trade, AFL-CIO Tells House Panel That U.S.–Mexico FTA Would Harm Workers," Bureau of National Affairs, *Daily Report for Executives*, 29 June 1990.

26. John R. Oravec, "Mexico Trade Pact Seen as Detriment to Workers," *AFL-CIO News*, 25 June 1990, 3.

27. Art Pine, "House Panel Embraces Idea of Mexico Pact: Lawmakers Cautioned That They Will Not Enact an Agreement That Sends U.S. Jobs South of the Border," *Los Angeles Times*, 15 June 1990, D5.

28. Anne Hazard, [Untitled], States News Service, 14 June 1990.

29. Fast track rules state that the Congress cannot amend a negotiated trade agreement and can only vote for or against the agreement as negotiated. The administration deemed this rule essential for negotiating an agreement with Mexico. The rule and its consequences are discussed more extensively in Chapter 4.

30. Richard Benedetto, "Bush Affirms U.S. Mexico Ties," Gannett News Service, 26 November 1990.

31. Speech by George Bush to Monterrery community, Federal News Service, 27 November 1990.

32. In contrast only 8 percent of Americans thought that it had hurt the United States, 14 percent thought that it had helped, and 78% of Americans either thought that it had made no difference or didn't know. "The Two Nations Poll: Where North Americans Stand on 32 Questions," *Maclean's*, 25 June 1990, 50. The poll involved samples of 1000 people in both Canada and the United States and was conducted by telephone between 1 May and 6 May.

33. "Canada Seeks to Join Mexico–U.S. in Trade Talks," Reuters, 24 September 1990.

34. William Claiborne, "Free Trade Foes Are Back: Canadians Seek to Defeat Joint Market," *The Washington Post*, 27 September 1990, A22.

35. Reuters, 28 November 1990.

36. As noted in chapter 2, classics in the realist tradition include Hans J. Morgenthau, *Politics Among Nations*; Kenneth Waltz, *Theories of International Politics*; and Robert O. Keohane, ed., *Neorealism and Its Critics*.

37. Robert O. Keohane, "Theory of World Politics: Structural Realism and Beyond," in Robert O. Keohane, ed., *Neorealism and Its Critics*, p. 166.

38. See the argument in Keohane, "Theory of World Politics," 158–203.

39. A considerable amount of literature on strategic trade policy investigates this point. See Paul R. Krugman, ed. *Strategic Trade Policy*.

40. See, for example, Oran R. Young, "Regime Dynamics: the Rise and Fall of International Regimes," in Stephen D. Krasner, ed. *International Regimes*, 93–113.

41. Robert Axelrod, *The Evolution of Cooperation*.

42. Robert O. Keohane, "The Demand for International Regimes," in Stephen D. Krasner, ed., *International Regimes*, 141–171.

43. The observation is made in Judith Goldstein and Robert O. Keohane, "Ideas and Foreign Policy: An Analytical Framework," in Judith Goldstein and Robert O. Keohane, eds., *Ideas and Foreign Policy*.

44. For an exploration of this role for ideas see Geoffrey Garrett and Barry Weingast, "Ideas, Interests, and Institutions: Constructing the European Community's Internal Market," in Judith Goldstein and Robert O. Keohane, eds., *Ideas and Foreign Policy*, pp. 173–206.

45. See in particular G. John Ikenberry, "Creating Yesterday's New World Order: Keynesian 'New Thinking' and the Anglo-American Postwar Settlement," in Judith Goldstein and Robert O. Keohane, eds., *Ideas and Foreign Policy*, pp. 57–86.

46. See William H. Riker, "Heresthetic and Rhetoric in the Spatial Model," in James E. Alt and Kenneth A. Shepsle, eds., *Perspectives on Positive Political Economy*.

47. Peter M. Haas, "Introduction."

48. See especially Alexander Wendt, "Collective Identity Formation."

49. E.E. Schattschneider, *Politics, Pressures and the Tariff*.

50. See, for example, Alexander L. George, *Presidential Decisionmaking*, and Alexander L. George, "The 'Operational Code.' "

Chapter 4

1. Classic texts in this tradition include E.E. Schattschneider, *Politics, Pressures and the Tariff*; Raymond A. Bauer, Ithiel de Sola Pool, and Lewis Anthony Dexter, *American Business and Public Policy*; and I. M. Destler, *American Trade Politics*.

2. A coalition of software, entertainment, and pharmaceutical companies, among others, threatened to withhold their support for NAFTA until Mexico passed a law to address the widespread piracy of intellectual property, but they could be counted on to be supporters once that law was passed.

3. "Manufacturing in Mexico: on Uncle Sam's Coat-Tails," *The Economist*, 16 September 1989, 82.

4. Comparing U.S. and Mexican wages is tricky, in part because fluctuations in the exchange rate can cause large apparent shifts in the ratio, and in part because of differences in fringe benefits.

5. Gene Zack, "Runaways to Mexico Spread Economic Woe," *AFL-CIO News*, 22 November 1986, 1.

6. Dinah Wisenberg, States News Service, 3 December 1986.

7. Statement by the AFL-CIO Executive Council on Mexico and the Maquiladora Twin-Plant Program, 16 February 1988.

8. AFL-CIO, The Maquiladoras: The Hidden Cost of Production South of the Border, February 1989.

9. Hearing before the House Ways and Means Committee, 21 February 1991.

10. Ibid.

11. David Haskel, "Free Trade With Mexico Under Intense Fire in the U.S.," Reuters, 17 February 1991.

12. Hearing before the House Ways and Means Committee, 20 February 1991.

13. Letter to the president from Lloyd Bentsen and Dan Rostenkowski, 7 March 1991.

14. Hearing before Senate Finance Committee, 12 March 1991.

15. Letter from Richard Gephardt to President Bush, 27 March 1991.

16. This scale has become standard for vote counting in Washington. The general rule was to be conservative in rating members, only putting them in the 1 or 5 categories when they were publicly committed one way or the other. Because members often wish to keep their options open, and rarely wish to offend, getting an accurate count is an art.

17. Sonia Nazario, "Boom and Despair: Mexican Border Towns Are a Magnet for Foreign Factories, Workers and Abysmal Living Conditions. World Business: A Special Report." *Wall Street Journal*, 22 September 1989, A1.

18. Lane Kirkland, "U.S.–Mexico Trade Pact: A Disaster Worthy of Stalin's Worst," *Wall Street Journal*, 18 April 1991, A17.

19. *Wall Street Journal*, 29 April 1991, A14.

20. Letter from President George Bush to Representative Dan Rostenkowski, 1 May 1991. Nearly identical letters were sent to Lloyd Bentsen and Richard Gephardt.

21. Federal News Service, "News Conference by the Coalition: Mobilization on Development, Trade, Labor and the Environment," 2 May 1991.

22. "Inside Track: Greens Put their Trade Case to President," *Greenwire*, 9 May 1991.

23. Gary Lee, " 'Fast Track' Sprint: Frenzied Lobbying on a Treaty Not Yet Written," *The Washington Post*, 23 May 1991, A21.

24. "Gephardt Says He Will Support Fast-Track But Reserves Right to Amend Mexico Pact," BNA *Daily Report for Executives*, 10 May 1991.

25. The law specifies that legislation be reported out of House committees no more than 45 legislative days (days that the House is in session) after introduction, voted upon in the House no more than 15 legislative days after discharge from House committees, reported out of Senate committees no more than 15 legislative days after the House vote, and voted upon in the full Senate no more than 15 legislative days after discharge from Senate committees. Regardless of how quickly the House acts, Senate committees cannot be compelled to discharge the legislation in fewer than 45 legislative days.

26. See Thomas C. Schelling, *The Strategy of Conflict*, and Jon Elster, *Ulysses and the Siren*.

27. In a sense, the vast majority of business interests were in this position too. They could be expected at the end of the day to endorse agreement, but in the

interim they would seek to influence the shape of the outcome. With respect to the fast track extension, however, they did not need a concession to ensure that their interests would be heard during negotiation. Environmental groups did.

28. For what constitutes an event for social sciences, see William Riker, "Political Science and Rational Choice," in James M. Enelow and Melvin J. Hinich, eds. *Advances in the Spacial Theory of Voting*, 163–181.

Chapter 5

1. See Gustavo del Castillo, "Private Sector Trade Advisory Group in North America: a Comparative Perspective," in Gustavo del Castillo and Gustavo Vega Cánovas, eds., *The Politics of Free Trade*, 21–50.

2. Juanita Darling, "Just Below the Surface: Reform of Mexico's Oil Industry Is Underlying Issue in the Free-Trade Talks, Breaking Down the Borders," *Los Angeles Times*, 15 June 1992, D1.

3. Gustavo Vega Cánovas, "NAFTA and the Auto Sector," in Gustavo del Castillo and Gustavo Vega Cánovas, eds., *The Politics of Free Trade*, 159–183.

4. The actual value content of a car could be considerably less than 50 percent and still qualify under the CUFTA. In a practice known as "roll up," a component such as an engine, which might itself be only 51 percent U.S.–Canadian, was treated as if it were 100 percent U.S.–Canadian when subsequently assembled into a car. A recent dispute between Canada and the United States over whether Hondas produced in Canada met the 50 percent standard made negotiators on both sides determined to eliminate roll up.

5. "Citrus, Vegetable Growers Tell Panel That NAFTA Could Ruin U.S. Industries," BNA Daily Report for Executives, 30 August 1991.

6. Steven V. Marks, "A Reassessment of Empirical Evidence on the U.S. Sugar Program," in Steven V. Marks and Keith E. Maskus, eds., *The Economics and Politics of World Sugar Policies*, 79–108.

7. Gustavo Vega Cánovas, "NAFTA and Financial Services," in Gustavo del Castillo and Gustavo Vega Cánovas, eds., *The Politics of Free Trade*, 187–222.

8. "NAFTA Public Hearings Conclude with Recommendations, Warnings," BNA *International Trade Reporter*, 18 September 1991.

9. "Free Trade: Enviros Blast Draft US-Mexico Green Plan," Greenwire, 18 November 1991.

10. "USTR Sued Over Lack of Environmental Impact Statements for GATT and NAFTA Negotiations," BNA *International Trade Reporter*, 7 August 1991.

11. Stuart Auerbach, "Raising a Roar Over a Ruling: Trade Pact Imperils Environmental Laws," *Washington Post*, 1 October 1991, D1.

12. "Boxer Pummels Trade Ruling," Greenwire, 24 September 1991.

13. Stuart Auerbach, "Raising a Roar Over A Ruling," D1.
14. Dianne Dumanoski, "Free-Trade Laws Could Undo Pacts on Environment," *Boston Globe*, 7 October 1991, 25.
15. "GATT: Boxer Pummels Trade Ruling," *Greenwire*, 24 September 1991.
16. Juanita Darling, "Tuna Turnabout; Mexico Announces a Dolphin Protection Plan," *Los Angeles Times*, 25 September 1991, D6.
17. "Gephardt, Other House Democrats Outline Parameters for NAFTA and GATT Agreements," *BNA International Trade Reporter*, 30 October 1991.
18. "Senate Finance Members Introduce Bill to Assure Adjustment Benefits Under NAFTA," *BNA Daily Report for Executives*, 31 October 1991.
19. "Free Trade Talks Reach Negotiating Stage—Mexicans," Reuters, 24 October 1991.
20. Keith Bradsher, "Few Gains Reported in 3-Way Trade Talks," *New York Times*, 22 February 1992, Sect. 1, p. 41.
21. "Environmentalist, Texas Group Cool to Bush Integrated Border Plan," *BNA International Environment Daily*, 26 February 1992.
22. Ibid.
23. Center for Public Integrity Staff, *The Trading Game: Inside Lobbying for the North American Free Trade Agreement* (Lanham, Md.: University Press of America, 1995).
24. "Citizen Groups Say Leaked NAFTA Draft Would Undermine U.S. Standards," *BNA International Trade Daily*, 26 March 1992.
25. Ibid.
26. Karen Tumulty, "Key Senator Assails Administration on Mexico Talks," *Los Angeles Times*, 22 May 1992, D2.
27. "Environmental Issues to Decide Fate of NAFTA, Representative Richardson Predicts," *BNA International Environment Daily*, 29 June 1992.
28. NAFTA, Article 712, paragraph 1.
29. "Southern State Legislators Say NAFTA Will Harm U.S. Agriculture, Environment," *BNA International Environment Daily*, 12 August 1992.
30. "Absense of GATT Deal Snags NAFTA Talks on Domestic Supports, Crowder Says," *BNA International Trade Daily*, 9 April 1992.
31. "Florida Agriculture Commissioner Calls for Excluding Winter Produce from NAFTA," *BNA International Trade Daily*, 28 May 1992.
32. Rod McQueen, " 'Prosperity Deal': Business Welcomes Free Trade Pact but Labor Fears for Jobs," *Financial Post*, 13 August 1992, Sect. 1, p. 1.
33. Maude Barlow, "NAFTA: 'A Corporate Charter of Rights and Freedoms,' " *The Toronto Star*, 13 August 1992, A23.
34. "Canada Opposition Says Not Supporting NAFTA Deal," Reuters, 12 August 1992.
35. "President Bush Announces NAFTA Accord, But Labor, Others Promise Renewed Attack," *BNA International Trade Daily*, 13 August 1992.

36. "AFL-CIO, Other Unions Blast Free Trade Pact as Prescription for U.S. Job Loss," BNA *International Trade Daily*, 13 August 1992.

37. "Environmentalists React Cautiously to Announcement that NAFTA Completed," BNA International Environment Daily, 14 August 1992.

38. The two-level bargaining approach is derived from Richard E. Walton and Robert B. McKersie, *A Behavioral Theory*, Howard Raiffa, *The Art and Science of Negotiation*, and David A. Lax and James K. Sebenius, *The Manager as Negotiator*. Robert D. Putnam, "Diplomacy and Domestic Politics" is responsible for spawning widespread interest in international relations. See also Frederick W. Mayer, "Managing Domestic Differences"; Peter B. Evans, Harold K. Jacobson, and Robert D. Putnam, eds. *Double-Edged Diplomacy*, and Leonard J. Schoppa, *Bargaining With Japan*.

Chapter 6

1. Senate Finance Committee Hearing to Consider the Nomination of Mickey Kantor to be United States Trade Representative, 19 January 1993.

2. For an overview of the environmental community landscape, see Daniel Esty, *Greening the GATT*.

3. Stewart J. Hudson and Rodrigo J. Prudencio, "The North American Commission on Environment and Other Supplemental Environmental Agreements: Part Two of the NAFTA Package," *National Wildlife Federation Report*, 4 February 1993, 2, 15.

4. Justin Ward and Jacob Scherr, "Testimony of the Natural Resource Defense Council before the Committee on Environment and Public Works," U.S. Senate, 16 March 1993.

5. Sierra Club, "Environmental Concerns Regarding the North American Free Trade Agreement," February 1993.

6. Laura Viani, "Free-Trade Pact Seen Ruled by Consultation," *American Metal Market*, 9 February 1993, 4.

7. Letter to Mickey Kantor from Defenders of Wildlife, et al., 4 March 1993.

8. Testimony of Thomas R. Donahue, Secretary-Treasury, AFL-CIO, and Chair Labor Advisory Committee on Trade Negotiations and Trade Policy, before the Senate Finance Committee on the North American Free Trade Agreement," 22 September 1992. (Prepared remarks.)

9. Statement by the AFL-CIO Executive Council on the North American Free Trade Agreement, 17 February 1993.

10. Stephen Franklin, "Unions Urge Clinton to Renegotiate Trade Pact," *Chicago Tribune*, 18 February 1993, N3.

11. "Gephardt Says He Will Vote Against Pact If Environmental Side Deal Not in Place," BNA National Environment Daily, 26 February 1993.

12. Tod Robberson and Jackson Diehl, "U.S. Urged to Act on Trade Pact: Mexican Leader Warns of Delay," *Washington Post*, 23 February 1993, A12.

13. Letter from Willard A. Workman, Vice President of the Chamber of Commerce of the United States, to Mickey Kantor, 8 March 1993.

14. Mickey Kantor, Testimony before the Senate Finance Committee, 9 March 1993.

15. Richard Gephardt, Statement to the House Ways and Means Committee, 11 March 1993.

16. Letter from Max Baucus to Mickey Kantor, 4 March 1993.

17. Mickey Kantor, Testimony before the Senate Environment and Public Works Committee, 16 March 1993.

18. "Canada Opposes Trade Sanctions," BNA *International Environment Daily*, 22 March 1993.

19. "Address by House Majority Leader Richard Gephardt Before the Citizen's Trade Campaign," Federal News Service, 25 March 1993.

20. Statement by the Citizen's Trade Campaign, issued 13 April 1992.

21. "Citizen's Trade Campaign Releases Policy Statement for NAFTA Supplements," BNA *International Environment Daily*, 15 April 1993.

22. Letter to President Bill Clinton from Senator John Danforth et al., 28 April 1993.

23. Letter to President Bill Clinton from William Archer and Robert Crane, 28 April 1993.

24. Letter to President Clinton from Bob Michel, Newt Gingrich, and sixteen other Republican representatives supportive of NAFTA, 28 April 1993.

25. "NAFTA: Enviro Groups Set to Back Pact if Arbitration Ok'd," *Greenwire*, 4 May 1993.

26. Jim Kolbe, Congressional Record, 20 May 1993.

27. Clyde H. Farnsworth, "3 Nations Disagree on Trade," *New York Times*, 22 May 1993, A33.

28. Ibid.

29. Letter to Mickey Kantor from the Business Roundtable, Council of the Americas, Emergency Committee for American Trade, National Association of Manufacturers, U.S. Chamber of Commerce, U.S. Council of the Mexico–U.S. Business Committee, U.S. Council for International Business, and USA*NAFTA, 4 June 1993.

30. John Maggs, "Senator Baucus Hits Businesses for Opposing NAFTA Side Deals," *Journal of Commerce*, 10 June 1993, 2A.

31. "Negotiators Report Progress on NAFTA Side Accords," *United Press International*, 9 July 1993.

32. David Haskel, "U.S. Insists NAFTA Side Deals Must Have Teeth," *Reuters Business Report*, 12 July 1993.

33. "Negotiators Still at Odds Over Some Trade Issues," *The Vancouver Sun*, 24 July 1993, 1.
34. The remarks were first reported in Katharine Seelye, "Canadian Prime Minister Is Challenging Convention," *Philadelphia Inquirer*, 25 July 1993, 1. They were reported in Canada over the next week. The interview took place on 13 July 1993.
35. "Canada Firmly Opposed to NAFTA Sanctions—Hockin," Reuters, 4 August 1993.
36. Letter from Max Baucus to Mickey Kantor, 28 July 1993.
37. Letter from Richard Gephardt to Mickey Kantor, 3 August 1993.
38. For a description of this meeting, see Robert Woodward, *The Agenda*, 314.
39. "Press Conference on the Topic of the North American Free Trade Agreement," Federal News Service, 13 August 1993.
40. Office of Representative Richard Gephardt, Press Release, 13 August 1993.
41. "News Conference With Labor, Environmental, Consumer Groups in Response to the NAFTA Accord," Federal News Service, 13 August 1993.
42. Edmund L. Andrews, "Accord Fails to Redraw Battle Lines Over Pact," *New York Times*, 14 August 1993, A45.
43. Transcript, "Inside Politics," Cable News Network, 13 August 1993.
44. This should not be surprising, since the original work on multilevel bargaining concerned labor negotiations. See Richard E. Walton and Robert D. McKersie, *A Behavioral Theory of Labor Negotiations*.

Chapter 7

1. Perhaps the most balanced reviews of the numerous analyses are U.S. International Trade Commission, Economy-Wide Modeling of the Implications of a FTA with Mexico and a NAFTA with Canada and Mexico, 1992, and United States Congressional Budget Office, A Budgetary and Economic Analysis of the North American Free Trade Agreement, 1993.
2. This argument is developed more fully in Frederick W. Mayer, "The NAFTA, Multinationals and Social Regulation."
3. Proponents pointed to a study by two Princeton economists, which concluded that more economic development generally leads to lower pollution levels. Gene M. Grossman and Alan B. Krueger, *Environmental Impacts of a North American Free Trade Agreement*, Working Paper 3914 (Cambridge, Mass.: National Bureau of Economic Research, 1991).
4. See H. Jeffrey Leonard, Pollution and the Struggle for the World Product (Cambridge: Cambridge University Press, 1988).
5. For a balanced assessment of NAFTA's effects on migration see Philip Martin, *Trade and Migration: NAFTA and Agriculture* (Washington, D.C.: Institutional Economics, 1993).

6. Statement by the AFL-CIO Executive Council on The North American Free Trade Agreement, 17 February 1993.

7. John R. Oravec, "Legislators Assail NAFTA in Border Tour," *AFL-CIO News*, 15 March 1993, 1.

8. Lisa Richwine, "Coalition Launches Grassroots Campaign to Defeat NAFTA," States News Service, 26 March 1993.

9. Citizen's Trade Campaign, "Citizen's Trade Campaign Policy Statement on NAFTA," 13 April 1993, press release.

10. Kim Moody and Mary McGinn, *Unions and Free Trade: Solidarity vs. Competition* (Detroit: Labor Notes, 1992), 1.

11. Andrea Durbin and Atlanta McIlwraith, "Summary of Organizers Strategy Meeting," 7 April 1993, memorandum.

12. Letter from Jim Jontz to "Activists," 5 April 1993.

13. "Hearing of the Senate Banking Committee," Federal News Service, 22 April 1993.

14. "Remarks by Pat Buchanan, Republican Presidential Candidate, to the Conservative Political Action Conference, Omni Shoreham Hotel, Washington, DC," Federal News Service, 20 February 1992.

15. Cable News Network, "Crossfire," 6 May 1993.

16. Cable News Network, "Crossfire," 6 May 1993.

17. Memorandum from Jeff Faux to Joan Baggett et al, 30 April 1993.

18. David S. Broder, "Panetta: President in Trouble on Hill; Agenda at Risk, Trade Pact 'Dead,' " *Washington Post*, 27 April 1993, A1.

19. "IUE Kicks Off Anti-NAFTA Grassroots Campaign During 'Fair Trade' Week," U.S. Newswire, 29 April 1993.

20. Center for Public Integrity, *The Trading Game: Inside Lobbying for the North American Free Trade Agreement*, 1993, 23.

21. Tim Weiner with Tim Golden, "Free-Trade Treaty May Widen Traffic in Drugs, U.S. Says," *New York Times*, 24 May 1993, A1.

22. "The Death of a Mexican Cardinal," *Los Angeles Times*, 26 May 1993, B6.

23. Dudley Althaus, "Salinas' Credibility Threatened; Poll Shows Doubts of Slaying Account," *Houston Chronicle*, 30 May 1993, A1.

24. Tod Robberson, "Drug Crime Spreading in Mexico; Salinas Presses Hunt for Cardinal's Killers," *Washington Post*, 26 May 1993, A1.

25. "Drug Agents Find 'Mind-Boggling' Tunnel Under U.S.–Mexico Border," *Atlanta Journal and Constitution*, 3 June 1993, A4.

26. "ABC Nightly News," 3 June 1993.

27. William Hamilton, "Harvest of Blame; Californians Turn on Illegal Immigrants," *Washington Post*, 4 June 1993, A1.

28. Dianne Feinstein, "Perspective on Illegal Immigration; We Can Get a Grip on Our Borders; the President Must Make Tough Enforcement a Policy Priority.

The Burden on California Is Overwhelming," *Los Angeles Times*, 16 June 1993, B7.

29. "Plugging the Border; Here We Go Again," *Arizona Republic*, 7 June 1993, A10.

30. "AFSCME Secretary-Treasurer Tells Blacks in Congress That Trade Pact Will Hurt African-American Workers and Communities," PR Newswire, 18 June 1993.

31. See Bob Woodward, *The Agenda*, for a gripping account of the budget battle.

32. Letter to President Bill Clinton from Representative David Bonior et al., 27 July 1993.

33. Indeed, the first week back from vacation in September was to be devoted to neither NAFTA nor health care, but to Gore's "Reinventing Government" initiative.

34. Eric Brazil, "Teamsters: Trial Run Shows NAFTA Hurts US, Mexico," *San Francisco Examiner*, 26 August 1993, 3.

35. Associated Press, "Perot and Jesse Jackson Join Forces to Oppose Trade Pact," *Los Angeles Times*, 27 August 1993, A4.

36. Pat Buchanan, "GOP's NAFTA Divide," *Washington Times*, 23 August 1993, E1.

37. "Morning Edition," National Public Radio, 31 August 1993.

38. Ross Perot with Pat Choate, *Save Your Job*, 41, 33, 6, 11, ii, 119–124.

39. NBC News, "Meet the Press," 29 August 1993.

40. Mancur Olson, *The Logic of Collective Action*.

41. See Terry M. Moe, *Organization of Interests*, and Joseph P. Kalt, *Economics and Politics of Oil Price Regulation*.

42. Anthony Downs, *An Economic Theory of Democracy*, 259.

43. Ibid., 239.

44. See for example, Peter M. Haas, "Introduction"; Judith Goldstein, *Ideas, Interests and American Trade Policy*; and Alexander Wendt, "Collective Identity Formation."

45. Major works in this school include George Herbert Mead, *The Philosophy of the Act*; Peter L. Berger and Thomas Luckmann, *The Social Construction of Reality*; Clifford Geertz, *The Interpretation of Cultures*; Victor W. Turner, *Dramas, Fields, and Metaphors*; Kenneth Burke, *On Symbols and Society*; and Jerome S. Bruner, *Acts of Meaning*.

46. Kenneth Burke, *On Symbols and Society*, 58.

47. Thomas Schelling, "The Mind as a Consuming Organ," in Jon Elster, ed., *The Multiple Self*, 179.

48. Ibid., 181.

49. See Clifford Geertz, *The Interpretation of Culture*, and Dan Nimmo and James E. Combs, *Subliminal Politics*.

50. Kenneth Burke, *On Symbols and Society*.
51. For a fascinating account of the creation of demand for diamond engagement rings, see Edward J. Epstein, *The Rise and Fall of Diamonds*.
52. See especially Victor W. Turner, *Dramas, Fields and Metaphors*.
53. The author's own experience with some of the protagonists in the NAFTA story is more consistent with the notion that the speakers believe what they say than the contrary. Indeed, at some level, the rhetoric may be more revealing of the basic thought patterns than the more elaborated versions devised for more sophisticated audiences.
54. For an example of an analysis making similar assumptions, see William H. Riker, "Heresthetic and Rhetoric in the Spatial Model," in James E. Alt and Kenneth A. Shepsle, eds., *Perspectives*, 46–65.
55. John Alan Belcher, letter, *Solidarity*, July 1993, 18.
56. "Larry King Live," CNN, 7 September 1993.
57. Pat Buchanan, "GOP's NAFTA Divide," *The Washington Times*, 23 August 1993, E1.
58. C. Vann Woodward, *Tom Watson*.

Chapter 8

1. Peter Behr, "Clinton Team's Lobbying Campaign Tries to Turn Corner on NAFTA," *Washington Post*, 11 October 1993, A14.
2. NBC–*Wall Street Journal* poll, September 1993.
3. "Press Conference with Vice President Al Gore, Senator Max Baucus (D-MT) and Representatives of Environmental Groups," Federal News Service, 15 September 1993.
4. "ABC World News Tonight," ABC, 8 November 1993.
5. John Harwood and Jackie Calmes, "Freshman House Democrats Feel Special Bind as Labor Applies Pressure for Anti-NAFTA Votes," *Wall Street Journal*, 25 October 1993, A22.
6. Ibid.
7. Edward Walsh, "In Anti-NAFTA Push, Perot Builds Support Among Clinton Backers," *Washington Post*, 19 September 1993, A8.
8. Greg Borowski, "Lansing Rally: Perot and Riegle Blast NAFTA, Use Each Other," *Lansing State Journal*, 20 September 1993, 1.
9. "Perot Criticized for Trade Stand," *Chicago Sun-Times*, 2 October 1993, 12.
10. Gary Wisby, "Perot Crowd Disappoints Organizers," *Chicago Sun Times*, 3 October 1993, 4.
11. Chart, *USA-Today*, 11 October 1993, 2A.
12. John W. Mashek, "GOP Senator Lashes Out at Perot, Says Billionaire Is Threat to Party," *Boston Globe*, 10 September 1993, 7.

13. J. William Middendorf, Jr., "Conservatives' Misguided Cases Against NAFTA," *The Washington Times*, 15 Novemnber 1993, A19.

14. "House Whip Says Votes near to Defeat NAFTA," *Reuters Business Report*, 26 October 1993, 7.

15. "News Conference with Representative David Bonior (D-Mi) Concerning NAFTA House Radio & TV Gallery," Federal News Service, 26 October 1993.

16. Keith Bradsher, "U.S. Says Chretien Will Not Undo NAFTA," *New York Times*, 27 October 1993, A10.

17. A year later, faced with almost precisely the same choice on the implementing bill for the Uruguay Round of the GATT, Hollings held the bill in the Commerce committee, forcing Congress into a rare post-election session.

18. Mikey Kantor, Testimony Before the House Ways and Means Committee, 11 March 1993.

19. "NAFTA: Bentsen Says NAFTA's $2.5 Billion Direct Cost Won't Be Offset by Taxes," BNA *International Trade Daily*, 16 September 1993.

20. Mark Z. Barabak, "One Ex-Opponent, Three Latino Groups Give Backing to NAFTA," *The San Diego Union-Tribune*, 28 October 1993, A10.

21. Hearing of the Senate Environment and Public Works Committee on Environmental Side Agreements of NAFTA, 19 October 1993.

22. Mickey Kantor, Testimony Before the House Ways and Means Committee, 19 October 1993.

23. Douglas Jell, "President Begins a Lobbying Blitz for Trade Accord" *New York Times*, 9 November 1993, A1.

24. Thomas B. Edsall, "Are Labor Tactics on NAFTA Real Threats or 'Tough Love'?" *Washington Post*, 16 November 1993, A24.

25. "Labor Reacts to Criticism by Clinton On NAFTA Efforts," BNA Daily Labor Report, 9 November 1993.

26. "Crossfire," CNN, 5 November 1993.

27. "Nightline," ABC, 11 November 1993.

28. "Larry King Live," CNN, 9 November 1993.

29. ABC News poll, 9 November 1993.

30. "Nightline," ABC, 11 November 1993.

31. NBC–*Wall Street Journal* poll, conducted 14–15 November 1993, released 16 November 1993.

32. James Welsh, "Sugar Sours on NAFTA: LA Group Says it Can Kill Treaty," *New Orleans Times-Picayune*, 2 November 1993, D1.

33. Kenneth J. Cooper, "NAFTA Split Parties, Crossed Political Lines," *Washington Post*, 18 November 1993, A1.

34. George Graham, "Trade Pact Vote Hanging in the Balance: Arm-twisting on NAFTA Will Go on to the Last Minute Before the U.S. Congress Decides," *Financial Times*, 15 November 1993, 4.

35. See Helen V. Milner, *Resisting Protectionism.*
36. See for example Richard Fenno, *Congressmen in Committees*; John W. Kingdon, *Congressman's Voting Decisions.*
37. See, especially, John W. Kingdon, *Congressman's Voting Decisions.*
38. R. Douglas Arnold, *The Logic of Congressional Action*, pp. 14–15.
39. This distinction was originally made in V. O. Key, *Public Opinion.*
40. R. Douglas Arnold, *Logic of Congressional Action*, 28.
41. Ibid., 69.
42. Ibid., 70.
43. Ibid., 84.
44. Joseph P. Kalt and Mark A. Zupan, "The Apparent Ideological Behavior of Legislators."

Chapter 9

1. See Alexander L. George, *Bridging the Gap.*
2. Graham T. Allison, *Essence of Decision.*

Selected Bibliography

Allison, Graham T. *Essence of Decision: Explaining the Cuban Missile Crisis.* Boston: Little Brown, 1971.

Alt, James E. and Kenneth A. Shepsle, eds. *Perspectives on Positive Political Economy.* New York: Cambridge University Press, 1990.

Arnold, Douglas R. *The Logic of Congressional Action.* New Haven, Conn.: Yale University Press, 1990.

Arrow, Kenneth. *Social Choice and Individual Values,* 2d. ed. New York: Wiley, 1963.

Axelrod, Robert. *The Evolution of Cooperation.* New York: Basic Books, 1984.

Bauer, Raymond A., Ithiel de Sola Pool, and Lewis Anthony Dexter. *American Business and Public Policy.* New York: Atherton, 1963.

Berger, Peter L. and Thomas Luckmann. *The Social Construction of Reality: A Treatise in the Sociology of Knowledge.* New York: Doubleday, 1966.

Bettelheim, Bruno. *The Uses of Enchantment: The Meaning and Importance of Fairy Tales.* New York: Knopf, 1976.

Bruner, Jerome S. *Acts of Meaning.* Cambridge, Mass.: Harvard University Press, 1990.

Buchanan, James M. and Gordon Tullock. *The Calculus of Consent: Logical Foundations of Constitutional Democracy.* Ann Arbor: University of Michigan Press, 1962.

Burke, Kenneth. *On Symbols and Society.* Chicago: University of Chicago Press, 1989.

Coase, Ronald. "The Problem of Social Cost," *Journal of Law and Economics* 3 (October 1960): 1–44.

Cornelius, Wayne A., Ann L. Craig, and Jonathan Fox, eds., *Transforming State-*

Society Relations in Mexico: The National Solidarity Strategy. San Diego: Center for U.S.–Mexican Studies, University of California, San Diego, 1994.

del Castillo, Gustavo and Gustavo Vega Cánovas. *The Politics of Free Trade in North America.* Ottawa: Centre for Trade Policy and Law, 1995.

Destler, I.M. *American Trade Politics,* 2d. ed. Washington, D.C.: Institute for International Economics, 1992.

Downs, Anthony. *An Economic Theory of Democracy.* New York: Harper-Row, 1957.

Edelman, Murray. *The Symbolic Uses of Politics.* Urbana: University of Illinois Press, 1964.

Elster, Jon. *The Cement of Society: A Study of Social Order.* Cambridge: Cambridge University Press, 1989.

Elster, Jon, ed. *The Multiple Self.* Cambridge: Cambridge University Press, 1985.

Elster, Jon. *Ulysses and the Siren: Studies in Rationality and Irrationality.* Cambridge: Cambridge University Press, 1979.

Enelow, James M. and Melvin J. Hinich, eds. *Advances in the Spacial Theory of Voting.* New York: Cambridge University Press, 1990.

Epstein, Edward J. *The Rise and Fall of Diamonds: The Shattering of a Brilliant Illusion.* New York: Simon and Schuster, 1982.

Esty, Daniel C., *Greening the GATT: Trade, Environment, and the Future.* Washington, D.C.: Institute for International Economics, 1994.

Evans, Peter B., Harold K. Jacobson, and Robert D. Putnam, eds. *Double-Edged Diplomacy: International Bargaining and Domestic Politics.* Berkeley: University of California Press, 1993.

Finlay, David J., Ole R. Holsti, and Richard R. Fagen. *Enemies in Politics.* Chicago: Rand-McNally, 1957.

Fenno, Richard. *Congressmen in Committees.* Boston: Little, Brown, 1973.

Geertz, Clifford. *The Interpretation of Cultures.* New York: Basic Books, 1973.

George, Alexander L. *Bridging the Gap: Theory and Practice in Foreign Policy.* Washington, D.C.: U.S. Institute of Peace Press, 1993.

George, Alexander L. "The 'Operational Code': A Neglected Approach to the Study of Political Leaders and Decision-Making." *International Studies Quarterly* 13, no. 2 (June 1969): 190–222.

George, Alexander L. *Presidential Decisionmaking in Foreign Policy: The Effective Use of Information and Advice.* Boulder, Colo.: Westview, 1980.

Goldstein, Judith. *Ideas, Interests and American Trade Policy.* Ithaca, N.Y.: Cornell University Press, 1993.

Goldstein, Judith and Robert O. Keohane, eds. *Ideas and Foreign Policy: Beliefs, Institutions, and Political Change.* Ithaca, N.Y.: Cornell University Press, 1993.

Grayson, George W. *The North American Free Trade Agreement.* New York: Foreign Policy Association, 1993.

Green, Donald P. and Ian Shapiro. *Pathologies of Rational Choice Theory: A Critique of Applications in Political Science.* New Haven, Conn.: Yale University Press, 1994.

Grieco, Joseph M. *Cooperation Among Nations: Europe, America, and Non-Tariff Barriers to Trade.* Ithaca, N.Y.: Cornell University Press, 1990.

Haas, Peter M. "Introduction: Epistemic Communities and International Policy Coordination." *International Organization.* 46, no. 1 (Winter 1992): 1–35.

Haggard, Stephan, and Steven B. Webb, eds., *Voting for Reform: Democracy, Political Liberalization, and Economic Adjustment.* Washington, D.C.: World Bank, 1994.

Hart, Michael. *Decision at Midnight: Inside the Canada-US Free-Trade Negotiations.* Vancouver: University of British Columbia Press, 1994.

Jervis, Robert. *Perception and Misperception in International Politics.* Princeton, N.J.: Princeton University Press, 1976.

Johnson, H.G. "Optimal Tariffs and Retaliation." *Review of Economic Studies* 21 (1954): 142–154.

Kalt, Joseph P. *The Economics and Politics of Oil Price Regulation: Federal Policy in the Post-Embargo Era.* Cambridge, Mass.: MIT Press, 1981.

Kalt, Joseph P. and Mark A. Zupan. "The Apparent Ideological Behavior of Legislators: Testing for Principal-Agent Slack in Political Institutions." *Journal of Law and Economics,* 33, no. 1 (April 1990): 103–31.

Katzenstein, Peter J., ed. *Between Power and Plenty: Foreign Economic Powers of Advanced Industrial States.* Madison: University of Wisconsin Press, 1978.

Keohane, Robert O., ed. *Neorealism and Its Critics.* New York: Columbia University Press, 1986.

Keohane, Robert O. and Joseph Nye. *Power and Interdependence: World Politics in Transition.* Boston: Little, Brown, 1977.

Key, V. O. *Public Opinion and American Democracy.* New York: Knopf, 1961.

Kingdon, John W. *Congressman's Voting Decisions,* 3d. ed. Ann Arbor: University of Michigan Press, 1989.

Krasner, Stephen D., ed. *International Regimes.* Ithaca, N.Y.: Cornell University Press, 1983.

Krugman, Paul R., ed. *Strategic Trade Policy and the New International Economics.* Cambridge, Mass.: MIT Press, 1986.

Lasswell, Harold D. *World Politics and Personal Insecurity.* New York: McGraw-Hill, 1935.

Lax, David A. and James K. Sebenius. *The Manager as Negotiator.* New York: Free Press, 1986.

Luce, Duncan R. and Howard Raiffa. *Games and Decisions: Introduction and Critical Survey.* New York: Wiley, 1957.

Lustig, Nora. *Mexico: The Remaking of an Economy.* Washington, D.C.: Brookings, 1992.

March, James and Herbert Simon. *Organizations.* New York: Wiley, 1958.

Marks, Steven V. and Keith E. Maskus, eds. *The Economics and Politics of World Sugar Policies*. Ann Arbor: University of Michigan Press, 1993.

Maxwell, Sylvia. *Governing Capital: International Finance and Mexican Politics*. Ithaca, N.Y.: Cornell University Press, 1990.

Mayer, Frederick W. "Domestic Politics and the Strategy of International Trade." *Journal of Policy Analysis and Management*. 10, no. 2 (1991): 222–46.

Mayer, Frederick W. "Managing Domestic Differences in International Negotiation: The Strategic Use of Internal Side Payments." *International Organization*. 46, no. 4 (1992): 793–818.

Mayer, Frederick W. "The NAFTA, Multinationals and Social Regulation." In Lorraine Eden, ed., *Multinationals in North America*, 509–524. Calgary: University of Calgary Press, 1994.

Mead, George Herbert. *The Philosophy of the Act*. Chicago: University of Chicago Press, 1938.

Milner, Helen V. *Resisting Protectionism: Global Industries and the Politics of International Trade*. Princeton: Princeton University Press, 1988.

Moe, Terry M. *The Organization of Interests: Incentives and the Internal Dynamics of Political Interest Groups*. Chicago: Chicago University Press, 1980.

Moe, Terry M. "Politics and the Theory of Organization." *Journal of Law and Economic Organization*. 7, no. 0 (Special Issue 1991): 106–29.

Morgenthau, Hans J. *Politics Among Nations: The Struggle for Power and Peace*, 5th ed. New York: Knopf, 1973.

Nau, Henry. *Domestic Trade Politics and the Uruguay Round*. New York: Columbia University Press, 1989.

Neustadt, Richard E. and Ernest R. May. *Thinking in Time: The Uses of History for Decision Makers*. New York: The Free Press, 1986.

Nimmo, Dan and James E. Combs. *Subliminal Politics: Myths and Mythmakers in America*. Englewood Cliffs, N.J.: Prentice-Hall, 1980.

North American Free Trade Agreeement Between the Government of the United States of America, the Government of Canada, and the Government of the United Mexican States, 1993.

Offerman-Zuckerberg, Joan, ed. *Politics and Psychology*. New York: Plenum, 1991.

Olson, Mancur. *The Logic of Collective Action*. Cambridge, Mass.: Harvard University Press, 1965.

Orden, David. "Agricultural Interest Groups and the North American Free Trade Agreement." Working Paper No. 4790. Cambridge, Mass.: National Bureau of Economic Research, 1994.

Oye, Kenneth A. ed. *Cooperation Under Anarchy*. Princeton, N.J.: Princeton University Press, 1986.

Pastor, Manuel Jr., and Carol Wise. "The Origins and Sustainability of Mexico's Free Trade Policy." *International Organization* 3 (1994): 459–89.

Pastor, Robert A. and Jorge G. Castenada. *Limits to Friendship: The United States and Mexico*. New York: Vintage, 1988.

Peacock, James L. *The Anthropological Lens: Harsh Light, Soft Focus*. Cambridge: Cambridge University Press, 1986.

Perot, Ross and Pat Choate. *Save Your Job, Save Our Country: Why NAFTA Must Be Stopped—Now!*. New York: Hyperion, 1993.

Price, David E. *Who Makes the Laws?: Creativity and Power in Senate Committees*. Morristown, N.J.: Schenkman, 1972.

Putnam, Robert D. "Diplomacy and Domestic Politics: The Logic of Two-Level Games," *International Organization* 42 (Summer 1988): 427–60.

Raiffa, Howard. *The Art and Science of Negotiation*. Cambridge, Mass.: Harvard University Press, 1982.

Rogatsky, Ronald. *Commerce and Coalitions: How Trade Affects Domestic Political Alignments*. Princeton: Princeton University Press, 1989.

Ruggie, John Gerard. "International Regimes, Transactions, and Change: Embedded Liberalism in the Postwar Economic Order." In Stephen D. Krasner, ed., *International Regimes*, 195–232. Ithaca, N.Y.: Cornell University Press, 1983.

Ruggie, John Gerard. "Transformation and Continuity in the World Polity: Towards a Neorealist Synthesis." In Robert O. Keohane, ed., *Neorealism and Its Critics*, 131–157. New York: Columbia University Press, 1986.

Schattschneider, E.E. *Politics, Pressures and the Tariff*. New York: Prentice-Hall, 1935.

Schelling, Thomas C. *The Strategy of Conflict*. Cambridge, Mass.: Harvard University Press, 1960.

Schoppa, Leonard J. *Bargaining with Japan: What American Pressure Can and Cannot Do*. New York: Columbia University Press, 1997.

Sears, David O. "Symbolic Racism." In Phyllis A. Katz and Dalmas A. Taylor, eds., *Eliminating Racism: Profiles in Controversy*, 53–84. New York: Plenum, 1988.

Sebenius, James K. "Negotiation Arithmetic." *International Organization*. 37, no. 2 (1983): 281–316.

Simon, Herbert A. "Rationality in Psychology and Economics." In Robin M. Hogarth and Melvin W. Reder, eds., *Rational Choice: The Contrast Between Economics and Psychology*, 25–40. Chicago: University of Chicago Press, 1986.

Snyder, Glenn H. and Paul Diesing. *Conflict Among Nations: Bargaining, Decision Making, and System Structure in International Crises*. Princeton, N.J.: Princeton University Press, 1977.

Snyder, Jack. *Myths of Empire: Domestic Politics and International Ambition*. Ithaca, N.Y.: Cornell University Press, 1991.

Steinbruner, John D. *The Cybernetic Theory of Decision*. Princeton, N.J.: Princeton University Press, 1974.

Stone, Deborah A. *Policy Paradox and Political Reason.* Glenview, Ill.: Scott Foresman, 1988.

Stone, William F. and Paul E. Schaffner. *The Psychology of Politics,* 2d. ed. New York: Springer-Verlag, 1988.

Tsebelis, George. *Nested Games: Rational Choice in Comparative Politics.* Berkeley: University of California Press, 1990.

Turner, Victor W. *Dramas, Fields, and Metaphors: Symbolic Action in Human Society.* Ithaca, N.Y.: Cornell University Press, 1974.

Tversky, Amos and Daniel Kahnemann. "Rational Choice and the Framing of Decisions." In Robin M. Hogarth and Melvin W. Reder, eds., *Rational Choice: The Contrast Between Economics and Psychology,* 67–94. Chicago: University of Chicago Press, 1986.

United States Congressional Budget Office. *An Economic and Budgetary Analysis of the North American Free Trade Agreement.* Washington, D.C.: U.S. Government Printing Office, 1993.

United States International Trade Commission. "Review of Trade and Investment Liberalization Measures by Mexico and Prospects for Future United States–Mexican Relations." Investigation No. 332-282, Publication No. 2275. Washington, D.C.: U.S. Government Printing Office, April 1990.

Vernon, Raymond. *Sovereignty at Bay: The Multinational Spread of U.S. Enterprises.* New York: Basic Books, 1971.

Walton, Richard E. and Robert B. McKersie. *A Behavioral Theory of Labor Negotiations.* New York: McGraw-Hill, 1965.

Waltz, Kenneth N., *Man, the State, and War: A Theoretical Analysis.* New York: Columbia University Press, 1959.

Weintraub, Sidney. *Free Trade Between Mexico and the United States?* Washington, D.C.: Brookings, 1984.

Wendt, Alexander. "Collective Identity Formation and the International State," *American Political Science Review,* 88, no. 2 (June 1994): 384–96.

Woodward, C. Vann. *Tom Watson: Agrarian Rebel.* New York: Rinehart, 1938.

Woodward, Robert. *The Agenda.* New York: Simon and Schuster, 1994.

Zaller, John R. *The Nature and Origins of Mass Opinion.* Cambridge: Cambridge University Press, 1992.

Index